FAITH AND MODERNITY

Contributors

Prof James D. Hunter, Professor of Sociology, University of Virginia, USA.

Philip Sampson. Social Worker specializing in child welfare, Portsmouth, England

Bishop Lesslie Newbigin, formerly Bishop of Madras, Church of South India, now leader of Church and Our Culture project, Selly Oak, Birmingham, England

Prof Harold A. Netland, Assistant Professor of Philosophy of Religion and Mission, Trinity Divinity School, Deerfield, Illinois, ISA

Prof David Wells, Andrew Mutch Distinguished Professor of Historical and Systematic Theology, Gordon Conwell Theological Seminary, USA

Elaine Storkey, Director of Christian Impact, London

Dr Stephen Williams, Assistant Director, Whitefield Institute, Oxford, England

Dr Tormod Engelsviken, Senior Lecturer in Missiology, Norwegian Lutheran School of Theology, Oslo, Norway

Prof James Houston, Professor of Spiritual Theology, Regent College, Vancouver

Lars Johansson, Director, Forum for Faith and Society, Örebro Theological Seminary, Sweden

Dr Craig Gay, Associated Professor of Interdisciplinary Studies, Regent College, Vancouver

Knud Jørgensen, Director of Information, Norwegian Church Aid

Dr John Steel, doctoral candidate, University of Maryland, and a Director of Trinity Forum, Washington, DC

Dr Vinay Samuel, Executive Director of International Fellowship of Evangelical Missionary Theologians, Oxford, England

Dr Os Guinness, a Director of Trinity Forum, Washington, DC

FAITH AND MODERNITY

Edited by

Philip Sampson, Vinay Samuel and Chris Sugden

Regnum Books International

Oxford

Akropong   Buenos Aires   Irvine, CA   New Delhi

Published by Regnum Books International
in association with Paternoster Press, P.O. Box 300, Carlisle, Cumbria
CA3 0QS U.K.

Regnum Books International

P.O. Box 70, Oxford, OX2 6HB, UK

17951 Cowan, Irvine, California 92714, USA

P.O. Box 76, Akropong-Akuapem, Ghana

Jose Marmol 1734, 1602 Florida, Buenos Aires, Argentina

Post Bag No. 21, Vasant Kunj, New Delhi 110057, India

01 00 99 98 97   7 6 5 4 3

A catalogue record for this book is available from the British Library

ISBN 1-870345-17-7

Printed and bound in Great Britain

Contents

LEVEL THREE: STRATEGIES IN CONFRONTING MODERNITY

Introduction

by the editors: Philip Sampson, Vinay Samuel and Chris Sugden

These essays repeatedly use the terms 'modern', 'modernity' and the corresponding forms 'postmodern' and 'postmodernity'. As these words have been used in a variety of senses elsewhere, we will review their meaning here, and set out the issues dealt with in the following pages. We begin with modern/modernity.

Among evangelicals, perhaps the most familiar sense of these and related terms arises from their use in apologetics, particularly in the work of Francis Shaeffer and the L'Abri Fellowship. In this sense, 'modern' refers principally to modern ideas, patterns of thought, philosophies, and their expression in art and literature. Modernity is the intellectual and cultural heritage of the Enlightenment project—namely, the rejection cf traditional and religious sources of authority in favour of reason and knowledge as the road to human emancipation. From this point of view, postmodernity refers to the progressive loss of confidence in, if not failure of, the enlightenment project since 1945. This accelerated in the seventies and eighties as the consequences of modernization became more apparent. For example, the environmental debate shows that science has not only failed to cure human ills but cannot do so. The debate suggests that science paradoxically contributes to the very problems it sets out to solve. The belief in progress is over. When reason is sovereign and human beings make their own rules, creation itself suffers.

The history of ideas approach to modernity and postmodernity continues to be important. But a second sense to these terms is just as vital but has been been relatively neglected. Christians are beginning to realize that there are social features to modernity and postmodernity which the church absorbs even as it rejects the ideas of the enlightenment. Guinness, Seel and Sampson all emphasize these specifically social effects. These effects are not limited to the social or political involvement of Christians in fighting the injustices of the contemporary world such as poverty or racism. The issue is wider and enters the heart of Christian practice and discipleship.

Modernity in this second sense refers not only to the enlightenment project, but to the social, economic and political developments associated with and sustaining it. The emergence of the democratic nation state, the progressive secularization and rationalization of society, economic growth, technological and industrial development, and urbanization have all transformed Western societies over the past 150 years. These changes are complex and have far-reaching consequences. The twentieth century has seen many benefits for the West, but also many unintended consequences. Seel, Guinness and Gay all point to aspects of these changes which have affected the church and which face us as Christians with challenges in our daily life, not least because the impact on us is covert and subversive. Thus Seel uses the example of McDonald's fast food to illustrate the rationalization of society in modernity: 'McDonalidization is the process by which the principles of the fast-food restuarant business are coming to dominate more and more sectors of North American society as well as of the rest of the world' (page 301). The values of McDonaldization (efficiency, calcul-ability, predictability and control) enter the church by the back door as Christians search to organize church institutions and to evangelize in the most effective way.

But, just as the enlightenment project is widely perceived to have failed, so the social fabric and processes of modernity are fragmenting. Early signs of this are sometimes seen in the 1970s oil crisis, with a loss of confidence in the inevitability of continuing growth (Harvey 1987:39), but the pace has accelerated since. Manufacturing industries are being displaced in the West by the service sector, with associated changes in the labour market; traditional political alignments are fragmenting into new social movements (such as environmental, feminist or even fundamentalist); Western economies are shifting emphasis from production to consumption; and communications technology permits the instantaneous dissemination of cultural images. From this social point of view, postmodernity refers to these shifts in the social, economic and political aspects of modernity. The terms 'information society' and 'consumer society' are sometimes used to describe these same shifts in social life. The church growth move-ment and some evangelistic crusades have accomodated to these social changes by marketing the gospel as a product for today's postmodern consumer; spectacle and image displace explanation and word; the service style is carefully matched to consumer preference; and the message is tailored to chime with felt needs, carefully excluding discomforting feelings.

A possible disadvantage of the term 'postmodernity', whether describing the collapse of the enlightenment project or the fragmenta-tion of social modernity, is that it might suggest that modernity is a spent force (see Seel page 292); that Christians need not be concerned with engaging with contemporary debate and social changes. To believe this would be a grave error, for the very opposite is the case. Modernity presents new issues just as challenging as those of post-modernity. Moreover, the transition from modernity to postmodernity is very uneven, demanding different responses in different settings. Partly because of this possibility for misunderstanding, some authors prefer the term 'late modernity' to 'postmodernity' in order to empha-size that issues remain. Other authors doubt that postmodernity represents anything essentially new, and use the term 'modernity' to include these more recent developments. Seel, for example, uses the term 'modernity' throughout to include social processes (such as consumerization) which others would regard as distinctively postmodern. Guinness (page 324) similarly uses the term 'modern' to include all aspects of the contemporary social world, restricting 'postmodern' to the collapse of the enlightenment project.

Despite these ambiguities, the term postmodern is now so widely used that to avoid it altogether becomes increasingly artificial. Moreover, it is valuable in highlighting the distinctive social and cultural developments of recent decades which might otherwise be so familiar to us as to become invisible.

Although modernity and postmodernity refer to different cultural and social developments, there is often no sharp distinction between them but features of continuity as well as of discontinuity. For example, Seel and Guinness discuss pluralization and privatization as aspects of modernity, but both processes are evident in the fragmentation of the social world produced by postmodernity. In modernity, pluralization referred to the distribution of power away from the central state, and between broad social or professional groups. In postmodernity this has been extended to fragment the social body into numerous smaller social groupings ('green', 'feminist', 'gay', 'fundamentalist', etc) each with their own agenda. Similarly, modernity relegated religion to the private sphere, denying it the authority of reason and knowledge which were reserved for the public sphere. Postmodernity extended this division into the public sphere itself, fragmenting the unified polity of modern democracies into a marketplace of competing interests and rationalities. Mrs Margaret Thatcher, the former Prime Minister of Britain, remarked 'there is no such thing as society' and thus exemplified the logical conclusion of this tendency. What was implicit in modernity has become explicit in postmodernity and is there ironically celebrated as a new source of democratic strength as representation is carried to ever more local levels.

To describe modernity and postmodernity thus is not to dismiss their culture and society as worthless or to encourage a simplistic rejection of the contemporary world. On the contrary, modernity has brought a respect for truth in science, and the development of decentralized institutions; similarly postmodernity has encouraged a cultural openness and the extension of democratic processes. Gay points to the role of Christian values in the foundation of social modernity, and both Guinness and Seel discuss the extended opportunities which this has provided for Christian mission. However, these benefits are neither unambiguous nor guaranteed, especially where they break free from the Christian norms which gave them birth (Gay). Even while modernity and postmodernity open up possibilities, they close others and exact their own price.

One response to the critique which postmodernity has leveled against modernity, especially against the enlightenment project, is to try to rehabilitate the premodern. An influential example has been MacIntyre's attempt to recover features of Thomism in order to revitalize social theory. A danger here is postmodernity's ability to absorb and transform past references, feeding upon them (Sampson page 39). Rather than providing a distinctive way forward, the pre-modern tradition becomes yet another colourful embroidery on the postmodern banner. Guinness (page 349) also notes this as a deficient Christian response to modernity itself. Storkey approaches this by arguing, not that a premodern tradition can revitalize those parts of modernity that other nostrums cannot reach, but that the Christian confession presents a unique starting point which is premodern in the sense that it rejects 'obedience to the modernist metanarratives of rationality, progress and scientific knowledge' (page 138).[1] This approach to the premodern is implicit in many of the other papers but is explicit in Engelsviken (page 167), Gay (final section) and Houston, and marks an important difference between the papers in this volume and other recent responses to the collapse of modernity.

The consultation did not address the impact of modernity on cultures of the non-Western world. Vinay Samuel's paper explores the connection between Western colonialism, Western mission, modernity and Hindu and Islamic societies. Japanese society had a well-worked-out strategy to respond to the forces of modernity. Its ability to absorb, accept and succeed technologically while maintaining an enviable continuity with its traditions poses a challenge which the Christian church has yet to face. China's strategy of modernization is also confienct of not repeating what it judges are mistakes of Western modernization.

The non-Western world is also in large part a world of poverty, and economic and political exploitation. Some postmodern theorists suggest that the increasing globalization of economy will lead to the development of cheap and relatively unregulated labour markets in the Two-Thirds World controlled by the West to produce manufactured goods. Modern industrialization without accountability to democratic regulatory systems will spread in the Two-Thirds World with its many disadvantages.

FOOTNOTES

1. For an excellent discussion of this and related issues see D. Lyon, *Postmodernity*, Open University Press, Milton Keynes, 1994

REFERENCES

Harvey, D (1987) *The condition of postmodernity*, Blackwell

LEVEL ONE:

THE ANALYSIS
OF MODERNITY

1

What is modernity? Historical roots and contemporary features

JAMES D. HUNTER

Nearly everyone nowadays senses deep within themselves a visceral unease about contemporary life. This feeling of disquiet is not what believers of all centuries have felt when they realize that their true home is not of this world. No, the tension, the dissonance, the emptiness is more acrid and unsettling than just that. Something, we sense, is unique about the nature and direction of our personal and collective existence and it is not all agreeable to us.

That ineffable sense of unease about our personal and social existence is our starting point. That sense, which for many Christians is becoming especially acute, signals existentially what is in fact a world-historical transformation, a consequence of which is the disintegration of the central institutions and ideals of civilization in the West. The catalyst for this transformation is 'modernization'; the epoch giving name to this change is 'modernity'.

Certainly most people of faith have not understood it as such, but in hindsight it is clear that the history of the Christian experience and witness in the West over the past two centuries is overwhelmingly the history of the church in confrontation with modernity. It is the central problematic in debates over soteriology, ecclesiology and missiology, not to mention popular piety; it is the central factor over which schisms and realignments in 'Christendom,' such as it is, have taken shape. In hindsight it is also clear that the drama played out in Western Christianity is part and parcel of the modern project in all of its great and glorious and horrific dimensions.

For its own part, it is as though Evangelical Christianity has been in a deep but agitated and restless slumber through all of

12

this. It is only now, in the late twentieth century, beginning to wake up and consciously grasp the monumental significance of what has and is occurring in and around it. A cynic would mutter 'tsk, tsk, isn't it about time?', but the fact that this recognition is happening only now and among a fairly small number of its intellectuals is a testimony to its subtle but profound influence. It is true, the power of any culture is measured by the extent to which its formulation of reality seems 'natural.' So it is (and perhaps especially) with the culture of modernity. Its structures of reality present themselves with such massive force that people who should know better, say evangelical historians and theologians, often scratch their heads and wonder what all of this talk about modernity is anyway. But rather than pursue it, all too many lapse back into dissecting and fighting the doctrinal battles of the sixteenth and seventeenth centuries. The abiding assumption for them, as it is for many people of faith, is that culture is morally neutral. If we can only get our doctrine straight and pray more, all will be well. That feeling of unease will disappear; all will be right again. Such an assumption is, to say the least, misplaced. The reason is that the challenge the Church now faces is nothing like it has ever before faced.

The task of coming to terms with the context in which the Church finds itself is not a task for independent intellectuals but one for the Church itself. At stake is its faithfulness to its creeds and traditions; at stake is its integrity as the spiritual body of Christ on earth. It is a huge and on-going undertaking. Questions concerning what is going on and what should be done need to be asked again and again at every level of church life.

Obviously, one could write volumes on these matters. My task in this essay is more modest. The first task is to place the concept of modernity in its intellectual context and to note upfront some of the analytical and empirical problems attending it. The heart of the essay, however, will be a review of the basic dimensions and dynamics of modernity and to sketch an outline of its consequences for faith.

Modernity as concept and paradigm

The term 'modern' comes from the latin, *modo*, meaning 'just now'. It originally meant something like 'recent', 'present' or 'contemporary'. It was first applied in the fifth century by church autho-

13

rities as a way of signifying the distinction between the Christian present and a Roman pagan past. As Jürgen Habermas notes, the term seemed to appear and reappear exactly during those periods in European history when people became aware of some new changes dawning against a vague backdrop of an ancient order receding.[1] Of course debates would always rage at these times as to whether the new was better than the old. Often enough, sentiment idealized the past, as in the Renaissance where classical antiquity was so venerated. With the French Enlightenment, however, the concept acquired a new meaning as a distinctive and superior period in the history of humanity, where in all spheres of life and culture, modern people were more knowledgeable, more refined, more sophisticated, and so on. The premise and promise of the 'modern' age would be 'the emancipation of humanity from poverty, ignorance, prejudice, and the absence of enjoyment'.[2] It is in this context that sociology, a pre-eminently Enlightenment academic discipline, latched onto the term.

This last point is worth highlighting. Sociology as a discipline emerged in response to modernity; its very identity during its classical period, centered on the task of figuring out the cataclysmic changes taking place at the time. In this light, one might hope that after 150 years the social sciences would now be able to offer a quick, clear and unified understanding of the phenomenon of modernity. The truth, though, is that scholarship on contemporary social change has disintegrated into a bewildering and often contradictory range of theories and perspectives. Dependency theory, world systems theory, developmentalism, and modernization theory are just the main ones.

The 'modernization' perspective, however, remains one particular, though major, angle of inquiry into the general matter of contemporary social change. This paradigm begins (in accord with its etiology) by suggesting that there is something qualitatively distinct about social life in our day from societies in times past. Indeed, following Tonnies, Durkheim, Maine, Parsons, and the like, all societies can be divided into one of two types: the traditional or 'premodern' type of society and the 'modern' type of society.[3]

Typologically, premodern societies are generally characterized by a population which is diffused throughout numerous, small, and isolated pockets in rural or quasi-rural settings. There is little technological sophistication and little division of labor.

Social relationships are personal, intimate, and essential, with the relations and institutions of kinship at the core of individual and social experience. Political hegemony is maintained by elites whose authority is based upon traditional sanctions. The culture of the community, *gemeinschaft*, is typically homogeneous. Consequently, social solidarity is based upon similarity of roles and of worldviews. All spheres of human life are bound by deeply rooted traditional modes of thought and behavior that are almost without exception, religious or sacred in character.

By contrast, modern societies are characterized by a population concentration in centralized urban areas. There is a highly intensified division of labor as well as a high degree of institutional specialization and segmentation. The economic sphere, but the production apparatus in particular, is based upon a highly sophisticated technology. Social relationships are largely impersonal and arbitrary with the primary mode of social organization in all spheres being bureaucratic. Political power is, at least ideologically, based in the populace. The society, *gesellschaft*, is further characterized by socio-cultural pluralism, a curious admixture of social and cultural worlds in various degrees of contract with one another. The worldview of modern man is typically rational and secular, not bound by traditional sanctions but critical and open to innovation and experimentation. Solidarity in modern society is based upon the interdependence which is fostered by role and institutional differentiation.

The problems with this model as originally formulated in the classical period of sociological theory were many. For one, the model has tended to fundamentally distort history, making the past flat and one-dimensional. There is, after all, an entire range of variations with regard to the manner and rate at which societies undergo the transition. No two societies go through transition exactly alike and this paradigm is insensitive to these substantive nuances of historical difference. In addition, this model presents the premodern/modern dichotomy in too exclusivistic terms. The concepts of the 'modern' and the 'premodern' are reified as categories, obscuring the connections between past and present. It does not account for the carry-over of traditional forces or symbols in even the most modern social worlds.[4] Moreover this paradigm is 'Western-centric', in the sense that it is assumed that the Western pattern of modernization is the model of ultimate form of modernization toward which all societies aim and converge. Perhaps the greatest danger of this model is that it serves to reinforce the ideological forms of nostalgia rampant, particularly in the U.S. We imagine 'traditional' society to be a time and place of idyllic simplicity, tranquility, security and happiness. Not only does this represent the abdication of memory, but dangerously distracts us from the challenges at hand.

Some social scientists have viewed these flaws as sufficient for abandoning the paradigm altogether. Perhaps we should. It is possible, though, to argue that these criticisms are more indicative of past tendencies rather than foibles inherent within the model.[5] I am not certain of this. What is clear is that there is no other language or set of concepts for discussing what is culturally distinctive about our age as compared to other periods of human history. Flawed though it may be, we are stuck with a typological model and should make the best of it. In the end, we gain in understanding far more than we would if we had to abandon the model altogether. But we should not forget the problems with the perspective, for our awareness of them will always urge upon us a measure of caution and modesty as we approach a basic understanding of its reality and consequences on our lives.

Modernity: toward a definition and description

WHAT IS MODERNITY?

First, modernity is a moment of human history of world-historical reach and consequences. As an 'epoch,' the defining elements of modernity can be seen as congealing, in incipient form, no earlier than the fourteenth century and no later than the sixteenth century in Western Europe. The hallmarks of this social and historical development were the spread of Western imperialism, the development of ascetic Protestantism and rational capitalism, and the widespread acceptance of scientific procedures. These changes intensified, however, in the late eighteenth and early nineteenth century. From this point on, the reality of modernity has spread (in various forms) to the furthest reaches of the globe.

More substantively, modernity can be defined as *both* a mode of social life *and* moral understanding more or less characterized by the universal claims of reason and instrumental (or means/ends) rationality; the differentiation of spheres of life-experience into public and private; and the pluralization and competition of truth claims. There may be other characteristics of modernity, but these are clearly among the most agreed upon and, by all accounts, the most important. Each calls attention to what is singular about our time. Consider first, the novelty of modern rationality.

Clearly there are a variety of ways of understanding and ordering experience. Modernity, however, posits an understanding and ordering of the world through an autonomous and human rationality. This plays out at two levels. At a philosophical level, rationality assumes the only reality to be that which can be appropriated empirically by the senses. This reality can be explained logically and scientifically in an ordered system of rationally-derived propositions. Such an assumption slams the door on the very idea of transcendence/supernatural. The world of Nature, of which humanity is a part, is all there is. It is the task of the sciences to explain this world.

Explanation, however, is not enough. It is essential to achieve mastery over the world through the practical application of rational controls on all aspects of everyday life, in our solving of the great human dilemmas, in our ordering of social relationships in organizations, in our rational management of everything from the day's activities to the next ten years of a career.

At both philosophical and practical levels, there is a presumption about the universal applicability of reason. At both levels the maximum control, predictability and efficiency is held up as the highest value. And at both levels rationality is severed from any transcendent notions of human good. Appeals to tradition or to positions of power are, by definition, illegitimate. Rather the only adequate and legitimate appeal is to consistency and efficiency. Intellectual and practical rationality is self-sufficient.

Because more traditional societies were locally-bounded and insular, social life was more or less integrated. But with modernity, one sees a strong tendency dividing life experience into public and private spheres. Practically speaking, this division tends to parallel the division between work and home; between career and family. What makes this separation between public and private so interesting and important (not to mention historically unique) is that each sphere tends to operate as different and unrelated realms of activity and meaning. The public sphere tends to be characterized by highly rational forms of thought, conduct and social relationship; the private sphere tends to be characterized by intimacy, particularity, and emotionality.

Then there is modern pluralism. Against the experience of more traditional societies which tended to be fairly homogeneous, modernity brings together distinct worldviews, belief systems or just points of view into close proximity to each other. What this means is that there is no unified perspective of reality but multiple realities from which one can choose.

Needless to say, traces of each of these defining features of modernity can be found in more traditional societies. What makes modernity distinct is the intensity with which these features are found.

INSTITUTIONAL CARRIERS

Clearly the way most scholars come to understand modernity is through the context of the history of ideas. Each of the three main characteristics of modernity I've just mentioned is just another name for Enlightenment ideas: reason and realism, the sovereignty of the individual in public and private life, tolerance toward diversity, and so on. This simple view of modernity, however, is fundamentally flawed. *The reason why modernity is so distinctive and powerful is that it is a dialectic between moral understanding* (e.g. the value of reason, the supreme importance of individuality, the value of tolerance and relativism), *and social/institutional life.* In practical terms, this means that the key ideas, values and characteristics of modernity mentioned above are 'carried' by specific institutions in three major spheres of human activity: the economic, the political and the cultural.

The first carrier of modernity is *industrial capitalism*. In classical Marxism the peculiarity of modern institutions is explained almost entirely in terms of the peculiar form of industrial capitalism. It is the particular form of property relations that are formative in the modern world, they argued. But as Weber correctly observed (and as Marxists later conceded, and now everyone knows), the real distinctive of modern society is something more basic and more consequential: applied rationality. In the economic sphere, then, what is unique is not so much the use of industrial and management technologies but the technologies themselves. Capitalism, then, would be just one form in which industrial and post-industrial economies could be rationally organized.

But the Marxists were not totally off-base in their contention about the special nature of capitalism. In industrial capitalism, the application of scientific rationality to the production of

18

goods, to the organization of labor, and to the distribution of goods in competitive markets was and remains *the* most innovative and efficient system ever created.

The critical point in all of this is that modern capitalism, or the technology and rationality that defines it, is not culturally neutral. Capitalism is probably the principal carrier of an ideology of rational control. It is here that modern individuals are socialized into a problem-solving approach to all of life and the quest for the most efficient means possible to accomplish one's objectives. The hard-nosed materialism of this reality fosters what is, in effect, a practical atheism toward everyday life.

Capitalism and urbanization not only dramatically weakened (and weakens) traditional and stable communities but also may be the key institutional carrier of a radical individualism; an ideology of self-sufficiency and moral autonomy that undermines the possibility of community.

Capitalism is also the institution through which social life came to be divided into public and private spheres. The rational organization of productivity through the factory system required the concentration of human labor in a single location, outside of the home. Where work and domesticity had been fused and interdependent, now they were sundered. The 'public' sphere of wage earning would become, for the middle classes and soon the working classes too, increasingly separated from the 'private' realm of kinship, family, and friendship. The creation of surplus wealth merely reinforced this, insofar as it freed up children and an increasing number of women from the need to be engaged in productive labor.

A second carrier of modernity is the *modern state*. The state is important because it is the principal carrier of a rationalist or bureaucratic form of social organization. It is the bureaucratic nature of authority that has tended to wash out differences between liberal democratic and authoritarian forms of political organization. Representation increasingly becomes a veneer for power politics waged in the insular setting of a bureaucratic monopoly. As Weber taught us, bureaucracy (especially in the state) is self-aggrandizing. It not only organizes political life, but over time all other major institutions—medicine and health care, education, welfare, the military, and so on—increasingly are organized under the sphere of state authority.

Here too the state is not culturally neutral. It is the principal carrier of componentiality in which knowledge and competencies, not to mention life itself, is compartmentalized rather than integrated. Consider too: the state (as in all bureaucratic structures) not only models abstract and anonymous social relationships but posits them as normative.

A third major carrier of modernity is *the 'knowledge sector'*: the contemporary institutions of culture formation and reality definition. Most prominent of these are the modern university, the media of mass communication, the arts, and popular culture.

It is chiefly through these institutions that pluralism and its competing perspectives of reality are presented. By their very nature, they are carriers of modern skepticism and relativism. As they have been transformed over the past two centuries by secular Enlightenment ideals, their capacity to engender a skeptical, relativist and disenchanted perspective is deepened. At another level, it is communication technology itself—television, radio, newspapers, popular music, and the like—that transforms our sense of space and time, that alters our sense of value, and that predisposes us toward superficiality and subjectivity. Jacques Ellul, Marshall McLuhan, Neil Postman, and Kenneth Myers are correct when they say that the medium is not neutral but is the message.

In sum, there is a strong isomorphism between the culture of modernity and the structures of modernity. The ideas and values of the modern age are not only intellectualized but they are embedded in powerful institutions, arguably the most powerful human institutions that have ever existed. All major areas of individual and collective life have been encompassed by its presence. It is a reality more than the sum total of its parts; it is something over which communities have little control and individuals even less.

LEGITIMATING IDEOLOGIES: PROGRESS AS A MORAL IMPERATIVE

However much anxiety one may feel about contemporary life, we can scarcely imagine it being any different. This, we say to ourselves, is just the way it is. We come to this conclusion, happily or unhappily, because modernity is a normative order whose overarching moral rationale and imperative is summarized by the word, progress. So much of the cultural and structural reality of modernity comes in its name.

Historically, the legitimating narrative of progress drew heavily from biblical sources. History has meaning. It is going somewhere. There is a purpose to all of our labor for there is an end for which we all can and must strive. But where the biblical ideal of historical movement articulated a *telos* in which the kingdom of God would be realized in the *eschaton*—emphatically a work of God—the ideal that emerged in early modernity was of inevitable, orderly, evolutionary progress toward the end of human perfectibility. The key difference, of course, was that the latter became a wholly secularized ideology in which humans, by their own effort, could achieve their own individual and collective improvement. The evolutionary assumptions were drawn from the powerful analog of nature. As organisms evolve from simplicity to complexity; from infancy to adulthood; from helplessness to mastery; so too would societies develop from small, isolated, hunting and gathering cultures to pastoral communities, to agrarian states, to advanced urban and industrial societies. In this natural movement, humanity evolves to a higher form of existence.

Progress, in this context, could only mean a rejection of the old, for the old is, by definition, obsolete. These themes have been played out in capitalism both in technological innovation and in the planned obsolescence of consumer goods; in politics both in the expansion of rights and in the (often hollow) rhetoric of change; in military technology, especially in the development of new weapons of large-scale destruction; in medicine and health care, particularly in the discovery and application of new interventions; in the arts in the endless quest for novelty in expression; in intellectual life in the expansion of the frontiers of knowledge. The theme of progress is also played out in therapeutic ideologies which portray the self as infinitely growing, actualizing, and realizing potential. The list goes on.

The limits of progress: modernity and its discontents

The rhetoric of progress, then, is not empty. Often enough it is backed by convincing evidence that society really has 'improved'. Medical advances, the decline of political and economic patrimonialism and the increase in fairness through bureaucracy, the creation of wealth—such examples cannot be dismissed by even the most curmudgeonly critic of modernity. Yet the rhetoric of progress is never totally believable for the simple reason that modernity creates its own discontents that quietly suggest to us that every 'advance' has cost us something too.

The list of discontents is long and complicated and invariably

21

inter-related. As Weber argued, rationalization makes the world orderly and reliable but it cannot make the world meaningful. Indeed, rationality deepens the 'disenchantment of the world', in which 'the ultimate and most sublime values have retreated from public life . . .'[6] Moreover, the expansion in choices we enjoy in modern times is often overshadowed by the constraints of a bureaucratic existence which can act as 'an iron-cage'. So too, the extraordinary mobility we have has gone far toward undermining the beneficent ties of kinship and community. Meanings we used to take for granted are now radically challenged. Thus, though surrounded by people, modern individuals can live with a terrible loneliness. On top of this, modernity often creates in people a sense of metaphysical homelessness.

One need not continue the litany to understand what Giddens calls the double-edged nature of modernity. Modernity has come with costs and benefits. In the realm of meaning and with regard to faith in particular, it seems as though there are mainly costs.

FAITH AND MODERNITY

And then there is faith itself at the heart of the matter. The beliefs of Christian faith in principle give meaning to the lives of individual believers and identity and purpose to churches. What are the challenges of modernity to belief? The paradox is clear: Christian faith is 'traditional' (that is, historically-rooted and continuous, enchanted and exclusivist) if it is anything at all; modernity is, by definition, post-traditional, secular and exclusivist. How is it possible for faith to survive against the world-disaffirming realities of modernity?

In general, there are three ideal-typical possibilities for a community of faith in response to modernity.[7] The first is *withdrawal*. This is the strategy chosen by such groups as the Amish and the old order Mennonites and Brethren denominations in the United States. Here, faith withdraws from any conscious interaction with the modern world. Studies of such groups show, however, that there is no complete escape from modernity's pressing, worldview changing realities. A second strategy is *accommodation*. Here, faith consciously embraces the cognitive and normative assumptions of the modern world, baptizing, as it were, the ideas and values of modern times with the waters of religious tradition. This is the strategy taken by liberal-modernists denominations. It takes expression in the embracing of Leftist political ideals, modern scientism, and not least, contemporary therapeutic techniques. What all share in common is a more secular/this-worldly orientation deprived of the mysterious and supernatural. The last ideal-typical strategy is *resistance*. Here, faith chooses to engage the modern world but to resist its secularizing effects in the effort to preserve its orthodoxy. This is the strategy chosen by fundamentalist movements around the world. The problem, as one might expect, is that even the heartiest fundamentalism is changed in the very act of engaging the modern world. Orthodoxy becomes something other than what earlier (premodern) generations of orthodox believers believed and practiced.

Evangelical Christianity certainly has its relationship with the resistances of fundamentalism, but overall, it is a faith that has engaged in a bargaining with modernity—accommodating here and there, resisting here and there. The preservation of orthodoxy, though, has been its priority. Despite this, Evangelical faith has changed in ways it has not intended.

The dynamic of change and transformation takes place on at least three levels.

THE STRUCTURAL RELOCATION OF BELIEF

Contrary to the hopes of the Enlightenment philosophers and predictions of secularization theorists, the claims of religious faith have not disappeared. They have, though, been thoroughly marginalized both to the experience of individual believers and in the play of institutions in society as a whole.

The marginalization of religious authority from the structures of power is a complex reality deriving from several sources. One dimension of this tendency can be seen in the contraction of organizational influence—a fundamental displacement of religious institutions in their various public roles by different agencies of the State. Another dimension of this can be seen in the estrangement of religious authority from the laity. On the surface this means there has been a decline in popular regard for the activities and pronouncements of religious institutions and a decline in the popular status of religious leaders. More importantly there is a decline in the ability of religious authority to compel action on the part of the laity. A third and arguably more important way to conceive of the marginalization of religious authority is in relation to the structures of cultural power, the power to create and maintain a definition of public reality.

The retreat from the once dominant role played by religious elites is not, I would argue, because religious institutions have submissively withdrawn from the burden of this task. It is, rather, a consequence of their being structurally displaced. In other words, where at one time there was little or no serious competition to define the symbols of public culture, there is now an overwhelming competition.

In virtually all of the countries of North America and northern Europe, the number of the religious élite has remained relatively constant *vis-à-vis* the total population—the ordinary people whose spiritual needs they serve—in some cases for over a century. In the U.S., there has been no appreciable change for 130 years. In Great Britain, Canada, and France the ratio remained relatively constant until the 1950s but soon after began to decline quite sharply. Though the data is less complete, much the same trend appears to have taken place in Germany and Switzerland as well. Through the same period, the number of the religious elite as a percent of other cultural elites (symbol specialists who also contribute to the definition of national public culture) has dropped consistently, dramatically and, as much as the findings can tell, uniformly through all of the countries. The drop was particularly dramatic in the postwar period. The reason, of course, has to do with the expansion of the ranks of secular cultural elites, once again, particularly since mid-century.

The point is also illustrated by the historical tendencies in cultural production. Across national boundaries, religious book production has increased in absolute terms just as knowledge production more generally has expanded. Yet as a percent of the total production of books in each country, the ratio has declined. The same pattern is seen in the publication of religious newspapers and periodicals in America as well. Cultural production has declined significantly relative to the production of all such publications.

Having once dominated the knowledge sector, religious elites have in the modern age now become only a small part of the knowledge sector. In the post World War II period, especially in the U.S., that tendency has intensified. Religious elites and the knowledge they promote have been structurally displaced.

A marginalization of religious belief also has a correlate in the lives of individual believers, where faith commitments become relegated to the private dimensions of family life and identity formation. In the public dimensions of the individual's life, faith

24

is seemingly irrelevant to the nature and conduct of business. There is, then, a structural explanation for the common complaint about 'the Sunday believer'.

Needless to say, the relocation of religious faith to the experience of individual believers and in the play of institutions in society as a whole creates tremendous countervailing pressures on the average believer to maintain fidelity to his commitments.

THE CONUNDRUM OF INDIVIDUAL BELIEF

Modernity, in brief, posits a crisis in the capacity of ordinary believers to believe what they say they believe. It is *not* that people stop believing as much as it is that the character of their belief changes.

Take as an example how the believer, in the context of modernity, approaches traditional doctrinal creeds. When traditional and creedal affirmations of religious truth are, to whatever degree, undermined by modern forms of rationalism or relativized by modern pluralism, they are simultaneously de-objectified. What was 'known' with a taken-for-granted certitude becomes, at best, a 'belief'. Further along in this process, it becomes a 'religious opinion' or a 'feeling'. Thus when believers approach a biblical story which their tradition regarded as an objective historical fact and say that they are 'open' to or 'comfortable' with the idea that it is just symbolic, or that it is 'not really important (to them) that it happened historically', religious truth devolves to religious opinion. The reality has been de-objectified.

The other side of de-objectification, though, is what social scientists call subjectivization. The emphasis shifts from a concern with the proclamation of an objective and universal truth to a concern with the subjective applicability of truth. In different terms, there is a shift from a concern with 'what the Bible states' to 'what God is telling us'. A shift from the former to the latter eases the tension arising from differences of opinion over what, in fact, the Bible does state.

THE CHALLENGE TO THE CULTURAL INTEGRITY OF BELIEF

At the level of cultural integrity, there is a subtle embrace of the cognitive and normative assumptions of secular modernity. It is not that the words or creeds or traditions are abandoned, but they come to take on new meaning.

At one level this development is seen in the eroding consensus

25

about what the Bible teaches about 'basic' points of doctrine. Evangelical theologians and lay believers give assent to such doctrines as the complete authority of Scripture, justification by faith through Christ alone, the divine origin and end of the world, the nature and purpose of the Christian mission, and so on, but the meaning they impute to these doctrines can vary considerably.

The variation, however, really points to a tendency over the century toward a broadening of the meaning of some of Evangelicalism's most basic religious symbols. Evangelicals, for example, all claim to accept the authority of Scripture, but when you get down to it, they show virtually no agreement as to what the authority of Scripture means. Another example is in the meaning of the 'Great Commission'. Evangelical seminarians in America, for example, are increasingly inclined to believe that those who do not hear the gospel may yet 'be saved'. My point is not to raise a theological argument but simply to point out that for generations, the missionary movement was motivated by a concern for the lost souls of 'the heathen'. Still a third example of this is the loss of any meaning to the word 'worldliness'. In America especially, the language of sin and evil is increasingly translated into the language of therapy.

In these cases, as in others, the meaning of such doctrines has become more inclusive. They mean *more* than they did even a generation or two ago. In brief, the cognitive boundaries of theological orthodoxy, once narrowly construed, have become variously widened. Insofar as this is true, theological orthodoxy is reinterpreted: the traditions are redefined in closer accord with the dominant assumptions of secular modernity.

IN SUM

In sum, the meaning of faith undergoes subtle but significant changes in the context of modernity. As Samuel Heilman has put it, the traditions of orthodoxy are 'worked-through'. The term, 'working through' is borrowed from psychoanalysis and refers to a process in which an individual (ego) confronts his resistances and, in so doing, learns to accept what he formerly repressed. The individual may still act the same way he did before this process, but now his actions are the result of deliberate choice rather than habit. In the same way, those who hold to one of the various orthodoxies, if they want to repeat the patterns of life and faith of their parents, must exert a much greater effort than their parents.

26

The contemporary world has undermined the taken-for-granted-ness of the traditions. As such the traditions are reinterpreted to make sense of the present, and the present is made comprehensible in traditional ways. In this way, the traditions come to mean something different from what they had meant to previous generations of believers.

At the very least, the binding address of faith—the inner imperative binding people to inherited rules and guiding them in day-to-day details of their lives—has weakened. Belief has not dissolved, but the feeling of serene certainty has. Truth is no longer something unconsciously assumed but something to which one must consciously and intellectually assent.

A WORD OF QUALIFICATION

Inevitably, the question of the universality of modernity and its consequences arises. Is modernity really just code for America? If broader, might it really be code for European hegemony? Is there something genuinely universal and world-historical about modernity?

If by modernity one focuses upon the individualism and consumerism of American society, the answer probably is no. If, however, one means by modernity the rationalization of economic life, the bureaucratization of political life, and the introduction of skepticism, doubt, and relativism into the moral life of societies, the answer is emphatically yes. Will the consequences of modernity (in this sense) be manifested in precisely the same ways in different societies around the world? The answer is no; the pressures modernity exerts are much the same but different cultures will have different coping mechanisms. As to how these pressures develop elsewhere in the world there are clues, yet in the particulars one must always be alert to subtle differences in each case.[8] At base, though, modernity is inherently 'globalizing' in its reach. Its consequences, therefore, will be felt (albeit somewhat differently in different settings) for centuries to come if the world lasts that long.

The perils of idealism

In light of all of this, one must reject the idealist assumption about the autonomy of ideas. For Christians theological clarity and devotional intensity are important, but in and of themselves, they will not be enough. Christian understanding must also proceed through self-conscious awareness of the subtle ways in which modernity affects faith and life. Christian understanding must further proceed with imagination about how the Christian community can maintain integrity to biblical revelation and to the legacy of Christian witness through the centuries. It is here that we find the structural antidote to the pressures of modernity. The urgency for Christians to deepen their understanding at both levels is nothing less than the call to faithfulness for this generation and generations to come.

Notes

1. Jürgen Habermas, 'Modernity and postmodernity', *New German Critique*, volume 22, 1981

2. Jean-François Lyotard, 'Interview', *Theory, Culture and Society*, volume 5, numbers 2/3, 1988, page 302

3. Concerning the typological distinction between premodern and modern societies and the typological tradition in modernization theory, see the excellent compendium in Tonnies, 1957, pages 12–29; compare Polanyi, 1944; Boulding, 1964.

4. For an elaboration of these criticisms, see Eisenstadt, 1973, pages 101ff.

5. It can be reasonably maintained that typological distinctions between premodern and modern societies do exist in spite of the many important historical differences between particular societies; that this position does not necessarily imply notions of convergence nor of Western-centricity; and that the classical paradigm is capable of accounting for remnants of traditional structures and symbols within the modern setting and is not inherently ahistorical. Societies can be understood as more or less 'modern' with ideal-types residing at either end of the continuum. Marion Levy, for example, simply draws the distinction between 'relatively non-modern' and 'relatively modern' societies.

6. Max Weber, 'Science as a Vocation,' in Gerth and Mills, *On Max Weber*, Oxford University Press, 1958

7. For a greater elaboration of the points that follow, see James D. Hunter, *American Evangelicalism: Conservative Religion and the Quandary of Modernity*, Rutgers University Press, 1983; *Evangelicalism: The Coming Generation*, University of Chicago Press, 1987.

8. Though a global impulse toward fundamentalism is one of the mechanisms for coping with modernity wherever it takes root, here too fundamentalism looks different in different settings, but with common characteristics which can still be discerned.

2
The rise of postmodernity

PHILIP SAMPSON

If *modernity* is the domain of progress through science, *postmodernity* has lost confidence in such progress, it has been disabused. Only two certainties remain. The first is the currency of the term *postmodern*. The number of entries in the Social Science Citations Index under *postmodern* and related terms[1] rose from 17 to 276 in the five year period to 1991. Its more popular usage has grown in parallel. In 1992 British television screened a three-part series on postmodernity ironically entitled *The Real Thing*, while 'postmodern' has become part of the language of critics and of cultural commentators. This brings me to the second certainty: if the use has mushroomed, its meaning is proportionately obscure. To shamelessly abuse Wittgenstein's aphorism: the mere use of a word does not guarantee its meaning. As one newspaper advised its readers: 'This word [postmodernism] has no meaning. Use it as often as possible'.[2]

Like love in the popular song, postmodernity is a many splendoured thing. Some see it as characterising the mode of production of late capitalism (Jameson), others identify an entirely new mode of activity (Poster); some consider it to presage new creative possibilities (Winter), others see its influence as sinister (Diederichsen); some see it as an essentially new condition (Lyotard), others doubt its existence (Rose), or consider that it articulates the position of dispossessed intellectuals (Bauman). Although I will return to these debates, my purpose here is not to resolve them. Rather, I will examine the rise of postmodernity and use it to map the territory of the modernity which has allegedly been left behind. In doing so I follow Bauman in reversing the usual relationship of modernity to postmodernity whereby the latter is derivative, a counter-identification with modernity.

> The *postmodern* discourse generates its own concept of
> *modernity*, made of the presence of all those things for
> the lack of which the concept of postmodernity stands.[3]

Indeed the anatomy of modernity emerges most clearly under the postmodern knife, regardless of the status we wish to give postmodernity itself. It is that anatomy as a response to God's word for culture and society[4] and its fragmentation in postmodernity which is the focus of this paper.

History of use and definitions

The term *postmodern* appears to have first been used by Federico de Onis in the 1930s,[5] but its currency dates from a reaction against high modernism in art and literature during the 1960s[6] and in architecture and style during the 1970s.[7] It became common coinage in the 1980s, extending its use to embrace the French post-structuralist debates (Foucault, Derrida, Guattari) and some North American pragmatist philosophers such as Rorty.[8] It remains a vague term in comparison with other, more empirically accessible concepts such as *post-capitalist* or *post-industrial*. Definitions take on a global, universal edge. For example, the postmodern is said to refer to:

> a number of related cultural tendencies, a constellation
> of values, a repertoire of procedures and attitudes.[9]

> a noticeable shift in sensibility, practices, and discourse
> formations which distinguishes a postmodern set of
> assumptions, experiences, and propositions from that
> of the preceding period.[10]

> a dominant cultural logic or hegemonic norm
> [transforming the cultural sphere in post 1945
> capitalism].[11]

Even the more whimsical definitions such as 'pessimistic wishful thinking'[12] or 'nihilism with a smile'[13] reflect this.

The evidence for postmodernity

These definitions are frequently criticised for their lack of specificity but a wide variety of evidence has been offered in their support. Perhaps the most plausible refers to changes evident in late industrial capitalism.[14] Modernity has been associated with the displacement of superstition, religion and tradition by scientific knowledge and technology, leading to industrialisation and social progress. The emergence of the democratic nation state, universal franchise and progressive secularisation have been taken as concomitant developments. (This is not, of course, universal. For example, Marx, Weber, Hooykaas, Goudzwaard and Islamic theorists all question one or more of these assertions.) But the last 20 years have seen a change, with the growing dominance of processes of consumption over those of industrial production in the West, giving priority to advertising, the media and service sector industries. Goods are valued for what they mean as much as for their use, and people find meaning in the very act of consumption. Advertising and product image become goods consumed for their own sake, rather than as representative of real products.[15] Signs signify other signs, rather than things, in an unending chain of signifiers for which MTV and television channel-hopping provide exemplars. The dominance of these processes is associated with the emergence of new technologies and communities—computers, telecommunication, the mass media, advertising, accounting, and publishing, which in the US had accounted for more than half the workforce by the mid 1970s.[16]

Once established, such a culture of consumption is quite undiscriminating and everything becomes a consumer item, including meaning, truth and knowledge. Whereas in modernity, meaning is rooted in a tradition of humanist ideals, it is now conferred through communities of product image, style and design. Whereas knowledge in modernity was grounded in science and underwrote humanist emancipation, it is now transformed into information and is targeted at a community of consumers. Research paradigms move from the modernist ideal of generating scientific knowledge, to policy oriented research serving managerial goals.[17] A new museum culture is emerging which no longer seeks epistemological classification under the rubric of progress but presents past, present and future as equivalent and themed according to a plurality of tastes and styles.[18] Professions are no longer normed by the growth in scientific knowledge but by managerial values.[19] Where modernity in the arts, including architecture, emphasized originality

and broke with tradition in the name of progress, postmodernism celebrates the past with references to a multiplicity of
traditions.

Bauman emphasises precisely these changes in meaning and
knowledge, the grand narratives of modernity, in his understanding of postmodernity. The self-confident superiority of the West
was legitimised by an ideology of modernity (progress, truth,
justice, meaning) which was provided by intellectuals. But the
postmodern culture of consumption has resulted in a much
tighter integration of the citizens of western democracies.
Citizens as consumers are seduced by the market into continued,
cooperative social participation and the language of modernity
has become superfluous to the legitimation of social forms. For
example, government social policy in Britain is no longer justified
by the kind of empirical and theoretical enquiry which Beveridge
conducted into the welfare state in the 1940s, but emerges from
the assumption that citizen-consumers are already integrated into
a market. The reflection of intellectuals is redundant and becomes
self-referential; postmodernism is the consequence: a reflexive
phenomenon of dispossessed intellectuals reflecting on their
own, reflecting 'the implosion of intellectual vision'.[20]

It is at present difficult to evaluate such evidence as debate has
a tendency to proceed by exemplary instances rather than by
conventional empirical research. For example, it is not clear how
people experience the new technologies, what new communities
they enable, or whether channel-hopping is any different from
browsing through a bookshop. Is the paradigmatic experience of
hyperspace in postmodern architecture and shopping malls
really new?[21] Is the consumerisation of knowledge and meaning
in the 1980s any different from its commodification as asserted
by Marx in the 1850s? Even the significance of tertiary sector
industries and the growth of information culture is still widely
debated.

From the high ground of modernity, such an information-
based consumer culture is either sinister or superficial. Electronic surveillance and control extends its invisible hand over the
lives of individuals and communities. The simulational world of
spectacle, experience and consumption provides a new opiate of
the people with Disneyesque nostalgia, shopping malls and
theme parks; Las Vegas style rules OK.[22] But, like any human
response to the cultural mandate, information culture opens up

32

new emancipatory possibilities even as it closes others. For example, cable TV has potential for minority broadcasting; computers allow for decentralized communication and social security provision as well as for surveillance; the voice of the citizen-consumer has sometimes restored human scale to architecture and human concern to impersonal bureaucracies; and the mere elitism of high modernism did not guarantee value. Winter argues that postmodernism provides an alternative to hierarchical social relationships of knowledge-creation and hence a democratic, educational base for enquiry.

Before I look at these features of postmodernity in more detail, I will briefly summarise the background of modernity which postmodernity takes as its protagonist.

Modernity and postmodernity

The concept of modernity is itself complex and may be analysed in a number of different ways with which other papers in this collection deal in more detail. I want here to note particularly two aspects of modernity: its Humanism, entailing a break with religion and with traditional legitimations; and the privileged role accorded to Reason as the path to human emancipation.

The Renaissance denotes a pivot for the rise of modernity and the demise of the pre-modern by inaugurating the modern with forms from antiquity. Clerical authority was displaced by a return to a Golden Age when men reflected upon themselves and their world. (I here employ the word 'men' deliberately, since a feature of modernity has been its patriarchy.) Somewhat paradoxically, therefore, modernity broke the shackles of tradition, religion and superstition with the hammer of a humanism forged in Greece and Rome. It was the Enlightenment which fused this humanism with Reason and Kant's three Critiques have taken pride of place in articulating this fusion as a modern vision.[23]

The experience of modernity, then, is to break with traditional hierarchies and justifications. Modern man invents himself and valorises the new in a heroism of self-discovery and self-revelation. The downside is the alienation of the anguished imagination evidenced in the Romantic movement and the sensibility of twentieth century modernism.[24] Modern man comes of age.

This Enlightenment project in the experience of social modernity re-read Christian themes to produce distinctive humanist responses to the scriptural norms for truth, justice, humanness and the role of rationality. These responses are sometimes known as *grand narratives*, for they retain the sense of transcendence of norms even as they undercut the origin of these norms in the God of the scriptures. An immense creative effort went into establishing an immanent basis for grand narratives, central among which was the emancipatory role of reason. The hope of modernity that reason brings progress and emancipation appeared to find support in the achievements of science and technology to such an extent that reason became restricted to an instrumental-cognitive explanation of the world, driving everything else 'into the realm of apparent irrationality'.[25]

Such beliefs were already shaky in the nineteenth century (see, for example, the works of the founding fathers of sociology), but events of the twentieth century have made them very implausible indeed. We can identify six interrelated areas in which difficulties steadily grew:

1. Technical reason increasingly appeared unable to bring the emancipation anticipated by the Enlightenment, especially in social and political life. This has led to the insight that it is the very form of technical rationality which inhibits human beings from finding their potential and to the search for universal forms of rationality which apply to the moral-practical interests of humanity; Habermas has devoted his life work to this project.

2. The very achievements of instrumental rationality which heralded such promise have turned sour: two world wars, industrial pollution, the environmental debate and nuclear armaments have all cast the accomplishments of science into shadow.

3. Poststructuralist theorists have shown that the highpoints of humanistic reform—for example, in penal justice, in the treatment of the insane and the development of clinical medicine—all these markers of humanity's progress are deeply ambiguous. Not only can reform be shown to arise from local, petty and ignominious interests rather than a liberal, humanist vision, but the very act of freeing human beings from inhumane treatment created new systems of domination. Moreover, knowledge and subjectivity are entwined in a will to power which inevitably ties them to subjugation and control.[26]

> From liberal and marxist perspectives discourses about
> society have the intention of furthering emancipation.
> Knowledge promotes freedom. This basic assumption
> characterises discourse since the Enlightenment. A
> serious problem arises, however, when it can be shown
> that such discourses become organised into disciplinary
> institutions . . . and begin to exert a powerful shaping
> influence (not unlike domination) on the social field.[27]

4. The very terms of humanist debate—'human', 'truth', 'justice', 'freedom'—have themselves been treated with scepticism as products of social context, discursive setting, and historical conditions.

5. There has been an increasing recognition of the links between the liberal humanist tradition and colonial history, with increasing criticism of the ethnocentricity of the West's self-confident assertions of superiority. Important contributions to this debate have come from women's studies, gay groups, and the anti-racist movement.

6. The changes involving production, consumption and experience discussed above have cut the social and cultural links with the grand narratives of modernity.

Postmodernity has had no inhibitions in announcing that modernity has been shredded by these problems and with it the authority of the modern intellectual, an 'enlightenment figure' articulating 'the grand metanarrative of emancipation'.[28]

By thus setting postmodernity against the fragmentation of modernity, it is conceived as a reaction against supposed freedoms, truths and certainties. Just as modernity was a break with traditional forms, so postmodernity signifies a break with modernity and a counter-identification with it.

> 'Modernism', as a category, is a vacuous self-
> congratulation, implying that historical periods (e.g.
> 'medieval', 'Renaissance', 'classical') have led up to this,
> here, now . . . In contrast 'postmodernism' is a despairing
> confession: we have no trustworthy explanation of who
> or what we are; we characterise ourselves only as coming
> *afterwards*, as disabused, as defined by a sense of lost
> certainty, of conscious ignorance.[29]

But in giving primacy to modernity in this way, postmodernity becomes derivative and parasitic. Many authors argue from the kind of evidence outlined above that this misses the positivity of postmodernity in its own right; that it overemphasises postmodernity as a reaction to the failure of the Enlightenment project, rather than as distinctive in its own right. Indeed, as I have already noted, Bauman reverses the counter-identification thesis and argues that modernity is a creation of postmodernity in that it only became visible qua *modernity* within a self conscious postmodern debate; modernity itself emerges as a postmodern phenomenon.

It seems likely that the interaction between modern and postmodern discourses is more complex than either of these alternatives. Jameson has noted that advocating the one does not necessarily imply rejecting the other.[30] Indeed, there are obvious advantages to such a mixed economy of use, not least the desire to have the best of both worlds in retaining the vision of modernity in a postmodern era.[31]

The postmodern universe

There is no straightforward way to characterise postmodernity. This need not surprise us, as the belief that everything is open to clear definition is part of the modernity which is surpassed. The classification which follows is therefore open to the objection that it snatches at a shadow, but it does have the virtue of mapping the ground on which the shadow lies.

METANARRATIVES

Lyotard defines as 'modern':

> any science that legitimates itself with reference to a
> metadiscourse [a transcendental or self-referential
> discourse] . . . making an explicit appeal to some grand
> narrative, such as the dialectics of Spirit, the
> hermeneutics of meaning, the emancipation of the
> rational or working subject, or the creation of wealth.[32]

Such grand narratives entail truth, justice, freedom and beauty; terms which, as I have noted, modernity inherited from Christianity and re-read in its own discourse. Of particular importance in modernity has been the narrative of emancipation

36

through science and reason. For example, while discussing the 'scientific approach' to social policy in 1956, Cormack and McDougall quote with approval Denison who wrote in the late 19th century:

> [A] Social Science policy... aims at utilising for
> the purposes of imperial, national, municipal and
> individual life, the great stores of knowledge... [which
> have been] created and accumulated, but which have
> not yet been employed to diminish the sufferings
> and to increase the happiness of humanity at large.[33]

The universal claims of modernity to progress and emancipation are here very clear and are beliefs evidently held with great fervour and conviction. But, as I have argued above, they are beliefs which have come to seem increasingly implausible. As a result, Lyotard argues that the defining feature of the *postmodern* is precisely an 'incredulity toward metanarratives'[34] (that is, the grand narratives of a metadiscourse).

But once such metanarratives go, humanity, understood in the Enlightenment sense, also goes. In Foucault's colourful phrase:

> [Humanity] would be erased, like a face drawn in sand
> at the edge of the sea.[35]

With the collapse of grand narratives to confer privileged status on the Western tradition of the past three centuries, no single account can take priority and we are left with a conflicting field of myths and stories. There is no single truth, only truths, each for its own public and occasion in what Habermas calls the localization of truth.[36] Knowledge becomes a commodity for chat shows. Postmodern law and justice no longer seek the unique truth but arbitrate between disjointed interest groups, each with its own truth.[37]

> [Post-structuralism subverted] the notions of truth,
> meaning and subjectivity held to be the defining
> features of Western metaphysics.[38]

One of the more radical consequences of this has been the implication for our understanding of justice. Modernity has generally been shy of promoting ethical claims but it has been more confident of establishing universal principles in the sphere of justice. For example, Rawls developed a theory of justice in the

37

long line of attempts to place it on a rational basis. Such has been the strength of postmodern arguments that Rawls has since accepted that his theory establishes justice as a rationally defensible concept only within the society from which it emerged; he leaves its validity open in a wider context.[39] To concede that the very concept of justice may be rationally incoherent outside of the Western tradition is a very long way from modernity's desire to establish it as a rational universal.

Modernity responded to God's norms for truth, justice and freedom in a way which took them seriously (as grand narratives), however unsatisfactory as a response it may have been in other respects. Postmodernity has made such serious responses unbelievable, incredible; but this also is a response to those norms, and one which is in this respect even more deplorable than that of modernity. It is worth noting that Christian critiques of modernity, in successfully uncovering the antinomies inherent in modern grand narratives, may reinforce postmodern 'incredulity' towards *any* grand narrative and become but another story in postmodernity's conflicting field of stories, with no more priority than any other. It is true that postmodernity is more open to religious accounts than was doctrinaire modernity, but the price of such openness is to demand that all accounts relinquish their claim to transcendent, unique truth.

THE REPRESENTATION OF THE WORLD

Christian doctrine informs us that God created and continually sustains the world outside of himself by his Word. Within modernity this was re-read to provide a justification for scientific knowledge of the world and hence for the grand narrative of emancipation through science. The Christian doctrine, shorn of its transcendent language, implies that the world, as object, can be conceptually represented by a subject who can know that that representation is true because concepts refer to things in the world. The project of modern epistemology was to show how this might work without the transcendent language; that it makes sense to pursue such a project was an article of modern faith. Postmodernity rejects that faith and with it the idea of reference. There is no given object world; concepts can have no unrepresented referent; and there is no knowledge outside of specific forms of discourse. Rather we represent one 'thing' in terms of another without end and none is granted priority or preferential reality; all is simulation. Moreover the only place to stand is within a representation. There is nowhere else to stand from which to judge whether this representation is true. It follows that knowledge of the world is no longer possible in the sense of modernity.[40]

This enables us to understand a common feature of post-modernity which may otherwise appear as a mere matter of style. Postmodern disciplines and discourses continually destabilize the process of representation by a variety of tropes: irony, quotation, parody, stylistic promiscuity, eclecticism, pastiche, jokeyness and playfulness, all aimed at distancing the reader or viewer from the representation. Thus postmodern design uses different typefaces and irregular left margin; film, a variety of visual references to different periods, genres and classic films; architecture, an eclectic mix of styles and decorative reference ironically juxtaposed; and literature, a plethora of genre, style, temporal reference and typography. Each in its own way makes the point that there is no fixed point of reference, no object world outside of representation, no knowledge of this world, and that style is nine points of the real.

The picture presented by modernity included an object world, scientific knowledge and causal accounts of how things work. Problems could be solved and humanity could progress by drawing upon our knowledge of the world to find the underlying difficulty and resolve it. All this has gone. We now have a surface of representations, without depth and without differentiation. Postmodernity celebrates surface over depth and transforms reality into the figural, into images.[41] Visual images are privileged over words; the immersion of the spectator over the objectivity of the observer. The body and bodily sensation receive a new emphasis.[42] A common paradigm for this is television channel-hopping, involving a series of disconnected images, each in its own present, and each enjoyed for its place in a surface of images with no narrative structure and no map. By contrast, the gospel relies upon the word rather than the image (Romans 10), and upon explanation rather than spectacle (Acts 8); it is difficult to see how the gospel can faithfully be conveyed within the tunnel vision of postmodernity.

THE LOSS OF HOPE

The hope of the Christian rests in the redemption accomplished by Jesus and applied to our hearts. Modernity denied itself this hope but tried to preserve another. The scriptural promises of freedom were re-read in modernity as humanist freedom: 'constant growth of man's ability, insight, and earthly happiness'.[43] The hope of modernity is that such freedom comes through science and knowledge; above all, through Reason.

This hope is modest compared with the Christian hope, what Lyon calls a 'black and white rainbow',[44] but it is still very significant in its own terms *if it is true*. But it is not true; and not even the shadow of the rainbow remains. This was a bitter disappointment to modernity and one response to such disappointment is the postmodern incredulity towards all metanarratives. Reason is displaced by reasons, each within its own discourse and for its own public. None is privileged. The rational project begun in the seventeenth century has collapsed, leaving a field of competing rationalities. But then there is no privileged rationality to adjudicate and therefore no rational basis for judgement; Habermas, probably the ablest defender of modernity, sees only the triumph of desire over reason in the postmodern vision of the world.[45]

With the loss of hope we also lose theories relying upon it. For example, social contract theory has had a long history in trying to provide a rational basis for social organization but this now appears as a very parochial affair, displaced by the closer integration of consumers in a market:

> . . .the rational sociality of the contract . . . gives way to the sociality of contact.[46]

Concomitant with this loss of hope is the marginalisation of rationality; science may be pragmatically successful but it cannot be true in any privileged sense.[47] Now I have not greatly emphasized it, but the faith in progress through reason had a background of actual accomplishments, beginning in the natural sciences of the eighteenth century but continuing in the nineteenth.[48] Although the role of the Reformation in providing the conditions for these accomplishments remains debated, that it had such a role is widely argued.[49] Science and knowledge are possible because the created world is attuned to the norms which govern it. Where rationality is given its place in obediently opening up God's world, there is hope for the future, for God has established his kingdom.[50] But in modernity, a particular form of rationality carried the hope of the world and collapsed beneath the weight. Postmodernity has recognised this and has rejected a false hope; but it has also rejected the possibility of any hope at all and with it the possibility of reason finding its true place in the world.

Fragmentation

Modernity, once so solid and self-confident, has fragmented. The genius of postmodernity has been its ability to build from the remains:

> [Postmodernism entails] an ever wider dispersal and dissemination of artistic procedures all working out of the ruins of the modernist edifice, raiding it for ideas, plundering its vocabulary and supplementing it with randomly chosen images and motifs from premodern and non-modern cultures as well as from contemporary mass culture.[51]

Huyssen is referring primarily to the arts but parallel considerations apply elsewhere. Incredulity towards metanarratives and the radical egalitarianism of representation in postmodernity have combined to prevent any one tradition or ideology from being granted priority in unifying all others. A key feature of postmodernity is therefore homogeneous plurality within fragmentation of cultures, traditions, ideologies, forms of life, language games, or life worlds.

This is an important transformation of hermeneutical theory. Within modernity, hermeneutics continued to privilege rational communication in order to provide a basis for debate and exchange between traditions.[52] In postmodern hermeneutics no such basis is possible as the privileging of rational communication is but another tradition which is on precisely the same footing as all others. There can be no rational basis, no evolutionary classification of ideologies or stages, no ethical distinction, no external viewpoint from which to judge and compare. The modern world fragments and the problem emerges of securing communication between traditions (or cultures etc.).[53]

This fragmentation of modernity could be described as either relativism or pluralism, depending upon how one feels about it, and it has become a central issue of debate. I am only able here briefly to illustrate a few consequences.

TIME

The linear, evolutionary time of modernity with its periodisation of past, present and future, fragments into a series of presents.[54] History in the modern sense becomes impossible; all history is history of the present. Thus postmodernity's relation to the past lacks a sense of progress or even evaluation. The past is not so much a historical 'there' as a repetition 'now' as pastiche, nostalgia and the superimposition of historical reference. From literature (Vonnegut or John Fowles) and film (David Lynch) to philosophy (Foucault[55]); from the heritage industry and museum culture to architecture; time is dislocated and fragmented.

SOCIETY, POLITICS AND JUSTICE

The modern, industrial, democratic nation-state has been associated with a centralised organization legitimized by the grand narratives of justice, emancipation and progress. Many social institutions have appealed to a similar justification: for example, the treatment of criminality as the product of an unjust, oppressive environment causing psychological maladjustment; or the welfare state's provision for poverty and disadvantage. The Social Science Policy of Denison noted earlier is an example of this.

Postmodernism has undone the assumptions on which all this was based. Universal justifications for social policies have been replaced by pragmatic arguments devised for particular occasions. Administration has become fragmented and decentralised, with proliferating networks of interaction. These become 'the organising concepts of a postmodern *administrative control apparatus*'.[56] Information technology facilitates rapid information exchange around these networks and the tailoring of supply to customer demand. The world fragments into designer cultures and communities, each a 'black box' referring only to itself and squeezing the voice of the subject.[57] The challenge for the church here is to take up its task in the reformation and renewal of all of life, rather than becoming another isolated customer centre, offering designer religion, the televangelistic marketing of religious products and images.[58]

This fragmentation undermines the common community of values, the basis for common interests and political action.[59] New social movements have emerged (e.g. the women's movement, gay and lesbian rights, anti-racism, ecology, environmental and peace movements), with a self-limiting radicalism which rejects the modernist project of speaking in the name of justice for all oppressed members of society.[60] Where the political interests of modernity were organized around questions of the distribution of goods and benefits, these new movements are concerned with forms of life.[61] This loss of political unity and power is for many commentators symptomatic of the inherently reactionary nature of postmodernity.[62] As citizens become consumers, integrated into society by the seductions of the market, and able to participate directly in political policy through technological innovation, representative democracy becomes a minority interest for those who are excluded from the market, for the oppressed, the poor.[63] Consequent tensions in the once unifying grand narrative of citizenship have emerged, with commentators divided on its future.[64]

Identification with the oppressed has a Christian background and found a place in the humanism of modernity. It is preserved in the political action of some poststructuralists such as Michel Foucault, but he is careful to maintain that this arises from the particular circumstances and not from a universal such as legitimized political action in modernity.

> [The poststructuralism of Foucault] cannot validate for
> [the right to justice of the oppressed and excluded] any
> superiority according to standards of truth claims that
> would transcend local arguments.[65]

The local demands of the new social movements displace the universal claims to justice of the poor and oppressed. Registered charities and voluntary organisations compete with one another for limited resources. To be merely poor is no longer marketable. How will their voice be heard?

Justice and the function of law are transformed. In modernity law sought to uncover the one unique truth on which judgment rests. In postmodernity law seeks to arbitrate between a 'flat, one-dimensional collage of disjointed agencies of control',[66] each of which establishes its own truth. Even advocates of postmodern jurisprudence have expressed concern at some of its consequences.[67]

As I suggested earlier, postmodernity opens up new possibilities even as it forecloses those of modernity. Many authors see the balance coming down heavily in favour of increased democracy, individual choice and empowerment. Fragmentation itself is seen as positive in pluralising social life and extending choices.[68] Consumer power and choice is enhanced. Interaction with senior politicians is democratised through the electronic town hall meeting whereby ordinary people from locations throughout the country can put direct questions through live TV links for national broadcasting. Policemen come out of their modern cars and return to the community in a blend of traditional beat-policing (walking a set route) with the latest electronic communications. Churches exploit the latest media technology and draw upon a wide range of traditions to present their message to an ever wider public. Such unqualified optimism is likely to be as disappointed as that of the modernity it displaces.

HUMAN IDENTITY

Scripture refers human identity outside creation to God as we image him in response to his word. Modernity locates human identity immanently within the world and at the centre of the world; human beings are reflexively related to themselves in self discovery and insight. The human subject was placed over against the object world in the natural sciences, and in due course over against itself, as the human being became both the subject and object of reflection in the human sciences. Humanity was at once aggrandised as subject and placed in doubt as object of enquiry. Even as human identity was placed at the centre, the search for an vital inner core of self began. The risk attending such identity is that of *alienation*.

In postmodernity this search for an inner self is abandoned. There is no inner self to find, no essence from which to be alienated. Postmodern identity displaced the inner core of an individual by a construction of images which are part of relationships:[69] the 'I' and 'me' are both discursive phenomena and we may choose which image to present, just as we choose other consumer products. There is no subject in the self, only a subject on the shelf. Where modern identity referred to a unity of past, present and future in a consensual narrative, postmodernity displaces this with fragmentation, local narratives and a series of presents.[70] The unity of the 'I' is 'more like the unity of a story than the unity of a thing'.[71] The risk attaching to such identity is that it will fall apart and the characterising metaphor of postmodern identity is therefore that of *schizophrenia* rather than alienation.[72]

> With postmodern consciousness begins the erasure of
> the category of self . . . we realise increasingly that who
> and what we are is not [so] much the result of our
> 'personal essence' . . . but how we are constructed in
> various social groups. The initial stages of this
> consciousness result in a sense of the self as a social
> con artist, manipulating images to achieve ends. As the
> category of 'real self' continues to recede from view,
> however, one acquires a pastiche-like personality.[73]

Goffman uses as an analogy of the self the image of a theatre where actors present performances for various audiences who cooperate in maintaining an agreed definition of the play/situation.[74] Tseelon argues that the 'Goffmanesque self is postmodern in that it consists of surfaces or performances'.[75]

> The immediacy of events, the sensationalism of the
> spectacle (political, scientific, military as well as those
> of entertainment), become the stuff of which
> consciousness is forged.[76]

Literature, music and film present instances of postmodern identity (for example William Burroughs/David Cronenberg, David Bowie, David Lynch) but the exemplary case of a self presenting a range of identities or performances is provided by Madonna, who draws on a multiplicity of representation, from Material Girl, through creator of her own sexuality, to the vulnerability of Monroe.[77]

THE DEMISE OF ÉLITES

Modernity has become associated with a variety of hierarchies: from the bureaucracies of social institutions; through the power of professionals; to the cultural elitism of high modernism. These hierarchies have been legitimised by grand narratives, particularly those which valorise knowledge and causal processes operating beneath the surface of appearances. With the collapse of grand narratives and the postmodern disdain for depth, hierarchies also collapse and with them the distinction between elite and mass culture.[78] Postmodernism celebrates mass, popular culture over the elitist high culture of modernism; consumers over professionals; the citizen over the expert.

Advocates of postmodernity see here new opportunities for democratization and the empowerment of the consumer-citizen. Others doubt that the mass culture of late capitalism is entirely admirable[79] or that the obliteration of hierarchies of value in politics will inevitably lead in a democratic direction.[80] As I will suggest below, postmodernity tends to produce its own distinctive hierarchies despite its best intentions.

The new certainties

Postmodernity reflects a loss of confidence in all the old certainties and justifications of Western society; and with them their hierarchies, elites and bureaucracies. The advocates of postmodernity see in this an opportunity to democratise institutions and professions which have previously been controlled by a self-serving elite: medicine, law, education and social welfare agencies have all been candidates. It is beyond the scope of this paper to discuss these claims in detail but there are a number of reasons to believe that it is more difficult to avoid new and equally oppressive certainties from arising than postmodern theorists allow.

Postmodernity disclaims a metanarrative of its own but a number of authors observe an inconsistency here. The very notion of a postmodern era makes appeal to the modern category of periodization. Foucault's universalization of power or the central place given to rhetoric by Derrida appear to privilege their own texts. Winter notes that Lyotard's seminal work, commissioned by a powerful institution, implicitly privileges itself as an authoritative generalization about knowledge, presents the 'outline of a "grand narrative" . . . a vision of decentralised knowledge creation',[81] and is set fair to raise a new elite.[82] Indeed some poststructuralists themselves propose a new integration point which might be described as anarchic aesthetics.[83] This emphasizes bodily experience, pleasures and sensation; surface over depth; rhetoric over logic; literature over philosophy; and the image over the word, in what Habermas has called the aesthetization of life and morals.[84] Quite what the consequences of such a scheme would be is difficult to say as poststructural theory is stronger on deconstruction than developing alternatives, but a form of postmodern certainty is visible in recent changes in the professions and those institutions associated with them.

Through the application of instrumental rationality in modernity, areas of expertise emerged, each with its own knowledge and skills; professional groupings were organised around these and there was a widespread consensus that, within their own field, such professional experts should have the last say. Take the example of medicine: where a dispute arises in the treatment of an illness, the court of appeal is the professional knowledge possessed by the expert physicians. This consensus is breaking down.

The emancipatory hope of modernity in medical progress and knowledge led to the establishment of the National Health Service in Britain after the Second World War; it was anticipated that medical advance would lead to a declining call upon that Service as the health of the population improved. This has not proved to be the case. Not only is the demand for health care ever increasing but the belief that scientific medicine is the solution now seems implausible. Alternative therapies blossom and medicine finds itself in a crisis. Moreover, there is no longer a consensus that the court of appeal competent to resolve this crisis is that of professional medicine itself. Indeed scientific medicine, far from providing the solution, is now part of the problem, with its ever-expanding repertoire of techniques and the resultant depersonalization of the patient.

Where then is the solution to be found? Certainly not in a socialist or liberal welfare model which were themselves based upon the hope of progress through the planned application of scientific knowledge and which are widely perceived to have failed. The postmodern critique of medicine has converged with its commercialisation to produce a post-modern solution—that of the new conservatism.[85] The problem, it is argued, was caused by the very liberal welfarism intended to solve it and the answer is to allow market forces to operate and regulate health care, with the consumer or customer acquiring a new authority over the expert. Turner quotes Friedman as arguing on free market grounds against the licensing of doctors, and as advocating a deregulated supermarket of health products. Orthodox medicine would have to compete with alternative therapies in the market-place of customer choice.[86] The professional élite, rooted in the knowledge of modernity, has been displaced by the empowered consumer-citizen.

Of course market forces demand efficient and effective organizational contexts, and this in turn requires a new generation of managers who become the competent authorities to resolve the problem. The consequent growth in management services in Britain has been meteoric. Moreover, as a postmodern phenomenon, management discourse provides its own justification beyond the reach of rationality in the modernist sense.[87]

> Market rationality is the ability to make right market
> decisions to be marketable.[88]

The important feature of this is that exactly the same considerations apply to other social institutions. For example, the criminal justice system (CJS) in Britain was, in the post-war period, legitimized by modern metanarratives of justice and the scientific treatment of offenders. Neither now seems credible, and the 'mission statement' of the CJS has become the *management of offenders*. Similar changes have taken place in law, education and social service provision. Churches in Britain turn to management models to guide their vision, with the 'church audit', five-year plan and statement of aims and objectives; by a curious irony, some even propose a 'mission statement'.[89] We see a new hierarchy of the management expert beginning to emerge. The demise of specific courts of appeal within each profession, the homogenized control of the market and the emergence of a new, universal group of management experts have been the paradoxical results of the postmodern desire to let a thousand flowers bloom. Such new power centres need intellectual support and who better to provide it than postmodern theorists? This increasing uniformity not only reverses the differentiations of modernity, but appears to run directly counter to Christian insights into the 'sphere sovereignty' of Abraham Kuyper.

Within Western democracies, the residue of modernity has provided a sense of direction to such developments; at best this can be sustained by a new authoritarianism of liberal rhetoric; at worst, it leads to the authoritarian irrationalism of the Right.

Dangerous liaisons

Whether we regard postmodernity as distinct from modernity or as another twist in its spiral, it is apparent at the very least that the contradictions of modernity are being posed in acute form. Advocates of modernity have been forced to face challenges not only in theory but in the very achievements formerly regarded as the jewels in its crown. Moreover, this has not only been from outside the camp; some of the most trenchant criticism has been from those who wish to perpetuate the tradition.[90] One might suppose that Christians should welcome the emergence of these difficulties with open arms as the inevitable collapse of an idolatrous intellectual pride. In some respects, however, we find ourselves allied with modernity; for example, in its rejection of irrationalism. Moreover, many of the metanarratives of modernity entail an understanding of justice, humanness and truth which we too wish to defend as serious and universal. This is not simply a theoretical debate, although that would be important enough in itself, but as I have tried to show it has implications throughout social, political and economic life. We can have some sympathy with Giddens when he writes:

> There is no need to release hold of [what Habermas
> calls] 'modernism' yet, to renounce the ideals of the
> Enlightenment as false gods to be replaced by a brutish
> acquiescence in the reality of power.[91]

But Giddens unintentionally shows us the limit of such alliances, for the 'ideals of the Enlightenment' precisely are false gods, and it is their vulnerability as idols which has undermined them. To stand they must take their place in the world God has made, having reference to him.

In other respects, we may be closer to postmodernity's rejection of arrogant and doctrinaire rationalism while always insisting that irrationalism and the universality of power are cures worse than the disease.

The debate over postmodernity provides an opportunity for presenting the gospel as the only foundation adequate to support the grand narratives which modernity took for granted. But to do so, we must become engaged with the world at all levels. The greatest irony would be for Christians uncritically to join the assault on a dying modernity only to find ourselves as but one story among many, unintentionally reinforcing the irrationalism of postmodernity.

Notes

1. A number of different terms are in current use. I will generally use *modernity* and *postmodernity* in preference to *modernism* and *postmodernism* as the latter often refer to a specific movement in art and literature carrying a slightly different range of meanings from those which I wish to emphasise. Other terms which appear are: postindustrialism, post-Fordism, postmaterialism, late or disorganised capitalism, the information society, and silicon city.

2. M. Featherstone, 'In Pursuit of the Postmodern: an introduction', in *Theory, Culture & Society*, volume 5.2–3, 1988, page 195

3. Z. Bauman, 'Is there a postmodern sociology?', in *Theory, Culture & Society*, volume 5.2–3, 1988, page 219

4. H. R. Van Til, *The Calvinistic Concept of Culture*, Presbyterian and Reformed, 1972; and H. Dooyeweerd, *A New Critique of Theoretical Thought*, Presbyterian and Reformed, Philadelphia, 1969

5. I. Hassan, 'The Culture of Postmodernism', *Theory, Culture & Society*, volume 2, 1985, pages 119–131

6. For example Warhol and Pop art; Vonnegut, Barth and Barthelme in literature. The range of others who have been called postmodern include: Bacon, Rauschenberg in art; Cage, Stockhausen in music; Pynchon, Burroughs, Ballard in literature; Greenaway and Lynch in film; Jencks, Venturi, Farrell in architecture; and Lyotard, Derrida, Baudrillard, Vattimo and Rorty in philosophy.

7. R. Venturi, D. Scott-Brown, and S. Izenour, *Learning from Las Vegas: the forgotten symbolism of architectural form*, MIT Press, 1972; and C. Jencks, *The Language of Postmodern Architecture*, Rizzoli, 1977

8. A. Huyssen, 'Mapping the Postmodern', in *New German Critique*, number 33, 1984, pages 5–52; and R. Rorty, 'Book Review', *London Review of Books*, 3 September 1987

9. I. Hassan, 'The Culture of Postmodernism', *Theory, Culture & Society*, volume 2, 1985, page 119

10. A. Huyssen, *After The Great Divide: modernism, mass culture, postmodernism*, Indiana University Press, 1986, page 181

11. F. Jameson, 'Postmodernism, or the Cultural Logic of Late Capitalism', in *New Left Review*, number 146, 1984, page 57

12. J. Gardner, 'Notes and Queries', *Guardian*, 7 September 1992, page 17

13. I first heard this phrase in a discussion at English L'Abri in 1992. [Wim

Rietkerk of Dutch L'Abri used it in his lecture, 'Postmodernity', given at the L'Abri Conference in Cambridge, December 1990.]

14. It is beyond the scope of this paper to discuss them here, but A.J. Garrood has produced a series of papers for the Ilkley Group of Christian sociologists which argue for a specifically Christian foundation for postmodernity. They are obtainable from Dr A. J. Garrood, 23 George Road, Guildford, Surrey, England GU1 4NP, and I commend them to the reader.

15. J. Baudrillard, *Simulations*, Semiotext(e) Inc., New York, 1983

16. T. Luke, 'From Fundamentalism to Televangelism', in *Telos*, number 58, 1983, pages 204–210; and M. Poster, *Foucault, Marxism and History*, Polity, 1984

17. R. V. G. Clark, 'Penal Policy Making and Research in the Home Office', in N. Walker, editor, *Penal Policy Making in England*, Cropwood Papers, 1976

18. D. Roberts, 'Beyond Progress: the museum and montage', in *Theory, Culture & Society*, volume 5.2–3, 1988, pages 543–557

19. W. McWilliams, 'Reducing the Role of Research', in *Probation Journal*, number 31.3, 1984, pages 87–88

20. Bauman [note 3]

21. Jameson [note 11]

22. Venturi and others [note 7]

23. J. Habermas, *The Philosophical Discourse of Modernity*, Polity, 1987

24. D. Frisby, 'George Simmel: first sociologist of modernity', in *Theory, Culture & Society*, volume 2.3, 1985, pages 49–67; D. Frisby, *Fragments of Modernity*, Polity, 1985; and M. Berman, *All That Is Solid Melts into Air*, Simon & Schuster, 1982

25. J. Habermas, 'Interview with Jürgen Habermas', *New German Critique*, number 18, autumn 1979, page 43

26. M. Foucault, *Discipline and Punish*, Penguin, 1977

27. Poster [note 16], page 160

28. Lyotard quoted by Featherstone [note 2], page 212

29. R. Winter, 'Postmodern Sociology as a Democratic Educational Practice? Some Suggestions', in *Br J Soc Ed*, number 12.4, 1991, page 471

30. F. Jameson, 'The Politics of Theory: ideological positions in the postmodernism debate', in *New German Critique*, number 33, 1984, pages 53–65

31. Bauman [note 3], pages 231-32. The weakness with this argument is apparent on page 231 where the value of the project of modernity is simply taken for granted and implicitly privileged above others.

32. J.-F. Lyotard, *The Postmodern Condition: a report on knowledge*, Manchester University Press, 1986, page xxiii

33. U. Cormack and K. McDougall, 'Casework in Social Service', in Morris, *Social Casework in Great Britiain*, Faber, 1954, page 25

34. Lyotard [note 32], page xxiv

35. M. Foucault, *The Order of Things*, Tavistock, 1970, page 387

36. Habermas [note 23]

37. A. Carty and J. Mair, 'Some Postmodern Perspectives on Law and Society', in *J Law Soc*, number 17(4), 1990, pages 395–410

38. A. Callinicos, *Against postmodernism: a marxist critique*, Polity, 1984, page 100

39. see first J. Rawls, *A Theory of Justice*, Harvard University Press, 1971; and later J. Rawls, 'Kantian Constructivism in Moral Theory', in *The Journal of Philosophy*, number 77, 1980

40. Baudrillard [note 15] and Lyotard [note 32]

41. Jameson [note 11]

42. S. Lash, 'Discourse or Figure? Postmodernism as a "Regime of Signification" ', in *Theory, Culture & Society*, volume 5.2–3, 1988, pages 322–336

43. R. Goudzwaard, *Capitalism and Progress*, Wedge, 1979, page 36

44. D. Lyon, *Future Society*, Lion Publishing, 1984, page 30

45. Habermas [note 23]

46. J. Baudrillard, *In the Shadow of the Silent Majorities . . . or the end of the social, and other essays*, Semiotext(e) Inc., New York, 1983, page 83

47. R. Rorty, *Philosophy and the Mirror of Nature*, Princeton University Press, 1979

48. Goudzwaard [note 43]

49. R. Hooykaas, *Christian Faith and the Freedom of Science*, Eerdmans, 1972; and M. Weber, *The Protestant Ethic and the Spirit of Capitalism*, Unwin, 1949

50. Lyon [note 44]

51. Huyssen [note 8], page 25

52. H.-G. Gadamer, *Truth and Method*, Seabury Press, 1975

53. Bauman [note 3], pages 225-26

54. Jameson [note 11]

55. M. Foucault, *The Archeology of Knowledge*, Tavistock, 1972

56. P. Wexler, *Social Analysis of Education: after the new sociology*, Routledge & Kegan Paul, 1987, page 157 (emphasis in the original). This does not necessarily result in the weakening of central control.

57. Carty and Mair [note 37], page 396

58. Luke [note 16]; see also Chapter 13 in this book: John Seel, 'Modernity and Evangelicals: American Evangelicalism as a Global Case Study'.

59. J. Gibbins, editor, *Contemporary Political Culture: politics in a postmodern age*, Sage, 1989

60. J. Cohen, 'Strategy or Identity: new theoretical paradigms and contemporary social movements', in *Social Research*, volume 52, 1985, pages 663–716

61. J. Habermas, 'New Social Movements', in *Telos*, number 49, 1981, page 33

62. Callinicos [note 38]; and Habermas [note 23]

63. Bauman [note 3]

64. D. Heater, *Citizenship: the civic ideal in world history, politics and education*, Longmans, 1990; and P. Wexler, 'Citizenship in the Semiotic Society', in B. S. Turner, editor, *Theories of Modernity and Postmodernity*, Sage, 1990

65. Habermas [note 23], page 281

66. Carty and Mair [note 37], page 404

67. C. Stone, *Postmodernism and Criminal Justice*, Institute of Criminal Justice, University of Southampton, Occasional Paper number 4, 1988

68. S. Hall, 'The Meaning of New Times', in S. Hall and M. Jacques, editors, *New Times: the changing face of politics in the 1990s*, Lawrence and Wishart, 1989, page 129

69. K. J. Gergen *The Saturated Self: dilemmas of identity in contemporary life*, Basic Books, 1990

70. Jameson [note 11], page 72

71. R. Harre, 'Social Sources of Mental Content and Order', in J. Margolis, P. T. Manicas, R. Harre, and P. F. Secord, editors, *Psychology: designing the paradigm*, Blackwell, 1986

72. Compare this sense of schizophrenia (which derives from Lacan's analysis of a pre-symbolic, fragmentary, imaginary order) with the texts of Laing which were still influenced by modern understandings of identity. Laing spoke of schizophrenia as a rational response to insane communication or as ontological insecurity: both are closer to forms of alienation from the *Other* and from *being* respectively. See G. Deleuze and F. Guattari, *Anti-Oedipus: capitalism and schizophrenia*, Athlone, 1982; D. Harvey, *The Condition of Postmodernity: an enquiry into the origins of cultural change*, Blackwell, 1989; Jencks [note 7]

73. Gergen [note 69], page 170

74. E. Goffman, *The Presentation of Self in Everyday Life*, Penguin, 1969

75. E. Tseelon, 'Is the Presented Self Sincere? Goffman, impression management and the postmodern self', in *Theory, Culture & Society*, volume 9.2, 1992, page 121

76. Harvey [note 72], page 54

77. C. Switchenberg, *The Madonna Connection: representational politics, subcultural identities and cultural theory*, Westview Press,, 1992

78. B. S. Turner, 'The Interdisciplinary Curriculum: from social medicine to postmodernism', in *Sociology of Health and Illness*, volume 12.1, 1990, pages 1–23

79. Jameson [note 11]

80. Habermas [note 23]; and D. Diederichsen, 'Spiritual Reactionaries After German Reunification: Syberberg, Foucault and Others', *October*, volume 62, pages 65–83, MIT Press, 1992

81. Winter [note 29], page 473

82. D. Kellner, 'Postmodernism as Social Theory: some challenges and problems', in *Theory, Culture & Society*, volume 5.2–3, 1988, pages 239–270

83. M. Foucault, 'On the Genealogy of Ethics: an overview of work in progress', in P. Rabinow, editor, *The Foucault Reader*, Penguin, 1984, pages 340–373; and M. Foucault, *The Use of Pleasure: the history of sexuality*, volume 2, Penguin, 1985

84. Habermas [note 23]

85. Turner [note 78]

86. the same, page 18

87. C. Humphrey, 'Calling in the experts: the financial management initiative (FMI): private sector management consultants and the probation service', in *Howard J*, volume 30.1, 1991, pages 1–18

88. Bauman [note 3], page 222

89. See Chapter 13 in this book: John Seel, 'Modernity and Evangelicals: American Evangelicalism as a Global Case Study'.

90. For example: M. Horkheimer and T. Adorno, *The Dialectic of Enlightenment*, Seabury Press, 1972

91. A. Giddens, *Profiles and Critiques in Social Theory*, Macmillan, 1976

Bibliography

Baudrillard, J., *Simulations*, Semiotext(e) Inc., New York, 1983

Baudrillard, J., *In the Shadow of the Silent Majorities . . . or the end of the social, and other essays*, Semiotext(e) Inc., New York, 1983

Bauman, Z., 'Is There a Postmodern Sociology?', in *Theory, Culture & Society*, volume 5.2–3, 1988, pages 217–238

Berman, M., *All That Is Solid Melts into Air*, Simon & Schuster, 1982

Callinicos, A., *Against Postmodernism: a marxist critique*, Polity, 1984

Callinicos, A., 'Reactionary postmodernism?', in Boyne, R. and Rattansi, A., editors, *Postmodernism and Society*, Macmillan, 1990

Carty, A. and Mair, J., 'Some Postmodern Perspectives on Law and Society', in *J Law Soc*, number 17(4), 1990, pages 395–410

Clark, R.V.G., 'Penal Policy Making and Research in the Home Office', in Walker, N., editor, *Penal Policy Making in England*, Cropwood Papers, 1976

Cohen, J., 'Strategy or Identity: new theoretical paradigms and contemporary social movements', in *Social Research*, volume 52, 1985, pages 663–716

Cormack, U. and McDougall, K., 'Casework in Social Service', in Morris, *Social Casework in Great Britian*, Faber, 1954

Deleuze, G. and Guattari, F., *Anti-Oedipus: capitalism and schizophrenia*, Athlone, 1982

Diederichsen, D., 'Spiritual Reactionaries After German Reunification: Syberberg, Foucault and Others', *October*, volume 62, pages 65–83, MIT Press, 1992

Dooyeweerd, H., *A New Critique of Theoretical Thought*, Presbyterian and Reformed, 1969

Featherstone, M., 'In Pursuit of the Postmodern: an introduction', in *Theory, Culture & Society*, volume 5.2–3, 1988, pages 195–216

Foucault, M., *The Order of Things*, Tavistock, 1970

Foucault, M., *The Archeology of Knowledge*, Tavistock, 1972

Foucault, M., *Discipline and Punish*, Penguin, 1977

Foucault, M., 'On the Genealogy of Ethics: an overview of work in progress', in Rabinow, P., editor, *The Foucault Reader*, Penguin, 1984, pages 340–373

Foucault, M. *The Use of Pleasure: the history of sexuality*, volume 2, Penguin, 1985

Frisby, D., 'George Simmel: first sociologist of modernity', in *Theory, Culture & Society*, volume 2.3, 1985, pages 49–67

Frisby, D., *Fragments of Modernity*, Polity, 1985

Gadamer, H.-G., *Truth and Method*, Seabury Press, 1975

Gibbins, J., editor, *Contemporary Political Culture: politics in a postmodern age*, Sage, 1989

Gardner, J., 'Notes and Queries', *Guardian*, 7 September 1992, page 17

Gergen, K.J., *The Saturated Self: dilemmas of identity in contemporary life*, Basic Books, 1990

Giddens, A., *Profiles and Critiques in Social Theory*, Macmillan, 1976

Goffman, E., *The Presentation of Self in Everyday Life*, Penguin, 1969

Goudzwaard, R., *Capitalism and Progress*, Wedge, 1979

Heater, D., *Citizenship: the civic ideal in world history, politics and education*, Longmans, 1990

Habermas, J., 'Interview with Jürgen Habermas', *New German Critique*, number 18, autumn 1979

Habermas, J., 'New Social Movements', in *Telos*, number 49, 1981, pages 33–37

Habermas, J., *The Philosophical Discourse of Modernity*, Polity, 1987

Hall, S., 'The Meaning of New Times', in Hall, S. and Jacques, M., editors, *New Times: the changing face of politics in the 1990s*, Lawrence and Wishart, 1989

Harre, R., 'Social Sources of Mental Content and Order', in Margolis, J., Manicas, P.T., Harre, R. and Secord, P. F., editors, *Psychology: designing the paradigm*, Blackwell, 1986

Harvey, D., *The Condition of Postmodernity: an enquiry into the origins of cultural change*, Blackwell, 1989

Hassan, I., 'The Culture of Postmodernism', *Theory, Culture & Society*, volume 2, 1985, pages 119–131

Hooykaas, R., *Christian Faith and the Freedom of Science*, Eerdmans, 1972

Horkheimer, M. and Adorno, T., *The Dialectic of Enlightenment*, Seabury Press, 1972

Humphrey, C., 'Calling in the experts: the financial management initiative (FMI): private sector management consultants and the probation service', in *Howard J*, volume 30.1, 1991, pages 1–18

Huyssen, A., 'Mapping the Postmodern', in *New German Critique*, number 33, 1984, pages 5–52

Huyssen, A., *After The Great Divide: modernism, mass culture, postmodernism*, Indiana University Press, 1986

Jameson, F., 'Postmodernism, or the Cultural Logic of Late Capitalism', in *New Left Review*, number 146, 1984, pages 53–92

Jameson, F., 'The Politics of Theory: ideological positions in the postmodernism debate', in *New German Critique*, number 33, 1984, pages 53–65

Jencks, C., *The Language of Postmodern Architecture*, Rizzoli, 1977

Kellner, D., 'Postmodernism as Social Theory: some challenges and problems', in *Theory, Culture & Society*, volume 5.2–3, 1988, pages 239–270

Lash, S., 'Discourse or Figure? Postmodernism as a "Regime of Signification"', in *Theory, Culture & Society*, volume 5.2–3, 1988, pages 322–336

Luke, T., 'From Fundamentalism to Televangelism', in *Telos*, number 58, 1983, pages 204–210

Luke, T. and White, S., 'Critical Theory, the Informational Revolution, and an Ecological Path to Modernity', in Forrester, J., editor, *Critical Theory and Public Life*, MIT Press, 1985

Lyon, D., *Future Society*, Lion Publishing, 1984

Lyotard, J.-F., *The Postmodern Condition: a report on knowledge*, Manchester University Press, 1984

McWilliams, W., 'Reducing the Role of Research', in *Probation Journal*, number 31.3, 1984, pages 87–88

Poster, M., *Foucault, Marxism and History*, Polity, 1984

Rawls, J., *A Theory of Justice*, Harvard University Press, 1971

Rawls, J., 'Kantian Constructivism in Moral Theory', in *The Journal of Philosophy*, number 77, 1980

Roberts, D., 'Beyond Progress: the museum and montage', in *Theory, Culture & Society*, volume 5.2–3, 1988, pages 543–557

Rorty, R., *Philosophy and the Mirror of Nature*, Princeton University Press, 1979

Rorty, R., 'Book Review', *London Review of Books*, 3 September 1987

Rose, G., 'Architecture to Philosophy: the postmodern complicity', in *Theory, Culture & Society*, volume 5.2–3, 1988, pages 357–372

Stone, C., *Postmodernism and Criminal Justice*, Institute of Criminal Justice, University of Southampton, Occasional Paper number 4, 1988

Switchenberg, C., *The Madonna Connection: representational politics, subcultural identities and cultural theory*, Westview Press, 1992

Tseelon, E., 'Is the Presented Self Sincere? Goffman, impression management and the postmodern self', in *Theory, Culture & Society*, volume 9.2, 1992, pages 115–128

Turner, B.S., 'The Interdisciplinary Curriculum: from social medicine to post-modernism', in *Sociology of Health and Illness*, volume 12.1, 1990, pages 1–23

Van Til, H.R., *The Calvinistic Concept of Culture*, Presbyterian and Reformed, 1972

Venturi, R., Scott-Brown, D. and Izenour, S., *Learning from Las Vegas: the forgotten symbolism of architectural form*, MIT Press, 1972

Weber, M., *The Protestant Ethic and the Spirit of Capitalism*, Unwin, 1949

Wexler, P., *Social Analysis of Education: after the new sociology*, Routledge & Kegan Paul, 1987

Wexler, P., 'Citizenship in the Semiotic Society', in Turner, B.S., editor, *Theories of Modernity and Postmodernity*, Sage, 1990

Winter, R., 'Postmodern Sociology as a Democratic Educational Practice? Some Suggestions', in *Br J Soc Ed*, number 12.4, 1991, pages 467–481

LEVEL TWO:

MODERNITY
AND
CHRISTIANITY
IN TENSION

3

Truth and authority in modernity

LESSLIE NEWBIGIN

If the reality which we seek to explore, and of which we are a part, is the work of a personal Creator, then authority resides in him who is the Author. But if this reality is the result of processes within itself, for example the outcome of a struggle for existence in which the strongest survives the rest, then authority is simply one way of describing superior strength. Power and authority are one and the same. The Christian tradition maintains that authority resides in Him who is the Author of all being. And since personal being can only be known in so far as the person chooses to reveal himself, and cannot be known by the methods which are appropriate to the investigation of impersonal matters and processes, authority must rest on divine revelation. Modernity has declined to accept this authority.

Divine authority

In the opening chapters of St. Matthew's Gospel, Jesus is heard teaching the people of Israel with the formula: 'You have heard that it was said to them of former times . . . But I say to you . . .' His hearers were astonished, because he taught as one having authority, and not as their scribes. Immediately Jesus heals a leper with a single authoritative word. The teaching of the scribes rested on the authority of the Torah: Jesus himself embodied final authority. Here is the point at which Christian teaching about authority finally rests. Christians have sharply disagreed about the ways in which this authority is mediated to the present life of the Christian community. These will be discussed in the second part of this paper. First, I will examine modernity's rejection of this central claim.

MODERNITY'S SUSPICION OF AUTHORITY

In speaking of 'modernity' we are speaking about that way of thinking which came to dominance in the intellectual leadership of Europe (though with roots running far back into the past). This way of thinking rejected appeals to revelation and tradition as sources of authority, except in so far as they could justify themselves before the bar of individual reason and conscience. Reliable and therefore authoritative knowledge of truth are not, in the view of modernity, to be found by faith in alleged revelation, but by observation of the facts and rigorously critical reflection on them. Typical of modernity is John Locke's definition of faith: 'a persuasion of our own minds short of knowledge'.[1] This may be contrasted with the famous slogan of Augustine: *credo ut intelligam*; I believe in order that I may know. Here faith is understood not as an alternative to knowledge but as the pathway to knowledge. We do not come to know anything except by believing something. We have to begin by believing the evidence of our senses, the veracity of our teachers and the validity of the tradition into which we are seeking apprenticeship. These may all have to be questioned at some stage, but we can only question them on the basis of things which we have come to know as the result of this kind of apprenticeship. We do not begin to acquire any kind of knowledge by laying down in advance the conditions upon which we will accept any evidence. We have to begin with an openness to a reality greater than ourselves in relation to which we are not judges but pupils.

Throughout the history of European Christianity there has always been another powerful element deriving from the tradition of Greek rationalism which achieved special impetus through the translation into Latin, during the tenth and eleventh centuries, of the great Islamic commentaries on Aristotle. This had an immense impact on the thought of western Europe, leading to the creation of the universities and the rise of 'the new science'. It also led to the great work of St Thomas Aquinas in which he restated the Christian tradition in the light of the new intellectual situation. Part of this restatement involved a distinction between those things which can be known by reason and those things which can only be known by revelation and faith. Among the former were included the knowledge of the existence of God and of the soul; among the latter were the Trinity, the Incarnation and the Atonement. The Jesuit theologian Michael

Buckley sees this as the point at which modern atheism had its origins. The arguments for the existence of God are always fragile. Buckley argues that a fatal step was taken when the church called in the help of 'The Philosopher' (as Aristotle was so often called) to provide assurance for faith, rather than relying for its assurance upon that which was given in Jesus Christ.[2]

The results of this step became apparent during the disturbance of thought which resulted from the new cosmology opened up by Galileo, Copernicus and Kepler. All the assured certainties seemed to be overturned. How could one be sure of God, the soul, or anything else? In this climate of extreme uncertainty René Descartes received a commission from a cardinal of the Catholic Church to develop a proof of the existence of God and of the soul. He found certainty in the existence of his own thinking mind and sought to build on this with logical arguments which had the clarity and indubitability of mathematics.

What are we to make of this demand for a proof of the existence of God which assumes that there are grounds more trustworthy than those given in God's own revelation of himself? If God really exists, is there not something ridiculous about one of God's creatures saying to him, 'I can demonstrate your existence without relying on what you tell me about yourself'? And is it not even more absurd for this creature to regard his own alleged proofs as the necessary basis for his attention to the divine revelation? Yet how otherwise can we regard the long tradition of 'natural theology' seen as the necessary prolegomena for the study of God's self-revelation in Christ as witnessed in scripture?

Descartes' method, which has dominated subsequent European thought, has in it the seeds of its own destruction. The corollary of that method was the famous 'critical principle'. Reliable knowledge is that which can be achieved by starting from indubitable certainties and building on them arguments which have the clarity and indubitability of mathematics. Reliable knowledge, for which the word 'science' is henceforth used, has mathematics as its working language. What falls outside the scope of this certain knowledge, is to be doubted. All claims to knowledge must pass through the fire of critical questioning so that claims to knowledge which are based merely on faith are to be distinguished from knowledge which can be certainly proved.

Augustine's maxim is therefore reversed. The pathway to knowledge is not faith but doubt. 'Honest doubt' is contrasted with 'blind faith' in the folk language of modernity.

THE 'POSTMODERN' REACTION

The Cartesian programme is inherently self-destructive for the simple reason that doubt, if it is to be rational, must rest upon something which is believed to be true. If I say, 'I doubt the proposition P' and am asked for my reasons, I will have to reply in one or other of two ways. Either I must say: 'Because I believe Q, and Q is not compatible with P', or else, 'Because P has not been proved'; and the latter assertion implies my belief that there are grounds on which P could be shown to be either true or false. In both cases my doubt is only rational if these beliefs are in place. Plainly both faith and doubt have necessary roles in the enterprise of knowing, but the role of doubt (necessary as it is) is secondary, and that of faith primary. We can know without doubting but we cannot know without believing. The Cartesian invitation to make doubt the primary tool in the search for knowledge was bound to lead to the triumph of scepticism and eventually of nihilism, as Nietzsche foresaw. The demand for a kind of indubitable certainty which does not depend on faith has led inexorably to despair about the possibility of knowing anything. We are in the situation which Nietzsche anticipated where rational argument ceases and the only arbiter is power and the will to power. Even science, the glory of our modern European society and still the most dynamic element in it, is no longer seen as a pathway to wisdom, to a true understanding of the human situation; it is seen as a means to power. The vastly greater part of all scientific work is now devoted to the search for power—military, industrial, commercial. If one looks at the characteristic products of contemporary European society in the areas of literature, drama, art and music, the picture is one of nihilism. Claims to know and speak truth are regarded merely as claims to dominance on the part of that section of society from which they emerge. There are successive 'regimes of truth' (Foucault) which succeed one another, each one repressing rival claims by the use of force until overturned by the next. There is no truth beyond this. The corollary on the personal level is narcissism, an obsession with the self, its development and its internal history.

There is profound irony in this story: the relapse into nihilism and narcissism is the end-product of the search for indubitable knowledge as distinct from the knowledge which is claimed to be available through faith in the divine revelation. Yet for those standing in the biblical and Christian tradition, this story should not be surprising. If it is really the case that God is the author of all being, including our own, then all claims to knowledge starting from elsewhere must end in confusion. The search for an authority prior to and more basic than the authority of God's self-revelation must end in failure. This statement has of course immediate implications for what is called 'natural theology', but its implications are far wider and cover the whole range of human knowing. R.A. Clouser in his book *The Myth of Religious Neutrality*[3] has shown convincingly how the great scientific theories take as their starting point some belief about what is ultimate and fundamental in the area of their study. In other words, they start from a belief about what religious people call 'god'. And, by definition, the starting point cannot be validated by any kind of *a priori* proof. It can only be validated, if at all, by its fruitfulness. And if it is true that the ultimate and fundamental reality is God as he has made himself known in that history which has Jesus Christ as its centre, then theories which take some other starting point, and which claim to give a comprehensive interpretation of the cosmos, must end in illusion. The biblical statement that 'the fear of the Lord is the beginning of wisdom' has a much wider range of importance than is commonly recognized. If fully understood, in fact, this small sentence would be seen to be subversive of the central thrust of modernity.

AUTHORITY: EXTERNAL AND INTERNAL

Modernity distrusts authority. It was born in a movement of emancipation from what were seen as external authorities. Its appeal was to the freedom and responsibility of the individual reason and conscience to judge between rival claims to truth. Kant's words provide its slogan: 'Dare to know'. There are many situations in which this is the most important thing to say. Authority which is merely imposed from outside is not true authority. We are so made that we need to see for ourselves that something is true or right. Yet, if this demand for individual freedom of judgment is taken as our sole guide to reality, we are in trouble. A visitor to the Uffizzi gallery in Florence came out and said 'I don't think much of the stuff here,' to which the janitor replied: 'It is not the pictures but the visitors who are on trial here.' Even as we claim freedom of judgment, we must know that in judging we are judged. A visitor went round a gallery with a guidebook in which the works exhibited were shown with one, two or three asterisks in accordance with their distinction as works of art. After looking at each picture, and then at the text of the guide book, the visitor was heard to murmur 'Good', 'Lovely' or 'Marvellous' in accordance with the indications given by the book. Even though we know that we are judged in our judging, we cannot escape from the responsibility for making personal judgment. But my personal judgment must be provisional, tempered by the recognition that I have more to learn. My judgment is not the last word. I have to be open to things which I have not yet understood. In this sense authority has to be external; it refers to a reality beyond myself. But, if it is to be authoritative for me, I must come to the point of recognizing its authority. It has to be internalized.

So the proper human relation to the reality with which we have to do is that of a learner, an apprentice. All our knowing comes to us through our apprenticeship in a tradition of knowing which has been formed through the effort of previous generations. This tradition is the source of the mental faculties through which we begin to make sense of the world. In this sense the tradition has authority, but it is not a purely external authority. We are responsible for internalizing the tradition by our struggle to understand the world with the help of the tools it furnishes. In this process the tradition itself develops and is changed. This calls for reverence for the tradition and courage to bring our own judgment to bear upon its application to new circumstances. The idea that we could construct an entire edifice of knowledge without reliance on the tradition by the exercise of our own powers of observation and reasoning (an idea which was certainly present in the formative process of modernity) is surely illusion. We are not in a position where we could lay down in advance the terms on which we will accept any claim to truth.

BY GRACE ALONE

But what are the implications of saying that authority must be both external and internal? If we are thinking not of secular knowledge but of the knowledge of God and of the recognition

65

of the authority of God, does it lead to a sort of Pelagianism? God not sovereign because we have to contribute our part to the recognition of his authority? Do we have to speak not only of divine revelation but also of a human 'capacity for revelation', without which divine revelation would be ineffectual? This is the battlefield on which Barth and Brunner waged their famous battle in the 1930s. To many people, at least in the Anglo-Saxon world, Brunner's seemed to be the reasonable position and Barth's angry 'No' seemed irrational. For Barth it was a matter of life and death to affirm that faith itself, the capacity to recognize and receive God's revelation, is God's gift and not man's achievement. This 'No' struck into the very heart of modernity. It seemed to be a direct assault on human freedom and responsibility.

We have hitherto talked as if the human search for knowledge was a disinterested search. At one level one would have to say that the human search for truth is something perfectly natural, something which we share with other animals. Animals need to explore their environment in order to discover where safety lies and where danger, where food and where none. The natural human curiosity which drives us to try to find out what the world is really like is continuous with this. But if, as the Christian tradition affirms, human beings differ from other animals in being so made in the image of God that they can find fulfilment only in the worship and love of God, then the search for a kind of knowledge of God which is not dependent on the grace of God is doomed to fail.

The human situation will be radically misunderstood unless we take account of what is told in the Christian tradition about the Fall. God's original purpose is that human life should be lived in faith in the goodness of God. God intended that we should know only good. The root of all the corruption that has stained our story is our determination to see for ourselves both good and evil and to arrogate to ourselves a position which we can never hold: as impartial arbitrators between good and evil. Because we seek to hold yet can never hold this position, we are shadowed by anxiety. We seek for assured knowledge, but the search does not have the innocence of the natural curiosity of the animal. We seek a security for ourselves which we were not meant to have, because the only security for which we were made is security in God, and his free grace. The search for certainty apart from grace has led to a profound loss of nerve, a deep scepticism about the possibility of knowing the truth. We are left shut up in ourselves.

If this is the human situation, God's revelation of himself can only be an act of redemption and forgiveness. It cannot be merely the communication of true information. This act creates (a new creation) the possibility of faith. In the communication of information between rational human beings, the listener exercises his own judgment on the matter being communicated. But when it is the act of one against whom I have offended and who takes the initiative to rescue me from my estrangement, then that act creates the possibility of my response. There is, as the New Testament repeatedly affirms, a new creation, and the Author of the new creation is necessarily the final authority. To seek elsewhere for grounds upon which the authority of the Redeemer might be validated would be to reject the act of redemption.

These assertions provoke the deep hostility of the 'modern' mind, but we cannot evade this confrontation. Every attempt to find grounds for accepting the authority of this revelation in something else must fail. The only way to communicate its authority is by the communication of the Gospel itself. It was said of Jesus by those who heard him that he spoke with authority and not as the scribes. The scribes had authority only in so far as their teaching rested on the authority of the Torah. Jesus did not rest his authority there but in the fact that his words and works were the words and works of the Father. Jesus did not cancel the human responsibility for judging. He asks his hearers, 'Why do you not judge for yourselves what is right?' We are not back in a pre-lapsarian innocence. And yet 'No one comes to me unless the Father who sent me draws him.' Faith in God's self-revelation is a gift of God not an achievement of the autonomous reason and conscience.

BY FAITH ALONE

In this context one can understand Barth's passionate attack on natural theology, and one can appreciate Buckley's judgment that a fatal step was taken in Christian theology when 'The Philosopher' was called in to underwrite the authority of revelation. If revelation were essentially the communication of information about God, then it would be appropriate to speak of the innate capacities of the human mind and conscience which enable us to grasp the revelation and make it our own. But if revelation is primarily the act of redemption and reconciliation, if we are speaking not just about information but about incarnation and its immeasurable costliness, then such talk is not appropriate. To use Barth's analogy, if I am drowning and a man risks his own life to save me, it may possibly be true that if I had been twice as heavy he could not have lifted me, and that in that sense I made some contribution to the rescue, but it would not be appropriate for me to make this claim. Even if we are thinking only of revelation as the communication of knowledge about God we have to reject the claim that this knowledge can be given added certitude by the support of natural theology for the 'God' whose existence natural theology claims to demonstrate is not the God whose character is rendered in the pages of the Bible, not the God and Father of our Lord Jesus Christ, not the blessed Trinity. This 'God' is a construct of the human mind and has therefore the essential character of an idol. Is idolatry a step on the way to the worship of the true God, or a threat to it? If our starting point is the kind of reasoning provided by 'the Philosopher' or his many successors, it becomes difficult to accept the possibility of a true incarnation and almost impossible to regard the blessed Trinity as anything other than a piece of mystification. If this is so, must we not say that the knowledge of God given through 'natural theology' is not merely a partial knowledge but is a distorted and misleading knowledge?

We have to reject the idea, so widely accepted, that rational thought can provide us with a kind of reliable knowledge which is neutral in respect of religious commitment and therefore capable of providing a secure foundation for a knowledge of God which does not depend on his own acts of revelation and redemption in history. This supposed neutrality is no neutrality at all, because all systematic human thought about the totality of our experience has to start from some belief about what is ultimate and fundamental—matter, spirit, life, reason or whatever. There is no neutral standpoint.

Natural theology is very tempting because it seems to offer a security which does not depend on faith alone. Even committed evangelical Christians hold a kind of rationalism which claims to possess indubitable certainty. But this is to fall into the enemy's trap. As Michael Polanyi has said, paraphrasing Einstein, 'Only statements which can be doubted make contact with reality.' Our knowledge of God is a matter of faith which is a gift of divine grace. We walk by faith, not by sight. We do not possess indubitable knowledge, but we press forward on the path of faith, looking for the day when we shall know as now we are known. A natural theology which purports to offer us grounds of assurance more reliable than those given to us in God's own revelation of himself in Jesus Christ does not serve faith but subverts it.

Two objections are commonly levelled against this position. The first is often presented as the accusation of 'fideism'. This term when used with hostile intent appears to rest on a theory of knowledge which in contrast to Augustine supposes that the invocation of faith as a necessary element in the enterprise of knowing excludes the intellect. The error of this supposition is the failure to understand that all knowing rests upon faith commitments. When a natural theology is proposed as the necessary preparation for the understanding of revelation, one has to uncover the (perhaps unexamined) faith commitments which underpin this theology. The criticism is sometimes expressed by using the phrase 'a leap of faith', as though a rejection of natural theology left one with no alternative except an irrational leap into the unknown. But that criticism misses the mark. We are speaking not of an irrational leap into the unknown, but of the responsible acceptance of a personal invitation: 'Follow me'. The act of following is an act of faith, not of rational calculation of the intellectual credentials of the one who calls and of the probable consequences of following. But it is not an irrational act. Rather one must ask about the credentials of a philosophy which supposes that more reliable clues are available for understanding the total mystery of human existence in this world than this personal invitation.

The other objection may be stated as follows: If the faith with which the believer follows Jesus is itself the gift of God, is not God arbitrary in his granting of this gift to some and not to others? This charge would stick if those whom God so calls and to whom is given the gift of faith to respond to the call were called in order to be simply the beneficiaries of this calling. But if, as the Bible makes clear, those so called are called not for themselves but that they may be the messengers of his calling for others, then the charge does not hold. And, secondly, while we are here seeking to probe the inner freedom of God himself to call whom he will, nevertheless no one who has been made part of the new creation in Christ would ever seek to claim any personal credit for their calling or their faith. If I interrogate my own experience, the ways by which I was brought to faith in Christ are very mysterious and beyond my own capacity fully to understand. It was the immeasurable grace of God. A personal decision or series of decisions is involved. But these pale into insignificance in comparison with the vast and immeasurable grace of God.

Something positive must also be said about natural theology. The territory which natural theology explores may be quite properly explored in the reverse direction. It is both possible and necessary, starting from the revelation in Jesus Christ, to explore all its implications in the realm of philosophy. Indeed this is often a very necessary part of the task of Christian witness. Any mind shaped by modernity will be fully furnished with beliefs and assumptions which seem to make Christian faith untenable or at least very questionable. Part of Christian testimony is to uncover the hidden assumptions behind these beliefs and to show how God's action in Christ, in redeeming and revealing, opened the way for a truer understanding of that which had been seen as calling it in question. This activity can have a very important role in helping others on the journey of faith. In that sense they may form part of the pathway to faith. But one must distinguish between the ways by which people are drawn to faith (which are as various as are the varieties of human nature and experience) and the foundation on which faith rests. This foundation cannot be anything provided by the philosopher. It can only be the action of God himself. The only ultimate authority in the new creation is its Author.[4]

The mediation of divine authority

The question now is: How is this authority mediated to us now two millennia after Jesus' incarnate life? To this question we turn. We must ask first what, according to the record, was Jesus' intention for the future of that work for which he was sent into the world by the Father?[5] Jesus did not write a book. He chose, called and prepared a company of people, he entrusted to them his teaching, and he promised them the gift of the Spirit of God to guide them in matters which were beyond their present horizons.

First, he formed a community and bound it closely to himself. This point is the central theme of the four Gospels. But the action of Jesus on the eve of his passion is surely the clearest and most unambiguous evidence of his intention. He was about to be taken from his friends in a shameful death. They would all leave him and flee, for they had not understood his mission. In the few remaining hours before his arrest and death, he acted and spoke in such a way that there could be no possible doubt that he intended them to remain a community committed to him beyond his death. 'This is my body given for you; eat it. This is my blood shed for you; drink it.' They did not understand, but they obeyed, and in obeying they came to know who he was. Nothing could more clearly and unambiguously reveal his intention that there should be a community continuing his life beyond his death, a continuing life together in this world, not just in the age to come.

Second, Jesus taught. Modern scholarship suggests that what is available for us is the spiritual experience of the early church, and the teaching of Jesus can only be perceived dimly if at all through this veil. This kind of scepticism if applied to all ancient history, would render it inaccessible. It is grounded, of course, in prior beliefs about what is the case. It is true that the sayings of Jesus have come to us in variant forms, but the variations are not such as to leave us in the dark about their substance. Much of this scholarly scepticism is grounded in the experience of those who have never known any culture but a literate one. Those who are familiar with cultures which do not rely on the written word, know how tenaciously oral teaching is treasured, preserved and handed on.[6] The teachings of Jesus, mediated to us in variant forms by the New Testament writers, have certainly been sharp and clear enough to challenge, disturb and sustain men and women through sixty generations in both literate and oral cultures.

Third, Jesus promised the gift of the Holy Spirit to lead them into the fullness of the truth, a fullness which was beyond their immediate possibility as a group of men and women shaped and limited by a particular culture at a particular moment in its history. And within the pages of the New Testament we can see this promise being fulfilled, as the first apostles combine faithfulness to the teaching of Jesus with freedom and boldness in making new decisions in new situations, relying on the promised guidance of the Spirit.[7]

In the contemporary debate among Christians about authority, four words are habitually used. We speak of the authority of scripture, of the church and its tradition, of reason and of experience.

SCRIPTURE

Christians are deeply divided on the question of the authority of scripture. For many centuries the Bible (*the* book) had a place apart from all other literature. Its authority was generally unquestioned. It provided the framework for the study of history and the natural world, as well as for the understanding of human life. During the last three centuries it has been subjected to critical analysis with the tools of modern scientific method. The result is the split between those who wish to affirm biblical authority by defending the factual accuracy of everything that it contains, and those who see the biblical material as an expression of human religious experience (and there are of course many other varieties of religious experience). In this situation it has become difficult or impossible to speak with intellectual coherence about the authority of scripture *vis-à-vis* any particular aspect of our culture.

This split is only one manifestation of a much deeper fissure in the culture of modernity as a whole. It might be described briefly as a breakdown of the unity between the subjective and the objective poles of human knowing. It is customary to trace this breakdown back to Descartes with his search for indubitable knowledge expressed in forms having the clarity and exactitude of mathematics. The centuries since then have been dominated by the ideal of a kind of knowledge which is objective in the sense that it involves no personal commitment on the part of the knower. It is 'factual', disinfected of all that personal interest might introduce. What is claimed to be knowledge but cannot be expressed in such 'objective' terms is a matter of personal opinion. It is belief rather than knowledge, and, as Locke has taught us, belief is what we fall back upon when knowledge is not available. 'Values' in this view are matters of personal choice; 'facts' are not. No logical ties can bind the two together. From 'facts', 'values' cannot be derived. The split is visible in the separation between science and 'the humanities' in the curriculum of the universities.

Given this situation, it is natural that the Bible has to be understood as belonging to one or other of these two halves of our culture. Some can only affirm the authority of scripture by regarding it as a collection of factually true statements. Others see in it material which expresses in symbolic and poetic form certain values, including various kinds of religious experience. If the first choice is made, one is on a collision course with the findings of science in spite of the efforts of the 'creationists'. If the second choice is made, the Bible simply has to take its place among the many varieties of moral and religious experience. It is part of the history of religions. George Lindbeck in *The Nature of Doctrine, Religion and Theology in a Post-Liberal Age*[8] proposes as an alternative to these two views what he calls a 'cultural-linguistic' model for the understanding of scripture. I find this helpful only if it is related explicitly to the deeper epistemological split of which the fundamentalist/liberal split is only a surface manifestation.

In his exposition of the 'cultural-linguistic' model for understanding doctrine, Lindbeck uses such phrases as 'myths or narratives . . . which structure human experience and understanding of self and world', 'an idiom that makes possible the description of realities', 'something like a Kantian *a priori*'.[9] Doctrine, in other words, is not so much something that we look *at* as something which we look *through* in order to understand the world. Here we are raising the epistemological question. All knowing involves a knowing subject, and knowing is only a possibility for a subject who has been inducted into a tradition of knowing embodied in language, symbol, story. Most of what we know is normally not the object of our attention. It is the framework by means of which we order our experience and make sense of it. It is, in Polanyi's phrase, the tacit component in all knowing. When Lindbeck uses the term 'cultural-linguistic' to describe his model for doctrine, he is rightly drawing attention to the fact that knowledge requires the ability to use a language and an accepted framework of understanding about 'how things are and how things behave' which enables us to make sense of experience. When we use language to communicate information or to share a vision, we do not attend to the words we are using; we attend *through* the words to the matter in hand. Only when the words fail to establish communication do we attend to the words in order to find better ones. And words are part of a culture, of a whole way of understanding and coping with the world which has been developed in a specific community. But this necessary subjective component in all knowing does not mean that it is robbed of its objective reference. It is saved from a false subjectivity by being published, made the object of public scrutiny and discussion, tested against new situations. Yet this scrutiny can only be undertaken by knowing subjects who are themselves depending on a culturally shaped tradition.

We seem to be nearing the end of a period in which it was believed that modern science could provide a corpus of universal truth which would be the possession of all human beings, whatever their culture differences. The enormous impact of Newton's physics has lasted until the present day, with its vision of a self-contained cosmos of particles of matter moving according to precisely determined mathematical laws, a world in which the human mind has no place. Paradoxically this dehumanized model had enormous human appeal. It gave birth to the idea of a universal reason equally applicable in all human cultures and of the universal rights of man simply as man and apart from the accidents of a particular society. But it created for Lessing the 'wide ugly ditch' between the universal truths of reason and the accidental happenings of history, and it provoked (most notably in Germany) the reaction in favour of the 'spirit of the nation', the *Volksgeist*, as the bearer of truth. In spite of all that has happened in the recent developments of physics to question the Newtonian vision, we are still left with a culture of science which is supposed to be universally valid for all peoples and a multiculturalism which brands as imperialistic any claim to discriminate between less and more valuable elements in culture, including the area of religious belief.[10] It is simply impossible to remain content with this bisection of human experience into two halves which have no rational connection with each other. This means that it is impossible to accept the terms of the fundamentalist/ liberal debate about the authority of scripture. Scripture, I suggest, functions (in Lindbeck's phrase) as the 'cultural-linguistic framework' within which the Christian life is lived and Christian doctrine developed. The Bible is (Lindbeck's language again) 'a narrative which structures human experience and understanding'. It is, however varied may be its texture, essentially a story which claims to be *the* story, the true story both of the cosmos and of human life within the cosmos. After one has done all the work that can and has to be done to analyze its structures and trace the origins of its different parts, it is in its total canonical structure a story. This story finds the clue to the meaning of cosmic and human history in the story of a particular people and of a particular man among that people. Like every telling of the human story it is a selection of a minute fraction of the available records and memories, on the basis of a particular belief about the meaning of the story. World history as it is normally taught in schools is the history of the development of civilization. We are, naturally, the civilized people, and we are the point of the story. The Bible tells the story from a different view of what is significant, from the belief that the point of the entire story has been made in the doings and sufferings and triumphs of the man Jesus.

At this point two important points must be made to avoid misunderstanding. First, when we speak of finding in Jesus the clue to the meaning of the whole human story, we are not speaking of a mere cognitive exercise. We are speaking of that act of atonement wrought in Jesus through which we are brought into a loving obedience to the will of God as it is exercised through all human and cosmic history. It is not merely a matter of illumination, of new understanding; it is a matter of reconciliation, of rescue from alienation, of obedient response to the divine initiative of love. It is illumination and new understanding only because it is first a divine action of reconciliation through which we are brought to that state in which we can say and know that God works all things together for good to those who love him. It is only through this act of atonement that Jesus becomes for us the clue to history.

Secondly, the word 'narrative' is sometimes used in theological discourse with the implication that the historical truth of the narrative is not important. The narrative which 'structures' our understanding of things might be nothing more than a story we tell to explain our experience, with no ontological status beyond our own imagination. It is of the essence of the Christian faith that this story is the true story. How do we understand the meaning of 'true' in this context? The Bible itself, in its canonical form contains accounts of happenings and of sayings which are in varying degrees discrepant. The crucial example (as we have already noted) is the existence of discrepancies in the accounts given of the ministry of Jesus in the four Gospels. Yet to any reader who stands within the same faith community as the apostolic writers, these are varying accounts of the same events and sayings, different human perceptions of things which really

75

happened. They share the character of all historical writing. However the Bible also deals with things which cannot be called history in this sense. Neither the creation of the world nor its ending are known to us through contemporary records. What the Bible tells us on these is imaginative interpretation arising from the fundamental truth about the human situation which is made known to us and believable by us through God's own redeeming acts.

The question: 'Which is the real story?' must determine everything else in our understanding of what it is to be human and what it is to handle rightly the natural world within which human life is set. The Bible, I suggest, functions properly in the life of the church when it functions as the true story of which our story is a part. Therefore we do not so much look at it as through it in order to understand and deal with the real world. To revert to Polanyi's language, the Bible ought to function primarily as the *tacit* component in our endeavour to understand and deal with the world. We have to *indwell* the story, as we indwell the language we use and the culture of which we are a part. But since we also live within this other culture, there is necessarily an internal dialogue within us. By all our cultural formation from infancy onward, we are made part of the story of our nation and our civilization. There is something to be learned here from the experience of a foreign missionary. As one learns to enter deeply into the mental world of another people, into their story, as one is drawn by the coherence and rationality of that other story, an internal dialogue is set up between this and the Christian story. That internal dialogue is the precondition for true interpersonal dialogue. But clearly the story functions effectively in providing the 'structure of understanding' only in so far as one really lives the story. The Bible cannot function with any authority except through the lives of those whose story it is, those who 'indwell' the story. We cannot speak of biblical authority without speaking of tradition.

TRADITION

Any discussion of authority must consider the significance of the fact that Jesus did not write a book. The only example recorded of Jesus' writing is of writing in the dust. He devoted his ministry (as far as we know) to the formation of a community which would represent him to those who would come after. He taught them in ways that would be remembered and passed on to others, but he did not provide a written text. Almost all the words of Jesus have come to us in versions which are not identical. To wish that it were otherwise would evidently be to go against the intention of Jesus. The fact that we have four Gospels and not one is cited by Muslims as evidence that the real Gospel (*Injil*) has been lost. But the church refused to substitute one harmonized version for the four disparate ones. On the one hand the New Testament writers insist that what they teach is (unless otherwise stated, for example, 1 Corinthians 7) a faithful rendering of the intention of Jesus. They are not originators but messengers. But, on the other hand, the teaching of Jesus and the stories of his ministry are told in words shaped to meet different situations.

The story which the Bible tells is tied to particular times, places, languages and cultures. If it were not, it would be no part of human history. It is told as the clue to the entire story human and cosmic, from creation to the end of time. It cannot function as the clue to the whole story if it is simply repeated in the same words. It has to be translated, and translation is (fallible) interpretation. The many-layered material of the Old Testament is witness to the repeated retelling of the fundamental story in new terms for new occasions. And Jesus expressly tells his disciples (in the Johannine interpretation) that although they have received a true and full revelation of the Father, they have yet much to learn which they cannot learn until later. They are promised that the Holy Spirit will guide them 'into all the truth'. In view of the perennial temptation to identify the Holy Spirit with the 'spirit of the age', the *Zeitgeist*, it is important to note that the promise is that the Spirit will glorify Jesus, for the Spirit will show the church how all things in the cosmos belong to him. Raymond Brown paraphrases the promise as 'interpreting in relation to each coming generation the contemporary significance of what Jesus has said and done'.[11] The church is not tied to a text in such a way that nothing will ever be done for the first time. In new situations those who 'indwell' the story of which Jesus is the centre will have to make new and risky decisions about what faithfulness to the Author of the story requires. There can be no drawing of a straight line from a text of scripture to a contemporary ethical decision; there will always be the requirement of a fresh decision in responsibility to the One whose story it is.

There can therefore be no appeal to scripture which ignores the continuing tradition of Christian discipleship. That would detach scripture from the story to which it is the clue. But the exact relation between scripture and tradition is a delicate matter. The tendency of Protestants to isolate the scriptures from the tradition is, of course, mistaken since no one has access to a Bible unless someone hands it over (*traditio*). But it is understandable in view of the long experience of the Roman Catholic tendency to treat scripture and tradition as though they were separate and parallel sources of authority.[12]

How is one to state the relation of tradition to scripture? On the one hand the New Testament is itself part of the tradition. It is obviously based upon oral testimony given at different times under different circumstances. But it claims to be authentic representation of that of which it speaks. 'I delivered to you . . . what I first received,' says the Apostle (1 Corinthians 15:3). On the other hand, the closing of the canon of scripture implies that what is included in the canon has a higher authority than that which is excluded. What is included has a normative role in relation to all further tradition. Not all of what has been handed on is to be accepted. The accusation which Jesus levelled against religious teachers of his time (Matthew 15:7ff), that they had made void the word of God by their traditions, has to be levelled against some forms of the Christian tradition. Development in Christian teaching is not a process which has its norm immanent in itself. The promise of Jesus to his disciples that the Holy Spirit would lead them into the fullness of the truth is linked to the promise that, in doing so, the Spirit will glorify Jesus. What the Spirit will show to the church is what belongs to Jesus, and every alleged teaching of the Spirit has to be tested by that criterion (John 16:14f). On the other hand, if the authority of scripture lies in the fact that it renders in narrative form the character of the One who is the Author of history and that it is therefore the clue to all history, we cannot follow this clue without taking account of the way that it has been followed in the past. The centuries which have followed the incarnation of the Word have filled out with further content the universal and cosmic implications of the incarnation, but all that has followed has to be judged by the criteria furnished by the events of the incarnation. The relation between scripture and tradition is thus reciprocal, but scripture is normative in relation to tradition. It often happens that someone who knows nothing of Jesus or of Christianity reads a Gospel for the first time and is captured by the sheer power of what he reads so that he or she turns to Christ in full submission. But such a reader will not learn what submission to Christ means except in the fellowship of the church. The book is the book of the community and the community is the community of the story which the book tells. Neither can be understood without the other.

Tradition, therefore, is not a source of authority separate from scripture. Rather it is only by 'indwelling' the scripture that one remains faithful to the tradition. By this 'indwelling' ('abiding') we take our place and play our part in the story which is the true story of the whole human race and of the cosmos. Reading the scriptures as our own story in a shared discipleship with all those past and present who acknowledge with us that this is the true story, we trust the promise that the Holy Spirit will lead us into the fullness of the truth. Neither scripture nor tradition furnishes us with an authority which dispenses us from the risky business of making our own decisions in every new situation. But we have the confidence that, though we may make mistaken decisions, the community which lives by the true story will not be finally lost (Matthew 16:18).

REASON

A long tradition speaks of scripture, tradition and reason as the three-fold source of authority in regard to Christian doctrine. It is a mistake to put tradition alongside of scripture as though it were a separate and parallel source of authority. It would be equally mistaken to think of reason as a separate and parallel source of authority. No one grasps or makes sense of anything in scriptures or in the tradition of scriptural interpretation except by the use of reason. And reason does not operate except within a continuous tradition of speech which is the speech of a community whose language embodies a shared way of understanding. Reason is a faculty with which we try to grasp the different elements in our experience in an orderly way, so that as we say 'they make sense'. It is not a separate source of information about what is the case. It can only function within a continuous linguistic and cultural tradition. We learn to reason as we learn, in childhood, to use words and concepts, those words and concepts which embody the way in which our society makes sense of the world. All rationality is socially and culturally embodied.

In the 'Age of Reason' and especially in the arguments used since the eighteenth century to defend the 'reasonableness' of Christianity, the word 'reason' was used to denote conformity with a set of assumptions derived from the science and philosophy of the time. The sociologists of knowledge have taught us to use the term 'plausibility structure' to denote the structure of beliefs and practices which, in any given society, determine what beliefs are plausible within that society. When 'reason' is adduced as a third source of authority alongside of scripture and tradition, is what is being appealed to simply the contemporary plausibility structure? This becomes especially obvious when we look at the 'self-evident truths' of which the eighteenth-century thinkers spoke. These truths are not self-evident. They are the product of a specific tradition of rationality. Reason operates within a specific tradition of rational discourse, which is carried by a specific human community. No supra-cultural 'reason' can stand in judgment over all particular human traditions of rationality. All reason operates within a total worldview which is embodied in the language, the concepts and the models which are the means by which those who share them can reason together. Christian doctrine is a form of rational discourse which has been developed in that community which finds the clue to the rationality of the cosmos as a whole in those events which form the substance of the biblical narrative and in the subsequent experience of those who have done the same. The fact that it is thus rooted in one strand of the whole human story in no way invalidates its claim to universal relevance. It shares this character with every other form of rationality.

This formulation does not lead to a total relativism because all human reasoning is subject to the test of adequacy. There are more and less adequate ways of making sense of human experience and of coping with the world in the light of what sense one can make of it. All forms of rationality are subject to this test. They are therefore (in vigorous societies) always being modified to take account of new experience. Sometimes the modifications are minor; sometimes they are cataclysmic. There is a parallel here with Thomas Kuhn's distinction between 'normal' science and the experience of 'paradigm shifts'.[13] A way of seeing things is proposed which 'makes sense' in a more adequate way than the one previously accepted. As Kuhn shows, no over-arching logical system can justify the switch from one vision to the other; it is a conversion to a different way of seeing things which always needs new language. The only test is adequacy to the reality which is to be understood and coped with. The new paradigm cannot demonstrate its 'reasonableness' on the terms of the old. But the success of the new paradigm will depend on the vigour and competence of those who have committed themselves to work with it. In every culture the Christian vision of how things are calls for a conversion and for the use of new language, none of which can be shown to be deducible from the reigning plausibility structure. It will convince people of its superior rationality in proportion to the intellectual vigour and practical courage with which those who inhabit the new plausibility structure demonstrate its adequacy to the realities of human existence. This will call for the most vigorous and exacting use of reason. In fact (and this is merely an aside) with the widespread breakdown of confidence in the universal applicability of the 'reason' of the eighteenth century, and the growth of movements like astrology and the 'New Age', one of the main functions of the church in the twenty-first century will be to defend rationality against the hydra-headed *Volksgeist*.

However, the test of adequacy does not claim to offer the kind of indubitable certainty which the Cartesian programme claimed. Final certainty belongs to the day of judgment. Until that day, the Christian is called to walk by faith, which is the gift of him who has reconciled us to himself through the cross. The idea that there is available to human beings a kind of indubitable certainty which is independent of divine grace is an illusion.

'Reason' has also been invoked as a source of authority, in contradistinction to 'revelation'. The reigning traditions of rationality in our culture are rooted in the specific history of Europe. These traditions rest upon the discoveries of the great scientists and philosophers and historians. In contrast the Christian tradition of rationality rests upon alleged revelations which cannot be experimentally checked but have to be accepted in faith. Is the idea of revelation compatible with the requirements of reason? We must look at two kinds of normal human experience which Martin Buber made familiar in his distinction between 'I and You' and 'I and it'. In the latter situation the autonomous reason is in full control. I analyze, classify, dissect. I decide what questions to put and force the material to answer my questions. Reason is in the service of my sovereign will. But in the other situation of interpersonal relationships, I am not in full control. I cannot force the other person to answer the questions I put. Of course I can treat the other person as an object in the 'it' world, and use the tools of science including eventually the tools of the neurosurgeon to find out how the brain of the person functions. But none of this gives knowledge of the other person as person. For that I must surrender control. I must listen and expose myself to question. And in thus surrendering sovereignty and moving to the position of one who is questioned, I have not abandoned the use of reason. I am still a rational person making rational judgments and drawing rational conclusions from data. The difference is in the role that reason is called to play. Reason has become the servant of a listening and trusting openness instead of being the servant of a masterful autonomy.

The question, therefore, is not whether or not reason is employed. The question is whether the total reality with which as human beings we have to deal is to be understood exclusively as lifeless matter, to be investigated by the autonomous human subject, or whether it is such that a proper knowing of it has more of the character of the kind of knowing which is the fruit of mature personal relationships. The question is not between 'reason' and 'revelation' but about what kind of reality it is that we are dealing with. If that reality is amenable to understanding along the lines which we follow in a personal relationship, then we may believe that a tradition of rational discourse could develop from the particular experiences of those to whom the Author of the universe has spoken and who have been alert and humble enough to listen. To 'indwell' such a tradition, to live with this paradigm, to endeavour to show in every new generation its adequacy to human experience, its power to 'make sense' of new situations, will be a fully rational enterprise. The proposal to set 'reason' against 'revelation' only arises if one is indwelling another tradition of rationality, one which sees the whole of reality only as an object for investigation. Within this tradition, of course, 'religion' is one of the matters for investigation. There are 'religious experiences'. In this tradition one says not 'God spoke to Moses', but 'Moses had a religious experience'. The latter formulation leaves the investigator in charge; the former does not.

But the long tradition of rational discourse which has followed from accepting the former as valid is not less rational than that which has been developed from the latter. Reason operating within the Christian (or Judaic or Muslim) tradition is still reason.

EXPERIENCE

The fourth word often used in discussions about the authority of the Christian message is 'experience'. It is a newcomer to theology. Until at least the beginning of the nineteenth century the word had the meaning which we now convey by the word 'experiment'. Apparently it has become popular in English theology as a translation of the German *Erlebnis*. Earlier theologians did not appear to need it. Scientists, at least in the natural sciences, do not seem to need it. Neither a scientist nor anyone else knows anything except by, in some sense, having an experience—seeing it, reading it or hearing it. But when a new star appears in the telescope of an astronomer, he doesn't describe it as a new astronomical experience; he talks about the star. Why is it otherwise in theology? Why say: 'Moses had a religious experience', rather than: 'God spoke to Moses'? Obviously because the existence of God cannot be 'objectively' demonstrated, whereas there is plenty of evidence to show conclusively that people have religious experiences, and these can be the object of scientific exploration. The most important factor in bringing this word into the theological debate is the impact of Schleiermacher's monumental effort to find a place for Christian belief among its 'cultural despisers' by finding the evidence for God in the 'feeling of absolute dependence' which, he held, is common to all. If Christian faith must leave the exploration of nature and history to those who operate on other presuppositions, it is in the world of inward feeling that it must find a habitation. Leaving aside such paranormal religious experiences as are the object of investigation by scientists, a great deal of Christian writing (and singing) is about inward experiences of peace and joy and penitence, rather than about realities outside the self.

In what sense can 'experience' function as a source of authority? For those who have had the kind of definable 'religious experience' which can be dated and described, such experience will seem an adequate basis for belief, even though similar experiences are produced by the use of drugs. But such

83

experiences, it would seem, are not totally unrelated to the rest of the person's experience of life. And they can only continue to provide authority for believing in so far as they enable the person to 'make sense' of the rest of experience. The great majority of Christians seem to hold the faith on grounds other than 'religious experience' in this narrower sense. They will, for example, continue faithfully to pray in private and worship in public along with others, even though there are long periods in which these exercises produce no vivid experiences such as those associated with the conversion of St Paul or St Augustine. They believe because they have been brought, perhaps from child-hood, into the life of the community which believes the Gospel, orders its life by it, and finds in so doing that its truth is confirmed in experience.

All experience is within a framework of interpretation. Even the primary experiences of sight and sound make sense only as the infant learns to relate the lights and noises that impinge on it to a real world which is there to be explored. The Christian Gospel provides a framework within which all experience is interpreted in terms of the wise and loving purpose of God. Something which, in another framework, is experienced as disaster, may, within the framework of Christian faith, be inter-preted as part of God's loving provision. The crucifixion of Jesus is 'folly' in one framework, 'the wisdom of God' in another. It would therefore be misleading to treat 'experience' as a distinct source of authority for Christian believing, because the character of our experience is a function of the faith which we hold. Church teaching advises us not to depend too much on special religious experiences (precious and needful as they may be from time to time) but to accept the call to walk by faith, trusting that this path leads to the vision of God of which all religious experience can only be a faint glimpse.

'Experience' certainly stands for something essential in any understanding of authority. God, according to scripture, desires that this authority be recognized and accepted in the heart, mind and conscience of every human being. He does not desire unwilling or uncomprehending submission to authority, which is the mark of slavery. The Christian believer willingly and joyfully submits to the authority of the one who (in Paul's words) 'loved me and gave himself up for me' (Galatians 2:20). But this authority is mediated through the living memory of a community which continually remembers, rehearses and relives the story which is the theme of the scriptures. In the church's liturgy the Bible story becomes a living tradition remembered again and again and, in the preaching of the word, reinterpreted and applied to contemporary discipleship. At the heart of all this is something which may be called experience. But it is specifically the experience of the contemporary power of the Holy Spirit of God, who is the Spirit of Jesus, to bring the atoning work of Christ home to the heart and conscience of the worshipping community.

All these four elements have their place in our recognition of and submission to the authority of God, but only as they are inseparably combined. Experience, considered apart from that which is experienced, namely the reconciling love of God in Christ, may be experience of something other than the one true and living God. Reason, considered as the possession of an autonomous human mind, excludes us from a whole range of reality. Tradition, uncontrolled by scripture, can stray far from the truth as it is in Jesus. And scripture, taken simply as the written letter apart from the quickening work of the Spirit in the life of the church, can become an instrument of bondage. In the end there can be no ultimate authority except the testimony of the Spirit of God in the heart and conscience of a man or woman. But the presence of the Spirit is promised to that community which 'indwells' that story of which the incarnation, ministry, death and resurrection of Jesus is the centre.

Notes

1. John Locke, 'A Third Letter on Tolerance', quoted in M. Polanyi, *Personal Knowledge*, page 266

2. Michael Buckley, SJ, *At the Origins of Modern Atheism*, Yale University Press, 1987

3. R. A. Clouser, *The Myth of Religious Neutrality*, Notre Dame University Press, 1991

4. Two of the papers in this volume raise a fundamental question about the grounds on which the Gospel is to be affirmed as true in the context of modernity.
In chapter 4, **Harold Netland** takes issue because I affirm that the presupposition of Christian theology is the truth of the Gospel and deny that this truth claim can be justified by reference to some more basic truth. He wishes to affirm that there are principles or criteria which are 'context-independent' and

thus can be used to evaluate alternative worldviews. He lists such criteria as non self-contradiction, coherence etc. He holds that 'such principles are ontologically objective in the sense that they are independent of the mental processes or psychological states on any human being'. But Indian philosophy denies the principle of non contradiction and regards it as one of the weaknesses of the Western tradition. There are no 'context-independent' criteria with which one could adjudicate between these two positions. Historians of science have pointed out that this Western conviction about the ultimate coherence of the cosmos is the fruit of biblical faith (see C. Kaiser, *Creation and the History of Science*, 1991). Moreover it is possible to construct coherent falsehoods.

Netland affirms that 'some beliefs must be such that they stand on their own without needing to be justified by more basic beliefs'. The subsequent history of these 'self-evident truths' is a sufficient commentary on this statement. It is true that tautologies are self-evident but, as Polanyi has said (paraphrasing Einstein), 'Only statements which can be doubted make contact with reality.'

Netland seeks to counter the claim that there is nothing more ultimate than Jesus Christ by referring to the ways by which the meaning of propositions is conveyed to us through signs written or oral. But this is beside the point; the same processes of interpretation are involved in communicating falsehood as in communicating truth. The point is irrelevant to the question of the justification of belief.

Netland does acknowledge that 'the very act of knowing anything at all is dependent on the sustaining and enabling grace of God', but the rest of the paper is devoted to demonstrating that there are other foundations on which our knowing rests.

In the same area of discussion, in chapter 5, David Wells attacks Barth on the ground that Barth speaks of God as the subject who addresses us rather than as the object of our scrutiny. His reading of Barth draws on the fantastic opinion of Cornelius van Til that Barth was controlled by a Kantian epistemology. It is hard to comprehend how anyone who had read the thirteen volumes of the Church Dogmatics could imagine that, for Barth, God is an unknown *noumenon*.

Both these writers have fallen into the modernist trap. They have accepted the modernist terminology of 'objective' and 'subjective' as though these words meant 'real' and 'unreal'. All knowing has obviously two poles: the knowing subject and the object of that subject's knowing. The ideal of a kind of 'objectivity' from which the knowing subject had been eliminated has been the great illusion of modernity. It has been popularized in the form of an idea of 'scientific knowledge' which is entirely 'context-independent' and in a vision of the cosmos as a vast mechanism which includes the human brain but has no place for the human mind. The counterpart of this has been the 'subjectivism' which both these papers rightly castigate. Excluded from the 'objective' world, the subject turns in upon itself and has to construct its own reality. The attempt to ascribe this kind of 'objectivity' to God is simply to ally oneself with the forces which deny God. God makes his sovereign reality known to us by addressing us as the supreme subject in an act of atonement which is also a word.

Neither the first disciples, nor any of their successors, became believers by attending to 'the logically prior (question) of the grounds upon which one is to choose a worldview in the first place' (Netland). This attempt to find 'context-independent' grounds for Christian faith is profoundly wrong. To be 'context-independent' one would have to be outside of history. One would in fact have to be God. This is exactly the temptation of modernism: 'You shall be as Gods', for only God is 'context-independent'. The position I am criticizing is in contradiction of the whole of scripture. Jesus said to his disciples: 'You did not choose me, I chose you.' The position affirms that we choose Jesus on the basis of 'context-independent criteria'. This position separates the knowing of God from the love of God. We are enabled to know God only through his own infinitely costly act of redemption through Christ. It denies the essential role of the Holy Spirit in bringing us to the knowledge of Christ. It asks for a kind of knowledge which does not depend on the grace of God. It falls into the Cartesian trap—a kind of certainty which rests upon the knowing subject, and not upon the faithfulness of the One whom we are enabled by grace to know. Paul says: I know whom I have believed (2 Timothy 1:12), not, 'I know the one whose existence I have demonstrated.' There is all the difference in the world between a certainty which rests wholly on the faithfulness of God, and a certainty which rests on a chain of human reasoning. The knowledge of God which is given us in Christ is, as Paul so strongly affirms, a new creation. It is not an edifice erected on the foundations of the old. It is the knowledge of the person who has to say 'I have been crucified with Christ, yet I live; yet not I but Christ lives in me, and the life I now live I live by faith in the Son of God who loved me and gave himself for me'. We walk by faith, not by sight. Every attempt to supplement faith with something else is a falling away from faith.

5. There is the view that Jesus had no intention for the future because he expected the immediate end of the present age. On this view the long centuries of Christian belief and practice are simply a mistake, based on the need to cope with the fundamental mistake of Jesus. Two immediate points may be made with reference to the scholarly view that Jesus was mistaken about the central message of the coming reign of God.

First, this view rests upon a selection of Jesus' sayings which speak of immediacy and ignores the many other sayings which speak of long patience. This is an example of a one-dimensional mind which cannot cope with the necessary tensions which are involved in a mature understanding of the human situation. Taken as a whole, the teaching of Jesus about the imminence of the new age calls for a combination of *alertness* with *patience* which is the mark of a good watchman. How else can this be communicated except by sayings and parables which stress one side or the other of the tension? If patience is taken alone, it can lead to drowsiness and sloth; if immediacy alone is stressed, it can lead to a kind of excitement which neglects the ordinary duties of the moment. Christian history is replete with examples of both. The temptation of the great historic churches is to ignore the notes of immediacy and to settle down to a long-term acceptance of things as they are. The temptation of those on the margins of society and the Church is to undervalue long-term perspectives and to live in a state of irresponsible excitement. Both poles of Jesus' teaching have to be held in tension.

Second, many New Testament scholars are eager to emphasize the fact that what we have in the Gospel record is the mind of the early church and not necessarily the exact words, *ipsissima verba*, of Jesus. Of course we have what the early church remembered of Jesus, not a tape recording of his words. But if the early writers were as free from dependence upon the exact words of Jesus as this view supposes, is it not odd that they should have recorded sayings which on this view had already been amply proved to be mistaken? Could these early disciples have understood the intention of Jesus better than some contemporary scholars?

6. See, for example, the work of Kenneth Bailey, based on long residence in the Middle East, in *Finding the Lost*, St Louis, 1989.

7. Is there any other way in which divine authority could be mediated to human beings? One would possibly be that God should make his authority known directly to every individual conscience without intervention of any other human agency. But no human being develops either reason or conscience except through participating in the intercourse of a human community, family, society, culture. Since no human experience is totally private, divine revelation could not be totally private. The other possibility is that divine revelation should be a matter of public history. It can only be in events which are limited to a particular time, place, culture. But the whole ongoing course of human history cannot be frozen forever at a particular point. Revelation only takes place if (as has been argued above) it is internalized, made part of a living human consciousness which must necessarily be the consciousness of a human being living in a particular time, place and culture. It is therefore hard to imagine how any other divine revelation could be authoritative for the whole of human history except one which embraced a living community, a tradition of teaching, and the continuing work of the divine Spirit illuminating the tradition in each new generation and each new situation, so that it becomes the living speech of God for that time, place and culture.

8. George Lindbeck, *The Nature of Doctrine, Religion and Theology in a Post-Liberal Age*, SPCK, 1984

9. the same, pages 32–33

10. See the fascinating study of Alain Finklekraut in *The Undoing of Thought*, London, 1988, a robust defence of the Enlightenment.

11. Raymond Brown, *The Gospel According to John*, volume 2, Geoffrey Chapman, 1971, page 716

12. It is well known that the first draft of the Vatican II document on revelation was entitled 'The Two Sources of Revelation'. This was rejected, and the final text, simply entitled 'Divine Revelation', begins with two chapters on 'Revelation Itself' and 'The Transmission of Divine Revelation'. The first, beginning from God's work incarnate in Jesus Christ, affirms that God 'can be known with certainty from created reality and by the light of human reason' and that he has spoken through the prophets and, last of all, in his Son. The second chapter speaks of Christ's commission to the apostles to preach the gospel to all, and of bishops as the successors of the apostles to whom this responsibility to transmit the gospel was entrusted. This tradition 'develops in the Church with the help of the Holy Spirit' so that 'the Church constantly moves forward towards the fullness of divine truth'. It follows that 'both sacred tradition and sacred Scripture are to be accepted and venerated with the same sense of devotion and reverence'.

13. Thomas Kuhn, *The Structure of Scientific Revolutions*, University of Chicago Press, 1970

4

Truth, authority and modernity: shopping for truth in a supermarket of worldviews

HAROLD A. NETLAND

> Then Jesus came to them and said, 'All authority on heaven and on earth has been given to me. Therefore go and make disciples of all nations, baptizing them in the name of the Father and of the Son, and of the Holy Spirit, and teaching them to obey everything I have commanded you. And surely I am with you always, to the very end of the age.'
>
> Matthew 28:18–20 (NIV)

The command of our Lord quoted above, generally known as the Great Commission, has traditionally been regarded as a concise expression of the mission of Christ's church in the world. Implicit in these verses, and the context of the New Testament in general which informs them, are certain assumptions about God, Jesus, and the nature of religious truth which are increasingly dismissed today as incredible. Among these are the following:

1 It is possible to know some religious truths.

2 Truth, including religious truth, is objective[1] and universally binding.

3 There is one eternal creator God who has revealed himself definitively in the Old and New Testaments.

4 There is one Lord and Savior for all humankind, Jesus Christ.

89

5 Christ's followers have an inescapable obligation to confront adherents of other religions with the gospel of Jesus Christ and to urge them to become disciples of Jesus.

These five propositions (and others as well) are basic to evangelical faith and would be regarded as non-negotiable by most evangelicals. And yet within much of the world today, certainly in Europe, North America, and much of Asia, each would be regarded as highly problematical. Under the impact of modernity, many people today embrace worldviews which cause them to dismiss such beliefs as naïve, intolerant and out of touch with the realities of the modern world.

Evangelicals engaged in ministry to those impacted by modernity increasingly find their efforts frustrated by the sharp clash between conflicting notions of religious truth, authority, and plausibility. Missionaries to non-Western cultures have long been aware of the need to understand adequately the worldview of the target culture before attempting to communicate the gospel. Recently those ministering in Europe and North America have begun to recognize the need for precisely the same kind of cultural analysis and 'contextualization' in evangelizing the West.[2] Not only does modernity present a challenge to evangelism but it also adversely affects Christian discipleship within the Church. For to the extent that one has bought into the mind-set of modernity one will resist the radical nature of genuinely biblical discipleship, which is based upon an exclusive understanding of religious truth and authority.

Modernity and religious truth

Modernity is a vast swamp fed by various social and intellectual streams, the cumulative effect of which makes traditional understandings of religious truth[3] and knowledge appear archaic and naive. We cannot review here the many factors which have led to the current milieu, but several key distinctives of the ethos of modernity should be briefly noted.

THE PRIVATIZATION OF RELIGIOUS BELIEF

In his seminal essay 'Mission in the Face of Modernity', Os Guinness speaks of privatization as a major trend shaping religious thinking in the modern world. 'By privatization is meant the process by which modernization produces a cleavage between the public and private spheres of life and focuses the private sphere as the special area for the expression of individual freedom and fulfillment.'[4] In a similar vein, Bishop Lesslie Newbigin has alerted us to the modern tendency to make a sharp dichotomy between the public world of 'facts', exemplified especially in the physical sciences, and the private realm of personal values, opinions, and preferences, with religion being banished to the latter.[5] Truth is said to belong to the public realm of 'facts' and not that of personal preference. And since religious statements are allegedly not empirically testable as are other 'public truths', religious beliefs are eliminated from the public sphere and are reduced to matters of mere personal preference and opinion. Just as some people prefer Mozart to the Beatles, so some people prefer Zen Buddhism to Protestant Christianity. The question of objective or universal truth is no more appropriate in religion than it is in music.

THE PLURALIZATION OF IDEOLOGIES AND WORLDVIEWS

Guinness further identifies pluralization as a significant modernizing trend. 'By pluralization is meant the process by which the number of opinions in the private sphere rapidly multiplies at all levels, especially at the level of worldviews, faiths, and ideologies.'[6] Postmodern theorists see this fragmentation and diversity extending into the public sphere, aided by the consumerization of culture. Diversity of belief and practice has of course always characterized our world. What is unprecedented today, however, is the degree to which people are aware of this diversity and the fact that in much of the world an astonishing variety of worldviews are live options for people right where they are. Someone living in a major urban center of Europe or North America can encounter sincere Buddhists, Muslims, Sikhs, Hindus, New Agers, Marxists, secular humanists, Mormons, Hare Krishnas and Scientologists as well as (hopefully) evangelical Christians. Multiple religious options are available even in highly homogeneous societies such as Japan, where hundreds of so-called 'new religions' flourish along with the major established traditions.

Now there is nothing in cultural or intellectual diversity in and of itself which is necessarily inimical to Christian faith. There is no reason to suppose that all Christians in all cultures must think and worship in precisely the same ways. Diversity is inherent in

God's creation. However, while fully acknowledging this, it is also important to note that the bewildering variety of intellectual and religious worldviews available today can have pernicious effects upon Christian faith and mission. Consider the following comments of Peter Berger:

> Modern man finds himself confronted not only by multiple options of possible courses of action but also by multiple options of possible ways of thinking about the world... [T]his means that the individual may choose his *Weltanschauung* very much as he chooses most other aspects of his private existence. In other words, there comes to be a smooth continuity between consumer choices in different areas of life—a preference for this brand of automobile as against another, for this sexual lifestyle as against another, and finally a decision to settle for a particular 'religious preference'.[7]

Berger notes that to speak in terms of 'religious preference', as many do today, implies that one might equally have made a different religious choice if desired. 'The notion of there being in some objective sense a *right* choice (a right model of car for everyone?) is out of place here.'[8]

Some significant consequences follow from this. For example, the availability of many alternative options tends to trivialize and relativize the significance of any one tradition. Particularly in the religious realm, where there are many competing voices each claiming to speak authoritatively, there is a marked tendency toward religious relativism, skepticism, or even suspension of judgment. There are so many conflicting truth claims; with each tradition claiming divine sanction for its assertions they cannot all be true, but how is one to choose among them? Loss of confidence in one's own tradition is not unusual. Berger observes that 'modern societies are characterized by unstable, incohesive, unreliable plausibility structures. Put differently, in the modern situation certainty is hard to come by.'[9]

Furthermore, this pluralization is amplified by the consumerism of postmodern society, encouraging the same mentality with regard to religion. The old advertising slogan of one of America's mammoth fast food chains sums up the current attitude well: 'Have it your way at Burger King!' The customer is always right, and his or her preferences rule. The desires and 'needs' of the consumer take priority over all else. This market-directed approach to religion finds expression in the eclecticism of the New Age movement, with its shameless borrowing and mixing of attractive teachings and practices from many different religions.

The postmodern displacement of truth by pragmatic utility is also reflected in a highly pragmatic view of religion, which emphasizes what religion does for individuals or society at large and minimizes questions of objective truth. Accordingly, one does not expect religion to provide 'objectively true' answers to fundamental questions about human origin and destiny. Various religions are to be evaluated pragmatically on the basis of how well they meet the needs and desires of their adherents. If an Indian happens to find that Vedanta Hinduism meets his needs, then that is right for him. If a Japanese finds Jodo Shinshu Buddhism fulfilling, then that is right for her. And so on. To speak of one religion or one religious figure being universally valid for all people in all cultures is thus to commit a category mistake.

THE PERVASIVE IMPACT OF RELIGIOUS RELATIVISM AND SKEPTICISM

Roger Trigg notes that relativism in its various forms has historically been an attractive option when people who had previously led settled and complacent lives were suddenly confronted with new and different ideas and practices.[10] It is hardly surprising, then, that an increasingly influential relativism has accompanied the growing awareness in the West of other cultures and religious traditions. The idea that there is religious truth which is objective and universally valid in all cultures and at all times is dismissed as a discredited vestige of a bygone age. Each culture and religious tradition expresses its own 'truth' in its own unique way.

Alongside relativism we must also mention the pervasive religious skepticism of the modern world. The roots of modern skepticism go back at least to David Hume and Immanuel Kant, although the more recent impact of Ludwig Wittgenstein should also be noted. Kant's contention that the mind plays a determinative role in organizing sensory data by imposing concepts or categories upon the raw data, thereby determining the form taken by our experience, and that all we can know are the *phenomena* or appearances, and never the *noumena* themselves, has been extremely influential in modern thought. Kant of course had assumed that the categorical scheme imposed by the mind was the same for all rational beings, and thus he was certainly no relativist. Those who came after him, however, emphasized even further the active part played by the mind in organizing and interpreting experience and creating frameworks according to which judgments about reality are made.[11] Postmodern theorists have increasingly asserted that there are many alternative ways of interpreting experience, each of which is legitimate, and that there is no single correct perspective on reality. What we can know is not reality itself but rather simply reality as it appears to us in our particular limited context.

So long as one accepts the terms imposed by modernity that religion be strictly relegated to the private sphere of personal preference, that it be evaluated pragmatically, and that talk of universally valid religious truth be abandoned, modernity is not particularly antagonistic to religion. So long as one is content to ignore the disturbing exclusive claims of Scripture, and is willing to replace the thundering 'Thus saith the Lord!' of the prophets with the soothing incantations of the therapist ('and how does it make you *feel*?'), modernity and religion can coexist in peace. However, when one rejects the parameters set by modernity and insists upon the public nature of religious truth, that truth in religion no less than in other spheres is objective and universal, and that religious truth is binding upon all humankind, when modernity is directly challenged in this manner it turns very hostile indeed.

In particular, modernity poses a direct challenge to the biblical perspective on two points: *First, the notion that one particular religious figure and one religious perspective can be universally valid, normative, and binding upon all peoples in all cultures—an assumption, central to the biblical understanding of Christ and salvation—is widely rejected today as arrogant and intellectually untenable in our pluralistic world.* Even within the broadly Christian community it is increasingly accepted that there cannot be just one savior and one religion for all of the world's diverse peoples.[12] *And second, even if in principle it is granted that one religion might be superior to the rest, and that one religious figure might be universally normative, why should we assume that Christianity and Jesus Christ are in this privileged position?* After all, why Jesus and not the Buddha or Muhammad or even Shirley MacLaine?

Engaging the plausibility structures of modernity

Ever since the Enlightenment the challenge to Christian faith in the West has been conceived largely in terms of secularism and unbelief, and certainly one should not minimize the impact of secularism today.[13] But the challenge posed by modernity goes much deeper than mere secularism. For in our pluralistic world the question is not simply that of the choice between theism and atheism, or Christian faith and secular humanism. Increasingly, whether in New York, Bangkok, Paris or Rio de Janeiro, the issue is: Given the many alternative worldviews available today, both secular and religious, why should one become (or remain) a Christian?[14]

THE NEED FOR AN INFORMED, SPIRIT-CONTROLLED APOLOGETIC

An integral component of effective evangelism and discipleship in contexts impacted by modernity must be a vigorous Christian apologetic which is capable of engaging the intellectual forces of modernity in informed debate, is sensitive to the values and mores of the target culture, and is conducted in conscious reliance upon the power and guidance of the Holy Spirit. *What is needed, in other words, is a Spirit-controlled apologetic which aggressively challenges the plausibility structures of modernity, which insists upon Christian belief as universally valid public truth, and which restores confidence in the normativity of the gospel of Jesus Christ.* Men and women today must be brought to the realization that Christian faith is not merely one of many equally legitimate alternative options, but that there is a significant sense in which they ought to accept Jesus Christ instead of opposing alternatives.

What is called for here is not simply a new apologetic gimmick—six easy steps to proving God's existence, the deity of Christ, and the resurrection which can be used to 'close the sale' in personal evangelism. Rather what is envisioned is a comprehensive long-term investment in challenging and changing the reigning paradigms and assumptions of modernity which shape people's values and thinking. An effective response must be comprehensive since it should address not only the educational and academic world but also the broader influences of the media and entertainment industries. And it must be a serious long-term effort since effective change on this level will not come overnight.

DEFINITIONS, CLARIFICATIONS, AND GUIDELINES.

It is essential to grasp a basic distinction between what might be called *theoretical apologetics* and *applied* or *context specific* apologetics. Theoretical apologetics is concerned solely with the objective justification of the Christian faith, irrespective of human response. Its purpose is to answer satisfactorily certain fundamental questions about the acceptability of Christian truth claims. Among these questions are the following: Can we know whether God exists, and if so, how? Is the Christian understanding of God, sin, and salvation significantly different from that found in other religions? Did Jesus actually rise from the dead, and if so, what is the significance of this? Theoretical apologetics is thus a highly rigorous and specialized endeavor, incorporating a variety of disciplines although epistemological issues are central.

Applied apologetics, by contrast, is very much concerned with human response to the proclamation and defense of the Gospel. It is the utilization of appropriate justification procedures and relevant data in the actual presentation and defense of the Gospel to a particular target audience. Thus its purpose is to elicit a favorable response from the audience it actively seeks to persuade. The methodology and level of sophistication of applied apologetics will vary greatly, depending upon one's audience. What is appropriate and effective in Kyoto may not be acceptable in Mexico City or Cairo. Considerable creativity and variety in approach are essential. But the answers to questions raised on the level of applied apologetics are logically dependent upon answers to corresponding questions in theoretical apologetics. Thus effective applied apologetics presupposes some familiarity with issues in theoretical apologetics.

Some guidelines for effective apologetics should be noted:

1. *We must recognize that apologetics in and of itself will not result in the salvation of anyone.* Nobody is argued into the Kingdom. Apologetics just as evangelism is ineffective apart from the power and work of the Holy Spirit, for ultimately it is the Holy Spirit who brings about conviction of sin (John 16:8–11) and who liberates the spiritually blind from the grasp of the Adversary and gives new birth in Christ (John 3:5; 1 Corinthians 2:14–16; Titus 3:5). But, of course, this does not make apologetics unnecessary any more than it renders evangelism optional. Both evangelism

and apologetics must be carried out with much prayer and conscious dependence upon the power of God. In our witness to an unbelieving world, primacy must always be given the simple, direct, Spirit-anointed proclamation of the gospel (Romans 1:16; Hebrews 4:12). But where appropriate, such witness should also be supplemented by an informed, sensitive response to criticism and questions, and demonstration of why one should accept the claims of Christian faith (1 Peter 3:15). Properly construed, then, apologetics is ancillary to evangelism.

2. *The focus of apologetics must always be upon leading the other person(s) into a direct encounter with the risen Lord Jesus Christ.* Discussions of doctrine and ideology, while perhaps interesting, are not the central concern. The distinctive feature of Christian faith is its ineradicable grounding in the historical person of Jesus of Nazareth—his life, death, and resurrection. The only Jesus that *can* be known is the Jesus of the New Testament; any other 'Jesus' is a figment of one's imagination. And Scripture is unambiguous on the uniqueness and normativity of Jesus as the one Savior and Lord for all humankind. Jesus himself was explicit: 'No one comes to the Father except through me' (John 14:6). Furthermore, the only Jesus we *need* to know is the Jesus of the New Testament. As Peter put it, 'Lord, to whom shall we go? You have the words of eternal life' (John 6:68).

Certainly it will on occasion be appropriate to challenge assumptions or beliefs which are incompatible with biblical truth, and this should be done with grace and humility. In such cases it is often most effective to challenge by raising probing questions rather than by arguing rigorously against a particular view. Throughout, however, the Christian apologist must remember that the objective is not to score debating points or to win arguments but rather to lead others to the point of seriously considering the claims of Christ.

3. *Proper applied apologetics will utilize morally acceptable and culturally appropriate means of persuasion.* This requires considerable understanding of the culture. Any activity which is manipulative or coercive, or which otherwise infringes upon the dignity of the other party, must be rejected. Nor is there any room in a genuinely Christian apologetic for ridicule of other religious figures, beliefs, or practices. It is a reproach to the cause

97

of Christ that Christians sometimes have been overly aggressive in evangelism and have engaged in caricature and ridicule of other religions. This is not only ineffective but much more importantly it is fundamentally unChristian. One can engage in vigorous apologetics while simultaneously demonstrating genuine respect for opposing views and acceptance of the other person as a fellow human being created in God's image and thus the object of God's limitless love.

4. *Effectively challenging the plausibility structures of modernity will require highly gifted apologists who are fully competent in their fields and who produce careful scholarship which is taken seriously by the broader academic community.* Unfortunately, few evangelicals today fall into this category. Popular apologetics directed at the ordinary person is important in its own right but it will hardly affect the opinion shapers of modernity. What is needed are men and women intellectually gifted by God who see the academy as a mission field and who have a sense of calling from God as agents of challenge and transformation within the intellectual world. This surely is one of the most demanding and difficult mission fields today. And yet the Church ignores it at its own peril. The Church at large must support such missionary apologists by recognizing the legitimacy of their missionary task and providing structures for encouragement and spiritual nourishment just as it does with missionaries in other contexts.

5. *Finally, while recognizing the importance of the intellectual dimension, surely the most powerful apologetic is a community of believers who have been radically transformed by the grace and love of Christ and who consistently manifest in their lives the qualities exemplified in Christ's life.* Jesus stated the basic principle to his disciples 2000 years ago: 'By this all men will know that you are my disciples, if you love one another' (John 13:35). The failure of the Church to live consistently as Christ's disciples undermines all other efforts to demonstrate the truth of Christian faith to a skeptical world. Particularly in the West, the glaring gap between what Christians profess with their lips and how they actually live has made the radical biblical claims about Jesus Christ and the possibility of new life in him sound hollow to modern ears.

ENGAGING MODERNITY: AN EXAMPLE FROM PHILOSOPHY

In much of the world today, anyone undergoing a university level education will directly or indirectly come under the influence of the major philosophical thinkers and movements of modern times. Academia tends to regard any claim to religious truth as problematic and views with amused incredulity those who hold that God has revealed himself definitively in the Bible.

Ever since Hume and Kant philosophy in the West has been largely critical of Christian faith, and in the earlier part of this century it was aggressively hostile to any kind of metaphysics. However, the changes within the Anglo-American philosophical community during the past twenty years are remarkable. Whereas in the 1940s and 1950s, under the influence of Logical Positivism, philosophers pompously declared that all talk of God was meaningless (thereby causing some theologians to scramble about madly trying to find creative ways to appease their critics and salvage their calling), by the 1980s Logical Positivism itself was a thoroughly discredited philosophical movement, and one of the most flourishing and vigorous branches of philosophy was philosophical theology. Many of the leading philosophers in the Anglo-American tradition today, teaching in some of the most prestigious institutions, are Christian theists. Philosophy journals today regularly carry articles dealing not only with religious epistemology in general but with classical theological issues such as the incarnation, divine revelation, the atonement, the divine attributes, etc.[15]

To be sure, the extent of the changes should not be exaggerated. No one is predicting that the American Philosophical Association will be taken over by evangelicals, and there are still plenty of atheists and agnostics who have no interest in religion of any kind as well as those who are virulently hostile to Christian faith. But the change in philosophical climate is significant. Some of the established paradigms of modern philosophy have been vigorously challenged and shown to be untenable. No longer is Christian faith routinely dismissed as philosophically unjustified. Some of the best work in epistemology today comes from Christian philosophers, and Christians are moving into prominent academic positions in secular universities.

What brought about the change? A variety of factors converged to make a change in attitude and direction within the philosophical community possible, but chief among them must be the efforts of an initially small group of committed Christian philosophers, led initially by William Alston and Alvin Plantinga, to establish a structure for fellowship and encouragement of Christian philosophers. The result was the formation of the Society of Christian Philosophers within the APA in 1978. Currently the Society has over one thousand members, including some of the most prestigious philosophers today, and publishes a highly respected journal, *Faith and Philosophy*.

No one has done more to change the contemporary philosophical climate than has Alvin Plantinga. One of the most respected and influential philosophers today, Plantinga has dramatically altered the terms of the debate over religious epistemology. Ever since the time of Hume and Kant, it has been widely accepted in the philosophical community that one cannot be justified in Christian belief unless he or she is able to demonstrate that such belief is justified. In other words, the theist was judged irrational unless he or she could demonstrate the rationality of Christian belief. The burden clearly rested with the theist. In a series of seminal articles Plantinga has challenged this reigning assumption, and has argued vigorously that belief in God can be what he calls 'properly basic', or in other words, that it can be 'entirely acceptable, desirable, right, proper, and rational to accept belief in God without any argument or evidence whatever'[16]. Plantinga has very effectively shown that common 'evidentialist objections', which maintain that theistic belief is somehow irrational unless one can demonstrate that it is epistemically justified, are themselves based upon highly problematic assumptions. He argues that a theist can be within his or her 'epistemic rights' in believing in God even though the theist is unable to give convincing reasons for that belief and even though such belief is not based upon sound theistic arguments. In Hoitenga's words,

> Plantinga's central position is that belief in God, that is, belief that God exists, does not require argument or evidence because it can be a properly basic belief.
> Indeed, for a fully rational human being, belief that God exists is in the foundations of the human noetic structure, just like beliefs that are self-evident to reason or evident to the senses, memory beliefs, and beliefs in other minds.[17]

Whether one is ultimately convinced by his 'Reformed episte-mology' or not, and there is today a vigorous debate over the acceptability of his thesis, it cannot be denied that he has almost singlehandedly shifted the terms of the debate over religious epistemology and has persuasively shown that the religious believer need not be in an epistemically inferior position to the agnostic or atheist. Although this in itself will hardly neutralize the challenge of modernity to Christian faith, this is an example of what one highly gifted and committed Christian thinker can do to help modify an aspect of the accepted plausibility structure. We can pray and hope that these positive changes within the philosophical community will be reflected in the educational climate of the next generation of university students.

Apologetics and alternative worldviews: the problem of criteria

We applaud the very significant achievements of Plantinga's Reformed epistemology, but some of its limitations should also be noted. In particular, Plantinga's argument for the 'proper basicality' of belief in God does not help us in responding to what I see as one of the central issues facing Christian mission in the face of modernity: Why should one be a Christian instead of a Buddhist or secular humanist or New Ager?

Here it is helpful to draw a distinction between what is frequently referred to as *negative* (or defensive) *apologetics* and *positive* (or offensive) *apologetics*. Negative apologetics is con-cerned with responding to direct attacks upon the truth or rationality of Christian faith and seeks to show that such attacks are unwarranted. The objective here is to show that the believer is justified, or is within his or her 'epistemic rights', in accepting the truth claims of Christian faith. Positive apologetics, on the other hand, goes beyond merely responding to criticism of Christian faith and is concerned to show that non-Christians too *ought* to accept the truth claims of Christianity. Thus the apologist here is very much on the offensive, trying to demon-strate that there is an important sense in which unbelievers too are epistemically obligated to accept Christian faith, or that it is unreasonable or irrational for them not to do so.

To the extent that he has shown that current forms of the evidentialist challenge are untenable, Plantinga has very effec-

tively engaged in negative apologetics. He has argued persuasively that a theist can be fully within his or her epistemic rights
in believing in God. But he does not go beyond that to show that
unbelievers and adherents of other religions are epistemically
obligated to accept the truth claims of Christianity as well.
Indeed, Plantinga's arguments can be applied equally to a
Buddhist or Hindu, and thus on Plantinga's premises the Zen
Buddhist can also be fully within his epistemic rights in holding
that belief in Emptiness as the ultimate reality is properly basic,
and the Hindu can equally claim that belief in Brahman as the
sole reality is properly basic. Plantinga's discussion is concerned
solely with the notion of *epistemic permission* rather than the
much stronger notion of *epistemic obligation*. And yet, this hardly
seems sufficient for our pluralistic world. What is needed is not
simply to be told that each religious believer can be within his or
her epistemic rights in believing certain things, but rather that
there are significant reasons why Christian faith is to be preferred
to other available alternatives. And for this positive apologetics is
inescapable.[18]

Anyone envisioning this kind of role for Christian apologetics,
however, will face some sharp critics. Some hold that this kind of
activity *cannot* be carried out and others maintain that even if it
can it *should not* be conducted. Critics in the former category,
often influenced by various forms of epistemological skepticism
and relativism, typically contend that it is simply not possible to
demonstrate that one particular religious worldview (e.g. Christian) is epistemically preferable to others. Those in the latter
category are frequently highly committed Christians who hold
that for various theological or moral reasons positive apologetics
is not an appropriate enterprise.

The issues involved here are complex and cannot be explored
fully, but given their importance in the present discussion they
should be given brief attention. One way to approach the matter
is to ask whether there are any criteria or principles which are
'context-independent' and thus can legitimately be used in
evaluating alternative worldviews.[19] If not, then clearly the kind
of apologetics called for above is impossible. The suggestion that
there are such criteria goes against the reigning 'orthodoxies' of
various modern and postmodern intellectual movements. Typically, all criteria are said to be merely the products of particular
nexuses or contexts, whether these be conceived of as linguistic,

cultural, historical, social, economic, or whatever. Different relativists emphasize different contexts: criteria for evaluation might be said to be relative to particular conceptual schemes, frameworks, forms of life, language games, modes of thought, *Weltanschauungen*, paradigms, etc. Thus, although such criteria can be employed for evaluation *from within* a given nexus, they cannot legitimately be used for making critical evaluations of competing worldviews *from the outside*. What is denied is that there is any truth, knowledge, or rationality norm independent of particular contexts.[20]

Thorough discussion of the issues is impossible here, but we might note three fundamental difficulties with any attempt to deny that there are principles or criteria which are context-independent and thus can be used to evaluate alternative world-views for truth. First, although the appeal of relativism is inspired in part by the observation of ideological and religious diversity, it is crucial to recognize that the empirical question of *what is in fact believed* is logically distinct from the normative question of *what ought to be believed*. Simply because there are many competing worldviews sincerely accepted by good people it does not necessarily follow that all are equally valid or that there are no legitimate criteria for selecting one particular worldview as true.

Furthermore, ever since the time of Plato it has repeatedly been pointed out that the mere assertion of the thesis of relativism, if intended to be accepted as true, involves one in incoherence or self-refutation. This can be demonstrated by taking cultural relativism, which maintains that truth and basic principles of rationality are internal or relative to a given culture, as an example. Criteria are said to be products of forces within the culture and thus cannot legitimately be used to make evaluations between various cultures. But if cultural relativism is in fact true, then it follows that the statement of cultural relativism must itself be true only within the context of the person asserting it. It cannot be regarded as true in any universal or trans-cultural sense. But if so, why should anyone who is not a member of that culture bother to accept the thesis of cultural relativism as true? Similar difficulties vitiate any attempt to restrict truth or rationality norms to a particular context, whether it be cultural, linguistic, social, historical, or whatever.

And third, it is often not appreciated that the price of

accepting relativism is forfeiture of the right to make judgments about the objective truth or falsity of worldviews. For if all criteria for making such judgments are internal to particular contexts, then clearly one cannot legitimately appeal to such criteria to make judgments about the truth of one's own view or to make evaluations about the truth or falsity of competing worldviews. The most one could say is that from one's own (relative) perspective worldview A is to be preferred to world-view B. This, however, amounts to nothing more than a statement of preference and has no bearing upon questions of objective truth.

If we reject a thoroughgoing relativism, it seems undeniable that there are at least some criteria or principles which are context-independent and can legitimately be used in appraising various ideological and religious perspectives. Elsewhere I have suggested ten basic principles which can be utilized in evaluating worldviews.[21] Although we cannot consider the principles here, I maintain that they are objective in the sense that they transcend particular social, cultural, or historical contexts and their validity is independent of their acceptance or rejection by particular persons—they are part of the 'stuff' of reality, so to speak.[22] Of course, recognizing the validity of such principles is one thing; applying them in actually evaluating specific worldviews is quite another (and an enormously complex) matter. Assessment of worldviews other than one's own requires in-depth understanding of the values, beliefs, and practices which shape the worldview in question, and must be carried out carefully in a gracious and humble spirit.

Some object that maintaining that we have access to context-independent criteria is simply untenable today in light of recent work in the sociology of knowledge which demonstrates the 'theory laden' nature of all our beliefs and judgments. Every belief reflects a particular perspective influenced by various socio-cultural factors. Appeal to some alleged 'neutral' criteria is a chimera.

To be sure, each person is rooted in a particular historical, socio-cultural setting; we are not disembodied intellects or Leibnizian monads. The issue, however, is not whether our beliefs and judgments are influenced by our surroundings. Clearly they are. The real issue concerns the nature and extent of such influence: Are our views *merely* the products of our environment, or are we able to transcend to some extent the cumulative influences of history, culture, society, etc., so as to apprehend truths which are themselves distinct from particular contexts?[23] Maintaining the former subjects one to the epistemological difficulties with thoroughgoing relativism noted above.

Curiously, there is a further objection to the role for apologetics outlined above which holds that any attempt to establish the truth of the Christian faith by appealing to allegedly neutral ('autonomous') criteria or principles of rationality compromises God's sovereignty and fails to take into account the noetic effects of sin. Presuppositionism,[24] or theological fideism as it is sometimes called, characteristically maintains that each person's worldview is ultimately based upon certain basic faith postulates, or presuppositions, and that there are no autonomous or neutral rationality norms by which to evaluate alternative worldviews. Every perspective—whether evangelical Christian, secular humanist, Buddhist, Muslim, even those of the natural sciences—is based upon fundamental assumptions which are themselves unprovable and are the object of one's faith commitment. Since every perspective is thus rooted in some faith commitment, Christian faith is no less 'rational' than any other perspective. Nevertheless, while maintaining that one's most basic assumptions are ultimately the product of a faith commitment, presuppositionists also contend that Christians are to judge every other perspective on the basis of God's self-revelation in Jesus Christ and Holy Scripture. As John Frame puts it,

> For a Christian, the content of Scripture must serve as his ultimate presupposition. Our beliefs about Scripture may be corrected by other beliefs about Scripture, but relative to the body of extra-scriptural information that we possess, those beliefs are presuppositional in character. This doctrine is merely the outworking of the lordship of God in the area of human thought . . . If Scripture is the ultimate justification for all human knowledge, how should we justify our belief in Scripture itself? By Scripture, of course! There is no more ultimate authority, no more reliable source of information, and nothing that is more certain by which Scripture might be tested.[25]

Few Christian thinkers have been as effective in calling the Church to grapple seriously with the challenges of modernity as has Bishop Lesslie Newbigin. Newbigin's writings present a penetrating and incisive critique of the ethos of modernity, and he forcefully calls for the Church to acknowledge the sovereignty and lordship of Jesus Christ over all of life, and to engage vigorously in evangelistic witness in our pluralistic world. However, some of Newbigin's statements make unnecessary and problematic concessions to presuppositionism.[26] Consider, for example, the following statements taken from his recent *Truth to Tell: The Gospel as Public Truth*:

> We are all Adam's heirs, and we in our particular culture are all heirs of Descartes. This becomes evident when we try to communicate the Christian faith to our unbelieving friends. When we try to do this, the answer comes: 'But can you prove it?' 'Can you prove to me that Jesus is indeed the true and living way?' 'What are the grounds on which I should choose to follow him rather than any of the others who have made similar claims?' We cannot answer that by offering some grounds, something supposedly more reliable than what is given to us in Christ. To do so would be to embark on an infinite regress, since we would in due course have to find proof that these grounds were reliable and then to show further grounds for this and so ad infinitum. What is really being asked, of course, is that we should show that the gospel is in accordance with the reigning plausibility structure of our society, that it accords with the assumptions which we normally do not doubt; and that is exactly what we cannot and must not do . . . We have to offer a new starting point for thought. That starting point is God's revelation of his being and purpose in those events which form the substance of the Scriptures and which have their center and determining focus in the events concerning Jesus . . . The Church lives by the faith that (to put it in a very truncated form) Jesus is Lord. That means that he is Lord not only of the Church but of the world, not only in the religious life but in all life, not merely over some peoples but over all peoples. He is

106

not just my savior, but the savior of the world. We have
no way in which we can demonstrate the truth of that
claim by reference to some supposedly more ultimate
realities.[27]

A number of significant and complex issues are raised in these
statements, but our concern here must be restricted to the
question whether there are any criteria or principles to which
we can legitimately appeal in deciding the truth or falsity of
alternative worldviews. Clearly there is a significant sense in
which the Christian, as a Christian, is not only entitled but is
obligated to judge alternative worldviews on the basis of God's
Word. Any values, beliefs, or practices which are incompatible
with Scripture must be rejected. But this is not the issue here. The
question here is the logically prior one of the grounds upon
which one is to choose a worldview in the first place. How does
one determine which perspective if any is in fact true?

Now this is not merely an academic question, for each of the
major religions claims to be true and to provide the standard by
which to evaluate competing perspectives. The Christian appeals
to the Bible as the supreme authority; the Muslim rejects the
Bible in favor of the Qur'an; the Zen Buddhist claims to have
direct access to ultimate reality through *satori* and *kensho*; the
Hindu appeals to the authority of the Upanishads and the
experience of *samadhi*; and of course Shirley MacLaine has her
own direct channel to religious truth. Simply appealing to
authority in and of itself settles nothing, for each tradition has
its own authoritative structure. The question is: Which 'authority'
is in fact ultimately authoritative?

Although there is undeniable appeal in presuppositionism
(after all, it *seems* to be merely drawing out the implications of
the doctrine of God's sovereignty over all of life), lurking beneath
the surface are some disturbing epistemological implications.
Presuppositionists are of course correct in insisting upon the
absolute sovereignty of God over every sphere, including human
knowledge. Ontologically, there is nothing more ultimate than
the Triune God, and epistemologically the very act of knowing
anything at all is dependent upon the sustaining and enabling
grace of God. Furthermore, the noetic effects of sin must be
acknowledged. Human depravity extends to the intellect, and the
knowing processes are affected by sin no less than the other

dimensions of the human person. As the apostle Paul reminds us, unregenerate persons characteristically distort and suppress God's truth in an effort to excuse their sin (Romans 1:18–32). Similarly, no informed Christian would deny that ultimately all persons fall into one of two mutually exclusive classes: those who recognize and respond appropriately to God as sovereign Lord (although their pilgrimage in this life may not be entirely free of sin), and those who persist in rejecting God and substituting something else apart from God as the focus of ultimate concern. Surely a genuinely biblical view of the person must insist upon all of this.

However, it does not necessarily follow from this that all knowing is ultimately based upon certain faith postulates or that there are no context-independent criteria for evaluating world-views which can be known. Not only is presuppositionism not demanded by Scripture but there are compelling epistemological reasons for not accepting it as well.

First, it must be admitted that not every belief can be justified on the basis of more basic beliefs or, as Newbigin points out, an infinite regress ensues. Some beliefs must be such that they 'stand on their own' without needing to be justified by more basic beliefs. A recurring theme in the history of philosophy has been the search for such 'basic beliefs' and formulation of acceptable procedures for their identification. But one must be careful here. It is one thing to recognize that knowledge is based upon certain epistemically basic beliefs which do not derive their justification from other beliefs, and then to try to identify them and to establish their relation to other beliefs. It is an entirely different matter, however, to suggest that every perspective is ultimately based upon certain basic presuppositions or faith postulates. In other words, *presuppositions* must be clearly distinguished from *epistemically basic beliefs*. A presupposition is generally held to be an assumption or postulate, that is, a belief which is assumed to be true, or is accepted as true, apart from corroborating evidence. There is a volitional element involved in a presupposition, since there is a sense in which one chooses to accept a presupposition, or as in some cases, a presupposition might be implicit in other beliefs one chooses to accept.

Epistemically basic beliefs, however, cannot be presuppositions for they are necessary for there to be any presupposition at all. For example, one cannot presuppose anything whether it be

God or some other object of ultimate commitment without appealing to (among other things) the principle of noncontradiction.[28] And the principle of noncontradiction cannot itself be a presupposition for it is a necessary condition for any presupposition whatever. Furthermore, in presenting their views presuppositionists make widespread appeal to principles and categories which are not presuppositions and which are logically independent of their particular system, e.g. general principles of adequacy, simplicity, coherence, consistency, and the logical principles of identity, noncontradiction, etc. Thus a presupposition, or faith postulate, cannot be what is most basic to worldviews, since it is itself dependent upon other more basic principles.

The same point can be made from a different perspective. Presuppositionists typically contend that there is nothing more ultimate than Scripture or Jesus Christ. Belief in God and his Word is the ultimate presupposition. But how does one know God's Word or learn about Jesus Christ? Presumably by reading the Bible. But reading anything, including the Bible, is a highly complex activity involving proper application of basic epistemological, semantic, and logical categories and principles. Minimally, application of fundamental logical principles such as those of noncontradiction and identity, and semantic and syntactic principles which enable one to derive meaning from the marks of ink on a page, and basic hermeneutical principles enabling one to interpret properly the data of Scripture are necessary.[29] Such basic principles cannot themselves be derived from Scripture since they are necessary for understanding Scripture in the first place.

On an even more basic level, in reading the Bible and thus encountering God's Word one holds in one's hands an empirical object: a book with a cover, pages, ink marks on the pages, etc. And in holding and reading a Bible one (presumably) accepts that one is holding an object with extra-mental reality, and that this experience is not simply the product of one's own consciousness, or indeed of some Cosmic Consciousness. Now to be sure, few if any persons reading the Bible ever wonder about its extra-mental reality, but this is largely beside the point. It is crucial to see that strictly speaking Jesus Christ, or Scripture itself, cannot be the epistemological starting point, since we come to know about Jesus and the content of Scripture through reading the Bible, and this very act presupposes, among other things, the reality of an external world, that one's senses are (generally) reliable, that one is justified in taking the object in one's hands to be a book which is to be read, and that appropriate logical, semantic, and hermeneutical principles can be applied in reading and understanding the book. Attempts to bypass epistemological issues by appealing directly to the Word of God as the epistemological starting point are untenable.

Furthermore, to the extent that presuppositionism denies the reality of context-independent criteria for the assessment of various worldviews, it is vitiated by the same difficulties plaguing relativism noted above. As with relativism, one accepts presuppositionism at enormous cost. For if all perspectives are ultimately based upon faith postulates, with no rational means of adjudicating between competing presuppositions, then not only does one forfeit the right to make claims of objective knowledge but one also loses the right to criticize alternative views as false. The most one could say is, 'Based upon my presuppositions, your position is unacceptable'. But it remains an open question why anyone should accept *those* particular presuppositions as opposed to any others.

Is maintaining the objective reality of context-independent criteria for evaluating worldviews really capitulation to the agenda of modernity? Is the attempt to demonstrate the epistemic warrant for accepting Jesus as Lord necessarily compromise with the reigning plausibility structures of secular society? Although one must always be vigilant in resisting the seductive lure of modernity, I see no reason for concluding that engaging in positive apologetics necessarily results in adopting the mind-set of modernity.

Indeed, might we not go a step further, and suggest that presuppositionism itself inadvertently makes unnecessary and unwarranted concessions to the contemporary mind-set? For in insisting that all perspectives reduce to certain 'faith commitments' and that there are no non-arbitrary criteria by which to settle cognitive conflicts between alternative worldviews, presuppositionism echoes the skepticism and relativism of a host of modern and postmodern thinkers. Enlightenment figures such as Voltaire certainly had an excessive confidence in the ability of reason alone to settle all disputes. But it seems that much of the contemporary world suffers from an opposite vice—excessive skepticism concerning our ability to know religious truth and to adjudicate between conflicting truth claims.

Contrary to the perspective of presuppositionism, I suggest that it is through the proper application of positive apologetics, under the sovereign direction of the Holy Spirit, that the reigning plausibility structures of modernity can be challenged and transformed, so that modern men and women come to accept the reality of the transcendent, open themselves to the liberating grace of God, and commit themselves to lives of radical discipleship of the one Lord, Jesus Christ.

Bishop Newbigin rightly castigates contemporary society for banishing Christian belief from the marketplace of ideas and reducing it to the status of mere private preference and opinion. He very properly calls the Church to engage modernity in debate and to insist upon the Gospel as 'public truth'. But if we expect the claims of Christian faith to be treated fairly in the public arena as genuine truth claims and not as mere private preferences, then we must be willing to subject the truth claims of the Gospel to rigorous scrutiny and the demand for corroborative justification, as are truth claims in all other domains.

Conclusion

Philosopher Diogenes Allen tells of someone coming to him and asking, 'Why should I go to church when I have no religious needs?' Allen very wisely replied, 'Because Christianity is true.'[30]

Why should one be a Christian instead of a Buddhist, or Hindu, or atheist, or New Ager? Because the central claims of the Christian faith are true. The effectiveness of evangelism and discipleship in the coming decades will be directly related to the Church's ability to challenge and transform some of the dominant assumptions of modernity which make it so difficult for many to accept the Gospel as truth.

May God raise up for His Church gifted men and women of vision and courage who understand the times and know what the Church should do (1 Chronicles 12:32) and who can demonstrate to a cynical and weary world through their lives as well as their words that in Jesus alone can one find the Way, the Truth, and the Life (John 14:6).

Notes

1. In this essay I use 'objective' to mean roughly 'having extra-mental reality or validity'. Objective truth, then, is truth which is independent of individual or collective states of consciousness and which obtains regardless of whether or not anyone happens to accept it as truth. On the notion of objectivity in epistemology see Roger Trigg, *Reality at Risk: A Defence of Realism in Philosophy and the Sciences*, Barnes & Noble, 1980.

2. See Lesslie Newbigin, 'Can the West be Converted?', *International Bulletin of Missionary Research*, 11, January 1987, pages 2–7; George Hunsberger, 'The Newbigin Gauntlet: Developing a Domestic Missiology for North America', *Missiology*, XIX, October 1991, pages 392–408; Craig Van Gelder, 'A Great New Fact of Our Day: America as a Mission Field', *Missiology*, XIX, October 1991, pages 409–418.

3. Truth theory is a highly technical and controversial subject in contemporary philosophy. Although the word 'truth' can be used in a wide variety of ways, in its logically basic sense truth is a property of statements or propositions such that a proposition is true if and only if the state of affairs to which it refers obtains; otherwise it is false. This definition of truth is not committed to any particular theory of truth, although it does accept the fundamental insight behind what have been called 'correspondence theories' of truth, that is, that a statement's truth is dependent upon the nature of objective reality. See Alan White, *Truth*, Macmillan, 1970; Lawrence E. Johnson, *Focusing On Truth*, Routledge, 1992; and Michael Devitt, *Realism and Truth*, 2nd edition, Blackwell, 1991.

4. Os Guinness, 'Mission in the Face of Modernity', in *The Gospel in the Modern World*, editors Martyn Eden and David Wells, Inter-Varsity Press, 1991, page 96

5. See Lesslie Newbigin, *Foolishness to the Greeks*, Eerdmans, 1986; *Truth to Tell*, Eerdmans, 1991; *The Gospel in a Pluralist Society*, Eerdmans, 1989. See also Richard John Neuhaus, *The Naked Public Square: Religion and Democracy in America*, Eerdmans, 1984.

6. Guinness [note 4], page 97.

7. Peter Berger, *The Heretical Imperative: Contemporary Possibilities of Religious Affirmation*, Doubleday, 1979, page 17

8. Peter Berger, 'The Pluralist Situation and the Coming Dialogue Between the World Religions', *Buddhist-Christian Studies*, 1, 1981, page 33

9. Berger [note7], page 19. Similarly, Guinness observes that when constantly confronted by other alternatives, one's commitment to any particular tradition remains somewhat tentative—after all, there are 'all those others...' 'Multiple conversions are now common, being 'born again' is trivialized and even testimonies are reduced to the status of a spiritual visiting card in need of updating in a spiritually mobile society.' Guinness [note 4], page 98.

10. Roger Trigg, 'Religion and the Threat of Relativism', *Religious Studies*, 19, 1983, page 297

11. See Patrick Gardner, 'German Philosophy and the Rise of Relativism', *The Monist*, 64, 1981, pages 138–54.

12. This is the explicit conclusion of John Hick's religious pluralism, but is also implicit in many other thinkers less radical than Hick. See for example John Hick, *An Interpretation of Religion*, Yale University Press, 1988; *The Myth of Christian Uniqueness*, John H. Hick & Paul F. Knitter, editors, Orbis, 1987; Paul F. Knitter, *No Other Name? A Critical Survey of Christian Attitudes Toward the World Religions*, Orbis, 1985; Stanley Samartha, *One Christ, Many Religions: Toward a Revised Christology*, Orbis, 1991.

13. Guinness reports that since 1900 the percentage of the world's atheistic, agnostic and secular peoples has grown from 0.2 per cent to 21.3 per cent, the most dramatic change on the entire religious map of the twentieth century. Guinness [note 4], page 99.

14. David Bosch states, 'It would probably be correct to say that we have reached the point where there can be little doubt that the two largest unsolved problems for the Christian Church are its relationship (1) to *worldviews which offer this-worldly salvation*, and (2) to *other faiths*.' David Bosch, *Transforming Mission: Paradigm Shifts in Theology of Mission*, Orbis, 1991, pages 476–477. Emphasis in original.

15. See Kenneth Konyndyk, 'Christianity Reenters Philosophical Circles', *Perspectives*, November 1992, pages 17–20.

16. Alvin Plantinga, 'Reason and Belief in God', in *Faith and Rationality: Reason and Belief in God*, Alvin Plantinga and Nicholas Wolterstorff, editors, University of Notre Dame Press, 1983. See also Plantinga's 'Is Belief in God Properly Basic?', *Nous*, 15, March 1981, pages 41–51; and 'Justification and Theism', *Faith and Philosophy*, 4, October 1987, pages 403–426. Plantinga's Gifford Lectures are forthcoming from Oxford University Press. For a helpful study placing Plantinga's contribution in the context of Western philosophy of religion in general, see Dewey J. Hoitenga, Jr., *Faith and Reason From Plato to Plantinga: An Introduction to Reformed Epistemology*, State University of New York Press, 1991.

17. Hoitenga [note 16], page 202

18. Paul Griffiths, in his recent *An Apology for Apologetics: A Study in the Logic of Interreligious Dialogue*, Orbis, 1991, sees clearly the need for a properly conducted positive apologetics. Griffiths is a Christian with a Ph.D. in Buddhist studies and teaches at the University of Chicago Divinity School. From this background and his experience in interreligious dialogue, he vigorously challenges 'an underlying orthodoxy' in current discussions of religious pluralism which maintains that 'mutual understanding between religious traditions' is the only legitimate goal of interreligious dialogue; that judgment and criticism of religious practices and beliefs of other traditions are always inappropriate; and that aggressive defense of the truth of the tenets of one's own tradition should be avoided (page xi). Griffiths convincingly shows this perspective to be deeply flawed and he correctly argues that it is often not only appropriate but also incumbent upon representatives of a particular tradition, such as orthodox Christianity, to engage in both negative and positive apologetics.

19. The philosophical significance of the question of criteria for evaluating cross-cultural worldviews was pointed out twenty years ago by Ninian Smart in his *The Science of Religion and the Sociology of Knowledge*, Princeton University Press, 1973, pages 12–13. See also Mary Ann Stenger, 'The Problem of Cross-Cultural Criteria of Religious Truths', *Modern Theology*, 3:4, 1987, pages 315–332. The discussion in the following pages makes use of some material earlier published in my 'Apologetics, Worldviews, and the Problem of Neutral Criteria', *Trinity Journal*, 12NS, 1991, pages 39–58, and is used here with permission of the editor.

20. There is an enormous amount of literature on the subject of rationality and relativism. Good discussions of the issues can be found in *Rationality and Relativism*, Martin Hollis and Steven Lukes, editors, Blackwell, 1982; *Relativism: Cognitive and Moral*, J. Meiland and M. Krausz, editors, University of Notre Dame Press, 1982; and Bryan Wilson, editor, *Rationality*, Blackwell, 1970. An incisive critique of various forms of relativism is found in Maurice Mandlebaum, 'Subjective, Objective, and Conceptual Relativisms', *The Monist* , 62, 1979, pages 403–423. Also helpful is Roger Trigg, *Reason and Commitment*, Cambridge University Press, 1973.

21. Harold Netland, *Dissonant Voices: Religious Pluralism and the Question of Truth*, Eerdmans, 1991, chapter five.

22. A question naturally arises here concerning the ontological status of such principles and their relation to God. I hold that such principles are ontologically objective in the sense that they are independent of the mental processes or psychological states of any human being. Like basic logical relations and propositions in general, they have extra-mental ontological reality and are part of the 'stuff' constituting reality. They are not, however, 'autonomous' in the sense of constituting an independent standard to which God himself is subject. Rather, they are grounded in the nature and being of God.

23. Ninian Smart observes 'even if it is granted that there are no pure descriptions, it in no way follows that all descriptions are equally impure. This is like the question of whether you can have value-free sociology. Well, some is more value-free than other sociology.' Smart [note 19], page 59. Similarly, Roger Trigg notes that 'although it is a truism that we cannot conceive of reality without conceiving of it, that does not mean that some of our conceptions may not be correct.' Trigg, *Reality at Risk* [note 1], page xiii. On this issue, Trigg's entire book is worth careful study.

24. For a vigorous recent statement of presuppositionism see John M. Frame, *The Doctrine of the Knowledge of God*, Presbyterian and Reformed, 1978.

25. the same, pages 45, 129

26. Criticism of Newbigin on this point in no way detracts from my appreciation of his contributions to the theology of mission. It is possible that differences between Newbigin and myself on this matter are due in part to the fact that we are each reacting against quite different emphases within modernity. Newbigin, it would seem, is responding to an excessive confidence in the powers of reason; the reductionistic rationalism and scientism most clearly exemplified in Logical Positivism earlier in this century. On the other hand, I am responding to an

opposite extreme, an excessive irrationalism and loss of confidence in reason to settle cognitive disputes that is characteristic of much contemporary thought.

27. Newbigin, *Truth to Tell* [note 5], pages 27–28; 33–34. Elsewhere, Newbigin states:

> No coherent thought is possible without presuppositions. What is required for honest thinking is that one should be as explicit as possible about what these presuppositions are. The presupposition of all valid and coherent Christian thinking is that God has acted to reveal and effect his purpose for the world in the manner made known in the Bible. Of course it is open to anyone to ask, 'Why choose this starting point rather than another—for example, the Qur'an, the Gita, or *Das Kapital* ?' But then one has to ask the questioner about the assumptions from which he starts, and which perhaps have not been examined.
>
> Newbigin, The Gospel in a Pluralist Society [note 5], page 8

28. The act of presupposing something ('I accept the Word of God as my basic presupposition . . .') implicitly negates the contradictory of what is presupposed ('The Word of God is not my basic presupposition . . .').

29. Christian philosopher Paul Helm observes that minimally the following five principles are necessary for understanding any passage of Scripture: (1) everything is identical with itself and distinct from anything else; (2) if A is identical with B then whatever is true of A is true of B; (3) no proposition can be both true and false; (4) if a proposition p is true, and q follows logically from p, then q is true; (5) if p and q contradict each other then they cannot both be true. Paul Helm, 'The Role of Logic in Biblical Interpretation', in *Hermeneutics, Inerrancy, and the Bible*, Earl D. Radmacher and Robert D. Preus, editors, Zondervan, 1984, pages 842–43.

30. Diogenes Allen, *Christian Belief in a Postmodern World: The Full Wealth of Conviction*, Westminster / John Knox Press, 1989, page 1

5

Modernity and theology: the doctrine of God

DAVID F. WELLS

I am to consider how modernity inclines those who live by its impulses to see God and what it inclines them to want from God. I am asking how the modern temperament, habits of thought and cognitive assumptions typically affect the way those who are psychologically modern think of God.

I am, then, asking what the psychological mechanisms seem to be, what the assumptions and intellectual connections are, which correlate the seemingly most plausible understanding of God with the modern environment. This public environment, of course, is one wrought by the interconnectedness of urbanization, democratic capitalism, technology and telecommunications, the whole of which makes the Enlightenment assumptions about human autonomy and the loss of all authority seem both normal and normative. This modern, public environment, moreover, is increasingly global. Its ligaments (urbanization, democratic capitalism, technology and telecommunications) link the globe together and produce a kind of shared, world cliché culture which is much the same whether it is encountered in Bombay, Copenhagen, Liverpool, Chicago or Sydney—the same consumer appetites, the same products to satisfy them, the same movies, the same rock music, the same clothes, the same food, and the same magazines. This is a very striking development. Until the twentieth century, cultures have always been *local*—defined by a people's history, religion, and ethnicity. While these local patterns are still present, what we are now seeing is a massive overlay, increasingly worldwide, of a culture which owes nothing to what is local and everything to what is not. This cultural overlay is owed to the fabric of expectations and the appetites which the capitalistic enterprise arouses, to the rationalization of life which technology produces, to the impersonal nature of large cities, and to the shallowness of the conceptual language which is spoken.[1]

If modernization is the social organization which has brought this about, modernity is the language that those who are modernized now speak. The external shaping of our world by the process of modernization typically creates an internal world of diminished cognitive horizons; appetites for affluence; a definition of meaning in terms of material possessions; an ethic which equates what is efficient (or what is self-serving) with what is morally right; and the relocation of all meaning from the outside world of creation and the public world of human organization to the inside, private world of intuition and of the self. This is modernity.[2]

In much of the Western world, however, modernity has seemed to flow along two quite different river beds, which have sometimes been distinguished as high culture, on the one hand, and low, popular, folk, or broad culture, on the other. It is a distinction often reinforced by class differences and certainly by those which are educational and economic. The distinction between culture which is 'high' and that which is 'low', however, is not primarily a distinction that is moral, or even aesthetic, with the one being invariably more elevated and the other always less so. Brahms may be more artistically refined than the Rolling Stones, and more beneficial to hear, but the destructive values of modernity are mediated down the one just as frequently and just as easily as down the other. Richard Rorty's postmodern philosophical emptiness is, after all, not much different from what Madonna personifies, nor is Carl Rogers' psychological narcissism hard to miss in the American magazines like *Self* and *Seventeen*.

What distinguishes these cultures, then, is mainly the number who can participate in them. High culture whether in music, literature, or art is by its very nature an elitist matter. Only the few have the ability, training and inclination to participate. Low, popular, or folk culture, by contrast, is where the masses play and find diversion. Any difference beyond this is that high culture is often distinguished from that which is low, popular, or broad by its self-consciousness and its critical awareness of its own thinking processes. Popular culture is often unaware of its internal mechanisms and not much interested in rectifying its ignorance. In most countries of the West at least, popular or folk culture is constructed upon a sinking literacy rate and a corresponding infatuation with the all-pervasive video culture. It floats upon the loss of the mental habits that go with the print culture and the corresponding ascendancy of those that cohere with television.[3] Those who live by and within high culture typically want to think about their world and about themselves in that world; those who are borne along by popular culture often wish to be spared such thought. The academic world, as a consequence, may imagine that it has no connections whatsoever with that other world in which television is dominant, the world of McDonald's, of Nike, of football and basketball heroes, of malls and quick-fix diet programmes. But that, I believe, is a fallacy.

What I wish to explore is the rather remarkable convergence in the perceptions that high and low culture offer on how God stands in our modern world. From culture that is high and from that which is low, from those who stand self-consciously within the flow of Enlightenment ideas to those who passively assimilate the interests of the modernized, public environment (in ways that are often inchoate and superficial), the same answers are emerging.

Here, then is my argument: the understanding of God—the vision of who he is and what modern people want from him—is typically built either upon the skewered connections between objective and subjective in the process of knowing or upon the dissolved contrast and nexus between what, in God's being and relation to creation, is transcendent and that which is immanent. These two sets of poles, the objective and subjective, and what is transcendent and immanent, are not, of course, referring to identical matters. The objective/subjective distinction is a matter of *epistemology*; the distinction between what is transcendent and what is immanent, in the contemporary world at least where classical theism is disintegrating, has frequently become a matter of *ontology*.

Western philosophical thought has, for the most part, observed this distinction. It has largely been dominated by two streams of thought which have flowed off the camber on the road which the Enlightenment has built, one going down one side and the other going down the other side. The one, predominantly epistemological, probably arises in Descartes, is greatly solidified in Immanuel Kant, flows through Søren Kierkegaard, into Martin Heidegger, Jean Paul Sartre, and then finally into some of the postmodern theorists like Richard Rorty. It is the tradition of thought that is much engaged with what can be known and how that is known. Increasingly it has come to assert the dominance of the inner, cognitive shape of the knower over what is externally known. In the process it strains the epistemological links to the external world and, finally, creates in the knower a growing sense of alienation. The other stream, which has much to do with ontology, probably arises in Spinoza, is redirected by Hegel, moves through many of the older Protestant Liberals, and now spills out in several directions such as Jürgen Moltmann, John Cobb and numerous other postmodern thinkers. This tradition is much fascinated by the infusion of the divine in creation and history, and comes to find either pantheism or panentheism irresistible.

In twentieth century theology, whether the primary mover has been an epistemological or an ontological interest, the frequent outcome has been the sundering of God's transcendence from his immanence, the denial or reduction of the one in the interests of advocating the other, and the almost inevitable tilt in this process toward immanence and away from transcendence. Stanley Grenz and Roger Olsen, in fact, have organized their entire account of twentieth century theology around these themes.[4] The Enlightenment shattered the inter-relations between God's immanence and his transcendence. On one side of what had now become a divide were: Kant, who reduced God to the immanence of moral experience; Hegel, to the immanence of speculative reason; Schleiermacher, to that of inner feeling; and Ritschl, to that of ethical culture. After the powerful neo-orthodox reaction, which reasserted the lost transcendence of God (but often at the cost of his immanence), an unbalanced and sometimes harmful stress upon the immanence of God has once again reappeared. Tillich so radicalized God's transcendence that he became unknowable (and hence the death-of-God theologians saw Tillich as their father) but then argued that God is the immanental 'ground' of all being. The later Bonhoeffer saw God as immanent in secular culture, the Liberation theologians as immanent in the experience of oppression, and the pluralists like John Hick as immanent in the religious spirit common to participants in all religions.

The Barthian attempt to reassert God's forgotten transcendence failed. But the need to see God as transcendent has never passed. In fact, the narrative theologians have tried to resurrect this dimension, arguing that the biblical narrative has the capacity to impart a transcendent dimension, a sense of mystery beyond the words of the text. Moltmann has also seen this need and has argued, in ways that place him within the Hegel-Marx family, that it is the future which is transcendent. The recovery of God's transcendence, not as an alternative to or substitute for his immanence but in relation to it, is now the great challenge facing the churches. Modernity has not only shattered the connections between God's transcendence and his immanence, it also inclines us to reinterpret the latter without the former, oftentimes subsuming God into the self in some fashion.

In today's popular culture, however, the same inclinations are also present because, I believe, they are reflecting the same modernized culture. Now, however, the lines become tangled; the distinction between epistemology and ontology becomes blurred. What starts out as an assumption about the dominance of the subject becomes expressed in a way which assumes the immanence of God in the self. In the most extreme case, the New Age movement, the self itself becomes divine. In other cases, the self is substituted for God. This latter is the premise beneath much of the therapeutic culture of the West especially the self-movement. Thus epistemology and ontology become folded into and then lost in one another, in the process inclining the West to be far more sympathetic to Eastern religious ideas than it has ever been before.[5]

I will try to illumine the *mechanism* by which, in both cultural streams, the subject comes to assert its dominance over what is objective, and what is transcendent in God's relation to creation and history then comes to be subsumed under what is immanent. The outcome is that the historic Christian understanding of God is massively changed. I can only illustrate the mechanism, as I see it, however, rather than give a full and complete survey of what has happened.

God in high culture

The stream of thought that arose in Descartes and was substantially formulated in Kant has been present in the Western world long enough for us to see with some clarity now its tendencies and outcomes. We have seen, in particular, how overwhelmingly difficult it is, once the Kantian world is entered, to preserve any objectivity in the knowledge of God. Without this there can be no binding revelatory address and hence no direct moral accountability before God, no particularity to Christian faith, no overarching meaning to life and history, no knowledge of God's overagainstness in relation to a fallen world and hence, in the end, no answer to the reality of evil. All of this can be seen quite clearly if we take soundings at three places, divided by about a century: Friedrich Schleiermacher, Karl Barth, and John Hick.

By far the greatest concentration of scholarly work has been done on Kant's epistemology on the way in which it transformed pre-critical thinking in which an objective world was thought simply to imprint its reality upon minds that were passive and inert, that were uninvolved in the transaction. It is important to see, though, that Kant's ambitions were much larger than this single interest. In the Dialectic of his *Critique of Pure Reason* it is quite clear that he is also pondering the peculiar burden which it is our lot to bear: that existence forces upon us questions which reason is not equipped to answer, what he calls 'antinomies'. This dilemma has created an opening for the entrance of post-Kantian theology into the discussion: modern theology has sought to provide the very answers Kant sought, usually without violating the framework he provided—a tall order indeed.

Kant's impact on religion can be followed out in a number of directions, but it is one of these which is of special interest here: the role of the subject in the process of knowing. Instead of beginning with the objective world, Kant begins with the subjective conditions for knowledge. The mind now becomes active in, and is a constitutive part of, what is known. Sensory perception is sorted into categories and, given the subject's freedom, is synthesized in ways which do not necessarily correspond to what is externally existent space and time, for example, being matters of the mind and not of the world. Subject and object thus become dancers in the ballet of knowledge, ever yoked, the shape the one provides for knowledge ever affecting what is known of the other.

Thus German philosophizing gave us *subjectivisch* and *objectivisch* in their modern connotations. This set the stage for the way that Western intellectuals began to think. In Britain, Samuel Coleridge was to the fore in transmitting the new thinking. Six years after his death, in 1840, Edward Fitzgerald wrote to

Frederick Tennyson to say that this strange word, *subjective*, which Coleridge has introduced into common parlance, had made 'considerable progress' and now a number of people fancied that they understood what it meant.[6] Wordsworth, after writing *The Prelude* in which he offered a minutely chronicled account of his inner life, admitted that it was unprecedented for an author to speak so much of himself. This, of course, was the beginning of the modern torrent of autobiographical writing as well as the modern literary obsession with the self as the source of meaning and morality that has spilled out across the twentieth century. This preoccupation and style have now become the norm not only in high culture but also in that which is broad as even a brief perusal of what is offered for sale on any magazine rack in an airport or supermarket will attest. This preoccupation with the self is one of the signatures of modernity.

There is a comparable development in theology to which we must now turn. Here, the initial conquest of the objective by the subjective is quickly followed by a fresh translation of the transcendence of God in terms that are wholly immanent. This of course, means a complete loss of what was once transcendent. The mechanism by which this happens is important for us to see. Kant had argued that reason cannot establish the reality and nature of God. Then, in his *Critique of Practical Reason*, he went on to propose that it is only in *moral* experience that such knowledge can be grounded, for this knowledge we have of ourselves as moral beings is inexplicable if God does not exist. Schleiermacher agreed with Kant that the reality and nature of God are not given by reason. He went on to propose that, instead, it is in *religious* experience that this knowledge is grounded. This had profound implications in the doing of theology. It also anticipates what in fact has become widely accepted in the broad popular culture of the modernized West: either experience is viewed as suffused with what is divine or the self simply offers itself as a substitute for the divine.[7] Clearly, popular culture has reached this conclusion with little knowledge of the learned discussions in the academy. This strongly suggests that both the academy and popular culture have been infused by a third reality, modernity, which is common to them.

The stepping stone from Kantian epistemology into modern ontology was made most adroitly by Schleiermacher. First in his *Speeches on Religion*, and later in his much more complex *The*

Christian Faith, he, too, repudiated an objective knowledge of God and, like the romantics,[8] reached down internally into his own being to find the grounding for his knowledge of God. Life, he asserts, consists in 'abiding-in-self' and 'passing-beyond-self', the former a matter of knowing and feeling, the latter of doing.[9] This latter category might, of course, have opened up into a fullscale assertion of divine transcendence in which the self is enabled to pass-beyond-itself into connectedness with God, even into a filial relationship with him through Christ. But that was not to be. This 'transcendence', this reaching by the self beyond itself, is reduced simply to the horizontal realm of action. The knowledge of God was then internally restricted to the self where the immanence of God was registered in feeling, specifically the awe of dependence. Thus did God become a kind of psychological deposit, a 'something' deep in the self. For Schleiermacher, Barth points out, God was the supposed correlate of the self-consciousness as its own reflection was projected into the absolute.[10] If the result was a God who was 'a little skinny', as Friedrich Schlegel charged, the reason was that God could be no larger than the self of which he was a reflection. As Barth went on to say, we cannot call 'God' by shouting 'man' in a loud voice. And the reason so much attention has been paid to this aspect of Schleiermacher's thought, he said, is the bad conscience from which modern theology suffers. Ours is an age 'whose theology suffers from a chronic lack of objectivity' so that 'we do not know what we are talking about when we talk about God but we still want to talk about him' and so theologians have repeatedly returned to Schleiermacher to see if perhaps he has not shown us how this might be done.[11]

Barth saw the deficiencies of Schleiermacher so clearly, and reasserted the lost transcendence of God so strongly. But he also found the scaffolding for his theology in Kant's epistemology. Barth uses *Gegenstand* of the objectiveness of God rather than speaking of God as the *Objekt*, as what is under the purview of the knowing subject. But Barth really does not think that God is to be found by our natural, epistemological radar: not in nature, not in human nature, and not in history. *Gegenstand* by contrast corresponds to what in English might be described as what is external to someone, the reality which is over against them. This is the sense that Barth wants to convey with respect to God. God is the One who is over-against us, never the One whom we peruse on our own terms and from our own vantage point.[12]

Nevertheless, Barth does immediately and extensively take up the Kantian framework,[13] at least in insisting that God is never an object in space and time who is read by the sinner as is the world by the knowing subject. God is never related to the sinner as an It but only as a Thou, never as Object and always as Subject. God, therefore, can never be subjected to human scrutiny, is never the target of the human process of counting, estimating, judging and passing sentence. Nor is God ever stumbled upon by the sinner as a scientist might stumble upon some new explanation of the world. No. God has stripped human nature of his revelatory presence. The creation is mute, except to the eyes of faith.[14]

Barth then finds the objectivity which he knows we need in our knowledge of God in his doctrine of the Word. But here, unfortunately, Kant once again intrudes and Barth cannot speak of the written words of Scripture in and of themselves as being the objective revelation. The Word only *becomes* revelation in its use by Christ, as the Holy Spirit so illumines the inner terrain of the sinner that the sinner is enabled to act in faith. Then and then only, is revelation given and God known. God is the Subject who makes himself known; he is not the Object who is discovered.[15] We are the objects upon whom *he* acts, never the subjects who act upon him.

Barth saw clearly the dire predicament into which theology in the Liberal era had fallen, what he spoke of as the chronic lack of objectivity in the knowledge of God. The result was that God became vague and misty, indistinguishable from merely human perceptions and intuitions about the meaning of life. His answer to this predicament was his doctrine of the inbreaking Word. This Word came from above and intruded upon the inner life of the sinner much as a lightening bolt might upon a landscape, its shafts of light brilliantly illumining the darkness. It proved to have been an impossible construct to hold. The stitching between the Protestant doctrine of the Word of God and the Kantian epistemology to which it was joined was altogether too frail. The rip was heard loudly and on all sides.

By the 1960s, theology was scattering far and wide. Once again, the old mechanism was at work. Though briefly arrested by Barth, the assertion of the subject in what is known was quickly linked up to fresh assertions that what has traditionally been thought of under the transcendence of God should now be seen under his immanence. Not all contemporary theology has moved in this direction, to be sure. Postmodern theologians, as David Griffin noted, 'registered their conviction that the noble and flawed enterprise called *modern theology* had run its course'.[16] They have abandoned their belief in the old Enlightenment project, in its optimism, in its expectation that reason will be able to pacify and understand the world, in truth, in meaning, in the intellectual categories in which theology has been conceived such as natural and supernatural, truth and error, transcendent and immanent. They repudiate the modern experience because it is not only made up of abundance but also of alienation, loneliness, rationalization, the abuse of nature, the abuse of minorities, and the estrangement within the self. The result is that God is now under fresh construction, using these materials of disaffection and protest. Yet even here, it is not uncommon to find some of the old Schleiermacherian themes.

In John Hick the line from the assertion of the subject in the knowing process to that of the immanence of God is clear. It is linked with the loss of a revelational objectivity in the knowledge of God. Hick tells us that while he was in university, he underwent an evangelical conversion.[17] Later, however, the problem of evil fractured his thinking. It became increasingly difficult for him to reconcile the idea of God's universally salvific will with that of the uniqueness of Christian faith.

In his most pivotal book he begins his resolution of these issues by identifying the central problem in theology. It is 'whether distinctive religious utterances are instances of the cognitive or of the non-cognitive uses of language'.[18] This is a Kantian question, and Hick's answer moves down a distinctively Schleiermacherian path. The reality of God is the 'ground', the substratum for which religious forms and rituals are the external expression. Unlike the postmodern proponents Hick retains some idea of truth and error and asserts that there will be an 'eschatological verification' of religious ideas. Nevertheless, he now argues for a hard form of religious pluralism: that God is to be found by, with, and under all religions. Neither Christ [19] nor Christian faith[20] can therefore be unique.

Alisdair MacIntyre in his Bampton Lectures[21] argued that modernity is by its very nature hostile to any expression of a traditional understanding of the transcendence of God. In consequence, theism takes one of two paths. If it retains its traditional character, it becomes increasingly incomprehensible to moderns. If it adapts itself to the modern mood (the word *mood* is now more appropriate than 'mind'), it becomes increasingly strained in its relation to historic orthodoxy. Where adaptation takes place in the modern period, James Turner has argued,[22] the pattern becomes quite predictable. Whereas the Deists rationalized away the oddness of God by eliminating his immanence in favour of a remote transcendence, we do the opposite. The contemporary concession to unbelief usually takes the form of sentimentalizing God, of eliminating his transcendence in favour of his immanence and then equating this with what is intuitively known in the self. It is to this self that external authorities are now subjugated, whether that of the Bible or of the Church. This perpetuates the vision of the autonomous self with which the Enlightenment was launched. This weakness, this unhappy capitulation, Peter Berger complains, has led to much of 'the wimpiness that is so characteristic of the theological milieux today'.[23]

God in broad culture

Martin Buber has argued that, as the sense of God has faded in the modern period, a compensation for this lost knowledge has been found in psychological thinking which has washed in to fill the empty holes in the modern psyche.[24] But this is only the first stage in the transformation. In the second, the self itself then disintegrates, which is the point many postmodern writers are now making.

The broader culture in the West has arrived at the same destination as that of the high culture of the Enlightenment not by the anguished contortions which we have been following but by a route not marked by much thought at all. In a nutshell, this is what appears to have happened: the reshaping of the world by modernization has increasingly robbed modern people of their external forms of connectedness; increasingly, they have relocated all reality internally. The self, however, is altogether inadequate to bear the entire burden of creating meaning. That means that each feeling, each intuition, must be blown up into grandiose proportions if it is to offer the kind of meaning which is large enough to be able to live by. This fails, and so moderns are increasingly drawn into themselves to see what potential might still be tapped, what fragments of authenticity might still be retrieved. That, in quick strokes, is the argument. By an entirely different route, then, this development has brought our broad, Western culture to the point of being obsessed with the autonomy of the self and to a corresponding rejection of all other authorities.

Reinhold Niebuhr observed that the self draws its substance from a threefold rootedness: in family, in community, and in craft.[25] Each of these connections is now either strained or lost to the modern self.

First, the family is besieged, not only by the plague of divorce, not only by the massive growth in illegitimacy, but also by the fact that the stresses and strains of modern life exact a painful toll on so many marriages in the modernized world. Families that function together are becoming an endangered species. And as they begin to malfunction, what has been the chief conduit for the transmission of values from one generation to another, becomes clogged. The new generation inherits a thinner set of values and expectations from their parents and hence is cast upon the wider culture for tutoring in the meaning of life. However, given the ambiguity of that life and given the multiple conflicting moral messages which television imparts, the young are increasingly forced to look inward for signals about the meaning of life.

Second, communities which are geographically defined have been mown down by modernization. Today, we are nearly all migrants in the very places where we live, our psychological connections are no longer to place. To be sure, this did produce some moments of exhilaration as people realized that they could escape the small town parochialisms. But the cost of this emancipation is to become anonymous, to belong everywhere and hence to belong nowhere, to have no connectedness. Where the self wanders the earth as a vagrant, belonging nowhere, something that is profoundly intrinsic to being human has been lost.

Third, the self's connection to craft has also been seriously diminished by modernization leaving many people perpetually dissatisfied with their work. Sometimes the problem is rooted in the fact that machines sever the link between the worker and the work, the product and its producer. At other times the layers of bureaucracy within the structures of management sever the personal links between ideas and products. Sometimes it is simply that the kind of work which is required by modernized societies is inherently undignified or boring. The old virtue of taking pride in one's work becomes harder and harder to realize.

Stripped of these forms of external connectedness, the modern person drifts in society like a speck upon the ocean, the currents beneath the surface moving what is above at will. Thus he or she, with no foot in any external reality, takes refuge in the one certain thing which remains: the self. The embrace of the self as the source of mystery, of meaning, and of hope becomes inevitable.

For all of the brave talk about the self and about its potential, Philip Rieff is undoubtedly correct to see in this the evidence of a 'disordering' of the self[26] from which three important consequences flow.

First, the whole of life is cast in therapeutic terms. All of life's maladies become wounds which simply need to be healed. The healing metaphor makes talk about sin and moral responsibility meaningless. Talk about evil disappears. Now that the self has been dislodged from the world, in its new freedom it finds only painful alienation—from family, community, and craft. This explains, I believe, the rather alarmed insistence that life is simply about recovery and internal healings of one kind or another.

Second, access to reality is now thought to take place through the self, through intuition, rather than through the understanding. This does for the broader culture what Kant and Schleiermacher did for high culture, though for entirely different reasons. Down both sides of the cultural divide, the cognitive dimension is assailed, with the result that the objectivity of God is lost. If he is to be found at all it will only be in the self. By an odd turn of events, modernity is in fact returning us to the older kind of paganism against which the biblical authors prophesied and wrote. Pagans then had no interest in history for history could yield no meaning for the present. When calamities struck, it was to the self that they listened to hear whatever intimations could be had about the disposition of the gods and goddesses. Again it is to the self that moderns look, only now its whisperings and intimations may not be rooted in the divine, for this is also a secularized age.

Finally, the reshaping of the world by modernization, and of the modern psyche as a part of that world, has given fresh opportunities to pride.[27] We usually think of pride as vanity, the relentless striving for success, the need to lord it over others, the appetite for power and attention, being puffed up and stiff-necked, all of which came into being in the first sin. Of this vice moderns may be no more guilty than anyone else. Nevertheless, it is important to see the shape which pride often assumes today. Pride is also that self-centredness which is pursued, protected and given shape as an alternative to submission to God and to being God-centred. It was for this reason that Dante pictured the proud man as one whose back is bent double under an enormous stone, so that he could never look up. The gaze of the proud never leaves the earth.

Modernity stokes these fires of pride in particular. Secular modernity marginalizes God who becomes an irrelevance to life. Therapeutic modernity proposes an alternative to God—the self. It is in the self that meaning and morality are sought. This dreadful tilt is made almost inescapable by the fact that the self typically finds no substantial connectedness in the world and is simply left to itself. The self revolves around itself. Harsh words of defiance against God are now entirely unnecessary. God has been quietly replaced in a spiritual *coup d'etat*; the sun is under eclipse, its bright light lost and obscured by the impenetrable thickness of the self. The initial sensation experienced is one of excitement, even exhilaration, at the complete freedom which has been won. The self is now free to be itself, to express itself in whatever manner it so chooses and to do this without reference to God, to what is ultimately right or, for that matter, to what anyone else may think or how they might be affected. In time, though, the exhilaration passes, and a weariness of soul sets in as the self creaks beneath all the functions which it is now being called upon to serve. The tension, anxiety, and bewilderment which usually follow have become the calling cards of modernity.

The recovery of God

God is sufficient to the needs of the twentieth-century, modernized self, but this will only be realized if he can once again be seen as being central in the world. This means that we must rediscover his transcendence—a transcendence which is held in relation to his immanence and which preserves that immanence from all of the modern variations on pantheism.[28]

There are two aspects to the transcendence of God. From one angle, God is transcendent because he is self-sufficient. He owes nothing to creation for his being and is dependent upon nothing outside of himself for the power to realize his will. From another angle, God is transcendent because of his utter moral purity which both sets him off from the creation in which sin reigns and defines who he is in his essential being. These two aspects of his self-disclosure are sometimes brought together in Scripture. If God is 'high and lifted up'(Isaiah 6:1), 'the high and lofty one who inhabits eternity' (Isaiah 57:15), if he is 'God and not man, the Holy one among you' (Hosea 11:9), part of the explanation of this awesome majesty, this greatness, is his transcendent goodness (see Psalms 93, 96–99; Luke 1:49; 1 Peter 1:16; 1 John 2:20; Revelation 4:8, 15:4, 16:5). This holiness does not supplant his aseity but interprets it in part: God is elevated over creation and is separate from it because of his incomparable goodness.

Returning now to the first of these themes, it is because God is self-sufficient that he can sustain the creation without being modified by it (contrary to process theology). Not only so but he can providentially direct all of its life to its ordained end, as well as acting in it. These acts are not only of a general kind in which he sustains the creation which he has brought forth; they are also the specific revelatory acts, in the flesh and bone of our history, by which he has made known his character and will. It is important, however, for us to see these acts from within the cultural contexts in which they appeared.

What we have in Scripture is a framework provided by God's redemptive acts whose meaning he himself provides.[29] The importance of this framework is not the narrative form in which it is given (as narrative theologians argue). It is true that narratives have evocative and suggestive power. But even if the Scriptures do evoke a sense of mystery, a sense of an Other, this is not the reason that God has so acted that today we have such a narrative. God's self-disclosure was tied to specific acts, because those acts, being external, secured and preserved the *objectivity* of God's revelation. Each generation was to be taught what God had done (Deuteronomy 4:9, 3:24; 1 Samuel 12:7; Psalm 103:7, 105:27) and was to commit it to memory (Deuteronomy 5:15, 7:18, 16:3, 25:17–9), for this history would reveal the nature and intentions of the God who had called them (Psalm 9:11, 66:5, 74:12, 77:11–2, 86:10, 96:3, 103:6, 105:1, 106:2).

This external history was important because pagans were in the habit of listening to themselves for clues about the intentions of the gods and goddesses, of keeping an ear cocked for the whisperings of intuition and the workings of their own nature, even as today we do with the help of our many psychologists. The point about this revelation was that it was not to be found within the psyche nor discerned by intuition. It was accessible to understanding, and its existence could no more vary from one person's interpretation to another's than could any other historical fact. Events had either happened or they had not. This framework of historical fact makes God's revelation public and preserves it from pagan habits of privatizing all truth. In the resurrection of Christ in which this line of redemptive acts comes to completion, Wolfhart Pannenberg says,[30] there is sounded God's public judgment on all religious mythologies, and on all private intuitions not in accord with it.

The objectivity of God's revelation is matched by the objectivity of his holiness, the second aspect to his transcendence. This, too, is a matter of peculiar applicability to paganism but even more pointedly to modernity. In a psychologized culture, there is a deep affinity for the relational which, in religious terms, carries over into an affinity for divine love and a corresponding uneasiness with his holiness. We who are modern find it infinitely easier to believe that God might be like a Rogerian therapist, one who empathetically solicits our knowledge of ourselves and passes judgment on none of it, than like Moses. The reason is that ours is a therapeutic culture, not a moral one.

The way this plays out is very simple. We are, typically, more interested in wholeness than in holiness, more intrigued with how we can feel good about ourselves than with being good. The problem with this neat little formula, of course, is that we can feel good about ourselves even when we are doing wrong. This is certainly true when we are inebriated which is one reason alcoholism is so serious a problem in many modernized countries. We can feel good too in states of considerable vacuity. We are not simply considering an innocent translation of ethical terms into psychological: there has been an exchange of one model of reality for another. The one that God has given us is a moral model, in which his moral character and ours should be central to our vision. Modernity strongly inclines us to embrace one that translates all of life's evil into the terms of disease, that focuses these in the self, that sees a remedy in terms of healing, and that sees this healing as as natural and as expected as the healing which nature provides for the body. It then casts God as the general provider of the one as much as of the other. God, therefore, is the means to our psychological wholeness.

This drift in our modernized thought, however inadvertent, has powerful consequences for the meaning of Christian faith. Indeed, it has the potential to destroy Christian faith. In this scheme, the death of Christ becomes an oddity which is without explanation. For the moral framework, the context of God's righteous anger with sin, is lost and without this Christ's death is an enigma. The conquest of the Christian message by this modern, psychologized understanding of the person inevitably translates the gospel message into yet another form of self-help, only in this version there is a religious component. This habit of psychologizing life, furthermore trivializes all of reality. The fact is that we live in a world of sometimes ghastly evil which is never conquered and whose real enormity is rarely ever understood within this sanitized world of well-to-do therapists. It is certainly never rolled back simply by a little tinkering with the psyche. Finally, this outlook grossly distorts the meaning of a life with God through Christ. The New Testament never promises anyone a life of psychological wholeness nor does it promise that we will be invulnerable to life's calamities. In the course of life, indignities are suffered, losses are incurred, damage is done, and deliverance does not always follow. After all, some of the faithful in Scripture were sawn in two, others were shipwrecked, most were scorned. The promise of the gospel is not that believers will be spared these experiences, nor that they will be able to settle down to the sanitized comfort of an inner life freed of stresses, pains, and ambiguities. The promise is simply that through Christ God walks with us in the dark places of this life, that he has the power and will to invest his promises with reality, and that such is his grace and wisdom, that even the shadows of life are made to serve our own best interests and his glory.

It is God whose presence, transcendent truth and goodness we seek, first in the Church, and then in the world whose substitutes for him have worn very thin. This redemptive presence, however, is only given on God's own terms and in his own manner. It is not the prerogative of those who are modern to establish the most easy and convenient terms on which to find

God. Specifically, unless God is once again seen to be objective, and therefore not subordinate to the caprices of the inner life, we can have no binding address, nor can we have a revelation which is given to all in the same way. We can have no Christianity which is universal in the sense that it summons all to the same kind of repentance in order to exercise faith in the same Christ. Unless God is understood to be transcendent in his holiness, the world is left without objective moral meaning, without accountability beyond the self and without assurance of his sovereign purposes in history. In the end it is without hope that, in his utter moral purity, God will be the final line of resistance to all that is wrong, and that the day will come when evil will be put forever on the scaffold and good forever on the throne.

It is, however, in and by his Word, preached in the power of the Spirit, that sinners are still summoned to know the God who has made himself known within the fabric of the space/time world, to acknowledge him in whom they live and move and have their being, and to see his holiness as what establishes both the moral standard of the world and the moral nature of all reality. This, indeed, is the framework within which God's acts, the death of his Son, and the final conquest of evil, alone are comprehensible. Without these connections there can be no Christian gospel.

Notes

1. Ninian Smart (*Worldviews: Crosscultural Explorations of Human Beliefs* Scribner's, 1983, pages 37–61) proposed that there are six basic worldviews operating globally today: i) the modern West with its pluralism and individualism; ii) Marxism, from Eastern Europe to Asia; iii) the Islamic crescent, centred in the Middle East and stretching down into Africa and out into Asia; iv) Old Asia, the religious substratum that stretches from India to Japan; v) the Latin South of South America; vi) smaller societies in the southern hemisphere, from Africa to the islands of the Pacific. This analysis is now obsolete in one respect and mistaken in another. The Marxist regimes have now mostly crumbled. Furthermore, it would be a large mistake to think that modernity is something exclusively Western, even if it is predominantly Western, because what is generating it are increasingly global factors. He is, however, correct in seeing that it does produce a worldview. A worldview is simply the dominant picture people have of their world, of its meaning. It may not have been refined in cogent ways and more commonly simply operates by assumptions which are expressed externally in dress, language, architecture, social organization, public symbols and, perhaps, rituals and myths.

2.   In this essay I have not clearly distinguished postmodernity from modernity. That there is a distinction seems clear; what its nature is less clear. Is it simply the next chapter in the unfolding of modernity or is it the beginning of a new cultural era? I have assumed the former but with this difference: after the 1960s it becomes increasingly clear that the Enlightenment project has failed.

3.   Neil Postman, *Amusing Ourselves to Death: Public Discourse in the Age of Show Business*, Penguin, 1985

4.   Stanley J. Grenz and Roger E. Olson, *20th Century Theology: God and the World in a Transitional Age*, InterVarsity Press, 1992

5.   For a comparative study, see Troy Wilson Organ, *Philosophy and the Self: East and West*, Associated University Presses, 1987

6.   Jerome Hamilton Buckley, *The Turning Key; Autobiography and the Subjective Impulse Since 1800*, Harvard University Press, 1984, pages 2–3

7.   Paul Vitz has argued that the practice of modern psychology has often produced a substitute religion. See his *Psychology as Religion: The Cult of Self Worship*, Eerdmans, 1977

8.   See Jack Forstmann, *A Romantic Triangle; Schleiermacher and Early German Romanticism*, Scholar's Press, 1977

9.   Friedrich Schleiermacher, *The Christian Faith*, H.R. Mackintosh and J.S. Stewart, editors, Harper, 1963, page 8

10. Karl Barth, *The Theology of Schleiermacher; Lectures at Goettingen, Winter Semester, 1923–24*, Dietrich Ritschl, editor, translated by G.W. Bromiley, Eerdmans, 1982, page 217

11. the same, page 193

12. See the helpful discussion in James Brown, *Subject and Object in Modern Theology*, SCM Press, 1953, pages 140–67

13. Cornelius Van Til was the first person to make the connection between Barth and Kant in a sustained way. See his *Christianity and Barthianism*, Presbyterian and Reformed, 1962

14. Karl Barth, *Church Dogmatics*, translated by G .T. Thomson and G. W. Bromiley, 5 volumes, T. & T. Clark, 1936–68, I, i, page 43

15. the same, I ,i , page 515; see also II, i, page 9

16. David Ray Griffin, 'Introduction: Varieties of Post Modern Theology', *Varieties of Post Modern Theology*, David Ray Griffin, editor, State University of New York Press, 1989, page 1

17. John Hick, *God Has Many Names*, Westminster Press, 1982

18. John Hick, *God and the Universe of Faiths: Essays in the Philosophy of Religion*, St. Martin's Press, 1973, page 1

19. See John Hick, editor, *The Myth of God Incarnate*, SCM Press, 1977. Though this was a collection of essays, Hick's own views are well represented in the authors who wrote in the book, and he has subsequently denied the divinity of Christ explicitly.

20. See John Hick and Paul Knitter, editor,s, *The Myth of Christian Uniqueness: Toward a Pluralistic Theology of Religions*, Orbis, 1988.

21. Alasdair MacIntyre, *The Religious Significance of Atheism*, Columbia University Press, pages 3–29

22. James Turner, *Without God, Without Creed; The Origins of Unbelief in America*, Johns Hopkins University Press, 1985, page 199

23. Peter L. Berger, *A Far Glory: The Quest for Faith in An Age of Credulity*, The Free Press, 1992, page 149

24. Martin Buber, *The Eclipse Of God: Studies in the Relation Between Religion and Philosophy*, Harper, 1965

25. Reinhold Niebuhr, *Reflections on the End of an Era*, Scribner's, 1934, page 104

26. See the brilliant analysis in Philip Rieff's *The Triumph of the Therapeutic: Uses of Faith After Freud*, Harper, 1968

27. See the powerful exposition of pride in Barth, *Church Dogmatics*, [note 14], IV, i, pages 413–78

28. What is sketched out here so briefly is given a full exposition in Carl F. H. Henry, *God, Revelation and Authority: Vol V; God Who Stands and Stays*, Word Publishing, 1982

29. The older Biblical Theology Movement proved to be an incomplete attempt to recover the importance of the biblical narrative because, I believe, it left the acts of God uninterpreted. See G. Ernest Wright, *God Who Acts: Biblical Theology as Recital*, SCM Press, 1953. On the demise of the movement, see Brevard S. Childs, *Biblical Theology in Crisis*, Westminster Press, 1970

30. Wolfhart Pannenberg, 'Focal Essay: The Revelation of God in Jesus of Nazareth', in James M. Robinson and John Cobb, editors, *New Frontiers in Theology: Vol. III: Theology as History*, Harper, 1967, pages 106–107

6

Modernity and anthropology

ELAINE STORKEY

In Charles Dickens' nineteenth century novel, *Hard Times*, Gradgrind's star pupil was asked to recite the basic 'facts' about 'Man'. He had no problems in obliging with an answer: 'Large brained, featherless biped, sir.' This simple response bore hopeful testimony to the benefits of a supposedly neutral, factual, and scientific education. In reality it demonstrated that this young protégé had thoroughly imbibed and appropriated a view of human anthropology which was biologistic, rationalist, reductionist and a product of modernity.

At least he could recite something, however remote from the reality of who we are as human persons. He could even rely on a kind of consensus, so that his neat formulations would be understood by those who heard, and his unimaginative teacher would give him the school prize for his impressive show of learning.

If we were to ask the same question in these latter days of modernity there would be no easy answer. It would be difficult even to ask the question. A substantive study of 'Man' is not where most of our human scientists are focused. It is too ontological. We are in the era of epistemology, where the process of knowing is more realizable than what can be known, and where the concept of a knower is even more of a problem.

We face a difficult task: to speak about a Christian Doctrine of Man in the latter days of modernity is like trying to put a Rembrandt self-portrait in a room where all but one of the paintings depict human beings as meat, dead, sliced up and weighed on the scales. In our determination to make Rembrandt's message visible we consider letting it stand alongside the only other paintings in the room, as a holdover from a previous era. It shows the confident face of a tyrant, proud in the optimism of human arrogance and self-sufficient power. It is soon evident that this juxtaposition will not work either. If only we could clear the room and let the Rembrandt's depths and humility of humanness speak to people without the confusion of other messages, our task would be easier.

In presenting an anthropology in modernity what language should we borrow? The very phrase Doctrine of Man is unusable. Sadly, even the notion of doctrine has become so affected by modernity and its capture of the rational that the word itself is in danger of becoming a liability. It fails to provide us with an activity within which we can communicate the fullness of who (and whose) we are. 'Doctrine' is something systematic in a random world; static, in a reality defined by change; singular, in a culture which espouses pluralities of meanings. And if by 'doctrine' we want to point people to biblical revelation, we must take care that the very word itself does not negate the truths we are trying to communicate.

What is Man that we need a doctrine of him? Is he a genetic accident, produced by complex evolutionary processes that have resulted in an ultra-sophisticated form of mammal life, or is he a freak of the universe; thoughtful, self-conscious life which ends, as Eric Fromm would have us believe, in nothing? Is Man some human particular, some culturally specific example of beha- vioured living, or is he some generic classification that includes all males of the species? Whatever he is, he no longer includes 'woman'. That in itself further compounds the problem for post- modern culture now insists that language creates reality. The notion of a doctrine of man creates an exclusive debate which leaves out half of humankind. In effect it removes Christian apologetics away from the area where so many of our end-of- modernity battles are being fought.

Some starting points

My standpoint is the truth of our creaturely identity before God. God has made us and we are in relationship with God whether we recognize it or not. The Bible speaks of humankind as God's image, as being both unique and communal, and as having an identity which is derived and not autonomous. A strong ontology is implied in the biblical story of human existence, as well as a teleology and a morality. The chief end of human existence is and

137

will be always to serve God and enjoy him forever, in both our personal and communal lives. How we can enjoy God is made clear to us. The norms of life offered to us in the biblical unfolding of our creatureliness, especially in the teachings of Jesus and the writings of the early church, define the way in which we are called to live and love. Yet our capitulation to sin has meant that we do not, by and large, live the way we ought. The image of God is marred and tarnished. Of ourselves we are powerless, alienated, fragmented, fearful. What makes a Christian anthropology good news, is the message that Jesus Christ, the Incarnate Word of God, came to share our humanity, and to redeem it through the Cross. Our wholeness depends on the quality of our relationship with God: whether we are forgiven and restored sinners, or still in rebellion; whether we receive love to give love, or are wrapped up in self-service and self-pity.

I am simply announcing this standpoint, not arguing for it. I would not argue for this within the terms of modernity, with reference to some external, timeless, objective norms of truth which my claims must obey. It would be difficult to argue for it also within the context of postmodernity, which has left behind the very notion of arguments about contesting truth claims. This fundamental anthropology comes to us in our creaturely given-ness and is something we respond to as much as argue for. We respond in millions of detailed ways and in many different cultural forms which are inevitably affected, informed or transformed by the responses we make.

This anthropic understanding is distinctly pre-modern. It does not obey the modernist metanarratives of universal rationality, progress, and scientific knowledge. Early Christian anthropology did not always sound like this. During the pre-modern era of medieval scholasticism it did not find great favour with philosophers and theologians. Already, Greek dualism had made its inroads into anthropology. Form-matter dichotomies, soul-body, rationality-materiality all infected the writers of the 'Christian' epoch. It so weakened their grasp of biblical truth that the onslaught of humanism had an easy ride.

Two major themes criss-cross questions of anthropology. One focuses on the nature of humanity itself—the 'doctrine of man' concerns. The other addresses the issue of what it is to be a person. The relationship of these two has often been at the heart of some of the confusions. Although human beings might generically be creaturely, and God's image (and 'rational'), the question then comes: what does this mean in specific terms: what is a person? Boethius (487–524) provided us with an idea which was to prove a most lasting concept. He defined a person as 'an individual substance in a rational nature'. The key elements of that definition individuality—distinctiveness, substantiveness, and rationality—travelled safely from the fifth century, through early humanism, into the Enlightenment and on to the very end of the twentieth century where it is now being savaged.

Of course Boethius was wrong, or was wrongly angled. To locate our human identity in some essential distinctiveness rather than in our relationality (especially our relationship to God), got anthropology off to a very bad start. Although there may have been no incompatibility for the early Church Fathers between a view of human personhood which focused on individual differentiation and rationality and one in which the individual derived ultimate meaning in relationship with God, the link was easy for the Enlightenment to sever.

The Enlightenment

The eighteenth century European Enlightenment defined modernity. Although anthropology went through various qualifications and refinements during those pre-modern conceptions, its underlying ontological reference point related it to God. The Enlightenment faced the future not with faith in God but with faith in human progress, reason, science, freedom and technology. At the very centre was its faith in autonomous human rationality. Human reason was not now a creature which needed to come humbly before the revelation of God before it could understand anything aright. Instead it had in its power the ability to unlock the secrets of the universe. Thus, the fundamental doctrine of the person changed from dependence on God to independence from any higher authority. It also changed from being relational to being avowedly individual. Because the dependent relationship with God had been severed, there was now no ontological basis for community. Autonomous human individuals do not readily give up their self-sufficiency to care for others in society. The contest between the twin giants of rational individualism and imposed collectivism began, fought out on the platform of the world stage.

There are two other fundamental points of Enlightenment departure: the ideals of autonomous science and of autonomous personality influenced the grand metanarratives of modernity for the next two hundred years. The 'science ideal' saw all of reality as reducible to mathematico-scientific formulations, which yielded causal explanations or necessary tautologous truths, whereas the 'personality ideal' stressed the freedom of the human spirit to control and subjugate nature and science and to express itself in its own wild imaginings. Many formulations— nature, freedom, determinism, free will, being conditioned by structures or authentically in control—all stem from this basic enlightenment dichotomy. They have been crucial in the debates throughout the history of modernity.

In the rest of this paper I consider subsequent elements in the crisis of modernity for the person: the impact of the human sciences and the way they appropriated this basic ontological dilemma of the enlightenment, the shift from ontologies to epistemologies, the notion of self-creation and the popular outworking of views of the person within the context of post-modernity, and the disintegration of the Subject. As a postscript I will end with a look at the feminist challenge, especially for those feminists within the church who have discarded a traditional Christian anthropology.

The impact of the human sciences

As post-Enlightenment culture took hold, the primary authority for articulating the meaning of human life fell to the disciplines of the human and social sciences. Each of these—economics, history, sociology and psychology—carried increasing weight as authorities. As disciplines they were born within modernity, and at their very beginning they absorbed the ethos of the science ideal.

Christian anthropology was rejected at the Enlightenment. The question for the early social scientists was whether they could provide an anthropology to replace that of Christianity. The great early theorists, Comte, Marx, Hegel, Smith, and Bentham tried. They had an optimistic view of and hope for humankind. Even as late as 1960 sociology was being heralded as a 'part of that great evolution of thought in Western civilizations which passes from religion through philosophy to science.'[1]

Within the discipline of sociology at least, the model borrowed from the physical sciences had internal contradictions from the beginning. Was the focus to be atomistic, looking at particles of society in a quasi-physicalist way? Was there something specifically organic about society which resisted this approach: where for example, the whole was greater than the parts? The resolution was never clear, and sociologists moved uneasily from a physicalist, atomistic viewpoint to an organic, universalist one. American sociologist R. M. MacIver provides an interesting example. Writing in 1917 he was easily distinguishing two kinds of laws: material and vital. Material laws were fixed, sequential and causal, whereas the 'vital laws' were unstable, changeful and relative. They were revealed 'in the will of the living'.[2] Yet over the next few decades he was converted from an orthodox positivism to the earlier thinking of Comte and Durkheim. As late as the 1960s he was reiterating a position in which:

> The line from the inorganic to the organic is
> continuous. The line therefore from the nonliving to
> the living is continuous and among the living from the
> simplest living forms of vegetative existence to the
> highest of the animal world.[3]

The espousal of the science ideal and the confusions within it were inevitably to produce problems within the social sciences for developing a theory of the person and for the first six decades of the twentieth century modernity was to be punctuated by attempts to develop an anthropology in quasi-scientific terms. The person was 'given' in a number of competing ways. With Freud it was in terms of fixed stages of development; with Skinner and the behaviourists it was in terms of learning theory and reinforcement histories; with Maslow it was in terms of a hierarchy of needs; with the socio-biologists it was of evolutionary, 'genetic predispositions'. The task was made more complex because the developing social sciences explicitly rejected any ontology of the person. The discussion was at the level of general assumptions. Thus social scientists, on the basis of a certain view of their discipline, came to conclusions of the person which later were to be seen as tendentious. This raised the underlying issue of what substantive understanding human scientists could have of the person.

Some were committed to the opposite pole: to understanding human personhood in terms of freedom and autonomy rather than as structured and constrained. Fromm, taking his cue from the existentialists, stressed the authenticity of human decision-making and the power of humans to make meaningful choices. Human beings were part of but also transcended nature. They were self-conscious and aware. They could organise and reflect upon their own existence and had within their grasp the power to change the direction and course of that existence. Yet, even for at Fromm this was, of course, where human autonomy stopped, for the centre of human existence lay the big existential dichotomy. In spite of self-consciousness and creativity, there was no power to change the ultimate end of life. Man was the only being who could reflect on his own significance and yet face the ending of that significance at death. Human beings could think about death, reflect on it, write, create stories, plays, envisage what it would be like for others without them, yet they could not prevent it. Here lay an insoluble dilemma. All the possibilities of human freedom ultimately had to contend with the limitations of mortality. All the infinite potential of the human spirit and imagination was never realizable within the span of life of any individual human. We would always have more self-conscious possibilities than we had time to actualise them.[4] For Fromm, the escape from the deterministic, 'science-ideal' into the freedom of the 'personality ideal' was ultimately limited by the sheer structure of temporality. This still did not lead him to abandon his humanistic starting-point; it simply led him to sorrow at the problem. The Christian who knows that God has put eternity into the human heart understands much of what Fromm leans towards, but without a Christian anthropology the dilemma cannot be resolved.

Experts and epistemologies

A focus on the 'personality ideal' was not yet mainstream social science. The optimistic hope that science would provide an anthropology continued down through to *Walden Two* and on to *Sociobiology*.[5] An old-style social scientist such as MacIver continued to think in the vein of substantive theories about the person in society, the economy, the state and history. Yet alongside this another development was taking place. Modern conceptions of social science have been deeply influenced by what we might call the shift from what is known to the process of knowing. Sociology, economics or psychology are no longer disciplines developing views of the human subject, but sciences which see themselves as committed to a well-founded basis for generating knowledge. They can be agnostic about the content of their discipline, but have belief in the epistemology. Modernity in this sense has slowly permeated Europe from about 1870, becoming dominant in some areas of culture (though not the political) by the First World War, and reaching a full expression from the late 1950s through to the 1970s.

Theorists who had a view of the person or society were open to the charge of being ideological, biased, committed, or meta-physical. Their knowledge was always open to challenge and was not part of a common scientific and academic corpus which could be accepted irrespective of ideological commitment. In the face of evident and contradictory ideological bias, socialism and fascism for example, many said that they did not know what the world was like and sought to maintain a basic agnostic position.

At the same time a new crusading faith was built into the approach. With the right attention to methodological exactness, and the right epistemic foundation, the human sciences could advance on an almost irrefutable basis. Consequently, faith in method has directed much research and produced many pro-nouncements about everything from human societies to human psyches. Positivism, descriptivism, logicism, phenomenology, behaviourism, structuralism, formalism, symbolic interaction-ism and other epistemic theories of knowledge have flourished and then often waned.

The anthropological 'crisis' which this movement created arose from the fact that the knowledge which emerged from this way of developing the human sciences was gnostic, the property of the social scientists but out of touch with people's day to day lives. It was self-referencing. Factor-analysis or equilibrium theory did not tell you how people live any more than redaction criticism tells you what the biblical text says. Sociologists did not tell people how to live with one another, political scientists what political life should be like, nor psychologists how to sort out your feelings. 'Ah,' you say, 'but they did not intend to'—which is precisely the point. The basis for knowing in the human sciences was presumed to be independent from life, religion,

143

ideology, beliefs, attitudes and actions. It could not offer anything to people in their everyday lives, even though it claimed to be authoritative in speaking about them. As a result, in the 1970s and 1980s the authority given to academics waned. They were otherworldly, out of touch and had missed the point. In Britain this transition went along with a rejection of the 'expert' and of the search for explanations as a whole. The effect was a growth of surrogate sciences, educational courses which were pragmatic and managerial in their basis. Business studies took over from economics, social policy from sociology, media studies from literature, computing from mathematics. Everywhere people were learning how to manage. There was no need to look to social scientists for explanations of patterns of behaviour based on their epistemic methods. So there is less interest now in knowing the answer to the question 'why?' After all, aren't the answers are obvious? People commit crimes because they are bad. Marriages break down because people are bored with each other. We do not need to be fed spurious knowledge we simply need to develop techniques for managing behaviour. The pro-liferation of 'how to' books, also coming from the Christian press, is only one of the many effects of this.

Creation and re-creation

Post-modernity is both a rejection of modernity and the ultimate development of the 'freedom' pole of the Enlightenment, for with the end of modernist utopias there are no constraints. The choice is ours. We may adopt, transform and accommodate any surfaces we choose to and design our own present.

Within the design come the choices over our morality, our sexuality and our anthropology. Within the social sciences there has already been the destructuring of the self. Human person-hood, as distinct from human particularity in a specific culture, time, ethnicity and gender, does not exist. We are constructed from our context and we imbibe the values of our culture. We learn how to be human beings. We learn our gendered beha-viour: how to be men and women. We either co-operate with the construction or we challenge and redirect it.

Once we recognize that the self is in the process of being constructed it is only a short step to the notion of self-creation. Glover articulates that step for us very clearly. We construct our own identity and take charge of our own lives. This is not done, however, according to some master-plan (some grandnarrative of modernity) but in terms of the everydayness of our experiences. We do it through story-telling:

> To varying degrees we take charge of our lives.
> Through controlling our actions by our own plans we
> become active rather than passive... Self-creation
> depends on the beliefs we have about what we are now
> like: on the stories we tell about ourselves. We tell
> other people what to expect of us, or else we send
> signals by actions or style. The stories vary. Applying
> for a job we tell a story about our competence and
> energy and how we have cared more about quantity
> surveying than about anything else in the world. To
> our family and friends we tell stories ranging over
> more of our life. But we also tell ourselves a story about
> ourselves. This is our inner story. It stretches back as
> far as we can remember, and we think of it as the one
> from which all the others deviate a bit.[6]

There is no aspect of our identity therefore which we cannot create. We write our own scripts. We may therefore vary the plot at will, and incorporate the scripts of others if we wish to. We may also unlearn the scripts which others have bequeathed us, including their sexual scripts. Our sexuality is also our creation, so to take one example, there is nothing 'given' about heterosexuality. It too is a product of the power concepts of modernity. There is nothing fixed about monogamy, either, and a plurality of couplings fits much more comfortably into a postmodernist culture. Fragmentation, surfaces rather than depths, are crucial in relationships, and the search for self or demands of intimacy may simply be too complicating. In a postmodernist advertisement for Smirnoff, a man sitting in the bath with his dog says, 'You don't have to be faithful to anyone unless you want to.'

It is not only in vodka advertisements that the implications of self-creation are felt in popular culture. In his book *Modernity and Self Identity*, Giddens describes the move from personalized to commodified experience.[7] This commodification is a crucial part of the end-of-modernity phase in our culture. It is also bound up with the notion of self-creation. We both create and market ourselves; our goods and products are personalized, pointing back not just to the owner but to the creator of cultural objects. Interior and exterior designs, Disneyland, landscaped gardens, warm, exciting bedrooms tell us we are having a good time, that we are relaxed, rich, intimate, or full of fun. Messages are planted which will come back to us, will be part of the story we are creating, as we are becoming part of the story which is being marketed in our name.

All this is because, as Jean-Francois Lyotard points out, there is no real Subject in the self. There is no universality, centrality, or stability to ground the world or life in society. He says, and who outside Christ could contradict: 'Each of us knows that our self does not amount to much.'[8]

The feminist challenge

Contemporary feminism elides the postmodern disenchantment with the metanarratives of modernity with a radical critique of patriarchal power which has undergirded modernist structures. No area of life is left untouched by a radical feminist analysis. Everything is addressed and challenged: politics, theology, linguistics, management and sexuality. I focus my own remarks only on anthropology, and limit my attention to those feminists who are writing to or about the Christian church.

The radical feminist looks carefully at traditional notions of the Christian doctrine of man and utterly rejects what she sees. It is not only inescapably exclusive, oppressive and self-alienating for women, but inevitably it is so for men also. Christian anthropology is seen as contingent on a God who empowers and elevates the male to a fundamental religious principle. This is a God who has invited men to capture, order, violate and debase female sexuality and at the same time to blame women for their failure to save the moral health of society. Most of all this is a God made in the image of men, who gives men permission to define the whole of reality in terms of the norm of maleness. It is not surprising, declares the feminist, that the church, along with society, politics, science, architecture, business, academia, and sexual relationships, have been constructed by and for the male.

Feminists who are on the edge of calling themselves post-Christian whether they are within or outside the church feel the only meaningful and faithful departure is to reclaim a different normative structure for humanity. In this, the critique is as much of the powerful rationalism and autonomy of the Enlightenment as of the patriarchy they see as undergirding the church and theology. The starting point is to discover our connectedness, our links with the earth, our mother, with the wind and seas and stars, our sisters. It is not to try to be some misbegotten image of a male God. Yet even here there is a contradiction. While rejecting the autonomy of the Enlightenment view of the person, there is a new autonomy of the post-Christian post-modern woman: the post-Christian feminist sees as the biggest need for liberation, to be liberated from dependence on an anthropomorphic God.

What now is the radical alternative? It is not to recreate a feminist anthropology in the image of the goddess, although that was a provisional way forward at an earlier stage of feminist theologizing. Nor is it to find in God a gender neutrality which will nudge us further towards New Age and pantheism, although this too has been the path trodden by some women. The radical movement has been to dispense with any anthropology which sees human personhood as derivative. God is not the name of anygod, anyman, anywoman, or anyforce. God is not a name at all.

It is thoroughly in keeping with the postmodernist repudiation of the grand schemes of modernity that post-Christian feminism rejects approximate solutions for its own anthropological dilemma. God is also our own creation. However it is not a substantive God, but a process; not a noun but a verb; not Being, but be-ing. Mary Daly, having already left the church and over the last twenty years having drawn out hundreds of thousands of women in her wake, has been the first to formulate this. God is the verb to be, uttered by self-authenticating, self-creating women who are done with the grand patriarchal schemes of both modernity and Christianity. The very statement, 'I am' shouted by those women who are coming into being, is the creating of god.[9]

We are used to Mary Daly however, and although her writings make our flesh creep she has less influence over the faithful who are wary of her vehemence against the Christian faith. Far more sinister are the feminist postmodernists who have stayed within the church, working in our midst to erode a Christian anthropology, to twist out of the very heart of the Eucharist any understanding of our humanity which still focuses on Jesus as the true authentic human, who has won for us the right of personhood. Among other women working from within the church is Carter Heyward, an American Episcopalian minister, whose book *Touching Our Strength* suggests that in the experience of Eros we become ourselves.[10]

The 'lesbian theology' of Heyward focuses also on god the verb. By accepting Mary Daly's assertion that traditional Christianity is a necrophilial religion centred on a dead man, she has no hesitation in replacing Christ with christa. Christa is the polemic sculpture of a woman on the cross, who, for many feminist post-Christians represents all the women who have given their bodies and spilt their blood for the sins of the world. In Heyward's words:

> For whereas the suffering and death of Christ signalled
> the woman-induced, sexual sin of the world over and
> against men of God, the suffering and death of christa,
> in fact, can represent the sin of churchmen, men of
> God over and against woman and our sacred/erotic
> power.[11]

It is not a reified christa but a movement of erotic connectedness which helps us to become god. Heyward's phrase is 'sexual godding'. We god with each other bodily, enjoying one another's surfaces and orifices, free from the agendas of others and the constraints of tradition. We write our own scripts, accept whatever of past narratives we choose—even bits of the Christian narrative if it pleases us. But by doing so we utterly corrupt and distort it, so that those who are not already deeply rooted in Christ cannot hear the scriptures, sing the hymns, tell the stories or celebrate the Eucharist in the same way and with the same simplicity of meaning framework again. For Heyward it is the process of sexual godding, with whomsoever we allow, which makes us human. In its focus on body and self-creation it also becomes the ultimate sacrament:

> 'I take her and stroke her playfully..... I take her and
> nibble a little. I take her and eat, take her and drink. I
> am taken, grasped and caressed by her power moving
> between us. Immersing myself in you, with you,
> through you, I move with you in the sensual wellspring
> of her love'.[11]

Conclusions on the journey

At the end of modernity there are categories which are rooted in a Christian anthropology that have ceased to carry weight in our culture: personhood, commitment, responsibility, love of neighbour, faithfulness, truth. For many people, including those within the church who are living a post-Christian 'gospel', these categories have ceased even to have meaning. They have gone along with the visions of the person embodied in the early modernist dream: sanity, reason, progress, education, happiness, morality and goodness.

I believe the task of the church is to reclaim the reality of our humanness, to cleanse it from the additions and subtractions to which it has been subject through Greek, scholastic, or modernist culture, and to reject the motifs of power and control which have been only too detectable by those who look on from the outside. We need to live the truth of human personhood in our lives and communities, praying that through our love for each other people will see that we are Christ's disciples. We need also to be confident that, when we tell the story of who we are from the pages of scripture and in the Incarnate Christ, we have on our lips and in our hearts the truth about the self and humanity that people are longing to hear. If our gospel is true, then they too are image-of-the-living-God, with eternity in their hearts and longing for wholeness. Whatever our culture denies, whatever our culture tries to affirm, ultimately, the human heart is still restless until it finds its rest in God.

Notes

1. D. Martindale, *The Nature and Types of Sociological Theory*, Houghton Miffin, 1960

2. R. M. MacIver, *Community, A Sociological Study*, 1917

3. R. M. MacIver, *The Challenge of the Passing Years, My Encounter with Time*, 1962

4. Eric Fromm, *The Art of Loving*, 1953

5. *Walden Two* is the utopian novel written by the Harvard behavioural psychologist, B.F. Skinner, to show how his theories could be used in society. Macmillan, 1948, paperback 1962. 'Sociobiology' is the self-proclaimed revolution in biology a generation later, by the Harvard genetic biologist,

E.O. Wilson, which tries to explain human behaviour in terms of a genetic determinism; see his *Sociobiology: the New Synthesis*, Harvard University Press, 1975.

6. G. Glover, *Understanding the Self*, Macmillan, 1988

7. A. Giddens, *Modernity and Self-Identity*, Polity, 1991

8. J.-F. Lyotard, *The Postmodern Condition: a report on knowledge*, Manchester University Press, 1987

9. M. Daly, *Beyond God the Father*

10. C. Heyward, *Touching our Strength: the Erotic as Power*, Harper, 1989

11. the same

Further references

Foucault, M., *The Order of Things: An Archaeology of the Human Sciences*, Routledge, 1989

Habermas, J., *The Philosophical Discourse on Modernity*, Polity, 1987

Lash, S., and Friedman, J., *Modernity and Identity*, Blackwell, 1992

Storkey, A., J., 'The Surrogate Sciences', *Philosophia Reformata*, 1986

Storkey, A., J., *The Epistemological Foundations of Consumption Theory*, Amsterdam, Free University Press, 1993

Taylor, C., *Sources of the Self: The Making of the Modern Identity*, CUP, 1989

Thompson, J. B., *Ideology and Modern Culture*, Polity, 1990

7

Modernity and morality

STEPHEN WILLIAMS

The word 'modernity', as it is used in this essay, is a broad and comprehensive rather than narrow and technical term. No attempt is made to define or address modernity in any conscious distinction from postmodernity. The relative definitions of 'modern' and 'postmodern' are in any case disputable and postmodernity is sometimes understood as a form of late modernity. The phenomenon I have in mind, however defined, is a recognizable feature of the contemporary Western scene; whether or not it is present elsewhere is not of present concern.

The historical background

Moderns have often found Christian morality problematic, indeed, obnoxious. We can get a grip on the way that the question of morality has brought 'modernity' into collision with Christianity by remarking on some features of intellectual history. Sometimes the story of the making of the modern mind is told as follows. Dogma held sway in Europe for a millennium and more. Then came the critical mind, heralded especially by René Descartes. With the dissolution of dogma under the impact of criticism the importance of human construction comes into its own, particularly human rational construction of the world, of life and of society. There is a tension between the domination of reason and rationality on the one hand and the creative will on the other. On the one hand, human rational constructions may be the product of the creative will: the will presses the intellect to discern rational order. On the other hand, that will refuses to be subject to any general or universal rationality. The house built by reason becomes a prison, for the tyranny of reason simply replaces the tyranny of dogma which reason displaced. If rational constructions successfully replicate reality, we are still subject to a given order. We are still not free. On account of this state of affairs, the critical mind implodes under the pressure of its own momentum. We end up culturally with the fragmentation and meaninglessness which have so long seemed to characterize the West. We are left with sheer will as the spring of life, now that revelation and reason have been dismissed.[1]

That story has some truth and some plausibility, but a significant dimension is missing. It has to do with morality. Descartes is rightly credited with great significance in the foregoing account. But we must probe his significance more deeply. In his recent study, *Descartes and the Enlightenment*, Peter Schouls argues for the fundamental nature of Descartes' philosophy of the will: the Cartesian enterprise is driven by the belief that the will is free and engagement in intellectual construction is the issue of this conviction.[2] To assess his impact on the Enlightenment, we should look not just at the *Discourse* and the *Meditations* but also at his essay on *The Passions of the Soul*.[3] Indeed, this last is:

> ... the only work in which he deals with an area of life
> in which he believes each individual can walk the road
> of progress to the end. Once that journey has been
> completed, the highest level of autonomy which is
> possible in that area of life has been reached: man then
> has exempted himself from being subject to God and
> has achieved complete mastery in that area of life. In
> this declaration of independence, *The Passions of the
> Soul* present what is perhaps Descartes' clearest
> articulation of the spirit which pervades the
> Enlightenment.[4]

The treatise is a monument to the ideal of moral self-possession and moral self-mastery. It was written at the behest of Princess Elizabeth of Bohemia, with whom Descartes developed a close intellectual relationship. This shows that there was much more in the early modern air than an intellectual crisis at the level of epistemology and scientific method. There was a moral crisis at the deepest social level at least amongst those with intellectual pretensions.

In his various writings Descartes reiterates the fond affirmation that his philosophical method is his own. The method is his, and he made it, and his hands prepared the whole scheme of things.[5] Descartes appears here as what has been termed the 'self-defining subject'.[6] It is a fundamental matter of human dignity to define oneself in the world. Even sources of modernity very different indeed from what we find in Descartes exhibit this feature. Thus in his recent comprehensive study *The Sources of the Self: the Making of Modern Identity*, Charles Taylor contrasts Descartes with one of his earlier intellectual foes, Michel de Montaigne.[7] According to Taylor, the Montaignian and Cartesian enterprises are flatly opposed to each other yet each influences the awakening Western self. Descartes is searching for the human essence, discoverable by scientific reasoning. Montaigne is searching for the human individual, discoverable by psychological observation. Both searches are alternative forms of a bid for freedom to 'let man be man' whatever we make of God. Here we have a revolution in human sensibility at the heart of post-Reformation moral philosophy and the coming of the modern world. When modern morality clashes with Christianity, it does so because Christianity is perceived as the foe of self-definition, since it locates us in a given moral order ordained of God.

The project of self-definition lies at the heart of the question of modernity and morality. To see how this stands in relation to Christianity, we recall the assault on Christianity made by Friedrich Nietzsche, the darling of postmodernity. According to Nietzsche, the end of theism, the death of God, spells the end of objectivity in the moral realm as well as the religious. He has nothing but contempt for those who seek to rescue moral objectivity from the fate of God. Writing of George Eliot, Nietzsche says:

> They have got rid of the Christian God, and now feel obliged to cling all the more firmly to Christian morality... In England, in response to every little emancipation from theology one has to reassert one's position... as a moral fanatic... With us it is different. When one gives up Christian belief one thereby deprives oneself of the right to Christian morality... Christianity is a system... If one breaks out of it a fundamental idea, the belief in God, one thereby breaks the whole thing to pieces... Christian morality is a command: its origin is transcendental; it is beyond all criticism, all right to criticize; it possesses truth only if God is truth—it stands or falls with the belief in God...[8]

Nietzsche is extremely cool here. Elsewhere he describes Christian morality, as it has been believed in for centuries, as a tissue of anti-human and stinking fictions,[9] but the last words in the quotation (from *The Twilight of the Idols*) indicate the problem modernity has with Christian morality. It is a stifling imposition. Its alternative is free creativity, and no one propagated the alternative more dramatically than Nietzsche. His famous doctrine of the Superman is bound up with his key, controversial, and on any account extraordinary doctrine of the eternal recurrence. This doctrine states that all that is and will be has already been. In the Bible of Nietzschean philosophy, *Thus Spoke Zarathustra*, he states in a nutshell the 'gospel' message which this extraordinary notion expresses:

> On one occasion Zarathustra strictly defines his task—
> it is also mine—the meaning of which cannot be
> misunderstood: he is affirmative to the point of
> justifying, of redeeming the entire past.[10]

The death of God leaves a vacuum to be filled by human creativity. Human creativity is fatally prevented by the disgusting remaining thought that perhaps we need redemption. We can create, then, only after the burden of redemption has been hurled aside, and this can happen only if I can truly say of everything that was that I had willed it to be thus. Remorse (which is pathetic weakness) and the need for forgiveness (which threatens to introduce talk of redemption) therefore have no place in a worthy human life. We should appreciate what Nietzche is doing: in pitting our creative humanity against the Christian doctrines of creation and of redemption, he is doing exactly what moderns need to do in order to raze the foundations of Christian morality. Divine creation means an order which is given and which we therefore can not create; divine redemption means a guilt incurred within such an order, a guilt dealt with by divine and not human action. These are the scandals modernity finds in Christian morality. How, then, should we respond?

Christian morality and freedom

One response is to offer counter-arguments in defence of some sort of moral objectivity and so clear the way for Christian moral beliefs in particular. After all, public rhetoric seems to feed on a widespread sense that certain things just are right or wrong. Every Western leader pronouncing on the matter takes it for granted that we are morally obligated to do what we can to try to resolve a crisis in one of the world's flashpoints, for the duty to alleviate suffering is taken to be the objective moral duty of humankind. Those who defend violence point to the moral obligation to secure the justice which can only come through violence, if it comes at all. 'Objective morality' means here a morality which should be binding on all. This militates against the idea of morality as one's individual creation, so at some point most people apparently appeal to moral obligation taken to be universally binding. If these obligations are human creations, they are yet binding on all and you cannot use your creativity to deny them. We thus have some sort of given order after all.

Alternatively, many say that we cannot know something to be morally right or wrong, because knowledge in these things eludes us. They presumably claim to know that this claim is true. How, exactly can it be known that we lack moral knowledge? Again, many assume that as long as we do not interfere with others, we should have freedom for moral creativity. Quite apart from the problem of who can decide and how we know what harms another, this statement assumes the paramount importance of freedom, but on what basis? Is it a moral dogma that impels us to say that moral freedom is so important? My point is not to refute the suggestion. It is to ask for its basis.

We could pursue discussions along these lines and try to undermine people's reasons, but even if we were successful, we might not change attitudes. Persuasion is more likely when we ally any such points to a demonstration of what true freedom looks like under the hand of God. Here we point to Jesus. Of the freedom of Jesus, we hear nothing explicitly in the Bible, yet the Bible portrays one who lives and moves in perfect freedom. He is free just at the point where we are not, just at the point where we have talked of our moral obligation to alleviate suffering. Those who have heard it said that we are to love our neighbour as ourselves know their failure. The combination of desire and power so to live fails us. If we constantly fail we are not integrated; we are inwardly alienated as we cannot match what we are humanly meant to be and to do with what we are humanly able or willing to be and to do. So it appears to those who are deeply sensitive to the imperious demand to love our fellows. As alienated and disintegrated we are unfree, yet Jesus wills, acts and responds as one to whom alienation and disintegration are themselves alien. In his orientation to others, including in the uniqueness of his vocation, freedom is perfectly displayed. Freedom is alienation banished, and such freedom is attained in communion with one he called Father. God is the enabler of this freedom, set in a context where the moral demand is strenuous to a degree that makes the very word 'moral' abysmally inappropriate. Indeed, the word 'moral' pales in the light of Jesus Christ. The Christian doctrine of redemption speaks of Jesus as infinitely more than the exemplar of freedom, and those who lament their own lack of freedom and concede the perfect freedom of Jesus will be quite prepared to hear of this doctrine. But Jesus is the author, as well as the exemplar of freedom, summoning the church, united to his risen humanity, to participate in that royal and serving liberty.

Dietrich Bonhoeffer expresses this in a particularly striking way. The crashing first sentence of his unfinished *Ethics* is:

> The knowledge of good and evil seems to be the aim of all ethical reflection. The first task of Christian ethics is to invalidate this knowledge.[11]

The reason for that is that knowledge of good and evil is a sign of the Fall. Humans were not created to know good and evil, only to know the good. Knowledge of good and evil, the sign of supposed ethical maturity, is a sign in fact of departure from what Bonhoeffer calls 'the origin'. Correspondingly, Bonhoeffer can proceed by saying that:

> The freedom of Jesus is not the arbitrary choice of one amongst innumerable possibilities; it consists on the contrary precisely in the complete simplicity of His action, which is never confronted by a plurality of possibilities, conflicts or alternatives, but always only by one thing. This one thing Jesus calls the will of God... This will of God is His life. He lives and acts not by the knowledge of good and evil but by the will of God. There is only one will of God. In it the origin is recovered; in it there is established the freedom and the simplicity of all action.[12]

The quest both to realize 'creativity' and to shrug off any sense of inward disintegration is the quest for freedom. Much more can be said about our response to the modern attitude to morality but surely the presentation of the concrete humanity of Christ as the one who loves in freedom must be central in a contemporary Christian riposte to the charges of stifling creativity and fostering alienation. It is not that one cravenly avoids speaking of God, the deity of Christ or the redemption. But it is in, with and before the human Jesus Christ that one must so speak in a culture convinced that Christianity is anti-humanist, even if that conviction proceeds not from intellectual sincerity but from willed perversity. At least, it must surely often be so.

It may be objected that thus far I have described modernity in terms of its moral form, talking in general terms of freedom and self-definition. The objection is that modernity has a far more specific programme and that therefore we must learn from those who have tried to analyze the fundamental human impulse in various ways connected with material greed, sex, power, the will to live, etc. Two things can be said in response to this objection. Firstly, an approach to 'modernity and morality' that took up a specific theme like the ones mentioned above could not justify in a short time the selection of that particular element as crucial. Having failed to do so, we would have landed ourselves with undue restrictions in the treatment of this theme. Secondly, even if we could show the centrality of some particular feature of the modern programme, we should in response still lead back to the freedom of Jesus Christ. The power of Bonhoeffer's essay on *Ethics* lies in its relentless christocentricity. He does not put an idea at the centre of ethical reflection but makes the person of Christ the reference point of it all. This is justified because Christian morality is nothing but the love of God and of neighbour. What is Christian in the love of God and of neighbour is the one in whom that commandment was perfectly fulfilled and whose concrete risen humanity is communicated to his church. That is the nub of our response even to more substantively specific diagnoses of the modern quarrel with Christian morality.

Another objection might be that the treatment has been woefully and depressingly individualistic, not in the sense of being abstracted from the sphere of human relations but in the sense of abstraction from the sphere of social structure and policy. This is a fair point and so we need to turn to the social realm. With all the rightful attention given these days to the socio-political form of Christian witness, we may forget that the social-structural is formed out of the intimately personal even while the social-structural itself forms the intimately personal. If socio-political structures require theological attention, the importance of personal moral conviction is enhanced. For 'attention' is something that persons give or choose not to give and the will to attend is a personal will. Hence the presentation of Christian morality in its modern context will require, as ever, the presentation of Christ personally to moral individuals so that the will is formed to attend to all that needs attention on a social-structural level.

Christian morality and the law

The presentation of Christian morality in relation to structures and institutions requires attention to a number of issues. One is the question of the grounds on which Christians publicly advance their convictions and recommendations. This question is historically bound up with epistemological questions concerning toleration where the strength of those grounds determines whether or not the law should be involved. John Locke, in his lengthy *Third Letter on Toleration*, argued that the coercive powers of the magistrate should be regulated by the fact that in certain matters the issue at stake had to do with matters believed but not known to be the case. And:

> How well grounded and great soever the assurance of
> faith may be wherewith it [a proposition] is received;
> but faith it is still, and not knowledge; persuasion, and
> not certainty. This is the highest the nature of the thing
> will permit us to go in matters of revealed religion,
> which are therefore called matters of faith; a persuasion
> of our minds, short of knowledge, is the last result that
> determines us in such truths.[13]

Where the epistemic status of beliefs is inferior to knowledge, coercion is unwarranted. The justification of law and its concomitant enforcement is here a function of the epistemic status of the beliefs in question. Locke's ways of relating faith and knowledge are not typical of his general philosophical treatment of religious epistemology. Elsewhere he speaks rather more strongly in favour of the epistemic status of faith.[14] It is as though you might be quite sure of something in a debate with your friends, but not justified in being quite as sure in the public, political arena. In the public domain religious believers must not think that things held by faith (rather than known to be the case) can be enshrined in law.

The difficulty is, of course, that it looks today as though no one can demonstrate anything in social morality. The sphere of bioethics is a testing-ground for the logic of public policy and reveals the fundamental lack of consensus on fundamental public moral issues. The attempt at rational demonstration seems doomed. How are rational first principles selected, and by whom? How do we rationally decide when personhood begins and what the limits are of human rights? In the light of these questions how can we move with rational confidence through the morass of problems and innumerable possibilities in bioethics? Appeal to intuition fares little better, for intuitions on fundamental issues can vary. On some things we have no intuitions at all but struggle to figure out the morality of the matter.

A bold reassertion of liberal social philosophy can help us. On such a philosophy, the key must be consent. For example, if the parties concerned agree to a contract for surrogate motherhood, then surrogate motherhood must be permitted in law. We cannot make any dogmatic moral appeal to the rights or wrongs of surrogacy, so consent must rule.[15] But this argument does not work. If society were composed of consenting adults, the argument might promise to get off the ground, but society is not so composed. What if my particular moral belief is that the embryo has rights despite being a non-consenting party in the surrogate contract? The proponent of surrogacy in this context must positively deny that there are such rights but why on earth should I accept it? Why should your insistence on the rights of the consenting individual or consenting individuals to carry out a certain project take precedence over my conviction that non-consenting individuals have rights? The argument could be extended, for example, to include animal rights.

In order to advance our Christian conviction, we must realize that everyone seems to have difficulty in producing universally acceptable grounds. That might not matter so much if it were just a question of conducting social arguments, but certain practices must be regulated by law and any such lack of regulation already favours the one rather than the other position. For example, if abortion is prohibited in law after a certain number of weeks, it may be held to violate the moral right of the mother to take decisions pro-abortion. If abortion is permitted in law up to a certain number of weeks, it may be held to violate the moral right of the embryo to life. In the end, the very refusal to frame a law much as the terms of any law which is framed, favours one position rather than another. If there is an explicit moral reason given for a law or for the lack of a law, that is a moral decision against one party. If one either frames or refuses to frame a law in order to protect freedom, that is still a moral decision against one party.

For this reason, Christianity is in principle at no disadvantage even though we may be tempted to think that it lacks compelling publicly demonstrable grounds for its position. For the same reason it is quite wrong to describe the issue as one of freedom and consent versus the imposition of a moral viewpoint.

One is bound to seek the widest possible grounds on which to commend a Christian perspective on social structures and institutions. Just how wide these can be and just what is a fit case for implementation in law depends entirely on the issue at hand. Christians believe that the failure to observe socially what they take to be universal ordinances of God must have some public consequences in the sense of objective social impact, but are they not public also in that some evidence can be offered? Public demonstration of Christian conviction or of the consequences of violating God's laws may well be difficult, but we can appeal to some outward elements in commending a Christian view of things, at least for those with ears to hear and eyes to see.

Here again, we must rest on Christ. Christ was a public figure, not just a literary invention. The documents of the Christian scriptures are a public phenomenon, written in readable languages. Christian social conviction springs from and comes to rest in the witness to a concrete humanity that occupied space and time. It traces its authority back to the authority of a lived life. In his *Ethics* Bonhoeffer wrote:

> In Soloviev's story of the Antichrist, in the last days
> before Christ's return the heads of the persecuted
> churches discuss the question of what is for each of

them the most precious thing in Christianity; the
decisive answer is that the most precious thing in
Christianity is Jesus Christ Himself. That is to say, that
in the face of the Antichrist only one thing has force
and permanence, and that is Christ Himself. Only he
who shares in Him has the power to withstand and to
overcome. He is the centre and the strength of the
Bible, of the Church and of theology, but also of
humanity, of reason, of justice and of culture.
Everything must return to Him; it is only under His
protection that it can live. There seems to be a general
unconscious knowledge, which, in the hour of ultimate
peril, leads everything which desires not to fall victim
to the Antichrist to take refuge with Christ.[16]

One fears lest these days are gone. Half a century after Bonhoeffer wrote those words the unconscious apprehension that once
drew people towards Christ seems to be vanishing. Yet Christ
remains all that Christianity has. To speak his name is not to
resolve all the social issues that perplex the makers of a modern
morality. 'Teacher, tell my brother to divide the inheritance with
me.' 'Man, who appointed me a judge or an arbiter between you?'
The dispute remains unresolved. 'Then he said to them, "Watch
out! Be on your guard against all kinds of greed..."'[17] Jesus
urges that we so dispose our spirit that all disputes, in the end,
will be tractable. And what greater authority can modernity find
to teach us how to dispose the spirit in moral matters?

Notes

1.   This is roughly the line that has been taken by Lesslie Newbigin in his various
works from the publication of *The Other Side of 1984*, World Council of Churches,
1983, *Truth to Tell: the Gospel as Public Truth*, SPCK, 1991

2.   Peter Schouls, *Descartes and the Enlightenment*, Edinburgh University Press,
1989

3.   See Cottingham, Murdoch and Stoothoff, editors, *The Philosophical Writings of
Descartes*, vol. i, Cambridge University Press, 1985, pages 325ff

4.   the same, page 172

5.   This is expressed in many places but the Discourse is as good an example as
any. See 'Discourse on the Method' in Cottingham, and others.

6. See CharlesTaylor, *Hegel*, Cambridge University Press, 1975, Part 1

7. Charles Taylor, *The Sources of the Self: the Making of Modern Identity*, Cambridge University Press, 1985

8. Friedrich Nietzsche, *Twilight of the Idols and The Antichrist*, Penguin, 1990, pages 29–30

9. See especially the discussions in Nietzsche, *The Genealogy of Morals*, Doubleday, 1956

10. Friedrich Nietzsche, *Ecce Homo*

11. Dietrich Bonhoeffer, *Ethics*, Macmillan

12. the same, page 30

13 I quote these words as they are found in an interpreter of John Locke who is influential as far as theologians go, namely Michael Polanyi in *Personal Knowledge*, Routledge and Kegan Paul, 1958. See pages 265–66, but he deviated a little in wording from that found in *Locke's Works*, London, 1823, VI. 144

14. Maurice Cranston is certainly right to say that in his Third Letter on Toleration 'Locke was forced ... to acknowledge a more sceptical attitude towards religion as such than he had previously admitted', *John Locke: a biography*, Longman, 1957, page 367. One has only to read Book IV of *Essay on Human Understanding*, P. Nidditch, editor, Clarendon, 1975, and the correspondence with Stillingfleet, *Works*, see vol IV) to appreciate this.

15. See Tristram Engelhardt, *Bioethics and Secular Humanism: the Search for a Common Morality*, SCM Press, 1991

16. Bonhoeffer, [note 11], page 56

17. Luke 12:13–15

8
Modernity and eschatology

TORMOD ENGELSVIKEN

This paper has three foci: modernity, eschatology and mission. The fact that our consultation is arranged by the Theology Working Group of the Lausanne Committee for World Evangelization indicates the missiological purpose of our endeavour.

As this paper was presented after the major foundational papers on modernity and post-modernity, I did not try to reinvent the wheel by attempting to define or analyze modernity and postmodernity. I simply presuppose the very incisive analysis and subtle critique that have been presented in earlier papers, and try to apply in a modest way some of those insights to my own theme.

In them, however, there was no attempt to define or analyze the concepts of mission and eschatology, or the relation between them, although several references were made to both. I first outline in very broad terms how mission and eschatology intrinsically relate to one another, and then see how they both apply to the issues raised by modernity and postmodernity. In my presentation of eschatology and mission I deliberately draw on some significant statements produced by the Lausanne Movement that I believe are very relevant to the theme of modernity. Thus this paper attempts to maintain some continuity with the theological tradition of the Lausanne movement.

The kingdom of God

After having presented the three main streams of mission theology in our century, the ecumenical, the evangelical, and the Roman Catholic, and their views of the goal of mission, the American Lutheran missiologist James Scherer concludes:

> All traditions agree that the kingdom of God is in some
> sense the final goal, but they differ on what that may mean
> and how it affects the ongoing task and priorities of the
> church during the interim period. Does the goal of
> mission remain making converts and planting churches
> wherever they do not exist, or does the expectation of the
> kingdom shift the church's priorities to activities which
> somehow anticipate a 'new heaven and a new earth'?[1]

This present consensus on making the kingdom of God the goal of mission and the overarching missiological concept implies an eschatological understanding of mission. Mission is the main task of the church in the interim between the first and the second coming of Christ, always carried out with a view towards the final consummation of God's plan of salvation.

Some of the reasons for the preference for the term 'kingdom of God'[2] in contemporary missiology are firstly its background in the message of Jesus himself, secondly its capability of conveying the comprehensiveness of the salvation that is offered in the gospel, and thirdly its dual meaning in expressing both the present and the future reality of salvation.

The proclamation and demonstration of the kingdom of God were central to Jesus earthly ministry as portrayed in the synoptic Gospels.[3] The kingdom has come near, it is already a reality to be entered into or received. Its power is being experienced in the present as sick are healed, lepers cleansed, dead raised, demons expelled, and most significantly, people enter into a new relationship to God as they turn to him and receive forgiveness of sins and new life through faith in Jesus. This new relationship to God based on forgiveness is the central soteriological gift in the kingdom. It is portrayed in various ways, for example, in Jesus' table fellowship with sinners and in many of his parables.

Still the kingdom is future. It has not yet come in power, in its fullness. Its coming is to be prayed for and expected as a future reality. This tension between the 'already' since the new aeon breaks into the present and transforms it, and the 'not yet' since the old aeon still exists, meaning that the evil powers: sin, the devil and death, are still operative in the world. It is in this tension, in this period of transition between the first and the second coming of Christ, that the church in mission is operating, not as identical with the kingdom but as the people of the kingdom, calling all people to enter the kingdom of God freely.

Neither in its present nor its future form is the kingdom the result of human achievement. It is a transcendent reality, the result of God's own intervention in human history. The incarnation was wholly God's initiative, and the central salvific act of Jesus, his death and resurrection, is signally God's work. Seen from the perspective of the church, eschatology is not merely future. The resurrection of Jesus from the dead to Lordship at the right hand of the Father, for the church an event of the past, is an eschatological event of greatest significance. He is the 'firstfruits of those who have fallen asleep' (1 Corinthians 15:20), a guarantee that also those who believe in him will rise by the power of the Spirit (Romans 8:11).

If the work of salvation fulfilled once for all in history by Christ and his present Lordship over the cosmos must be seen solely as the result of divine intervention, even more so the return of Christ, the resurrection of the dead, the final judgment, and the establishment of God's ultimate and eternal kingdom. This is not to deny the relationship of God's kingdom to the realities of this world, as God acts in, with and through the world, even to the point of establishing eschatological 'signs' that are the results also of of human activity. It does mean, however, that no human efforts can bring about the kingdom of God, or that humans can set the timetable for God. He is the sovereign Lord.

Luther as missiologist: an untapped source?

Martin Luther's missionary thinking can be characterized as 'theocentric missionary eschatology'.[4] Mission is always the work of the Triune God. The later term *Missio Dei* would well fit his basic understanding of mission. The goal of mission is the coming of the kingdom of God. The concept of the kingdom of God in Luther's thinking is not completely identical with that of recent exegesis and mission theology (but whose is?). He has, however, caught its essentially soteriological content, as he expresses it in the Large Catechism:

> What is the kingdom of God? Answer: Simply what we
> learned in the Creed, namely that God sent his Son,
> Christ our Lord, into the world to redeem and deliver
> us from the power of the devil and to bring us to

himself and rule us as a king of righteousness, life,
salvation against sin, death, and evil conscience. To
this end he also gave his Holy Spirit to teach us this
through his holy Word and to enlighten and
strengthen us in faith by his power. [5]

Interestingly, the dual nature of the kingdom, both as a present
and a future, an individual and a universal reality, is also
emphasized by Luther:

God's kingdom comes to us in two ways: first, it comes
here, in time, through the Word and faith, and
secondly, in eternity, it comes through the final
revelation. Now we pray for both of these, that it may
come to those who are not yet in it, and that it may
come by daily growth here and in eternal life hereafter
to us who have attained it. [6]

According to Luther, the coming of the kingdom to people 'in
time' takes place through the preaching of the gospel throughout
the world.

Another characteristic of the kingdom of God as portrayed in
the synoptic gospels is its antagonistic character. The ministry of
Jesus that brings the kingdom close, launches, as Bosch says,

an all-out attack on evil in all its manifestations. God's
reign arrives wherever Jesus overcomes the power of
evil. Then, as it does now, evil took many forms: pain,
sickness, death, demon-possession, personal sin and
immorality, the loveless self-righteousness of those
who claim to know God, the maintaining of special
class privileges, the brokenness of human
relationships. [7]

This antagonistic dimension is also strongly emphasized by
Luther,

So we pray that thy kingdom may prevail among us
through the Word and the power of the Holy Spirit,
that the devil's kingdom may be overthrown and he
may have no right or power over us, until finally the
devil's kingdom shall be utterly destroyed and sin,
death, and hell exterminated, and that we may live
forever in perfect righteousness and blessedness. [8]

I might be suspected of introducing Luther here for the sake of a confessional repristination of a Lutheran theological tradition. However, it is an attempt to present an aspect of the 'rich but untested potential' in Luther's missiology developed as it was before the major onslaught of modernity and 'firmly grounded in the biblical world view'.[9] Luther's understanding of 'the mission of God contrasts sharply with humanistic missionary attitudes of later periods'.[10] It could therefore be that Luther's missionary vision with all its practical limitations could help the church to recover a sense of theocentric and transcendent missionary eschatology in a time of anthropocentric preoccupation with self and the present (or immediate future).

Mission and eschatology in Lausanne documents.

Professor O. G. Myklebust suggests that there are three 'types' of mission theologies, the 'geographical', the 'eschatological' and the 'historical'.[11] In the eschatological understanding of mission the spread of the gospel throughout the world is a condition for and a preparation for the end of this aeon. Mission is a ministry of expectation, receiving power and inspiration from the promise that every knee will bow and every tongue confess that Jesus Christ is Lord to the glory of God the Father (Philippians 2:10f).[12] Myklebust mentions a number of missiologists representing this position and includes also 'authoritative declarations' such as the 'Wheaton Declaration', the 'Frankfurt Declaration' and the Second Vatican Council's 'Decree on the mission activity of the Church'.[13]

There is no doubt that this view also is characteristic of evangelical mission as represented by the Lausanne Movement. In the Lausanne Covenant (LC), eschatology seems to be emphasized primarily in three respects.[14]

Firstly, it is mentioned in connection with the uniqueness and universality of Christ (LC, Article 3), where salvation is understood eschatologically and seen on the dark background of eternal lostness:

There is no other name by which we must be saved. All men and women are perishing because of sin, but God loves everyone, not wishing that any should perish but that all should repent. Yet those who reject Christ repudiate the joy of salvation and condemn themselves to eternal separation from God. To proclaim Jesus as 'the Saviour of the world' is not to affirm that all people are either automatically or ultimately saved, still less to affirm that all religions offer salvation in Christ.

Through this statement the LC stands firmly on the biblical doctrine of Christian exclusivism, with emphasis on the two possible eternal outcomes, rejecting universalism in both inclusivist and pluralist forms. This eschatological position has been reiterated in the Manila Manifesto (MM), which defines the gospel in clearly eschatological and exclusivist terms:

> The gospel is the good news of God's salvation from the powers of evil, the establishment of his eternal kingdom and his final victory over everything that defies his purpose.[15]

> We have no warrant for saying that salvation can be found outside Christ or apart from an explicit acceptance of his work through faith.[16]

Secondly, eschatology is especially spelled out with reference to the personal, visible and glorious return of Christ to consummate his salvation and his judgment (LC, Article 15). The promise of his coming is seen as a spur to evangelism in light of the word that the gospel must first be preached to all nations (Matthew 24:14). It will involve the perfection of God's kingdom, a new heaven and earth in which righteousness will dwell and God will reign forever. On this background 'the notion that people can ever build a utopia on earth' is rejected as a 'proud, self-confident dream'.

The same view is expressed in the MM,[17] where there also is a warning against confusing the kingdom of God with a Christianized society.[18]

Thirdly, eschatology is associated with spiritual conflict or warfare. The article on the Return of Christ continues:

> we also remember his warning that false Christs and false prophets will arise as precursors of the final Antichrist.

In articles 12 and 13, the questions of spiritual conflict and freedom and persecution are addressed in an eschatological context.

> We believe that we are engaged in constant spiritual
> warfare with the principalities and powers of evil, who
> are seeking to overthrow the Church and frustrate its
> task of world evangelization.... For we detect the
> activity of our enemy, not only in false ideologies
> outside the Church, but also inside it in false gospels
> which twist Scripture and put people in the place of
> God. We need both watchfulness and discernment to
> safeguard the biblical gospel.

It is exactly in this context of spiritual conflict and attack on the
Church and its gospel that the LC raises the issue of what we
today would call modernity:

> We acknowledge that we ourselves are not immune to
> worldliness of thought and action, that is, to a
> surrender to secularism ... The Church must be in the
> world; the world must not be in the Church.

In the MM there is also an important reference to 'spiritual
warfare', with emphasis on the role of the Word, the Spirit and
prayer. Although the eschatological context is not spelled out, it
is implied in the following:

> Every true conversion involves a power encounter, in
> which the superior authority of Jesus Christ is
> demonstrated. There is no greater miracle than this, in
> which the believer is set free from the bondage of Satan
> and sin, fear and futility, darkness and death.'[19]

While the relationship between eschatology and mission seems
to be focused in these three areas in the LC, the report from the
consultation on Evangelism and Social Responsibility in Grand
Rapids in 1982 raises the issue of the relationship between
history and eschatology in a broader sense. In doing so the
consultation underlines the general human need for hope, and
points out how false dreams have been fabricated, 'visions which
come out of our own minds, and not from the Lord'. Among the
false dreams are modern ideologies, like 'dogmatic and Messianic
Marxisms' which proclaim

> a bogus millennium which recognizes neither the
> Creator of the world, nor his Christ. Yet they anticipate
> that by changing social structures, frequently by

violent means, they will by human effort alone bring about a fully just and perfect society.[20]

With the demise of Marxism as a viable ideology in East Europe and other parts of the world, the threat from this direction has been reduced considerably, but the ideological 'winner', called Western democracy and market economy, may also harbour a dangerous challenge to Christian eschatology, as noted in the report:

> We also reject the Messianic Western dream which aims at erecting a counterfeit materialistic Kingdom... selfish secular materialism pursues its own economic growth irrespective of the need to conserve the environment and to serve the development of the poorer nations. It is characterized by self-absorbed individualism and insensitive affluence, which are incompatible with Christian let alone truly human values...[21]

While the Grand Rapids Report refuses to take a stand as far as differing millennarian views are concerned, it focuses on the kingdom of God as the central model of salvation. The reason given for this choice is significant: 'The Kingdom is a richly suggestive concept, with significant applications to the modern world.'[22]

Distinguishing between the kingdom of God as a present reality and a future expectation, it is said that after the physical presence of Jesus has been withdrawn from the earth, it is the Holy Spirit which establishes it in the lives of his people. 'His rule takes the form of both total blessing (salvation, in fact) and total demand (obedience and service).'

The Grand Rapids Report enters into the debate on the signs of the kingdom, and places them primarily within the church, and not in the world! While the church cannot be identified with the kingdom, it is the community in which God's kingly rule is revealed. The church is an eschatological community, 'witnesses to the divine rule, and... the firstfruits of the redeemed humanity (James 1:18)... it lives in an uneasy tension between the "already" and the "not yet", between the present reality and the future expectation of the kingdom.'[23]

The signs are set in the context of Jesus' destruction of the devil's work (1 John 3:8): 'The signs of the Kingdom were evidences that the devil was retreating before the advance of the King.'

The seven signs of the kingdom that are enumerated have great significance as they capture the central 'visible' marks of the kingdom, or as the report phrases it,

> Jesus did more than preach the Kingdom; he
> demonstrated its reality with 'signs of the Kingdom',
> public evidence [sic!] that the Kingdom he was talking
> about had come.

The signs of the kingdom are the following: 'Jesus himself in the midst of his people, whose presence brings joy, peace, and a sense of celebration', 'the preaching of the Gospel', 'exorcism', 'healing and nature miracles', 'the miracle of conversion and new birth', 'the people of the Kingdom, in whom is manifested that cluster of Christlike qualities which Paul called "the fruit of the Spirit" ', and 'suffering'.

'To suffer for the sake of righteousness or for our testimony to Jesus, and to bear such suffering courageously, is a clear sign to all beholders that we have received God's salvation or Kingdom.[24]

These signs of the kingdom that are irruptions of divine reality and power into our world for all to see (though only faith understands them), may be helpful as criteria for the critical contextualization of the gospel in the modern world. Such a critical contextualization will involve an affirmation of some and a confrontation with other salient features of modernity. It may be that critique and confrontation are most needed today since, for a long time, the church and its theology have been marked by compromise and accommodation to modernity in such a way that biblical eschatology has been all but lost in the large mainline churches, especially among their many nominal members.

Eschatology or futurology?

Over twenty years ago, the title 'Eschatology or Futurology?' was used for the introductory chapter in a book about eschatology by Hans Schwarz.[25] The background for the title is the increased interest in the future exemplified by modern science, literature and art. This interest is not only an expression of a natural curiosity, but is seen as matter of life and death. 'The future must become calculable if we are to guarantee our own survival.'[26]

Schwarz points out that although some theologians are redis-covering the dimension of the future, eschatology in traditional terms is of diminishing interest:

> A Christ-centered and God-provided final
> transformation and new creation of man and of his
> environment seems to be an old-fashioned idea finally
> to be discarded. In the eyes of most people, including
> many theologians, man must take the shaping of his
> future into his own hands'.[27]

This seems to be an accurate description which still holds true today. [28] Although we may notice an increasing scepticism as to the possibilities of humans to shape their own future, the need for it is strongly emphasized by historians and futurologists alike.

On the other side, among large groups of conservative Christians there is a very strong interest in eschatology, often almost to the exclusion of other concerns. Hal Lindsay's book *The Late, Great Planet Earth* and all its successors illustrate this interest. However, this interest is often concerned solely with the apocalyptic aspects of eschatology, and often involves highly speculative views. One often gets the impression that this literature is a Christian parallel to books on secular futurology or New Age futurology. Its driving motivation seems to be to secure one's life in the immediate future by a 'knowledge' about things to come which is drawn partly from a speculative exegesis of the Scriptures and partly from an 'interpretation' of current world events and trends that often is strongly nationalistically and ideologically biased. One cannot wait for God but has a desire to know in a detailed manner what will happen in the immediate future. In that way one may control and secure one's life in the time to come. This speculative and apocalyptic eschatology that may also involve heated arguments about topics such as the millennium, the great tribulation, the return of Christ and the role of the church, is hardly an eschatology that may serve as an answer to the present crisis of modernity and the evolving postmodern paradigm. Eschatology is not a Christian version of futurology, although it obviously has great relevance as far as our understanding of the future is concerned. Evangelical Christians concerned with biblical eschatology must find their way between secular futurology and religious apocalypticism.

For this reason, we need to recapture the intrinsic inter-relationship between eschatology and the total content of the Christian gospel. Eschatology is not a 'speciality' for particularly interested people; the Christian revelation is eschatological in its very structure and content.

Schwarz points out that Luther's famous quest, 'How do I find a gracious God?' is not unrelated to the question of death, judgment and eternal life.[29] One of our main challenges today as evangelical Christians is how to relate the situations and quests of modern people, Christians and non Christians alike (the context), to the eschatological outlook of divine revelation, or maybe even more importantly, how to communicate biblical eschatology (the text) in an adequate and relevant way to people influenced by the ideas and moods of modernity and postmodernity?

Progress

A basic characteristic of modernity is belief in progress. There is no doubt that this concept has a root in Christian eschatology. It has, however, been secularized and is today most often understood in wholly immanent terms. An axiomatic presupposition for this belief is a linear understanding of time where time runs from a beginning towards a goal. This concept of time has its origin in the Judeo-Christian worldview, where creation and consummation stand at either end of history. Although presupposing it (and rightly so), the proponents of modernity have logical difficulties with linear time apart from a beginning and an end. Linear time without creation and eternity both resting in the sovereign power of a transcendent God is a difficult concept indeed.

Christian eschatology connects the past and the future, creation and consummation. Belief in creation *ex nihilo* by a transcendent God opens up belief in an ultimate intervention by the same God to bring history to an end and and to fulfill his salvific design for humankind.

The optimism of progress in the eighteenth and nineteenth centuries has been thoroughly shaken in the twentieth, and it is pessimism that dominates as we approach the twenty-first century.[30] In a strange way optimism and pessimism have changed place: while Christians earlier often were embarrassed by the violent and graphic apocalyptic imagery of the New Testament, young secular people today are familiar with it through books, movies, television, cartoons, music and science fiction! But it is not only fiction: the news media reinforce the mood of doom and imminent destruction that characterize large groups of young people in the Western world. At the same time that the present world seems to turn uglier, the transcendent world, or life in the hereafter, is seen as merely bliss. The fear of judgment or hell is gone. In a quiz show on Swedish television in 1992 the contestants were asked to guess how many out of 100 randomly selected people believed that they would go to heaven if there was such a place. The answer was 90! Although this is hardly a reliable statistical figure, the general impression is that life after death will mean happiness for all. The increase in belief in reincarnation as a definite possibility and 'research' into 'near death experiences' seem to corroborate this notion.

The deep searching question that must be asked is: What is the goal of progress? Does it lie within the process of progress itself? Or is there a human destiny given by God beyond this-worldly progress?

Christians ought to speak openly of the limits of growth and progress. They should not be embarrassed by the sometimes scary biblical stories and images of the end time which indicate a deterioration of the human condition rather than an improvement. Christians ought to speak realistically both of human sinfulness and of what sustainable growth and progress would mean in a world created by God with limited resources.

At the same time biblical eschatology provides hope through faith in the transcendent intervention of an almighty God, recreating the cosmos and making it an eternal home for a saved humankind (this is not an excuse for not caring for this world or its people). Biblical eschatology does not, however, guarantee a blissful outcome for all, either in this world or in the world to come.

The notion of salvation and judgment, of communion with God and separation from him, based on each individual's personal relationship to the God who will establish the new heaven and earth, is basic to the biblical revelation. Neither a general pessimism nor optimism are in accord with biblical eschatology. It is a matter of faith and hope, since it is our Creator and Redeemer who determines the final outcome.

The meaning of life and history

Modernity has led to a widespread loss of meaning and purpose resulting from causal reasoning and a lack of teleological orientation. In the postmodern era nihilism seems to replace the 'grand narratives' of modernity. But man cannot and will not live without meaning and purpose.[31]

Christian eschatology offers meaning and purpose, and therefore hope. In postmodernity the categories of contingency and unpredictability have opened up for a less rigid causal understanding of the world. This is an opportunity for a Christian understanding of history, since a transcendent God leading history towards an end seems at least conceivable. In a Christian eschatological perspective each person has immeasurable worth and is destined for an eternity in communion with God. The worth and ethical responsibility of humans as created in the image of God set them apart from the rest of nature—animals and plants included!—and gave them an obligation to 'work it and take care of it' (Genesis 2:15), but not to destroy or exploit it.

It is only as created in the image of God with personal responsibility that humans can and must be held accountable for their lives on the day of judgment. The inevitability of either eternal salvation or lostness, harsh as it may seem to modern people, nevertheless gives them a dignity that makes them and the way they lead their lives ultimately significant.

God's revelation of his absolute and holy will and his work of redemption through Christ cannot be reconciled with religious or ethical pluralism. The uncompromising biblical description of sin with its temporal and eternal consequences, and the promise of total salvation by grace through faith are uniquely able to reach people both in their deepest desperation and highest aspirations.

As uncertainty, individualism and shallowness are typical of many modern people in their attitude to meaning and morality, Christian eschatology objectively grounded in the resurrection of Jesus as a historical (and meta-historical) event and looking forward to resurrection, judgment and eternal life may provide both a personal assurance and a depth to religious convictions that differ sharply from postmodern relativism, making the Christian faith an attractive alternative for people looking for ultimate truth.

In this context biblical eschatology repudiates the notion of one redemptive history including all people. Christ is the Lord of all history, but he leads his people to salvation through a special salvation history (*Heilsgeschichte*) within world history, closely associated with the kingdom of God as the realm of salvation and the church as the people of the kingdom. Wherever the notion of one history is accepted, universalism is the result.[32]

The plausibility of Christian eschatology

It must be openly admitted that the Christian church in its proclamation of the Christian message, and particularly of biblical eschatology, suffers from an acute credibility problem in a pluralistic and relativistic world. Some people simply cannot believe it, even if they want to!

It seems to me that an important answer to this problem lies in the 'signs of the kingdom' as 'public evidence'. It is important, however, not to construe these signs too narrowly. It has in recent years been proposed by some charismatic church leaders that 'signs and wonders', especially healing and other miracles, are an integral and normative part of the church's evangelistic ministry.[33] This has been strongly debated, but there seems to be an emerging agreement among evangelicals that miracles still do occur, that they are signs and anticipations of the coming kingdom, and that the message of the kingdom should not only be proclaimed but also demonstrated. As people experience or witness a divine intervention interpreted in the setting of the gospel, it may lead to new openness among non-believers and a strengthening of faith among those who already believe (compare Acts 14:3).

There are several 'signs', however, as pointed out in the Grand Rapids Report. Healings and exorcisms as important as they are are only some of them. The signs of the presence of Jesus, the preaching of the gospel in the power of the Spirit, the miracle of conversion and new birth, the fruit of the Spirit exhibited in love, joy, peace, and righteousness, and patient and courageous suffering for Christ's sake, are all signs. They may not be as conspicuous and spectacular as a healing miracle but nevertheless have a profound convincing and convicting impact on non-believers. Although Christian apologetics has an important role to play, the role of the Holy Spirit in bringing modern people to faith in Jesus should be emphasized. (This is not to say that the Spirit may not also use apologetical work.)

The eschatological character of the gift of the Spirit is brought out in passages that speak of the Spirit as 'a deposit, guaranteeing what is to come' (2 Corinthians 1:22; 5:5) and as 'the firstfruits' (Romans 8:23). The Spirit can only serve this function if he is personally 'experienced' in the present. It seems that in a time when 'spirituality' with a transcendent referent is in vogue, Christians should not shy from presenting the work of the Spirit of God as a alternative 'plausibility structure' to religiously seeking people today. What else does a counselor do but make his own testimony and those of his clients 'plausible' (compare John 15:26–27; 16:7–10).

Spiritual encounter and conflict

The eschatological texts of the New Testament envisage consistently a spiritual battle being waged throughout history and coming to a climax before the return of Christ.[34]

Jesus' conflict with Satan and his victory over him and his evil spirits is a central feature of Jesus' ministry and has deep eschatological significance. 'But if I drive out demons by the Spirit of God, then the kingdom of God has come upon you' (Matthew 12:28).

The church under pressure of rationalism has been embarrassed to speak of personal evil intelligences hurting and destroying human lives and opposing the work of God. At most one has dared to speak of 'demonic structures' and 'forces' in a depersonalized way. Today we observe stark and naked evil both in individual and collective life; occultism and Satanism are 'in' among young people in several Western countries. The church should no longer shirk its responsibility to confront the Satanic powers in the name of Jesus and call them by their right name. 'Modern' evils such as abortion, raw materialism, sexual promiscuity, drug addiction and alcoholism, the destruction of marriage and family life all are examples of the works of Satan through which he keeps people in bondage and destroys human dignity and community.

Although 'peace' is one of the fruits of the Spirit, there is no peace between truth and falsehood, good and evil. The biblical eschatological perspective also includes false doctrine and apostasy within the church. Modern demands for a visibly united church may lead us to avoid the struggle for evangelical truth and righteousness, and the unmasking of false doctrine and sin within the organized church.

It is even possible that a regression will take place, especially in the Western world, that only a remnant is left who will remain faithful to the coming Lord and his word. Ecclesiastical triumphalism and exclusive emphasis on quantitative growth among evangelicals may be more symptomatic of a modern success-orientation than true concern for the expansion of the kingdom of God.

The danger of materialism

Last but not least we would like to point out that cultures marked by the values of modernity represent a temptation that very few are able to resist, the temptation of wealth. While the desire for riches probably is evenly distributed among humankind, material resources, technology, education, transportation, information, the market economy and the ideology of capitalism have combined to create opportunities for amassing wealth on the part of large numbers of people as never before in the history of the world. Riches tend to create the conceit of power, independence and security. It also tends to make people insensitive to the need of others in less fortunate circumstances. In addition to the injustice and suffering caused by the production and uneven distribution of wealth in the world at large, wealth also binds people to this world and makes them forget about the coming world.

It is worth noting that the New Testament, including Jesus' own teaching, contains far more warnings against the danger of riches and the service of Mammon than against any other god or religion. *While modern Western Christians sometimes are very worried about syncretism in other cultures and religions, they largely ignore Jesus' words about the danger of wealth and affluence.*

The parables of the Rich Man and Lazarus (Luke 16:19–31), the Rich Fool (Luke 12:13–21) and the story of the Rich Ruler (Luke 18:18–30) all contain eschatological warnings. For a person who 'stores up things for himself but is not rich toward God', who lives in luxury and ignores the sufferings of his neighbour, or who prefers his wealth to being a poor disciple of Jesus, the kingdom of God is closed now and forever. While the church often has promised the poor heavenly bliss after death, it very seldom has proclaimed God's eternal judgment on the selfish rich.

178

To be credible the church has to confront the lifestyle of affluent western society. Only a simple lifestyle will do.[35] Radical as it may seem, I believe that a real spiritual renewal of the church in rich societies and an effective missionary outreach to modern people only will be possible when the Spirit of God has convicted God's people of the sin of materialism. Jesus' words, 'But seek first the kingdom of God and his righteousness, and all these things will be given to you as well' are spoken to people who worried about material things (Matthew 6:33).

In the two parables of Jesus just mentioned, *death relativizes all riches and earthly security*. Modern people also die. As people who have received the gift of eternal life through faith in Jesus, we should exemplify in our lives by love, service, and humility what it means to be a pilgrim people on the way to our eternal home and in that way call others to join us. Only as we serve him and proclaim him as the conqueror of sin, the devil and death will Jesus draw modern people to himself today.

Notes

1. James A. Scherer, *Gospel, Church, & Kingdom, Comparative Studies in World Mission Theology*, Augsburg, 1987, pages 235–236

2. For reasons that cannot be discussed here, I prefer the term 'kingdom of God' to 'reign of God'. It brings out more clearly the basic soteriological character of the kingdom as the realm in which all the benefits of salvation are present.

3. For example, Mark 1:14–15; Matthew 4:17; Luke 6:20. See David J. Bosch, *Transforming Mission. Paradigm Shifts in Theology of Mission*, Orbis Books, 1991, pages 31–32

4. See Scherer [note 1], pages 55–59

5. *The Book of Concord: The Confessions of the Evangelical Lutheran Church*, translated and edited by Theodore G. Tappert, Fortress Press, 1959, pages 426–427

6. the same, page 427

7. Bosch [note 3], pages 32–33

8. *The Book of Concord* [note 5], page 427

9. Scherer [note 1], pages 65–66

10. the same

11. O. G. Myklebust, *Misjonskunnskap. En innføring*, Oslo, Gyldendal Norsk Forlag, 1976, pages 24–38

12. the same, pages 29–30

13. the same, pages 30–31

14. This does not mean that eschatology does not undergird the other aspects of the Lausanne Covenant, but it seems to be especially significant in these areas. The text of 'The Lausanne Covenant' is included in *The Manila Manifesto, an elaboration of The Lausanne Covenant fifteen years later*, Pasadena, California, Lausanne Committee for World Evangelization, 1989.

15. *Manila Manifesto,* [note 14], page 8; compare also page 10: 'To those who repent and believe in Christ, God grants a share in the new creation'.

16. the same, page 13

17. the same, pages 10, 14

18. the same, page 16

19. the same, page 18. The MM has a large section on 'The Modern World' ending with the following statement inspired by Os Guinness' plenary speech at the congress, 'But we determine in the future to take these challenges and opportunities seriously, to resist the secular pressures of modernity, to relate the lordship of Christ to the whole of modern culture, and thus to engage in mission in the modern world without worldliness in modern mission' (pages 29–31). This consultation in Uppsala is one result of this 'determination'.

20. *Evangelism and Social Responsibility. An Evangelical Commitment* (A Report from the Consultation in Grand Rapids), Paternoster, 1982, pages 36–42

21. the same, pages 36–37

22. the same, page 29

23. the same, page 30

24. the same, pages 31–32. A reference to the signs of the kingdom set in the context of 'spiritual warfare' is also found in the Manila Manifesto, which balances the extremes with a statement like this, 'Although the miracles of Jesus were special, being signs of his Messiahship and anticipations of his perfect kingdom when all nature will be subject to him, we have no liberty to place limits on the power of the living Creator today. We reject both the skepticism which denies miracles and the presumption which demands them...' (MM [note 15], page 18). See also David F. Wells, *God the Evangelist. How the Holy Spirit Works to Bring Men and Women to Faith*, Eerdmans, 1987, pages 79–91.

25. Hans Schwarz, *On the Way to the Future. A Christian View of Eschatology in the Light of Current Trends in Religion, Philosophy and Science*, Augsburg, 1972, pages 11–26

26. the same, page 11

27. the same

28. Typically, in Norway there is an organization that calls itself program-matically 'The Future in Our Hands', fighting for a radically different economic and environmental policy.

29. Schwarz [note 25], page 14

30. The gap between the rich and the poor countries of the world after 200 years of 'evolution' and 'development', the population explosion, the Aids epidemic, the impending ecological disaster, unemployment, the nuclear threat (both in terms of proliferation of armaments and of pollution) and social unrest all give substance to pessimism.

31. For the importance of meaning and purpose to life, see especially the works of psychiatrist Viktor E. Frankl: 'The Will to Meaning', *Journal of Pastoral Care*, XII, 1958, pages 82–88; *Man's Search for Meaning, An Introduction to Logotherapy*, Beacon Press, 1962; *The Doctor and the Soul, from Psychotherapy to Logotherapy*, Knopf, 2nd edition 1965; *Psychotherapy and Existentialism: Selected Papers on Logotherapy*, Washington Square Press, 1967: *Logotherapy, Foundations and Applications*, New American Library, 1968.

32. This is one of the major fallacies of the ecumenical mission theology of the 1960s associated with J.C. Hoekendijk and the study program on 'The missionary structure of the congregation', where 'shalom' or 'humanization' became the goals of *Missio Dei*. This theology is a classical example of how the influence of modernity and its occupation with this worldly concerns led a large part of the churches and their theologians astray and caused them to lose their eschatological bearings. (See Klaus Bockmühl, *Was heisst heute Mission? Entscheidungsfragen det neueren Missionstheologie*, Giessen, Brunnen-Verlag, 1974; Peter Beyerhaus, *Mission in urchristlicher und endgeschichtlicher Zeit*, Giessen, Brunnen-Verlag, 1975; and Scherer [note 1], pages 107–125.) Unfortunately the same emphasis on 'one history' is found within much of the present liberation theology.

33. For example, see John Wimber, *Power Evangelism: signs and wonders today*, Hodder, 1985; and Wells [note 24], pages 87–91.

34. For example, Matthew 24; 2 Thessalonians 2; Revelation 13

35. 'All of us are shocked by the poverty of millions and disturbed by the injustices which cause it. Those of us who live in affluent circumstances accept our duty to develop a simple life-style to contribute more generously both to relief and evangelism', The Lausanne Covenant, pages 51–52, cp. 'An Evangelical Commitment to Simple Lifestyle', Lausanne Occasional Paper, No. 20, 1980. This particular statement in the Lausanne Covenant has prevented many evangelical Christians from signing the covenant, not because they disagree with it in theory, but because they are not willing to practise it.

9
Modernity and spirituality

JAMES M. HOUSTON

What we are seeing at the end of the twentieth century is the collapse of the mindset of the Enlightenment, with its assumptions and hopes. The new era of thought that is opening before us will affect every aspect of our lives. It is in this context that we have to re-examine our theological reflections.

Why is there such an interest in spirituality today? Christians, members of other faiths and secularists all recognize that the whole of life cannot be included in a materialistic or scientific interpretation. The protest against reductionism is widespread. The curious phenomenon is that, while some Christians are suspicious of spirituality, an increasing number of secular academics are protesting for its recognition while remaining unaware of the philosophical and theological implications behind this spiritual quest. What we as Christians need to recognize is that spirituality, as it deals with all of human life before God, should be understood as the application of Christian principles to everyday life. That is why I resist teaching spirituality as a departmental discipline; rather I see a need for all informed Christians to practice their faith in a integrated life.

The practice of Christian faith is Christian spirituality. It is the experience of the reality of God in all aspects of our lives, as we relate to the world authentically and with understanding. Christian praxis (the application of Christian principles to everyday life) looks inward to God as well as outward to the world. It cannot be reduced to 'me and my God' or even to 'me, God and a small circle of like-minded friends'. Such a spirituality would lack a proper social, historical and political context. Augustine has written: 'Let me know Thee, O God, let me know myself, that is all!' We might add 'let me experience Thy presence Lord, so that I may be a presence for Thee in this fallen world'. In the quest of spirituality we need to take our world seriously and diagnose the malaise that we call modernity.

There are three signs that suggest we are entering into a new era of history. First, the new confidence of science in assuming that 'we now know how to know'. In spite of this confidence, the canons of science cannot take mankind beyond certain frontiers; thus science is becoming increasingly metaphysical. Second, with the practical applications of science to technology the machine threatens 'the abolition of man'[1]. Thirdly, it was assumed that the Enlightenment would eliminate superstition and unexamined authority, especially in religion, making it possible, for the first time in history, to have proper rational judgments. But those three assumptions—the confidence of science, the application of science, and the victory of rationality—have been negated by the events of the twentieth century. This period has seen the genocide of over 167 million human beings by tyranny that has been ideologically and politically motivated. Modern culture has got exactly what it wanted, only to find it has become utterly menacing.

Langdon Gilkey[2] described this disillusionment of modernity. It has developed autonomy only to find itself sliding into narcissistic subjectivity. It wanted to subjugate and dominate nature for its own purposes but found those purposes ignoble or concupiscent and itself menaced. Praising rationality it tried to exclude all that could not be proved empirically, only to find cross-disciplinary speech impossible, and consideration of standards, aims, or purposes a heavy burden. It tried to rationalize social existence, only to find it had created problems for strong individuals and community alike. Modernity tried to eradicate the religious, only to find that demonic social ideologies dominated its historical scene. Rather than having created a rational society, new religious cults and the occult are replacing our tamed churches, and there has been an upsurge in religious fundamentalism that has hitched a ride on the technological culture. Science and rationality were confident that they could rule the world: they have lost the battle.

For two hundred years the Enlightenment has assumed that Western civilization was superior to others: now that assumption is being questioned. Today no European power is dominant. The United States alone has this western inheritance as a superpower but is being threatened by the economic potentials of countries on the Pacific rim. At the same time, the juxtaposition of religious faiths, East and West, is generating a global pluralism never

183

experienced before. The science, technology, and industrialism of the West have spread around the world, to be assimilated in new ways by the religions and cultures of different societies. Economic inequalities are now rapidly becoming equalized, while at the same time the secularized faiths of the West are assuming religious equality as the standard for all the world's religions. What is called religious truth is being eliminated by a phenomenological pluralism. Many liberal Christians are acknowledging salvation to be available to all faiths, since they believe that Christianity has been identified too closely with a culture in demise.[3] Yet the survival of Christianity through two millennia has been precisely because it has not been identified wholly with any given culture. Its transcendence of culture marks its true character, speaking within, yet also challenging each culture from without.

In the light of these challenges, we have to decide what we mean by 'modernity'. Are we referring to the developmental and institutional changes that have come from science and technology? Many may focus on these changes, seeking to study their effects on religious life.[4] Or do we mean by modernity the defects generated by the Enlightenment mind-set, so that we may more accurately speak of our times now as 'postmodern'? I believe it is the latter. As we seek to interpret the relevance and meaning of spirituality for the postmodern mind, we must first ask what that mind is, and secondly we must find a definition of spirituality.

What is the postmodern mind?

The postmodern intellectual climate is being shaped by a great diversity of cultural and intellectual cross currents.[5] These range from pragmatism, existentialism, psychoanalysis, and Marxism, to feminism, deconstructionism, and postempiricist philosophy of science. It is recognized that human knowledge is determined subjectively by many factors. What was previously accepted as objective is now regarded as ambiguous and unconvincing. Because it is assumed that there are no absolutes the quest for knowledge is seen as endless self-revising. Reality is no longer perceived as fixed but caught up in kaleidoscopic changes. Nor is the mind now viewed as the passive receptor of an external world with its own ordering but as being active in creating its own realities. So all human interpretation is perceived as merely interpretative and no interpretation is accepted as final.

The concept of paradigms, or mental models, first popularized by Kuhn in the 1960s, shows the mind's interpretative character[6] then T.F. Torrance introduced the concept into historical theology,[7] and it has been recently applied to missiology by David Bosch.[8] The paradigmatic approach has its own intrinsic historical value but a context-perspective encourages a relativism of approach and laxness of concern for truth *per se*. Western thought is becoming relativised within its own cultural heritage and this has led some people to assume that the world and God are not objects-in-themselves, but only part of a pre-interpreted context. Hence the nature of truth, as of reality, is becoming ambiguous. As Richard Tarnas has argued, 'one must now recognize the insuperable solipsism of human awareness against the radical illegibility of the world'.[9] Postmodern man now exists in a universe that is disoriented, free-floating and with no foundations.

The Cartesian frame of doubt has now reached its zenith for in a systematic scepticism everything must be uncertain. Truth is no longer a fixed point like the traveller's north star. The affirmations of Augustine and Anselm have been rejected, namely that understanding is grounded upon faith, not scepticism. This crisis of belief has been well expressed by T.S. Eliot: 'Men have left GOD not for other gods, they say, but for no god; this has never happened before'.[10] The loss of structures and limits has also removed the focus upon 'worldviews'. Properly speaking, there can be no postmodern worldview, for the only absolute left is the critical consciousness of the thinker—a consciousness that, by deconstructing all, is forced by its own logic to then deconstruct itself.

Pluralism, complexity, relativism, and ambiguity thus intensify the alienation and narcissism of postmodern humanity.[11] In postmodernism no perspective, whether religious, scientific, or philosophical, can have the upper hand. This indefinite open-endedness is generating a renewed interest in the syncretisms of earlier ages, the gnosticism or paganism of the classical world, the hermeticism or occultism of the Renaissance age, or Neolithic fertility cults with their goddesses. The lack of objective social and personal values are shown by psychedelic exploration, ecofeminist experimentation, and the individualist experimentation of new cults. In them, each one feels compelled to work out their own relationships with an alien world and an abstract society. There is a need for a more holistic approach to knowledge: one that will enable Christians to be revitalised by the depth of the postmodern challenge.

What is spirituality?

In the context of postmodern moral weightlessness we see a contemporary interest in forms of spirituality. There is a thoroughly postmodern distinction now being made between those who say they are not religious (because of the inconsistencies and offences they see in organised religion), and yet who say they are on a 'spiritual quest'. Something of the 'beyond' suits the postmodern discontentedness well. Spirituality is identified with the individual quest as well as with the questioning of institutionalism, so the contemporary breakdown of traditional values and communal life is compensated for by a renewal of 'spirituality'. If Christian spirituality is defined as the practice of the Christian life in the real world, a postmodern definition is: 'the ways individuals seek to renew spirit and soul in their lonely lives'.

Technocracy may be viewed as particularly anti-spiritual. When technical-mindedness takes over, the person at the machine is depersonalised and despiritualized. Political ideologies, whether marxism, socialism or capitalism, have also despiritualized the individual, so from both the ideological left and the ideological right we witness a strong outcry for 'human rights'. Professionalism and functionalism also reduce the fullness of personhood to something less than genuinely human, because of the dictates of the market, a Ph.D., or indeed any other socially recognized goals. When institutions fail to meet individual needs, whether churches, universities, financial organizations, or governments, we can expect postmodern spiritualities to flourish. So a second definition of such spirituality is: 'the inward quest of the individual, or the group, to find personal and spiritual rationality in the inward quest, in an impersonal environment'.

However, postmodernism is characterized by intense subjectivism. Expressing the 'divine' within one's self is merely a stage in the spiritual pride of egoism. The New Age movement expresses this self-preoccupation in the psychology of self-fulfilment. It has no sense of the boundaries of the sacred, no

186

reverence for the otherness of God, and therefore no Hebraic 'fear of the Lord'. New Age Spirituality uncritically accepts narcissism. Determined by loneliness and self-preoccupation, New Age spirituality may be defined as the acme of metaphysical selfishness.

HISTORICAL DEFINITIONS

'Ways of seeking to renew the soul in a lonely life', 'the inward quest in an impersonal environment', 'the acme of metaphysical selfishness': these three definitions of spirituality all express postmodernity. But how was spirituality defined in the past? The abstract latin noun *spiritualitas* was first used by Jerome in the fifth century, in a letter that urged its reader so to act by the indwelling Spirit of God as to advance in spirituality, and thus act as a spiritual person.[12] This follows the New Testament usage of being indwelt by the Holy Spirit to become spiritual, and not live according to the flesh (1 Corinthians 2:14–15). This biblical and early Fathers' definition of Christian spirituality might then be: 'living in Christ, so that by his indwelling Spirit all our experiences of life are motivated, interpreted, and lived by the Gospel, to enjoy a new being'.

This definition remained until after the twelfth century, when the rise of scholasticism led to a sharper distinction between spirit and matter. 'Flesh' was now an admixture of the Pauline usage, combined with the anti-material disdain of the body in the widespread practice of the ascetic life. From the thirteenth to the sixteenth the centuries a further definition developed: the juridical notion of spirituality as the clerical estate.[13] In keeping with this late medieval tradition, Pourrat's definition is: 'Spirituality is that part of theology which deals with Christian perfection and of the ways that lead to it.'[14]

By the seventeenth century there was a popular reaction in France to 'salon mysticism', quietism, and other non-ecclesial expressions of *La Spiritualité*. But though the influence of such Catholic writers as Archbishop Fenelon, Madame Guyon, and Miguel de Molinos were deliberately suppressed within their own church, their influence grew rapidly in certain Protestant circles, such as the Moravians, and Methodists. Their quest for piety and perfection took on new force. These terms replace 'Catholic spirituality', while within official Catholic circles the very word spirituality tended to disappear in the early eighteenth century. In Puritan life, the term 'godliness' was commonly used to express spiritual seriousness. All these movements would see spirituality then, as an oxymoron, which has only been imported into Protestant circles since Vatican II.[15]

The re-establishment of the religious orders in France, banished by the French Revolution, led to a new and somewhat artificial emphasis on 'traditions of spirituality' later in the century. These were used of the various religious orders. Louis Bouyer criticized this as the tendency to reduce the spiritual life to certain states of consciousness as if they were nothing more than mystical experiences.[16] This in turn has tended towards syncretism for by focusing upon the religious experience itself, it is easy to assume that common experiences of religious consciousness transcend all doctrinal distinctive in a universal *gnosis*. Such a psychological focus defines spirituality as 'the science of interpreting the extraordinary gifts of mystical prayer, reserved for the very few of the faithful'. At the same time the notion of 'spiritualities' as expressing the quintessence of various religious traditions, whether Benedictine or Cistercian, Anglican or Wesleyan has further degenerated into broader notions such as spiritualities of Black, Feminist, or native Indian communities. What they really express is more of a political expansion of consciousness of the marginalized in society.[17]

Since the late 1930s, the West has begun to recognize the distinctive spirituality of the Eastern Orthodox Church. This tradition has been neither influenced by the strong classical tradition of the West nor dominated by the West's Enlightenment rationalism. Because of that, the dualism of the western mind, apparent in the distinction between dogmatics and spiritual theology, or between theory and praxis, is unknown within Orthodox theology. It knows of no dichotomy between a theology that is understood and a mysticism or spirituality that is experienced and lived. The dictum of Evagrius Ponticus that 'theology is prayer and prayer is theology', rejects any separation between a rational understanding and a contemplative experience of the truth. Vladimir Lossky would define Orthodox spirituality as mystical theology, where 'spirituality and dogma, mysticism and theology, are inseparably linked in the life of the church... so no sharp distinction can be made between the realm of common faith and that of personal experience'.[18]

During the last twenty years or so, the goal of Christians in the West has been wholeness, rather than enlightenment. As Rowan Williams has expressed it: 'Spirituality becomes far more than a science of interpreting exceptional private experiences; it must now touch every area of human experience, the public and social, the painful, negative, even pathological byways of the mind, the moral and relational world'[19] It is thus the urge to shift Western theology from a merely descriptive series of deductions from revealed premises, towards more serious reflections upon Christian experience, whether personal or communal. This new thrust of Christian spirituality may be defined as: 'the dynamic experiencing of the Christian faith that is not exclusive to one particular tradition of the church yet is grounded upon doctrinal foundations. It is expressive of an intimate, living relationship with the triune God, that seeks not perfection but the maturity of and wholeness of life, as begraced by God. Its foundations, are those of mere Christianity. It is not limited to a concern for the interior life, but is integrative of all aspects of human life, its social relationships and obligations'.

Christian spirituality is thus concerned about the whole breadth and depth of human life. It must face all the pressures and insights that challenge the western mind-set in its transition from 'modern' to 'postmodern' and must face them in every area whether psychoanalysis, deconstruction, or postcritical philosophy. Moreover, it implies all that must be faced by the Christian in the quest of a deeper spiritual understanding and the experience of the Christian life. The question 'What is a Christian?' must haunt us incessantly, in the light of contemporary life. We must also discern the diverse cultural traditions that would bias perceptions of how the Christian life should be defined or what priorities should be given to its actions in the world. For example, American activism may give more emphasis to the politicalisation of faith, whereas the older European cultures may tend to be more privatized in their expressions of faith. While the expansion of personal consciousness tends to isolate us in depth, in spite of a common doctrinal framework, personal awareness and public conscience tends to pull Christians apart because of their diverse concerns. We can group all these issues under four major topics: Christian Spirituality and Modern Consciousness, History, Personhood and the Holy Spirit.

Christian spirituality and modern consciousness

Modern spirituality is associated with six major areas of human concern: mysticism, the paranormal, scepticism, depth psychology, ethics, and openness to other religions. These all contribute to the popular interest in spirituality. Spirituality is openness, the protest of the human spirit to self-enclosure and the tyranny of -isms that would box us in. The closed, rationalistic mind-set is a particularly modern feature that is being challenged. Contemporary globalisation is forcing us to be open to other cultures and religions while human consciousness is expanding by explaining new avenues of mind and spirit. But we may question both the inwardness of narcissism in self-love, as well as the wholehearted surrender to superstition. As G.K. Chesterton once commented, if you open your mouth, make sure you know what you are eating. The opening of the mind and spirit are even more serious if this leads to the poisoning of our souls.

DIRECT EXPERIENCE OF GOD

The Church has been ambivalent, if not divided, about mysticism because it has two basic features. Firstly, it claims the possibility of direct experience of God. Yet *mysterion* means a secret, so the mystic has often been viewed as a deviant from normality. Moreover, orthodoxy has often suspected that mysticism is associated with neo-platonism. Recent studies show that this is reacting too strongly against mysticism *per se*.[20]

Bernard McGinn has recently observed, 'a recognition of the interdependence of experience and interpretation can help avoid some of the false problems evident in scholarship on mysticism'. The issue is not, 'Was this person really a mystic because he or she claims to have had the kind of experience I define as mystical?' but, 'What is the significance of her or his writings, autobiographically mystical or not, in the history of Christian mysticism?'[21] Paranormal behaviour is one thing, but the sheer mystery of the timeless intersecting time implied in the mystery of the Incarnation is another. Moreover, the cultural changes that have influenced the interpretation of the mystical consciousness of God's presence is another realm for reflection. Though mysticism is part of every religion we must distinguish it from the mysticism of Christianity where there is direct experience of the presence of the Triune God.

There is a literary protest, led by such novelists as Saul Bellows and William Golding, that modern 'explanation' has been explaining itself to death and that the human spirit must have 'space for mystery' in life. The artist Marc Chagall has expressed it as follows:

> Mystic! How many times they have thrown this word at my face, just as formerly they scolded me for being 'literary'! But without mysticism would a single great painting, a single great poem, or even a single great social movement exist in the world? Does not every individual or social organism fade, does it not die, if deprived of the strength of mysticism? ... it is precisely the lack of mysticism that almost destroyed France.[22]

How much more should the Christian protest against the prejudiced mind that, desirous of its own rational control, ignores the reverential posture towards the mysteries of God. Experiencing him may defy conceptualization or verbalization, in part or in whole: its purpose is not information but transformation; not description, but helping others to share in similar experiences.

THE PARANORMAL

A second element of spirituality is the paranormal. The psychic dimension of man is more profound than positivism can claim to explain. Indeed, positivism is a species of impersonalism that refuses to accept the fullness of what it means to be human. Scientific investigation of the paranormal is not the same as a religious interest into the human condition that may manifest paranormality, for while the former looks at its phenomenal character, the latter looks at its experience. Christian spirituality would go beyond both the interests of the scientific and the psychical in a conscious commitment to personal transformation. Receptivity to deepening openness to the Spirit of God, and discerning what is of the Holy Spirit rather than what is of the human spirit implies self-surrender to the divine presence. A fearful fascination and involvement with the spirit world can make one more narcissistic or more evil. It is vital to seek a true doctrinal framework of faith within which to experience that genuinely spiritual content of consciousness which allows a genuinely spiritual mode of being.[23] We should share the concern of the medieval Christian to avoid the sin of spiritual curiosity.[24] The concern of curiosity is not the same as the concern to be more loving, though both may seek spiritual pathways.

SECULARISM AND SPIRITUALITY

The secular spirit is sceptical of the spiritual life. Positivism cannot recognize the spiritual, for the dogmatic rejection of any claim that cannot be tested by science, denies the validity of any mystical experience. Perspectivalism cannot see the spiritual either for it rejects any claim not based on a direct experience of reality. And according to impersonalism, truth can only be known impersonally so pure reason exists without reference to a knower.[25]

Sometimes one or other of these three positions has some legitimacy but they claim too much for themselves. Social science cannot rightly claim to possess all knowledge regarding the human condition. Spiritual experiences cannot all be hallucinatory and subjective. The spiritual dimension is not the only dimension of a human being, but it does exist and not only in the private domain. Spirituality is not merely a matter of inwardness, separated from the social and political outer world. Thus scepticism has reinforced the need to see the religious life as both personally and publicly spiritual.

Openness has always been characteristic of spirituality and mental health[26] but a new creative force for modern openness is psychoanalysis. We are beginning to discern the inner space that counselees are communicating, in contrast to those who resolutely reject self-understanding that has been given through others. They differ to the extent to which they will be open or closed and it is difficult for any of us to appraise how self-centred we all are, and therefore to appraise our openness.[27] Openness has often been judged negatively in terms of self-inflation, with its associated vices of selfishness and pride, rather than in terms of self-deflation with its sense of shame and defeatedness. Both pride and shame are self enclosing.[28] Donald Evans has pointed out the distinction between *open responsiveness* and two forms of *closedness: subjectivism and objectivism*. Subjectivism is a form of closedness in which the world becomes my experience of the world and in which I am preoccupied with my feelings about it. When I subjectivise other people, I control them. Objectivism means I view the world from a distance, and become detached from it. As a spectator, I dwell in my own world, safe from intrusion. So subjectivism and objectivism are both one-sided forms of self-inflation, of experience and feeling, and of intellect and will.

Creative psychotherapy should be seen more as an art than technical device, for the therapist must be *personally* effective in the exercise of relational skills such as empathy, insight, caring, presence, and assurance. There must be appreciative love. The therapist must also uncover the counselee's *creative* as well as *destructive* potentials. Moreover, the deeper we enter into the repressed layers of unconsciousness, the more destructive these tendencies appear to be, either of narcissism or of masochism. Judgment and intuition are thus required together with determination and commitment on the part of the therapist. Psychotherapy reveals how we transfer our passions not only to our relationships with others but also to our relationship with God. This is often manifest in our attitudes and experiences in prayer. Yet the essence of Christian spirituality is the surrender of our whole being to God; this is the expression of our love for him, and our experience of him. Unlike secular therapy which is self-analysis and self-cultivation, Christian spirituality is concerned with conversion as the gift of God's grace.

The spiritual openness of some people is seen in the serene demeanour and warmth of personality that they express, in their kindness and loveliness of spirit. They are God-centered, radiant people who love life. Such godliness comes when conversion is an ongoing process of transformation. Spirituality associated with mysticism, the paranormal, scepticism, and depth psychology is also concerned with ethics because experiencing God means becoming involved in a process of transformation. This is why Bernard Lonergan describes himself not as a theologian, but as a theological therapist. By this he means that spiritual theology has to enter through the mind into the heart, in a therapy of interiority.[30] Out of the theory of spirituality there must come praxis, the practical outworking of spirituality. It is the experience of the grace of Christ, given by God through his Holy Spirit. Spiritual growth is the result of an ever deeper and closer walk with God, made possible only by the indwelling presence of the Holy Spirit.[31]

For some, the mystical life of Christian spirituality has seemed too idealistic; this was the view of Ernst Troeltsch who saw the romanticism of Schleiermacher as the end product of this spiritual idealism.[32]

But the dualistic opposition between flesh and spirit, so long held by the medieval mystics, disappears with Schleiermacher, and what disappears also is the asceticism which marked earlier spiritual traditions. The personalness of faith also disappears and with it the historicity of Christianity. To be true to the life of the Church, we need to relate spirituality to its historical foundations.

It is in its syncretistic tendencies, which contradict the particular and specific, that religious pluralism negates the historicity of the Christian faith. In the older textbooks on the history of spirituality (such as in Pourrat's volumes, written shortly after the First World War), theological presuppositions assume a basic uniformity overarched by the superiority of the monastic life as 'the more perfect expression' of spirituality. Consequently, Pourrat pays little notice to lay movements.[33] In Louis Bouyer's history of spirituality, written in the 1960s, he criticizes Pourrat for focusing upon a more mystical theology. Nevertheless he too stresses the essential oneness of Christian spirituality.[34] But the new World Spirituality project of twenty five volumes, which was begun in 1985, has an overtly pluralistic objective even though its general editor Ewert Cousins is a Roman Catholic. The objective is now to promote an emerging discipline, that of 'global spirituality'. While there is factual and specialist material given in each volume for each religion, the assumption is now that it is the *phenomenon* of spirituality that is being studied, rather than a spirituality that has arisen from a particular religious confession. Spirituality is no longer reserved for the uniqueness of the Christian faith but seen as a science in its own right. It is a 'gnostic science' now falling within the orbit of comparative religion, and no longer within the discipline of Christian spiritual theology. We see the modern liberal spirit replacing cultural anthropology with spiritual anthropology. This syncretistic intent is clearly stated by the general editor Ewert Cousins: 'by drawing the material into the focus of world spirituality, it can provide a perspective for understanding one's place in the larger process. For it may well be that the meeting of spiritual paths—the assimilation not only of one's own spiritual heritage but of that of the human community as a whole—is the distinctive spiritual journey of our time'.[34]

Christian spirituality and history

I believe that the current interest in spirituality expresses the crisis of Western society. There is an increasing awareness of the reductionism implicit in modernity, without the recognition that the gnostic spirit is creating a worse situation by its refusal to acknowledge the Otherness of God. For man cannot fill his own 'God-shaped' vacuum by himself. Only God can do that. The spiritual wasteland challenges us to be aware of the forces that have brought us to our present dilemma. Part of our dilemma is the indifference of the modern spirit to the study of the past: that is why a historical approach to spirituality is essential.

In his book *After Ideology*, David Walsh points out that all the great historians of our time, such as Arnold Toynbee, Christopher Dawson, Alexander Solzhenitsyn, and Eric Voegelin, have turned to history in order to diagnose the causes of the horrendous events of the twentieth century. When Solzhenitsyn began his analysis of the gulag and the Russian revolution in 1917, he found he had to go back to the ambiguities of the Renaissance. There he found the ideas that have so powerfully influenced the ideologies of our times: the 'autonomy of man from any force higher than his own'; the 'lack of any intrinsic evil in man'; and the refusal to admit 'any higher task than the attainment of happiness on earth.'[36] Solzhenitsyn sums it up in his acceptance speech for the Templeton prize: 'Men have forgotten God'.[36] Likewise Voegelin identifies modern consciousness with Gnosticism as he looks back, not only to the Greek world but to the revolt of man against God which he discerned in the ancient Near East.[38] Albert Camus identified the communist ideology as a Christian heresy born of Christian origins, for as Gnosticism divinized human nature, so Communism has exalted a secular saviour with a secular eschatology. Today, partial reforms have been introduced in Russia and elsewhere, but the key issue is the degree to which the principle of ideology has been abandoned in the Western or pseudo-Christian, secularized world.[39]

The great need of modernity is the quest for order in society but it will not be resolved by reciting maxims and rational arguments. Order can only come through personal participation in the righteousness of God. This has been made possible by the historic reality of the incarnation when God entered into history to participate in the life of man. The emergence of order, truth and love radiate from that historic event. The divine presence of Christ, as the sole mediator between man and God, is what Christian spirituality is all about. Modern man's aberrations and distortions of the western heritage of Christian faith can only be put right by repentance and conversion towards the God against whom we have rebelled. Any understanding of this remains shallow, however, without a recognition of the deep connections between spirituality and history. It is in this that evangelicals remain shallow, for their perspective is scarcely two centuries old.

There are two errors to avoid: that of the historists and that of the theologists. The historicist takes the past seriously unlike the modernist yet canonises the pastness of the past, isolating it from the present. He does not understand that Christian spirituality is dynamic, with the communion of saints an ongoing vitality that is made possible by the Spirit of God throughout past, present and future. The historicists ignore the grace of God, seeing the mystics frozen within their own medieval past and having no relevance for Christians today. The second error is to subsume the history of spirituality into a theology is neither spiritual or historical. It was the concern of Bernard Lonergan when he insisted that spirituality is a more adequate foundation for theology than doctrine. By this he meant that the foundation of theology is the converted person's experience of faith. Of course theological reflection extends beyond one's own converted existence, but experience is the key to theological sensibility.[40]

The recording of one's personal experience is a necessary aspect of the history of spirituality. But who is permitted to have a history? If on the scales of God only hearts have weight, spiritual historiography differs significantly from secular histories because it has very different priorities and values. Like the biblical *anawim* 'the poor in spirit', the saints of God are usually marginalised by secular society and their influence in being the salt of the earth is not acknowledged. On the other hand hagiography has also presented a distortion of the saints' influences within society. As Phyllis McGinley observes, the saints 'lost their tempers, got hungry, scolded God, were egotistical or testy or impatient, made mistakes and regretted them. Still they went doggedly blundering their way to heaven. And they won sanctity partly by willing to be saints, not because they encountered no temptation to be less'.[41] Perhaps religious leaders should be criticised on their politics of hagiography more than the saints themselves.[42]

The existence of saintly people is a much more important fact than is commonly recognised. They demonstrate the reality of spirituality and it is crucial for the witness of Christianity that each generation should have such exemplars of faith. Abbe Huvelin calls them 'living images painted by Christ himself for his Church that He might recall of her own features to her mind and console her in her widowhood.'[43] It is a tragedy that this need for living images of Christ has been mixed and adulterated by ecclesial politics. Because of this we should ask who creates or controls spirituality within the life of the Christian community. Is it the religious orders, or the clergy, or the majority over the minority? Models of sanctity have differed in various spiritual traditions, a fact that has tempted contemporary believers not to take seriously any of the historical models—nor indeed the possibility of true sanctity.[44] Charles Peguy said, 'the only tragedy is that we are not all saints'.

Calumny has also given a bad name to movements that were deemed to be threatening to the ecclesial *status quo*. It is now apparent that the medieval women's movement, the Beguines, was not as inherently unorthodox as it was officially claimed to be.[45] The same may be true of the *illumbrados* in fifteenth century Spain and the quietism associated with Molinos in seventeenth-century France. The history of spirituality challenges secular history, discerning its processes with accuracy and wisdom. Social dissent, political oppression and the voices of conscience, as well as the movements of spirituality themselves, all need to be recognized, heard, and judged within the history of the past; only by that will we be better able to diagnose our own times.

All specialist histories require two competences: a historical sense, and a technical skill. But in the history of spirituality, other than what comes from the Roman Catholic magisterium, the bias of what is assumed to be spiritual theology often lacks a critical theological criteria. It is more often pietistically providential, rather than critically aware of the dangers of teleology.[46] What distinctions should we make between the manifestation of the human spirit and the manifestation of the Holy Spirit? In pentecostalism and in the charismatic movement we may find it hard to draw distinctions. As for the written record, some Christians will see a spiritual tradition popularised by a current classic of devotion to be of permanent importance, while others see it primarily within its own historical and cultural context. For example, are the Exercises of Ignatian spirituality of permanent significance to the church, as the Jesuit Karl Rahner has asserted,[47] and is the expression of Puritan godliness of like centrality for evangelicals? There is a temptation to use the history of spirituality as an apologia for the traditional norms and attitudes of our own part of the church. In doing so, we may forget that the radicalism of the original movement of spirituality was that it challenged and reformed the abuses of its own times.

Christian spirituality and personhood

The loss of faith in transcendence has led to the modern despair of having any integrated outlook or any consistent worldview. Contemporary studies on the history of spirituality often assume that broad historical surveys are no longer possible by one scholar. This is the editorial view of the series on World Spirituality, already referred to.[48] The death of metaphysics, with its loss of human moral unanimity and the current nihilism, deeply divide the self from the external world. The postmodernist philosopher Huston Smith has defined the postmodern mind as 'one which, having lost the conviction that reality is personal, has come to question whether it is ordered in a way that man's reason can lay bare'.[49] The fifteen volume *Encyclopedia of the Social Sciences* has no article on the person. A recent philosophical study seriously suggested the abolition of the 'person' to be replaced merely by the 'individual'. Yet the heart of Christian spirituality is personal experience of God in prayer and communion with divine personeity. This is where Christians are being most challenged to renew their theological perspective in the pursuit of personal faith.

At the end of the nineteenth century, R.J. Illingworth saw personality as 'our canon of reality, the most real thing we know, and by comparison with which we estimate the amount of reality in other things'.[50] Three examples from the Gifford Lecture in our century demonstrate the shift of thinking that followed that definition. In 1907, A. Seth Pringle-Pattison said: 'The essential feature of the Christian conception of the world in contrast to the Hellenic may be said to be that it regards the person and the relations of persons to one another as the essence of reality, whereas Greek thought conceived of personality however spiritual, as a restrictive characteristic of the finite, a transitory product of a life which as a whole is impersonal'.[51] Clement C. J. Webb (1919) claimed that the words 'person' and 'personality' were really theological terms, used primarily of the triune character of God.[51] In 1953 John MacMurray related the decline of Christian influence in society to the trend towards depersonalization. 'Such a decline betrays and in turn intensifies a growing insensitiveness to the personal aspects of life and a growing indifference to personal values. Christianity in particular is the exponent and guardian of the personal...'[53] He saw that philosophy had failed to deal with the whole of human experience for the fundamental error of critical philosophy was the primacy it gave to the self as an isolated thinker or ego, that is the Cartesian error. He would reverse the priority of thought over action, placing primacy in the self as agent, relationships being viewed as actions with others.[54] However, he failed to lift religion above a humanistic communal enterprise because he was unaware that the ontology is grounded.

This is where our understanding of the Trinity needs to be revitalized in our Christian faith to-day. For too many Christians it has become unitarian. In *Being as Communion*, John Zizioulas reaffirms the Cappadocian Fathers teaching, that 'the being of God is relational being... that "God", has no ontological content, no true being, apart from communion'.[55] Mankind has been made in the image and likeness of God; because of that central fact our humanity can have neither true existence nor true relationships without communion with him. For that reason we have been given the double command, to love God and to love our neighbour. Another Orthodox theologian, Kallistos Ware, maintains that it is by meditation, rather than by subordination, that we are called to 'unify ourselves and the world around us', holding the spiritual and the material 'as an undivided whole'.[56] This is the essence of current environmental issues in which the interpenetration of the material and the spiritual is seen as a global issue for humanity in the wellbeing of the planet.

T.F. Torrance also advocates the central importance of the doctrine of the Trinity today for our acceptance of personhood:

'It is only through a divine Trinity who admits us to
communion with himself in his own transcendence
that we can be consistently and persistently personal,

with the kind of freedom, openness, and transcendent reference which we need both to develop our own personal and social culture and our scientific exploration of the universe. I believe that it is in a radical renewing of our personal and inter-personal structures that comes from communion with God, that we are to look for a healing of the deep splits which have opened up in our modern civilisation. But this means that what we need is the recovery of *spiritual being, which is open to personal reality and not imprisoned in its own self-centredness.*[57]

The essence of the gnostic heresy that pervades secular thought today is to ground ontology upon the world as it is, and on the human condition in its fallen state. This is the ancient Greeks' view of the person and led to their tragic protest of the human spirit pitted against the cosmic impersonal. The true observation of the person is still not possible today from the humanistic perspective, for only openness to the Spirit of God, as embodied in Jesus Christ, can manifest and sustain the person.[58] Christian spirituality today is the protest against frames of mind which are either free-floating in human *hubris* or self-enclosed in ultimate doubt. Openness to personhood is a theological, rather than an anthropological reality. We must seek an eschatological orientation as people in the process of becoming persons-in-the-Triune-God. Colin Gunton has written, 'The triune God has created humankind as finite persons-in-relation who are called to acknowledge his creation by becoming the persons they are and by enabling the rest of creation to make its due response of praise'.[59]

The call of Christ can redeem us from being merely isolated individuals. Significantly it is Christ who calls, for as he is humanity-and-divinity, we can find in his person God's redemptive call to us. Individual identity is thus redeemed by our response to Christ by his Spirit. The call creates new possibilities, inviting the transformation of the lonely 'I' into a glorious 'we'. Personal obedience to God in Christ is the path to be followed. Self-renunciation is essential, for 'whoever will love his own life shall lose it', but conformity to Christ turns out to be true individuation, a freedom from the imprisoned ego. Ecclesial community expresses this inspired response to discipleship for the Church is where Christian persons are relating to one another, united in their worship of God. This definition highlights the *intrinsically personal* character of Christian spirituality.

A new interest is being shown in personal story-telling and in the role played by exemplary morality. In place of abstract morality, there is a fresh focus upon the personal influence exerted by individuals within society. In a series of books entitled 'Constructive Postmodern Thought', Robert Inchausti observes:

> As we move into the last decade of the twentieth century, it is becoming increasingly evident that the most progressive and lasting political innovations in this century have not come from the expected sources: violent revolutionaries or avant-garde social theorists. Rather they have come from the practical achievements of moralists and religious reformers, simple and straightforward people...These reformers base their movements upon such pre-industrial values as personal integrity and transcendental obligation.[60]

The author may not understand the theological issues but is at least searching for spiritual values that may enhance our humanness.

Survival at the dead end of modernism is sought either in deification for its own sake or else in community.[61] But 'community' is a clichéd advocacy that has no substance without the ontology outlined above. This Scott Peck betrays when he insists: 'my basic identity was (and still is) that of a scientist before that of a religious person'.[62] Speaking of being a scientist in relational life is a form of angelism. Nor can we afford to sink into mental obscurantism which is what emotionalism is. Christian spirituality cannot afford to be either.

Conclusion: spirituality and the Holy Spirit

The crisis of modernity is a challenge for us to broaden and deepen our perspective, in protest against the reductionism in so much contemporary life and thought. It challenges us to awaken the recovery of the historic reality of faith, as well as our sense of the loss of the reality of personal relationships. It refuses to generalise when the particular has to be preserved, and yet rejects the selfism that inhibits and prevents us from openness to the grace of God. Modernity can make us aware that personal experience can never be substituted by mere description and can make us more open to being more transformed in holiness of life.

Spirituality is not so much a mental discipline as a confessional journey of the heart before God. It is as broad as the search for a genuine humanness and deeper than any challenge given by psycho-analysis. It is a spiritual pursuit that stands in judgment of what our society calls normal life. Augustine's *Confessions* are a worthy example of what spirituality is all about. On the one hand, it lays bare the soul before God, as a confession of sin. On the other hand, it is 'a confession of faith, of faith in the God who created, who judges and who forgives'.[63] Above all, spirituality is the place we give to the operation of the Holy Spirit—though we frequently confuse him with our own spirit.

Hans Urs von Balthasar noted that in the early centuries of the Church the roles of teacher and pastor were usually conjoined and that many of the early Fathers reproduced in their own lives what they also taught. 'What they taught they lived with such directness... that the subsequent separation of theology and spirituality was quite unknown to them.' But 'as time went on, theology at prayer was superseded by theology at the desk, and this brought about the cleavage now under discussion. "Scientific" theology became more and more divorced from prayer, and so lost the accent and tone with which one could speak of what was holy.'[64] Von Balthasar insists that spirituality should never be a separate field of study but rather 'the subjective aspect of dogmatic theology...what makes the objective teaching of the church come alive in the individual'.[65] Wittgenstein has argued that 'to imagine a language means to imagine a form life', and speaks of the tendency of much philosophical language to get cut off from the circumstance which gives meaning to our language.[66] How much more then should theology be conjoined with spirituality.

The academic return to spirituality may be not unlike the charismatic movement in the last decades. Whatever significance glossolalia has had on individuals, at least it was associated with an experience of breaking down and opening up. One is opened up to a new experience of God's indwelling Spirit leading to a new reliance upon God rather than upon one's self. Perhaps spirituality in the academy may have a similar result.[67] If so, spiritual theology will challenge conventional epistemology in theology. As Kierkegaard said, 'only the truth that edifies, is the truth for you'. To open up the possibility of teaching and exemplifying trinitarian spirituality is the Christian quest. Though the quest may be too exacting or unacceptable for some nominal believers, it may lead to the further breakdown of folk religion, or indeed of institutionalised Christianity. Karl Rahner has therefore predicted: 'the devout Christian of the future will either be "mystic", one who has experienced something, or he will cease to be anything at all'.

What we can say about 'spirit' is however what is most elusive and mysterious about our nature. It is that extra dimension that makes us more than physical beings. It is a capacity of being able to go outside and beyond ourselves. We are not closed but open beings. Most importantly, we are able to receive renewal of spirit by receiving the Spirit of God within us, to move our from a self-centred mode of being, into a new openness.[68] Spirituality is in simple terms the process of becoming persons in the fullest sense for 'what is born of the Spirit is spirit'. Yet Christian spirituality is broader than the spiritualization of the individual. The Church is the community of the Spirit, the corporate spiritual entity that God has called us to be, in order to go out from itself.

However, it is not from our notions of what is spirit or spiritual that we can arrive at who the Holy Spirit is. As T.F. Torrance said: 'through the ineffability of his own personal mode of being then, the Holy Spirit confronts us with the sheer ineffability of God, for in him we are in immediate touch with the ultimate being.'[69] His Spirit is capable of being most intimate with us, yet in his holiness he is ineffably the Holy Spirit. He is distinctly and uniquely personal, yet inseparable from the Father and the Son. He dwells within us, yet he does not eliminate our distinct and unique identity. He enables us to call God, 'Abba' in the intimacy of a new and mediated relationship in the Son, yet he also enables us to call Jesus, 'Lord'. The Holy Spirit comes to us in power, yet he comes gently. Our knowledge of the Spirit comes from the knowledge of the Son so that the New Testament writers frequently speak of the Spirit that indwelt Christ. Coming from the communion of the Father and the Son, the fellowship of the Holy Spirit is what unites us with the Father and the Son. Thus Christian spirituality can never be disassociated from the triune God for it takes its character from the mystery of the Trinity.

Our spiritual life is not only for this short span of earthly existence but will continue in a life beyond death. Christian personhood is never fully defined: it opens us to the eternal future. Eternal life participates in the relational life of God as an infinite future, as well as in the present possession of the believer. Neither a spiritual life that is already full achievable in the here and now, nor a spiritual life to be begun and lived solely in the beyond, could satisfy these requirements. Humanity's deepest longings are for eternal life begun here on earth as touched by the prevenient Spirit of God and yet fully experienced only in eternity. The New Testament uses metaphors to describe this prospective life: 'the first-fruits' and the 'earnest of our inheritance'. As Jesus was raised by the Spirit from the dead, so likewise we shall be raised. It is the claim of the indwelling Spirit that our lives can bear the fruits of love, joy, peace and other evidences of moral transformation of character. Spiritual experience bears witness to the reality that in ordinary life we can transcend its ordinariness, what Christopher Nash describes as 'Easter in Ordinary'. This is both a present reality, and also what participates in 'the life of the age to come'. For the apostle Paul, what is spiritual, *pneumatikos*, denotes a quality of relational life that only God can give. Therefore we pray: Come, Holy Spirit come..Integrate our theology and our spirituality as one, in heart and mind before Thee Amen.

Notes

1. C. S. Lewis, *The Abolition of Man*, Collins, 1949

2. Langdon Gilkey, *Society and the Sacred*, Crossroad, 1981

3. the same, pages 157–170

4. James Davison Hunter, *American Evangelicalism*, Rutgers University Press, 1983, pages 4–7

5. See David Harvey, *The Condition of Postmodernity*, Blackwell, 1989

6. Thomas S. Kuhn, *The Structure of Scientific Revolutions*, University of Chicago Press, 1964

7. T.F. Torrance, *Reality and Scientific Theology*, Scottish Academic Press, 1985

8. David Bosch, *Transforming Mission, Paradigm Shifts in the Theology of Mission*, Orbis Books, 1991

9. Richard Tarnes, *The Passion of the Western Mind*, Harvey Books, 1991

10. Quoted by Michael Harrington, *The Accidental Century*, Penguin, 1967, page 173

11. Tarnes [note 9], page 398

12. Philip Sheldrake, *Spirituality and History*, Crossroad, 1991

13. Gordon S. Wakefield, editor, *A Dictionary of Christian Spirituality*, SCM Press, 1983, pages 261–3

14 P. Pourrat, *Christian Spirituality*, Burnes, Oates, and Washbourne, London, 1922, vol. 1, page v

15. T. Hartley Hall, 'The Shape of Reformed Piety', in Robin Maas and Gabriel O'Donnelt, editors, *Spiritual Traditions for the Contemporary Church*, Abingdon Press, 1990, page 202

16. Louis Bouyer, *Introduction to Spirituality*, Liturgical Press, 1961, pages 17–18

17. For example see Procter-Smith, 'Feminism and Spirituality', in Maas and O'Donnelt [note 15], pages 430–443

18. Vladimir Lossky, *The Mystical Theology of the Eastern Church*, James Clarke, 1973 pages 13–14

19. Rowan Williams, *The Wound of Knowledge*, Darton, Longman & Todd, 1979, page 2

20. James M. Houston, 'Reflections on Mysticism. How Valid is Evangelical Anti-Mysticism?' in Markus Bockmuehl and Helmut Burkhardt, editors, *Loving God and Keeping His Commandments*, Brunnen Verlag Giessen, Basel, 1991, pages 163–181

21. Bernard McGinn, *The Foundations of Mysticism*, Crossroad, 1991, vol.1, pages xiv-xv

22. Marc Chagall, *Chagall by Chagall*, edited by Charles Sorlier, translator John Shepley, Harry N. Abrams, 1979, page 12

23. Donald Evans, *Spirituality and Human Nature*, State University of New York Press, 1993, page 147

24. *Curiositas*, was a serious vice in the Middle Ages, inimicable to the contemplative life. Few studies on medieval thought recognise the repugnance with which curiosity was held in medieval society.

25. Evans [note 23], page 101

26. See Heinz Kohut, *The Analysis of the Self*, International Universities Press, 1971

27. Evans [note 23], page 42

28. Gerald May, *Will and Spirit*, Harper, 1982

29. Evans [note 23], pages 42–43

30. Vernon Gregson, *Lonergan, Spirituality and the meeting of Religions*, University Press of America, 1985, pages 10–15

31. David G. Benner, *Psychotherapy and the Spiritual Quest*, Baker Books, 1988, page 34

32. Ernst Troeltsch, *The Social Teaching of the Christian Churches*, translator Olive Wyon, University of Chicago Press, 1981, vol. 2, pages 791–95

33. P. Pourrat [note 14]

34. Louis Bouyer [note 16]

35. Ewert Cousins, 'World Spirituality', in Bernard McGinn and John Meyendorff, editors, *An Encyclopedic History of the Religious Quest*, volume 16, 'Christian Spirituality', Crossroad, 1985, page xiv

36. David Walsh, *After Ideology*, Harper, 1990, page 90

37. Alexander Solzhenitsyn, 'Men have forgotten God', translator A. Klimoff, *National Review*, 22 July 1983, pages 872–876

38. Eric Voegelin, *Order and History*, Louisiana State University Press, 5 volumes. For a good summary of his thought see Eugene Webb, *Eric Voegelin: Philosopher of History*, University of Washington Press, 1981

39. Walsh [note 36], pages 51–54

40. Gregson [note 30], pages 16–21

41. Phyllis McGinley, *Saint-Watching*, Viking Press, 1961, page 6

42. Lawrence Cunningham, *The Meaning of Saints*, Harper, 1980

43. Quoted by Patrick Sherry, *Spirit, Saints and Immortality*, State University of New York Press, 1984, page 84

44. See Peter Brown, *The Cult of the Saints*, SCM Press, 1981

45. Sheldrake [note 12], pages 133–159

46. the same, pages 83-102

47. Karl Rahner, *The Dynamic Element in the Church*, E.T., 1964, pages 85–7

48. Cousins [note 35]

49. Huston Smith, *Beyond the Post-Modern Mind*, Crossroad, 1982, page 7

50. R.J. Illingworth, *Personality, Divine and Human*, Macmillan, 1894, page 43

51. A. Seth Pringle-Pattinson, *The Idea of God*, Oxford University Press, 1907, page 238

52. C. C. J. Webb, *God and Personality*, London University Press, 1919, pages 61ff

53. John MacMurray, *The Self as Agent*, Faber, 1957, page 30

54. John MacMurray, *Persons in Relation*, Faber, 1961, page 28

55. John D. Zizoulas, *Being as Communion*, St. Vladimir's Seminary Press, 1985, page 1

56. Kallistos Ware, 'The unity of the Human Person according to the Greek Fathers', in A. Peacocke and G. Gillet, editors, *Persons and Personality*, Oxford University Press, 1987, page 102

57. T.F. Torrance, 'On being a Person. Towards an Ontology of Personhood', in Christoph Schwobel and Colin E. Gunton, editors, *Persons, Human and Divine*, T. & T. Clark, 1991, pages 33–46

58. T.F. Torrance, 'Human Capacity and Human Incapacity, a theological exploration of Personhood', *Scottish Journal of Theology*, 28, 1975, pages 401–448

59. Colin Gunton, 'Trinity, Ontology, and Anthropology', in Gunton and Schobel [note 57], page 61

60. Robert Inchausti, *The Ignorant Perfection of Ordinary People*, State University of New York, 1991, page 1

61. Christopher Lasch, *The Culture of Narcissism*, Norton, 1978; and *The Minimal Self*, Norton, 1984

62. M. Scott Peck, *A World Waiting to be Born*, Bantam, 1993, page 347

63. Jaroslav Pelikan, 'Writing as a Means of Grace', in William Zinsser, editor, *Spiritual Quests*, Houghton Mifflin, 1989, page 91

64. Hans Urs von Balthasar, *Word and Redemption*, Ignatius Press, 1965, page 51

65. the same, pages 87–88

66. Quoted by Sherry [note 43], page 7

67. William M. Thompson, *Christology and Spirituality*, Crossroad, 1990, page 9

68. John Macquarrie, *Paths of Spirituality*, SCM Press, 1972, pages 44–47

69. T.F. Torrance, *The Trinitarian Faith*, T. & T. Clark, 1988, page 205

10

New Age—a synthesis of the premodern, modern and postmodern

LARS JOHANSSON

It is four o'clock on an ordinary afternoon in Stockholm. People are already queuing for a meeting that will take place at seven o'clock. Messages from a spirit entity called Ambres, who is claimed to have lived in Egypt three thousand years ago, are due to be transmitted via Sture Johansson, a channeller who became world famous through the Shirley MacLaine movie *Out on a Limb*. As the session starts, several public figures strive to find a place to stand in the crowded room. All this is happening in what is perceived to be one of the most secularized and modern countries in the world. How are we to interpret this fascination with messages from an old Egyptian? I believe it has something to do with the dynamics of modernity and post-modernity.

In spite of repeated claims during previous decades that they are dead, the spiritual and 'God' have lately made a strong comeback. In sociological theory, the triumph of the secular has been taken as a practically unshakable dogma and the disappearance of religion as being more or less irreversible. But the concept of secularization itself has proved to be very slippery and has therefore created a lot of debate.[1] One phenomenon which questions the thesis of a secular society is the growth of numerous new religious movements during the last decades.

Many theories have been presented which have tried to explain this upsurge of new religions. Most are related to what has been labelled a crisis in modernity.[2] Some argue though, that the return of religious interest in the West must not be seen in terms of a failure of the ideals of modernity but rather is a reconstitution of modernity within itself.[3] In spite of such considerations, many of the formative ideals of 'the modern project' (Habermas) have lost their compelling power. Conditions of life in contemporary Western societies are also such that the metaphor of homelessness becomes useful both in the physical and spiritual sense. Today, the word 'crisis' is frequently used to describe the situation in most sectors of society. In my presentation I will give examples of elements within modernity which contribute to the growth of new religions and the New Age (NA).

Most sociologists concentrate their studies of new religions on the organized New Religious Movements (NRM). This fails to recognize wider phenomena such as the NA. Studies have also shown that NRMs in general are very small and do not attract people the way they used to. Beckford rightly suggest that we use the term 'movement' in a double sense, also being aware of the broad shifts of people's religious ideas outside the organized movements, in society at large.[4] By focusing on these general movements we reach a better understanding of the plausibility of the NA.

Several studies in Sweden have shown that more people than expected have some sort of belief in God which most often is not the Christian one and that they also pray to this higher power. In a wider European perspective there are ample indications that a Christian worldview has been replaced by a general belief in the transcendent.[5] One can argue that there has been a major shift in Western society, not so much from belief to unbelief as from belief to seeking. A move away from any commitment to doctrine and dogma, and towards a high valuation of individual intellectual growth and the pursuit for truth, is coupled with a readiness to believe in almost any alternative and occult teaching.[6] Commenting on changes in the American spiritual climate, Anthony and Robbins say that many are becoming 'seekers of self-fullfilment' with a 'mystical orientation' that makes them attracted to monistic systems.[7] They find this trend to be one of the most influential in the contemporary climate of moral ambiguity.

In Sweden are many signs of similar developments. A vague and rather open spirituality with an individualistic profile is becoming more popular. Basic ideas from Eastern thought and the Western esoteric tradition are gaining in acceptance. These combine with elements of folk religion and beliefs of a neopagan character, a concept often used by those who try to summarize what is going on in New Age. So what is its background?

The New Age in context

The NA phenomenon can be traced back to the late 1960s and early 1970s. During the countercultural 1960s, a time which Wuthnow calls 'the decade of religious turbulence', many young Americans turned for inspiration to the varied traditions of the East and to Western occultism. The NA emerged out of this search for alternative spirituality. Melton sees in this period a very special combination of circumstances. Religious hunger has been experienced periodically in Western history, but now, for the first time in many centuries, it has coincided with other factors such as the presence of a number of Eastern religious teachers and a new wave. 'The New Age Movement was and is the attempt to find the social, religious, political, and cultural convergence between the new Eastern and mystical religions and the religious disenchantment of many Westerners'.[8]

The NA vision is of a radical mystical transformation on an individual level that is believed will have tremendous consequences for society and the world. The spiritual evolution of humanity will bring in a New Age. In order to achieve this transformation you can freely use almost any tool or technique from the many different spiritual traditions of the world, including Western therapeutical novelties. The impact of these ideas have been remarkable in the West.[9] In Eastern Europe there is a massive input of different cults and sects[10] as well as a fascination with the NA.

Trying to understand the relationship between the NA and modernity/postmodernity I employ both philosophical and sociological aspects since the NA is a reaction against certain Western ideas as well social conditions. From a sociological perspective Peter Berger argues that it is a mistake to deduce modern consciousness as well as reactions against it (de-modernizing consciousness) from scientific and intellectual theories.[11] The themes he is dealing with are rooted in pre-theoretical consciousness, being expressions of an underlying social-psychological reality. Theories, he claims, are later legitimations of particular circumstances.

The difficulties in making clearcut distinctions between ideological and social factors are seen in the many attempts to define modernity and postmodernity. Berman says that between modernization and modernism there is 'modernity', a concept that unites the two others and denotes everything that happens at the cultural level, such as the spirit of the age, and the socio-psychological experience of many. He describes modernity as a mode of vital experience of possibilities and perils, a maelstrom of perpetual disintegration and renewal.[12] This experience, as it is deepened through structural changes and the media, creates what can be called a postmodern cultural condition. There are reasons to regard what has been called postmodernity as a phase of modernity itself.[13]

Defining the origins of modernity one can include four modern revolutions: the scientific, political, cultural and technical,[14] including not only the structural aspects but also theoretical discourse. The same goes for postmodernism which at one and the same time deals with philosophy, aesthetics, the condition of society and the spirit of the age.[15]

In this paper, I will describe some ideological and structural aspects of the modern and of the postmodern with regard to the NA. The NA vision seeks to go beyond modernity by making use of the premodern and the modern, thereby entering into a new phase that could be called postmodern. There are points of contact between the NA and the postmodern, but also points of disagreement. The NA protest against modernity strongly reflects the dynamic and ideals of modernity. This bewildering spirituality looks to me like a combination of premodern, modern and postmodern themes. Its highly individualist mix of ancient as well as modern motives and methods is a postmodern trait. The postmodern character of the NA lies more in its approach to the traditional than in its ideas, although some of the ideas resonate with the postmodern. I find it valuable to seek a deeper understanding of the NA as a reaction to, and a reflexion of, the contemporary context since this may contribute to a discussion about the role and character of the Christian message and the Church in modernity or postmodernity. In the last section of this paper I will also briefly highlight some tensions between the NA and the Christian faith.

A crisis of worldview

SCIENCE AND RATIONALITY

I first came into contact with the NA through the debate on the 'new worldview' during the late 1970s. The NA was and is a strong protest against the worldview of Newtonian science, the science of modernity.[16] But is also a reaction against an important element of modernity on the structural level, in functional rationality, which has had a strong impact on everyday life through technological production and bureaucracy. 'Functional rationality means, above all, the imposition of rational controls over the material universe, over social relations and finally over the self.'[17] It is in this light that one must see Weber's words about the 'disenchantment of the world' as characteristic of Western development with its growth of bureaucratic social forms (the iron cage).

Identifying the reactions against functional rationality in the early youth-culture and counterculture of the 1960s, Berger sees elements of nature worship and mysticism expressed in the ecological movement and the resurgence of new religions.[18] The NA, as a development of the counterculture, is expressing its discontent with modernity in a number of more explicit ways.

This protest has to a very high degree a scientific character, thereby reflecting its dependence on modernity. Even more striking is its frequent use of scientific models and language to legitimate premodern views. The former enemies, science and religion, are now best friends. Science has become a handmaid for a new spirituality.[19]

Advocates of the NA talk of a new Copernican revolution,[20] a paradigm shift, using Kuhn's theory of scientific revolutions. The Newtonian worldview is regarded as incomplete. The mechanistic/materialist view is too reductionistic. It has led to a devaluation of nature and its exploitation, and to a reification of man. The Cartesian division between mind and body is a particular target, including the idea that the thinking subject is set apart from the causal, material and unthinking nature. Drawing on Einstein, NA advocates emphasize that matter is a form of energy but they expand this distinction and add consciousness, saying that matter, energy and consciousness are one continuum.[21] The Heisenberg uncertainty principle of quantum physics, which on the microlevel questions a deterministic view of the world, is often developed in a distinctly Eastern fashion in that human consciousness is seen to play a part in creating reality.[22] Parallels are drawn between modern physics and Eastern mystics as they both view the cosmos as an interconnected web of relations.

James Lovelock's Gaia hypothesis about the development of the global ecosystem is taken much further by NA writers such as Peter Russel and Rupert Sheldrake. Russel says that Gaia is only just on the threshold of consciousness, a process crucially dependent on human choices. Sheldrake argues that the purposive organizing principle behind Gaia is a morphogenetic field.[23] With its origin in Greek mythology, Gaia the Earth Goddess is attractive also to the followers of neopaganism,[24] which is now one of the strongest formative elements in the NA.

Because of the nineteenth century incorporation of evolutionary thinking in the esoteric tradition (Theosophy), evolution is a key theme in the NA. The evolutionism of modern biology is often criticised for its lack of values, intention and insight into human destiny.[25] With reference to the old gnosis and hidden wisdom of premodern mythology, the Romantic movement and the nineteenth century occultists, one is now talking of the evolution of human consciousness as the primary purpose of the cosmic process. One New Ager describes the 'expanded vocation' of connecting her own growth urge to the force that is evolving the Universe, 'I had discovered a purpose related to the evolution of the world'.[26] Modern concepts such as chance and necessity lose their power and are replaced by a teleological view of the world.

Scientific references are found throughout NA literature. Quotations about research into psychic and near-death experiences, and the human brain, also confirm the NA vision. Discussing Karl Pribram's hologram theory on parts with the capacity to reflect the whole and applying it to the brain and the entire cosmos, brain researcher Marilyn Ferguson comments: 'If the nature of reality is itself holographic, and the brain operates holographically, then the world is indeed, as the Eastern religions have said, maya: a magic show. Its concreteness is an illusion'.[27]

Many signs indicate that NA writers are using modern science to promote a premodern vision of the world. They hope to see a new synthesis between the old and the new. For example, David Harris sees, 'the marriage of science with religion as bringing about the next stage of our evolution'.[28] The NA and one of its

213

strongest growing branches, Neopaganism, have a strong reaction against the 'disenchantment of the world' that Weber wrote about. One of the most important figures in the development of the New Age scene delivers this prophecy: 'Twenty-first century man will ... learn how to talk and listen to plants ... to commune with devas of the wind ... to cure with etheric invocation ... he will humanize technology with animism'.[29]

One commentator says that what New Agers are criticizing is not science or the scientific method, but 'scientism'.[30] But some of them make strong claims from a supposedly scientific position. Capras' arguments create the illusion that modern physics determines a unique worldview when he asserts the confirmation of Eastern mysticism by physics, with several phrases such as 'Quantum mechanic tells us ...' and 'Modern physics forces one to believe ...'.[31]

In general, the degree of scientific justification in NA literature is very high. Modern shamans and mystics seem to need doctorates in psychology or physics. The simplistic and often absolute scientific claims made in NA books on the popular level suggests that the general plausibility of science is creating a kind of normative pattern also for New Agers. In a society which is still dominated by science you sell your commodities by an appeal to science.

Campbell argues that one kind of rationalization in modern society leads not to secularization but to a systematization that subsumes symbols under higher principles. This type of rationalization may occur in systems of thought which enthrone the feelings, the will, or the imagination, thus having the effect of making nonrational criteria a more powerful cultural force.[32] The NA is an expression of this type of rationalization.

In spite of this, the NA levels a protest against the dominant Western view of rationality. The Cartesian separation between mind and matter, developing into the idea of a detached reason with the capacity to gain objective knowledge, is rightly criticized but the alternatives presented tend to be extreme. According to the NA, human rationality is normally regarded as a function of the lower ego and there are many ways of knowing the world besides the rational. These correspond to different levels of reality and states of consciousness. Some even try to show the need and possibility of developing state-specific sciences with regard to these different realities.[33] Reason is seen as valid in some situations but there are many other ways to knowledge. Most of them are regarded as superior to reason since they are held to be immediate forms of knowledge and therefore self-authenticating. They have the character of a Gnostic knowing.

Ultimate reality is encountered beyond the rational in an intuitive experience that cannot be expressed in words. *A Course in Miracles* (ACIM), probably the most influential single book in the NA at the moment, states that 'God does not understand words, for they were made by separated minds to keep them in the illusion of separation'.[34] In the NA, ultimate truth is generally noncognitive and inexpressible in mere language.

Ideas need not cohere with each other or correspond to any reality. The real criterion of truth is pragmatic: 'Does it work?'[35] Beliefs are judged according to their functionality on an individual level: 'Does it work for me?' ACIM proclaims that you need not believe, accept or welcome its ideas as long as you use them. You are not asked to judge them at all, only to use them.[36]

NEW AGE AND TECHNOLOGY

The development of modern society is described by a New Ager as a development from magic to technology, thereby reducing the sacred qualities of life.[37] Since one of the effects of modernization is said to be the invasion of technology into almost every area of life, one can ask whether the sacred vision of the NA has suffered from this. Jacques Ellul sees a close connection between the new religions and technology, and explains their origin from the fact that some religions, such as the Eastern ones, lend themselves more readily than others to technicization.[38] But the contemporary climate also has certain effects. 'In the mental space of technological cultures, the highest philosophies deteriorate into recipes. It is always a matter of finding an exterior procedure demanding the least effort (an eminently technological trait) to obtain the same apparent result'.[39] The effect of functional rationality on evangelicalism has also been said to produce a spirituality with rigorously standardized prescriptions including 'principles', 'rules', 'steps', 'laws', 'codes', and 'guidelines'.[40]

New Age handbooks on Higher Consciousness, Affirmations and Creative Visualization are full of standardized prescriptions. A leading Swedish New Ager says that affirmations are commonly called 'scientific prayers'.[41] Shirley MacLaine summarizes the many techniques she is exploring by the expression, 'spiritual technologies of the new era'.[42] It is within one's power to effect any change in the world since the outer world is a reflection of our thoughts and thoughts can be changed. We can even choose our parents and create our own death during the cosmic journey.[43] Human consciousness is also described as a computer that needs to be reprogrammed, an exquisite mechanism which you need to learn how to operate in order to fully realize your potential for a happy life.[44]

This technological tendency is visible not only on the popular level where it is influenced by contemporary ideals of instant success: it is also common within the more countercultural strands of the NA. Modern shamans have added new methods for altering consciousness: flotation tanks, strobe lights, hypnotic inductions, New Age music, and an array of technically advanced 'mind altering machines'.[45] The counterculture has turned into a combination of hightech spirituality with ancient wisdom, a blend of the ultramodern with the premodern.

The other day I read an obituary notice saying: 'My beloved mother ... has today changed frequency and gone over to another dimension'. Maybe we are seeing the beginning of a change in language/imagery with regard to life and death. Will a techno-spiritual language become normal in the postmodern era?

New Age and the postmodern, part 1

The fascination with the sacred, the divine, or the infinite, in contemporary postmodern thought illustrates an affinity with religious or mystical discourse.[46] The postmodern rehabilitation of myth is related to the deconstruction of the metanarratives of the Western tradition (Lyotard) leaving modern man with a plurality of narratives and values.[47] One of the metanarratives that has been disclosed is reason. Central to the critique of reason is language. All thinking begins and ends in language. Philosophy is seen as rhetoric in disguise. There is no independent vantage point outside of language. Particularly interesting is the postmodern disclosure of the relation between power and knowledge.[48] The Western rational discourse has exercised control and domination. The concept of Truth is itself authoritarian. Here we find a close parallel between postmodernism and NA. The latter is strongly critical of the dominant rationality expressed in big science which is male and which defines itself within a culture of power.[49] Instead, New Agers seek a soft science which is feminine and intuitive. Evil is defined as a reductionist simplicity that is easy to predict and control.[50]

A further connection between the NA and the postmodern is the strong emphasis on subjectivism and the fact that the distinction between subject and object is dissolved.[51]According to postmodern discourse we no longer share an objective reality; all is simulation (Baudrillard) and reality is transformed into a series of disparate images. The New Agers, though, affirm a basic unity beyond the mental images of ordinary life. In the experience of this fundamental unity of reality, the subject and the object are being fused.

The NA teaching on a plurality of truths, the individual and the present, is very much in step with postmodernism. An individual can choose from a variety of truths and techniques, old and new, in order to have a heightened awareness of the present. The discrepancy is revealed in the different attitudes to the ultimate. In its holistic vision, the desire to include every aspect of life into a totality, the NA is more modern than postmodern.[52] Postmodernism is a total acceptance of the ephemerality, fragmentation and discontinuity of life.[53] It is hostile to monism, unification, totalization and global solutions and sees such things as dangerous because they hide various kinds of despotism. As we shall see in the last section of this paper, the NA vision represents a solution with a totalitarian inclination.

In the tensions between the Enlightenment and Romanticism we find clear parallels between the modern and the postmodern, the modern and NA. On the Enlightenment side we have a heavy emphasis on science, universal principles, and rationality. On the romantic side there are deep doubts about science, and a reliance on intuition and feeling rather than reason. But both believe in the personal significance of the individual, and that through the individual it is possible to understand the whole.[54]

NEW AGE AND THE SELF

The question of human identity is as old as man himself. Ever since Greek philosophers as Socrates and Protagoras we find an anthropocentric urge developing in Western thought. In Pico della Mirandolas' *Oration on the Dignity of Man*, written during the Renaissance, we see for the first time in the modern West a vision of human nature as unfulfilled potential, of life as an adventure in self-development.[55] (Though many regard Descartes as the founder of the modern philosophical obsession with the self, a concern which develops further through Rousseau, Kant and their followers.) Solomon claims that: 'The story of modern European philosophy is the protracted prognosis of self-transformation'.[56]

Though the grand ideas of the self have long been with us, they have not gained widespread influence until fairly recently. It has taken a long process of socio-economic change to create the right climate. Examples of this change provide a background for a deeper understanding of the NA phenomenon. NA is as much a child of modernity as it is a protest against it.

One explanation to our modern climate of expressivism and selfism is provided by Inglehart's discussions of 'the silent revolution'.[57] Drawing on Maslow's 'hierarchy of needs', he claims that people naturally turn to 'non-material' goals once they have become physically and economically secure. According to him, when people's basic needs have been met in our affluent Western culture, they move on to higher needs, the highest of all being 'self-actualization'.[58]

The split between the public and the private, between society and the individual has had profound effects. Traditional patterns for social behaviour as well as belief systems and external authorities have changed or been eroded and modern humanity is left alone to find meaning and identity in life. The tension between the individual and society can be described with the help of several concepts.

◇ 'De-traditionalization'[59]: Humanity is no longer in contact with traditions which speak with a demanding external voice and authority. 'De-traditionalizing' means a process whereby the action of authority with internal voice becomes prominent: in R. Bellah's words it involves 'the internalization of authority'.

◇ 'De-institutionalization' is a process whereby the patterns of human behavior and social relations become unstable and traditional definitions of reality become unreliable.[60] The public sphere in modern society is not affected by this process but still cannot provide a pattern of identification since it is experienced as overly rational, abstract and incomprehensible. Questions of meaning and identity are delegated to the private sphere which then has to compensate for the impersonal character of the public sphere. The modern dilemma is that the private sector has become enfeebled and unstable through de-institutionalization.

◇ The increased 'pluralization of social life-worlds'.[61] Many individuals are not only uprooted from their original social milieu, but are also migrating through numerous social contexts during one life-span as well as in everyday life. This social mobility has its correlate/correspondence in cognitive and normative mobility. What is true and right in one social context may be wrong in another.

De-traditionalization, de-institutionalization, pluralization and alienation from the public sphere, are conditions that create a crisis of meaning, psychological anomie, and homelessness. These circumstances are felt to be intolerable and bring about a protest which has been called the 'demodernizing impulse'. It is seen as the source of 'the new religious consciousness'[62] and the youth culture and counterculture of the 1960s.[63]

A closely related phenomenon is **expressivism** which can be associated not only with 'the silent revolution', but also with the following two aspects:

1. Modern humanity is said to protest against the patterns of a public sphere which is abstract, impersonal, rational and utilitarian. This reaction bestows higher value on the concrete and personal, than on experience, feeling, and the subjective.[64] Humanity is searching for the more real and natural.

2. A consequence of de-institutionalization is **subjectivization**. The question of personal identity becomes complex through the loss of stable institutional patterns in the private sphere. As a result, personal identity turns out to be a matter of private choice. This also necessitates a turning within, to the subjective, in order to reflect and ponder over the options that are at hand.[65] Subjectivization can then be defined as a structural process where people are forced to turn inward to find meaningful life patterns and a stable identity.[66] This process also fosters subjectivism which is a preoccupation with the undiscovered complexities of one's individual subjectivity.

All of these concepts—de-traditionalization, de-institutionalization, pluralization, the silent 'expressive' revolution, subjectivization, the existence of a public sphere which has an alienating effect—can be used to shine some light on the predicament of people in modern society. They also serve as backgrounds when we seek to understand the NA phenomenon as an expression of modernity. Describing the demodernizing consciousness, Berger writes that the anthropological assumptions of the protest against modernity are profoundly modern: 'The concept of the naked Self, beyond institutions and roles, as the *ens realissimus* of human being, is at the very heart of modernity'.[67]

Because of the focus on the self, the turning within, and the increased demands for authentic self-expression, psychology has become a major force in the West.[68] Many claim that it has become a substitute for religion or even a secular religion.[69] In one of the strongest formative elements of the NA, the development of humanistic psychology into The Human Potential Movement and transpersonal psychology, we see an explicit fusion between psychology and religion. Eastern philosophy is married with Western psychology. This is not surprising since they both diagnose the problem of humanity as basically psychological: people suffer from a lack of knowledge of their true nature and the proper insight will lead to liberation.

Some affirm that psychology will have a major role to play in uniting the different spiritual traditions of the world, 'Therapy will universalize the traditions'.[70] Leading transpersonal psychologists claim that different mythologies represent a type of sacred psychology through which each one of us can learn to contact the divine essence of our being.[71] Here I find an interesting parallel with the way the NA use the natural sciences. In the NA we see a fusion between modern science/psychology and premodern, ancient wisdom.

One proponent says that the increased awareness of human potential could take political form in a fight for the right to be yourself, thereby echoing Inglehart's description of 'the silent revolution'. Drawing a parallel with the fight for democracy during previous centuries, it is claimed that the right to explore the self and inner liberation must be the main objective in life, also demanding the right of support from the whole of society.[72] The NA is also distinctively modern in its democratic ambitions and presentations of instant solutions. The secrets of the esoteric tradition are openly proclaimed in the NA with the goal that everybody shall have a direct connection with the spiritual world, each one of us becoming a channeller or medium. During one weekend session you are supposed to learn how to be a shaman or do tantra yoga, practices which outside the NA context are considered to require years of arduous training.

As a remedy for a fragmented society with no basis for social coherence New Agers argue for the need of religious revival through a rediscovery of the sacred.[73] As the alternative to secularization and the split between sacred and profane they often present primal and non-western cultures where all of life is sacred.[74] From old myths we can also learn the secret of non-duality.[75] ACIM teaches that One-mindedness is the word from heaven, and that all forms of duality are creations of the lower ego.[76]

THE COSMIC SELF

The quest for the true self becomes crucial since society is seen as a reflection of fragmented personalities. The established patterns in society become a great problem since they predispose us towards a rational and dualistic view of ourselves and the world. NA regards the ego function of our personalities as particularly conditioned by society. The rescue is to be sought within each person, in a space beyond conditioning.[77] The NA cure for most of our modern problems can thus be summarized in the slogan 'the only way out is in'. This journey within can be described as an ongoing process where you get in touch with your inner feelings, 'inner child', 'inner wisdom', 'inner voice', in order to fully realize yourself.[78]

This process has not only a therapeutic value with regard to self image and social relationships but has also a cosmic dimension. Concepts as 'The Higher Self', 'Inner Self', transcend the social context and unite the individual with the universe as a whole. In this we find an integration of microcosmos (the human soul) into macrocosmos, a fundamental oneness with everything there is. Humanity is thus given a cosmic identity.

One writer perceptively remarks the difference between concepts of the self in the NA and the East.[79] In the East one loses one's self in the whole as the individuality of a drop of water is lost when it falls into a pail of water. In the NA we find a reversal

221

of the process, the single self becomes important. One could say that the pail of water comes into the drop. The self becomes the prime reality.

Two influential NA writers even describe the Higher Self as a visible person in the inner realm that one can communicate with.[80] This depiction of the self strengthens Berger's thesis about the fundamental anthropological assumption behind the protest. The Self has been refashioned in line with Western concepts of the self in modernity.[81]

This may also indicate the psychological difficulties involved in relating an abstract concept of Ultimate Reality to an All. The increase of the channelling phenomena in NA circles, where a lot of spirit entities/personalities actually become the formative influences for people, may serve as an example of this point. This is an important link to Christian teaching as I will show in the last section.

THE OMNIPOTENT SELF

In the nineteenth century romantic vision of the self, even the nature of the 'external' reality was incorporated into the realm of the human mind and made dependent on the faculties of human knowledge. The mind was thought not only to discover reality, but to constitute it.[82] The occult traditions affirm that everything in the world is energy and that this energy conforms itself to thought.[83] The capacities associated with the Higher Self in the NA are quite in line with romantic and occult views. While New Agers differ about the extent to which we create reality[84] it is clear that their most popular books all affirm that the self has a godlike ability to create reality.[85] The total power of the self is particularly manifested in the new supermen and superwomen of the NA.

This empowerment of the self must seem very attractive in a society where people are on the one hand, powerless, and on the other hand, part of a strongly competitive climate, while being impregnated by the success fantasies of the media. Through new spiritual techniques the individual will pass from the position of slave to that of a master, becoming an active, creative agent instead of a passive dependant.[86] Reading NA books, magazines and adverts is like wandering through a hall of mirrors where all the images of the true self compete in telling you that you are absolutely wonderful and omnipotent. One writer strongly recommends the use of a mirror as one utters the positive affirmations.[87] If, as Lasch suggests, we live in a narcissistic culture, this spirituality has a lot to do with it.

If you have total power you also have total responsibility for the reality you experience. Listening to a New Ager claiming that even a child who has been abused must somehow have wanted it, makes this new meaning of responsibility rather cynical.[88]

THE SELF AS A COSMIC TRAVELLER

Another aspect of the NA-self is reincarnation. The fusion between Eastern views on reincarnation and evolutionary optimism in the Western esoteric tradition is taken up by the NA. Whereas in the East the reincarnation model ultimately proves the illusory character of the self, the Western innovation turns out to secure the self.[89] Ruppert sees this as an expression of a modern impulse. Drawing out the implications of this in relation to MacIntyre's concept of selfhood, in which self-identity is related to an individual's narrative that links birth to life and death,[90] it is possible to see the attractiveness of an extended narrative where the self gets numerous chances to actualize itself. Reincarnation is not a curse as in the East, but a blessing, a positive opportunity for self-improvement on our cosmic journey. Reincarnation is also attractive since it gives a rational explanation for the inequalities and negativities of life, although it should be remembered that the law of karma and reincarnation introduces a strict causality which is not very far from the reductionist functionality of modern society from which the NA tries to escape.[91]

THE MYSTICAL SYNTHESIS

In times of rapid social and cultural change, when people experience a dissonance between the observed reality and the beliefs and values of their culture and the established religions, we find an increased interest in mysticism.[92] The direct experience of a transcendental reality offers either the possibility of reform, or a new synthesis with which to meet those psychological needs which become urgent in times of unrest.

Mysticism becomes a solution, not only to fragmentation and social pluralism but also to religious pluralism. The vision of a universal religion that originated in the Western esoteric tradition is taken up by the NA. In the mystical experience you pass beyond the exoteric, outer forms of different traditions and reach the esoteric, underlying core of common truth behind all religions. The claim that the mystical experience is that which provides the primary clue to what is real, is very attractive in our tolerant society, providing a strong argument for the NA in which they hope that we will all come to recognize only one universal religion.

NEW AGE—COUNTER CULTURE OR MAINSTREAM?

A unifying concept for Paul Heelas' description of the NA is 'self-religion'. Identifying the contemporary forms of these self-religions he sees a tension between two different wings of the NA. The first one is countercultural and seeks liberation from the institutions of modernity, in particular those involving commitment to the materialistic life.[93] The response to modernity is defined as a reaction from the mainstream, a hankering after some 'non-modern' sense of the natural. The second response has a different relationship to modernity. During the 80s many New Agers became active in the world of big business and began to tap the powers of the self in order to promote not only spiritual but material success.[94] While the tendency to instrumentalize religion has its roots in modernity, these people and groups still do not devalue the spiritual dimension. This spirituality reflects, on a general level, the patterns of postmodern consumer culture.

New Age and the postmodern, part 2

THE CONSUMING SELF

A parallel between the NA and the postmodern can, according to Heelas, be seen in the way NA is sometimes being used. The 'cultural logic of late capitalism' (Jameson) has generated a postmodern consumer culture where those involved can treat different spiritual provisions as 'consuming delights'.[95] Through 'de-traditionalization' we have seen an internalization of authority (Bellah). One does not relate to external authority but rather has an internal authority as a consumer.[96] Instead of standing before a consuming God who sets limits, people today are increasingly consuming 'God' or religion, treating it as providing commodities that the individual, out of his self-informed authority can choose from. Commitment to the theistic order is eroded by a 'what's in it for me' attitude. People choose the components of the religious sphere which best suit their own particular consumer requirements. Berger sees this also as a consequence of the pluralistic situation, where religion has to be marketed, 'religious traditions becomes consumer commodities'.[97]

THE SELF—SOMEBODY OR NOBODY?

The ideal of the individual as an autonomous, self-determining entity can be seen as the fundamental cultural assumption of modernity. Postmodernity on the other hand, involves a fragmentation and dissolution of the subject, who is said to live in the perpetual present, devoid of any meaningful existential continuity with the past.[98] The French philosophical deconstruction of the subject claims that the modern subject is a late invention in history, a creation of the modern. The grand vision of the cosmic or higher self in the NA seems to be a powerful metanarrative which stands in sharp contrast to the de-centered self which one finds among advocates of the postmodern.

In spite of this magnificent Self and evidence that at least some New Agers endow the Self with a type of higher personality, it is possible to see a further connection between NA and the postmodern. One of the most influential NA teachers describes the ultimate goal as you develop your consciousness by these words: 'As our perception of "self" or "somebody" disappears, we become "nobody" '.[99] After a survey of different Western philosophical images of the Self, starting with the grandiose views of the Self in Rousseau and the Romantics and ending with postmodernism, Solomon concludes: 'Between the Self as an absolute Spirit and the Self as nothing at all there is, it turns out, very little difference'.[100] The inflated and cosmic Selfs of the romantic movement and the NA are almost identical and both run the risk of collapsing into postmodern nothingness.

THE NEW AGE AND THE FUTURE

A graffiti in the Stockholm underground railway says 'The Future is dead': it illustrates the contemporary mood, particularly among young people. 'The modern project' with its belief in progress through science, enlightened reason and rational planning, is today in a severe state of crisis. This loss of confidence in the future is important for understanding the attractiveness of the NA. In a culture which needs utopias we find a powerful alternative expressed in the vision of a new era, made possible through the development of human consciousness. Building on the inclusion and elaboration of evolutionary teaching within the esoteric tradition, particularly Theosophy, NA goes even further. The movement looks not only for a personal transformation of those who adhere to it, but for a broad social and cultural transformation as well.

NA presents a hope for the coming of a new golden age. This theme is quite foreign to the traditional occult world and must be seen as the intrusion of a social vision into the occult.[101] This involves several cooperative programmes by which people are called to draw upon additional sources of spiritual energies, in order to save the planet, work for peace, feminism, interfaith cooperation, animal rights and reforms in the business and educational sectors.

The influential New Ager Barbara Max-Hubbard writes:

> In my forties I felt at the beginning of life almost a
> second adolescence. I became convinced that we stand
> upon the threshold of the greatest age of human
> history. Anyone who can see the opportunities will
> emancipate their own potential through involvement.
> Personal and planetary growth are not merely parallel,
> they are one.

> We live at the most marvellous moment in human
> history. Everyone now alive is involved in the greatest
> of upheaval since humanity emerged out of the animal
> world. We are at the dawn of 'conscious evolution',
> when the creature-human first becomes aware of the
> processes of creation and begins to participate
> deliberately in the design of our world. We are the first
> generation to awaken to the awesome fact that we are
> affecting the future by our every act, from the number
> of children we have and the kind of food we eat to the
> creation of new life forms and new worlds in space.

> A powerful movement of action for life is spreading
> throughout the world. Untold individuals are building
> a 'cathedral of action', an edifice of effort to transcend

the limitations of the present and to create a desirable future for humankind. Each embodies a gift, a shining act of excellence which is incorporated into the cathedral.

....we are not working alone. The laws of attraction are working with us. The power that organised the Universe is organising us! [102]

This glorious vision seems to be a spiritualized version of the utopian dreams emanating from the Enlightenment. Even from within the NA movement, some are critical of the imminent emergence of a New Age. To claim that one is a part of the most advanced turn in history, that this will be completed in a few years and that one also has a leading role to play in this global transformation is classified as extreme narcissism.[103] Taken literally it says, 'I am participating in the most important and powerful transformation which has ever happened in history'. Some leading New Agers already interpret the NA as a metaphor for personal growth, rather than a future period or event.[104]

New Age and the postmodern, part 3

Are there aspects of the NA on this level which parallel the postmodern? At first sight there are big differences. The postmodernists say that the totalizing visions and narratives of progress are no longer tenable. Lyotard argues for a shift away from faith in human progress, describing the collapse of over-arching narratives which locate people within a history that has a definite past, present and future. Postmodernity heralds the rise of competing and contradictory views of what 'reality' might actually be. 'Because we can never acquire knowledge of the world apart from our existence in localized interpretive communities, global projects become impossible, leaving us only with the recognition and celebration of differences and discontinuities, even within ourselves'.[105]

In spite of this clear indication of discrepancy one can point to some similarities between the NA and the postmodern. Lyon mentions the globalization theme which, in our postmodern phase is an accelerating phenomenon spurred by the development of new information and communications technologies.[106] The NA is said to speak about the reunion of the self with the cosmos against the backdrop of motives which paradoxically rely on archetypical products of modernity, the TV and the satellite. The leading NA publisher in Sweden told me that the core of the NA is the globalization of the spiritual world impulse achieved with the aid of modern technology.

Lyon also connects the postmodern and NA with the *fin de siecle* if not millennialism of the later parts of the nineteenth century.[107] During that time there was a strong anti-enlightenment rhetoric in many circles. Motifs from that period also appear in the postmodern discourse. There was also a positive alternative present in millennialistic expectations. NA is an expression of the later phenomenon but with a broader vision.

I hope this presentation of modern, premodern and postmodern themes has shown the composite nature of the NA. Reaching beyond modernity, it reflects both the pre-modern and the modern. Modern traits are seen in relation to science, technology, the self and the grand narrative of a utopian vision. The combination of pre-modern and modern motives leads us into a new phase, a New Age, that may be called postmodern religion. Some postmodern features of the NA are displayed in relation to the subjective, pluralization, consumption, globalization and even in an indirect way, to the self. This spirituality 'compensates for postmodern failure to transcend modernity completely. It offers optimism and unity in place of anxiety and difference'.[108]

A Christian response

Having seen the NA reaction against modernity, what should be the contours of a Christian response? In a number of ways Christians have embraced a worldview which is becoming outdated and is rejected by the New Agers. The NA flight to premodern sources of inspiration depends to a certain degree on the fact that most of them have come in contact with only a static Christian faith. The dynamic, organic and relational aspects have been obscured as we have capitulated to modernity. But at present there is a disillusionment with both established solutions and institutions. The church, as well as its message, is seen as a part of the establishment, and is therefore not attractive among the ones who seek alternative ways to live and think. NA rejects Christianity as being part of a discredited system.

Any type of Christian faith which feeds too much on modernity runs the risk of being regarded as inadequate. At the same time NA reflects, to a large degree, patterns integral to modernity. One could thus argue that Christian faith and practice needs to reflect the same patterns in order to be relevant (for example with regards to self-actualization), but at this point the Christian response to modernity is even more radical than the NA one. The call to a renewal of the Christian faith is motivated not only by the breakdown of modernity and its NA alternative but, first of all, by the gospel itself. Through a deepened loyalty to the Word of God and a rediscovery of our own tradition we may be a credible alternative in a postmodern society.

SCIENCE AND CREATION

New Age writers present a relevant critique of scientism and the mechanistic/materialistic worldview of Newtonian science. But they unite their criticism with a negative evaluation of the Judeo-Christian tradition which is said to have created a dualistic view of the world. The belief in a male deity, a distant omnipotent power ruling the world with immutable laws, not being fully present in a fallen world, is said to have contributed to our present problems.[109] The NA solution most often implies that new scientific theories are promoting a different worldview, more in line with Eastern mysticism. These metaphysical interpretations are not only questionable, but also create the false notion that we must regard as outdated a Christian understanding of the world.[110]

NA draws simplistic parallels between the negative consequences of Newtonian science and Christian teaching. Can the Christian faith be blamed for exploitation and modern reductionist views of humanity? Moltmann helps us to discover what has happened to the Christian understanding of creation and nature under the conditions of modernity.[111] As scientific materialism develops, God is excluded as an explanation, and theological reflection on creation is reduced to a matter of personal faith. Science and theology are separated from faith and the human understanding of the world. Faith as primarily a matter of personal, human salvation in post-Reformation theology is a part of a defensive strategy towards the scientific and philosophical attacks of modernity. This adaptation creates a dualism, with a privatized faith and little room for creational theology.

The modern division between the sacred and the secular

229

accepted by the church is challenged by the ecological crises and the NA response. The church needs to move beyond the dualistic and monistic interpretations (the NA) to recover the holistic relationship with creation which is found in the Bible and tradition.[112] This is fuelled by the relational character of the Christian faith and a Trinitarian perspective. In Trinitarian theology the relationship between God and the world is a personal one, God and the world being ontologically distinct realities creating a ground for genuine relationships.[113] The world is a product of the free and personal action of the triune God and is what it is only by virtue of its continuing dynamic dependance upon its creator. This God does not act from a distance or from above but from within. In Romans 8 we see that: 1) God is radically committed to his world but never merged with it; 2) the evil which afflicts creation has been defeated in God the Son; 3) God the Spirit (not the universal spirit of the NA, but the spirit of the risen Christ) is at work within creation; 4) the Spirit of Christ has been given to us, which means that we participate both in the renewal, and in the suffering and groaning of creation. This passage is a resource for 'a "creation spirituality" which neither idolizes creation nor abuses it, nor withdraws from it as if it were basically evil, but can speak of sharing in the redemption of creation in the knowledge that this is what God has begun in Christ and will one day complete'.[114]

One reason why an eastern worldview has become more plausible for many scientists today may be the silent adaptation of theology to a Newtonian worldview. Another reason may be that Christians are being silent while the scientific community engages in 'God-talk' both on the academic and popular level. We need to enter into this dialogue in order to challenge its presuppositions and highlight areas that create new openings for faith. On the other hand, the Christian faith must be aware of the dangers involved in depending too much on scientific theories. The NA marriage between science and religion can prove to be risky; NA religion may be widowed since science has a history of changing its mind. It is also relevant to question the future role of science in the New Age. With the retreat into different mental states and incommunicable subjective experiences it is likely that the NA framework will ultimately bring about the end of science.[115] The Christian faith assumes a stable physical order and the possibility of various degrees of public verification.

REASON AND EXPERIENCE

As a Christian I find it easy to agree with the NA critique of Western rationality and its dominant role. Sadly enough, the church has in different ways accommodated itself to this aspect of modernity. Liberal theology produces a reductionist theology that leaves little room for the supernatural. The counter-reaction from strong fundamentalism produces a very rationalistic theology. Some thinkers argue that evangelical apologetics are often made from an acceptance of the enlightenment view of reason and the need of sufficient evidence.[116] Contemporary epistemological moves away from the modern agenda include a more holistic approach, the search for knowledge as a practice dependent upon tradition, a communal achievement.[117] These may challenge us to reconsider our views of rationality and make us better equipped to meet the present situation.[118] In fact, Christian theology is in a strong position to offer a model of rationality which will throw light on many of the problems which our culture faces.[119] The basis of such an alternative view of knowledge is a concrete relation, a kind of knowledge by acquaintance. Gunton exemplifies this by the Christian community, which through worship but in other ways as well, is brought into a Trinitarian relationship which is both rational and imaginative, both deeply personal and communal, both spiritual and material.[120]

NA spirituality represents the search for an experience of wholeness in a highly rational and fragmented society. The starting point for the NA vision is a transformative experience. Truth is encountered in a mystical experience, not via creeds, dogmas or written revelations. Such external authorities merely block the way to the inner realm. According to NA, truth comes from within. Through the aid of many different techniques and methods one is supposed to unlock the door to an inner room of harmony and beauty.

Although this is by no means a Christian ideal, it represents a tremendous challenge for the church in several ways. New Agers claim to have first-hand knowledge. They regard Christians as having second-hand knowledge, relying too much on external authorities, most of the time merely repeating what they have heard or read. Joseph Campbell writes that a priest is a civil servant, whereas a shaman is someone who has had an experience.[121] The lack of spiritual vitality in the Church is to a large degree dependent on our accommodation to modernity.

Preaching and worship have often become means of information rather than transformation. What goes on in the church tends to be routinized and thoroughly planned activities with little room for transcendence. The Bible challenges us to have a personal first-hand knowledge of God. The worshipping community also needs to reflect a living encounter with God. Such an encounter is not just an affair between the individual and God but a process through which all creation is brought back to its Creator.[122] In order to be relevant to postmodern society and true to its origin, the Church needs both its charismatics and its mystics.

The NA claim to mystical first-hand knowledge runs the risk of ending up in subjectivism and solipsism. Any experience needs to be weighed against external factors and, in practice, most New Agers rely on external authorities such as channellers or mediumistic written revelations. The NA charge against Christians falls back on themselves. They are in a similar position. It is impossible to live without some kind of dependence on external authorities. You are always a part of a tradition, a society, something outside your self. Every tradition also has some basic beliefs which, in one way or the other, are formulated in words and concepts and are embraced in a fairly uncritical way. I have met several New Agers who are very dogmatic on a number of issues. Belief is a matter of choice made from a whole range of considerations. For example, is the twentieth century Jesus presented in *A Course in Miracles* more reliable than the Jesus of Nazareth recorded in the Bible?

POWER AND LOVE

A common feature of the NA and of the postmodern discourse is a reaction against a connection between power and rationality in modernity. The NA also more explicitly addresses the relationship between power and religion, reacting not only to dogma in general but to the institutionalized church of power and the god of power. New Agers frequently refer to the failures of the church throughout history, particularly its treatment of dissenters and all the religious wars that have been fought in the name of Jesus. This church of power has suppressed truth and also hidden documents it has considered dangerous. While some of this critique, sadly, is accurate, there are also attempts to rewrite history which range from speculation to pure falsification.[123]

How true to Christian teaching is this God of absolute power that the NA rejects? We need to question the versions of classical theism which understand God as being primarily omnipotent, eternal, and changeless, remote from the world. In the incarnation and the cross God reveals himself as a suffering God. McGrath writes: 'the glory of the omnipotent Lord of all creation gave himself up to the shame and powerlessness of the cross. The hands that flung the stars into the heavens were surrendered to the nails of the cross'.[124] This giving of himself in unselfish love reveals the deepest mystery of God. It is a love which flows forever in the triunity of Father, Son and Spirit. 'To be God is to be a communion of giving and receiving. The self-giving and receiving that is God takes temporal and spatial form in Jesus' *kenosis*. The Father gives up the Son in the overflow of his love for the world, and receives him back, glorified, through the Spirit'.[125] The love of God belongs to the heart of his being.

God's love becomes a suffering love because of humanity's unwillingness to live in communion with the creator. As God in Jesus takes upon himself our independence and pride on the cross this self-giving love reaches a climax. Through this we know what love is (1 John 3:16). By contrast, the NA concept of love refers to an undifferentiated cosmic energy which represents wholeness rather than holiness. This cosmic love, beyond good and evil, turns out to be a very weak ethical foundation for personal or social action. The God of the Bible is a moral being who in his radical love reveals himself as wholly opposed to evil. Reaching out in love to his world he is wounded by the full weight of its evil. Atoning for a moral rebellion, God the Son suffers unto death in order to bring new life. The prize of this re-creation is high. The holy and consuming love of God can therefore not be trivialized into a postmodern consumer item for that love is unique, finding no equal in other religions. No other god has wounds. John Stott writes: 'only one act of pure love, unsullied by any taint of ulterior motive, has ever been performed in the history of the world, namely the self-giving of God in Christ on the cross for undeserving sinners...if we are looking for a definition of love, we should not look in a dictionary, but at Calvary'.[126] This holy love provides us with a stronger ethical foundation for personal and social action than any amoral cosmic love ever can.

The incarnational love of God becomes important as we approach seekers within the NA. Christians often tend to be hard and judgmental towards dissenting people and opinions. We also have a habit of projecting our own failures onto external factors, forgetting that our real enemy lies within. People today struggle intensely to find solutions to life's problems. They try out the alternatives that are at hand. A probing question to the church in the West is why so few of these seekers come in contact with a living Christian witness. We should not blame them for their choice of perspective but rather ask ourselves where we were when the choices were being made. In spite of all the disagreements between us we also have or should have some things in common with New Agers. For example, the NA discontent with life in the West should also be ours.

Christians during the 1990s need to find the right balance between dissociation and identification. On the one hand, we are called to define the boundaries between classical Christian faith and the new religious teachings, and in order to do it in a credible way we need increased knowledge of these new spiritualities. This encounter will, at the same time, lead us to a new discovery of the basic truths of the Gospel. On the other hand, we also need to identify with seekers of the NA. We must be willing to talk to them and share their critical moments, to allow them space in our lives and churches. The incarnational pattern of Christ shows us a way.

Sadly however, we seldom relate to these people. Life in the Christian colony seems to be enough to fill our diaries. It is time to ask hard questions about our priorities as individuals and churches. If we reserved some time every week for fellowship with people who do not share our values and lifestyle, we would see a change in church statistics. Our contemporary spiritual climate challenges us to break out of the iron cage of the institutionalized church.

At present there is a widespread distrust of established solutions and institutions in society. The Church and its message is associated with the establishment and seems to represent no positive alternative for those who seek change. Sociological and theological considerations beg us to question all sorts of Constantinian ambitions. With the end of the Christendom period, the church in a postmodern society can no longer cling to earlier notions of power and security. The church also serves a Lord who in his death challenged the entire system of domination. What does it mean to embody the love of God today? Surely, the church must regain its character as a counterculture. By being true to its teaching, a new people with alternative values and life patterns may be created. A visible and living community of faith is the most credible form of witness. 'The overriding political task of the church is to be the community of the cross'.[127] It means both daring to take God's account of reality more seriously than Caesar's and daring to participate in a revolution-ary way in the victory of Christ over the powers. Despite NA unease about the cross, I suspect that a community who lived out its values would be highly attractive, especially with the present deconstruction of the public sector and increase of social problems in the West. The church does not have a social strategy but is in itself, through its life, a social strategy.[128] By imitating Christ in self-giving love and compassion the church will have a countercultural impact.

MAN AND RELATIONSHIPS

The preoccupation with the self is a feature of both modernity and the NA. As the West today suffers from a general hangover from the 1980s it seems as if even the self has its melancholy moments. The early 1990s show signs of a deeper search for community and corporate images.[129] In spite of this trend I believe that the internal tensions in modernity will make any corporate endeavour problematic. The high demands for indivi-dual freedom and flexibility, self-actualization and change will continually collide with concerns for the common good. This is also a dilemma for the church today. To a large degree we have accepted the priority of the self and ended up with a basically therapeutic message. (In the following pages I will focus on the relational character of the Christian faith and highlight some of the internal tensions in the corporate vision of the NA. What are the problems that the NA self struggles with and how do they relate to a Christian understanding?)

Advocates of the NA present many valuable psychological insights about the way egocentricity works and how it separates us from God, from each other, and from our own true identity and creation. Both the NA faith and and the Christian faith are wrestling with the problem of selfishness. Both grapple with how to overcome the separation between God and humanity. A new union between God and humanity is the solution to the problem of selfishness. Despite that there are big differences. The NA suggests that there is not, and has never been, any real separation between God and humanity. All separation is unreal. The diagnosis is psychological. Abandon your wrong conceptions about a finite self and you will experience that you are unselfish, infinite, and identical with God and the whole universe. The goal is to merge with the higher impersonal cosmic energy that is God. This may have unpleasant consequences. The ultimate NA solution to the problem of selfishness is the dissolution of the self. The individual is swallowed up by the impersonal mass.

This is the result of an ideology driven by fear of the 'other'. This aspect of the NA is much in line with contemporary culture as Begbie observes: 'The dogma that freedom means escaping the authority of the "other" whether God, parents, the state, or whatever is very deeply rooted in our age. Yet it is profoundly mistaken'.[130] He goes on to explain why, by describing human relationships. '... persons are what they are in relationship to others, by virtue of what they give to and receive from each other. We come to self-fulfilment in relationship ... It is not that we "happen to have" relations; our relationship with others is part of what it means to be human. And yet, at the same time, we become persons when we respect people as unique and distinct, as other than ourselves. My freedom depends on being rightly related to others and on my distinctiveness from other people.'[131] In spite of the New Ager's relational talk, the obliteration of all distinctions leads, not to freedom, but to the obliteration of the human person. Even if the NA combination of a plurality of options with a common goal seem to solve the basic tension between freedom and solidarity, its corporate vision ultimately ends up in a collectivism with totalitarian inclinations.

As the image of God, humanity stands in relationship not only to their fellow men and the rest of creation, but first of all to God. The distinction between God and his creation permits a genuine and fulfilling relationship. As humanity asserts itself and turns away from a God who desires mutual fellowship, we are faced with a relational and moral problem, not a psychological one as in the NA. It is not mind power but the power of God's love that can heal this broken relationship. When God in Christ freely carries the weight of our independence and rebellion we see how far he is willing to go in order to restore what has been lost. This God is not the impersonal 'Force' of the NA but a personal and loving Father who seeks communion with his children. The growth of the channelling phenomenon in the NA, with its personified spirit entities, may be an example of the psychological difficulties involved in relating to an overly abstract ultimate reality. It may be seen as yet another sign that the human heart, at the deepest level, has a desire for Someone rather than Something; we need, as Buber said, an I-Thou relationship rather than an I-It approach. The Christian story is about a God who calls us to intimate personal friendship with himself.

The real clue to an understanding of humanity as the image of God is to be found in the concept of the person. To be a person is to be made in the image of God, a God who is a communion of persons inseparably related.[132] 'Our personhood is grounded in a God who is neither three entirely separate persons, nor a completely singular Person, but a community of distinct Persons who are inseparably bonded in self-giving love. God's unity is a unity of distinct persons-in-relationship'.[133] This is the heritage of the Trinitarian theology of the Cappadocian fathers. The nature and being of God is personal communion. 'There is no true being without communion. Nothing exists as an "individual", conceivable in itself. Communion is an ontological category'.[134]

The quest for the true and naked self, beyond institutions and social conditioning, which we find in modernity and the NA is a dead end because human beings are basically relational. A human being is constituted by its relatedness to others. The Western concept of personal identity is, in fact, derived from the early Trinitarian theologians.[135] The recent high evaluation of individual self-actualization indicates that our culture is losing contact with its roots. The contemporary search for community is at the same time a sign of hope and a serious challenge to the church to move beyond self-religion and live out the true meaning of its nature. '..a church that has shaped its life around the needs and demands of the individual has sold its birthrights'.[136] The Church is called to show, on the finite level, the inner life of communion in God.[137]

The NA claims to present a new holistic vision of humanity as a cure for Cartesian dualism. But their solution is not holistic enough. It represents a reductionist view since the ultimate goal of humanity is a spiritual and non-related existence. A biblical holism is more comprehensive and realistic because it affirms the value of the physical reality, including the body, as well as the spiritual and intellectual. It also sees humanity's problem as basically relational and it provides a way to restored relationships. The NA elevation of finite humanity to divine status is not only unrealistic but blasphemous since humanity and the rest of creation constantly depend on its Creator. This divinity is a heavy burden to bear since the new superman has a total responsibility as creator of his own life as well as of history. The law of karma and reincarnation introduces a strict causality which is impossible to evade. There is little room for human frailty and failure. The Christian description of the human predicament is, in this light, an affirmation of humanity and its everyday experience. There is a freedom in being limited. Moreover, freedom is also bestowed by grace. Humanity does not need to carry bad karma through endless reincarnations since Christ carried all our burdens on the cross once and for all. Forgiveness can be received in one moment through grace. Our dilemma, as well as its solution, is personal and relational. There is no karmic mechanism at work.

The technological spirituality of the NA is very different from the relational spirituality of the Christian tradition. In spite of NA talk of 'letting go' there is a focus on manipulation and mastery of cosmic energy. Its magical worldview assumes that the basic solution to our common problems is the empowerment of the self. Reacting against the power of 'the other', one affirms the power of the self. This shift is complicated by the fact that all moral distinctions are being obliterated. If 'All is Love' it is hard to know when you manipulate or hurt others. NA books display a dangerous naivety in these matters. The cosmic force beyond good and evil provides no corrective in this techno-magical approach to power. The holy love of God provides a better framework for our relationships with fellow humans and with God. Any kind of manipulation violates a true relationship which, by contrast, is characterized by mutuality, giving and receiving. Martin Buber said: 'whoever knows the world as something to be utilized knows God the same way.'[138] Even Christians are called to move from technique to trust. Christian spirituality is, as James Houston says, first of all a transforming friendship.

The Future Modernity represents in many ways, especially in Sweden, an attempt to build a heaven on earth through rational planning and social engineering. A Swedish writer remarks that the thoroughly planned welfare state has abolished the existential dilemma of dependence.[139] In an affluent society where everything is taken care of, Christians easily adopt a pattern in everyday life in which they do not need one another, let alone God. We become accommodated settlers who enjoy the good life without having to worry much about the future since that will be taken care of, on an individual basis, by an intervention from God. Through an identification with the present order and a privatized faith we accept the status quo in society. New Agers are presently occupying both the prophetic void and the 'service void' which the church has failed to fill.[140] The NA takes a clear stand against cultural sins and vices such as materialism, racism, neglect of the poor and the oppressed, environmental abuse and the like, and therefore challenges the church to inner renewal and outward action. The NA is also meeting needs in areas the church has neglected. They are in the forefront of reforms in health care, education, and business personnel 'development', and have led the way in a number of social innovations.[141] By contrast, Christian initiatives tend to be more supportive than transformative of established institutions and social processes.

The drive behind the NA critique of society and social activities, the factor that unites a spirituality of almost painful plurality, is a transformative vision of the future.[142] There is a common commitment to making the world a better place. From a Christian standpoint this vision is problematic in several ways. It is a cosmic humanism which places humanity at the centre of the stage of history. The Bible also teaches that the new order is not an inherent quality in humanity. The kingdom of God is a gift from God. Moreover, the NA does not involve a future radical defeat of evil since evil is only an illusion. In spite of considerations like these I believe that NA eschatology is a challenge to the life and teaching of the church. Much Christian preaching is emptying this present age of significance out of concern for the age to come.[143] The coming of the kingdom is located in a distant future at the end of time. But the New Testament teaches the presence of the future in the here and now. The future has already happened in and through the work of Christ; the new age has come. Salvation is thus much more than a personal insurance against future trouble. The inbreaking of God's kingdom, God's future, brings a whole new reality into human life which has profound social and ethical consequences. Participation in the life of this kingdom by faith involves a prophetic nonconformity to the world. It assumes the Lordship of Christ over both our private and public lives. It manifests itself in the preaching of the good news, works of the Spirit and acts of social justice. Its scope is both personal and communal, local and global. This kingdom is yet provisional since Christ will come again and perfect God's purpose for this earth and the whole universe. A new world will be born, a transformed and transparent creation glorified in God, and glorifying God who is all in all. The Spirit of God enables anticipations in the present of this promised perfection. Have we lost the eschatological drive to live transformed lives in this present age? Today we must address people's need to experience a transformational reality. 'Scripture speaks of a covenant people joined together in a pilgrimage toward the wholeness and healing of creation in Christ. This transforming vision must shape our proclamation of the gospel and the reality of our lives together in congregations.'[144]

CONCLUSION

The church in the postmodern society needs: 1) to question its allegiance to modernity in a number of areas, 2) to listen carefully to the New Ager's response to the present crises in society and, 3) to discover the treasures of its own heritage. Christians need to move from fear to faith, from theory to practice, from periphery to centre. We are often afraid to meet people with other convictions. This fear is to a large degree dependent on a lack of rootedness in our own faith and a lack of knowledge of other faiths. Today we need to grow in knowledge and faith. By daring to bring ourselves and the Gospel out to the crossroads where the choices are made, we will discover that the Christian faith can stand the test of this present time.

Even if theological and intellectual clarity is needed as we face NA seekers, we will seldom get far with advanced theoretical disputes. New Agers are more attracted by the experiential qualities of our faith. A personal testimony can often be more fruitful than right apologetics. We do of course need to share both our experiences and balanced arguments. The problem is that many Christians are bad at both. Most people who turn to the NA do so out of a personal crisis. They struggle with life on a very basic level, trying to make sense of their situation in a complex society. Any Christian faith that seeks relevance today therefore needs to be very practical.

Christians often become deeply worried as they are confronted with the NA because of all the striking similarities in vocabulary and practice. The NA challenges us to ask whether we have our identity in socially conditioned behaviour or in the outward manifestations of the faith. It stirs us to seek the deeper meaning of the Christian words that we commonly use. It calls us to move from the periphery to the centre. It urges us to approach the cross. Only there do we actually see what makes the Christian faith unique. Only there do we meet Someone who has the power to save even the most self-centred human being.

Writing this last section I was interrupted by a telephone call from a young pastor in deep distress. The reasons were, firstly, that several younger Christians were dropping out of church and giving up the faith because they are unable to cope with the complexities of being a Christian in modern society. Secondly, a young woman, whom he considered to be a solid Christian, had suddenly told him that she had become a Buddhist. He was not only shocked but felt unable to have a fruitful discussion with her because of his lack of knowledge. There can be no more urgent task for the church than to pray, fast and reflect over the future of Christianity in the West.

Notes

1. A Swedish sociologist suggests that we use the expression 'religious change' in order to avoid certain conceptual difficulties and get a more useful concept with regards to what is happening in society (Gustafsson, Göran, Tro, Samfund, Samhålle, 'Sociologiska perspektiv', Libris, 1991, page 206).

Very good surveys of the debate can be found in:

Karel Dobbelaere, 'Some trends in European Sociology of Religion: The Secularization Debate,' Sociological Analysis, 1987, 48, 2: pages 107–137;

David Lyon, The Steeple's Shadow, On the Myths and Realities of Secularisation, SPCK, 1985.

Also a shorter version by Peter B. Hamm, 'The Sacred and secularisation', in L. Driedger and L. Harder, editors, Anabaptist-Mennonite Identities in Ferment, Occasional Papers no. 14, Institute of Mennonite Studies, Elkhart, Indiana, 1990.

A particular problem is how you define religion. Different patterns emerge depending on whether you apply a substantive (content) or functionalist definition. New patterns also appear in the tension between collective and individualistic interpretations of religion as seen in the different concepts of civil, common (folk) and implicit religion. Analyses of these concepts, in different contexts, may lead us to question the impact of secularization and show that religion is still very much with us. While recognizing that religion has lost its status in public institutions, Thomas Luckman sees new social forms which have taken over some of the traditional functions of religion. The family, sexuality and individualism, for example, are given a sacred status in modern society and forms elements of what he calls 'the invisible religion'. Here we perceive a connection with N. Luhman's word, 'The social structure is secularized—the individual is not'. (Dobbelaere, page 124).

At the end of the 1970s Peter Berger wrote that modern secularity was in a state of crisis. 'The most obvious fact about the contemporary world is not so much its secularity, but rather its great hunger for redemption and for transcendence.' (Peter L. Berger, *The Heretical Imperative, Contemporary Possibilities of Religious Affirmation*, Anchor/Doubleday, 1979, page 184).

Secularization is often seen as a product of modernization and of having a worldwide effect, also influencing other cultures which are in the process of becoming modernized (P. Berger, *The Sacred Canopy, Elements of a Sociological Theory of Religion*, Anchor/Doubleday, 1969, page 108).

Secularization need not be inevitably linked with modernization, something which the Asian development can show us (G. Baum, 'Modernity: A Sociological Perspective', *Concilium*, 1992/6, page 5).

It is common to link modernization to secularization in the West through the concept of 'de-institutionalization'. The de-institutionalization of religious reality in society immediately precedes, and indeed is a prerequisite of the secularization of religious world views (James Davison Hunter, *American Evangelicalism, Conservative Religion and the Quandary of Modernity*, Rutgers University Press, page 14).

2. Some of the motives are as follows:

◇ According to various writers they are a response to the process of rationalization and the phenomenon of secularization which it brings in its train. The end product is a world bereft of the sacred, of magic and mystery. New religions are thus a response to secularization.

◇ The rapid changes in a transitory postmodern, postindustrial society are also seen as hard to absorb at an emotional, psychological and intellectual level and therefore makes people prone to seek a new synthesis in life.

◇ It has further been suggested that the new religions are a response to the crisis of community in Western societies, some of them also trying to provide a new sense of community which has been lost in society.

◇ It is also common to explain the new religions with reference to a general crisis of meaning and a loss of value consensus in society, this being a consequence of modernity.

◇ Anthony and Robbins, following Bellah, associate the new religions with a crisis in American Civil religion.

Useful surveys can be found in:
Dick Anthony and Thomas Robbins, 'Spiritual Innovation and the Crisis of American Civil Religion', in *Daedalus*, III (1), Winter 1982, pages 215—234

Eileen Barker, 'Religious Movements: Cult and Anticult since Jonestown', *Annual Review of Sociology*, 1986, 12, pages 329–46

Robert Bellah, 'The New Consciousness and the crisis in Modernity', in Charles Y. Glock and Robert Bellah, editors, *The New Religious Consciousness*, University of California Press, 1976

P. Berger, B. Berger and H. Kellner, *The Homeless Mind*, Penguin, 1974

Peter B. Clarke, *New Religious Movements*, Centre for the Study of Religion and Society, Pamphlet Library number. 4, 1984

Peter B. Clarke, 'The Occult and Newly Religious in Modern Society': part II, in *Religion Today*, volume 7, number 3, summer 1992

James Davison Hunter, 'The New Religions: Demodernization and the Protest Against Modernity', in Bryan Wilson, editor, *The Social Impact of New Religious Movements*, The Rose of Sharon Press, 1983

R. Wuthnow, 'Religious Movements and the Transition in World Order', in Needleman/Baker, editors, *Understanding the New Religions*, Seabury, 1981

A thorough and extensive survey is John A. Saliba, *Social Science and the Cults, An Annotated Bibliography*, Garland Publishing, 1990

3. Claude Geffr and Jean-Pierre Jossua, 'Editorial: Towards a Theological Interpretation of Modernity', *Concilium*, 1992/6, page ix

4. James A. Beckford, 'Introduction', in J.A. Beckford, editor, *New Religious Movements and Rapid Social Change*, Sage Publications, 1986, page x

5. Dobbelaere [note 1], page 127

6. Colin Campbell, 'Some comments on the new religious movements, the new spirituality and postindustrial society', in E. Barker, editor, *New Religious Movements: A Perspective for Understanding Society*, The Edwin Mellen Press, 1982, page 6. Page references are made to a prepublished photocopy.

7. Anthony and Robbins [note 2], page 231

8. Gordon Melton, *Encyclopedic Handbook of Cults in America*, Garland Publishing, 1986, page 107. A valuable resource is Melton, Clark, Kelly, *New Age Encyclopedia*, Gale Resarch, 1990

9. See, for example, Paul Heelas, 'The New Age in a Cultural Context, the Premodern, the Modern and the Post-modern', *Religion*, volume 23, number 2, April 1993, pages 112–13

10. Thomas Gandow, *New Religious Movements in the New Europe, Update & Dialog*, no 1/1993

11. Berger and others [note 2], *The Homeless Mind*, page 182

12. Marshall Berman, *All That is Solid Melts into Air, The Experience of Modernity*, 1982. Reference made to the Swedish edition, *Allt som är fast förflyktigas*, Arkiv Förlag, 1987, page 13

13. Baum [note 1], page 8

14. J. C. Scannone, 'The debate about Modernity in the North Atlantic World and the Third World', *Concilium*, 1992/6, page 78

15. To sort out the conceptual confusion, Philip A. Mellor suggests that the terms 'postmodernism' and 'postmodernity' can be distinguished on the following grounds: '... "postmodernism" signifies a particular approach (or series of related approaches) to the interpretation of contemporary culture. It is characterized by the assumption that "a crisis in modernity" has occurred, involving a loss of the "master narratives" which have shaped Western culture and consciousness since the Enlightenment..."postmodernity" is surely something rather different: this term refers (or ought to refer) to the kind of cultural environment which actually exists (or might exist) in the aftermath of this "crisis of modernity" the postmodernists tell us about'. Philip A. Mellor, 'Reflexive traditions'; Anthony Giddens, 'High Modernity, and the Contours of Contemporary Religiosity', *Religious Studies*, 29, pages 11–127, 1993, Cambridge University Press, page 112.

16. Mary Farrel Bednarowski, 'The New Age Movement and Feminist Spirituality: Overlapping Conversations at the End of The Century', in James R. Lewis and J. Gordon Melton, editors, *Perspectives on the New Age*, State Univerity of New York Press, page 169

17. Berger and others, *The Homeless Mind* [note 2], page 181

18. the same

19. It is worth noting that the spiritistic mass movement and the revival of the esoteric tradition during the nineteenth century should be seen as a protest, providing a third way out between scientific materialism and Christianity (Geoffrey Ahern, 'Esoteric New Religious Movements and the Western Esoteric Tradition', in E. Barker, editor, *Of Gods and Men*, Mercer University Press, 1984, page 171; Håkan Arlebrand, *Det Okända, om Ockultism och Andlighet i en ny tidsålder*, Libris, 1992, page 172). By including evolutionary teaching (Blavatsky, Steiner) and making scientific claims (Steiner) they gained a higher degree of plausibility.

20. Willis Harman and Howard Rheingold, *Higher Creativity*, Jeremy P. Tarcher, Inc. References are made to the Swedish edition, *Inspirationens ögonblick*, Förlagshuset Hagaberg, Vallentuna, 1987, page 199

21. William Bloom, editor, *The New Age, An Anthology of Essential Writings*, Rider, 1991, page xvi

22. Fritjof Capra, *The turning point: Science, Society and the Rising Culture*, London, Wildwood House, 1982, page 77

23. Lawrence Osborn, 'The Machine and the Mother Goddess: The Gaia Hypothesis in Contemporary Scientific and Religious Thought', *Science and Christian Belief*, volume 4, April, 1992, page 35

24. Roman Schweidienka, 'Der Neue Kult um Mutter Erde', *Esotera*, 1/1991, page 91

25. Theodore Roszak, *Unfinished Animal—the Aquarian Frontier and the Evolution of Consciousness*, Faber, 1976, page 96

26. Barbara Max Hubbard, 'The Evolutionary Journey', in Bloom, editor, *The New Age, An Anthology of Essential Writings*, Rider, 1991, page 4

27. Marilyn Ferguson, *The Aquarian Conspiracy—Personal and Social Transformation in the 1980s*, J. P. Tarcher, 1980, page 180

28. Quoted in Brooks Alexander, 'Holistic Health from the inside', *Spiritual Counterfeits Project Journal*, August 1978, page 9

29. William Irvin Thompson, 'Introduction' to David Spangler, *Revelation the birth of a New Age*, Findhorn Publications, 1978, page 9

30. Scientism being 'a metaphysical construct which takes as one of its basic assumptions the belief that the scientific method is the only valid route to truth and that it therefore provides us with a comprehensive view of reality.' Ernest Lucas, 'Scientific Truth and New Age Thinking', *Science and Christian Belief*, volume 4, April 1992, page 22

31. Clifton/Regehr, 'Capra on Eastern Mysticism and Modern Physics', *Science and Christian Belief*, number 1, 1989, pages 57, 66

32. Campbell, 'Some Comments on the New Religious Movements' [note 6], page 8

33. Charles T. Tart, *States of Consciousness*, E.P. Dutton, 1975, page 206

34. *A Course In Miracles: The Text, Workbook for Students and Manual for Teachers*, Tiburon, California: Foundation for Inner Peace. London: Arkana, 1988, *Manual for Teachers*, page 53. ACIM is more sharply dualistic than other NA books in its description of the contrast between ordinary human experience and ultimate reality. The growing influence of this book may intensify this trait in the NA.

35. Lawrence Osborn, *Angels of Light, The Challenge of the New Age*, Daybreak/ Darton, Longman and Todd, 1992, page 10

36. *A Course in Miracles, Textbook* [note 34], page 2

37. Roszak [note 25], page 164

38. Jacques Ellul, *The Technological Society*, Continuum Publishing Company, 1980, page 174

39. the same

40. Hunter, *American Evangelicalism* [note 1], pages 74, 82

41. Annastina Wrethammar, *Tänk dig ett bättre liv, Om affirmationer och positivt tänkande*, Trevi, 1988, page 77

42. Shirley MacLaine, *Going within*, Bantam, 1989. References are made to the Swedish edition, *Resan Inåt*, Pan/Nordsteds, 1990, page 141.

43. L. Hay, *You can Heal your life*, Hay House, 1987. References are made to the Swedish edition, *Du kan hela ditt liv*, Energica förlag, Orsa, 1988, page 22. Sondra Ray, *Loving Relationships*. Reference are made to the Swedish edition, *Kärleksfulla relationer*, Livskraft förlag, Stockholm, 1984, page 18

44. Ken Keys Jr, *Handbook to Higher Consciousness*, Living Love Center, 1975, page xv, and in passing

45. Gary Doore, 'The New Shamans', *Yoga Journal*, Jan/Feb, 1989, page 44

46. Hans Joachim Turk, *Postmoderne*, Mathias-GrunewaldVerlag, Mainz, Quell Verlag, Stuttgart, 1990, page 80; John Milbank, 'Problematizing the Secular—The Post-Modern Agenda', pages 30–44, in Philippa Berry and Andrew Wernick, editors, *Shadow of Spirit, Postmodernism and Religion*, Routledge, 1992, page 30. The whole book, *Shadow of Spirit*, deals with this interesting field. Quasi-religious thematics are present in postmodernist texts, page 31. According to Milbank, even the secular is composed of rearranged fragments of religious discourse and makes up its whole substance, page 37.

47. Lyotard defines postmodern 'as incredulity toward metanarratives', Jean-Francois Lyotard, *The Postmodern Condition: A Report on Knowledge*, Manchester University Press, 1987, page xxiv.

48. D. Harvey,*The Condition of postmodernity*, Blackwell, 1989, page 45; Ernest Gellner, *Postmodernism, Reason and Religion*, Routledge, 1992, page 30

49. Thompson in David Spangler and William Irvin Thompson, *Reimagination of the World, A Critique of the New Age, Science, and Popular Culture*, Bear and Company, 1991, page 83

50. the same, page 132

51. Gellner [note 48], pages 24, 29, 40. The connection with the NA is not made by Gellner, but by me as I see striking similarities in these contemporary moves from objectivity to subjectivity.

52. Turk [note 46], page 13

53. Harvey [note 48], page 44

54. Robert C. Solomon, *Continental Philosophy since 1750, the Rise and Fall of the Self*, Oxford University Press, 1988, page 14

55. Roszak [note 25], page 7

56. Solomon [note 54], page 21

57. Paul Heelas, 'The Sacralization of the Self and New Age Capitalism', in N. Abercrombie and A. Warde, editors, *Social change in Contemporary Britain*, Polity, 1992, page 149

58. A striking illustration of this diagnosis is found in the personal testimony of New Ager Barbara Hubbard [note 26], page 3

59. Paul Heelas, 'The Limits of Consumption and the Post-modern "Religion" of the New Age', in Nicholas Abercrombie, Russell Keat and Nigel Whiteley, editors, *The Authority of the Consumer*, Routledge, 1993, page 4. Page references are made to a prepublished photocopy of the paper.

60. Hunter, *American Evangelicalism* [note 1], page 14

61. Berger and others, *The Homeless Mind* [note 1], page 165

62. Hunter, *The New Religion* [note 2], page 7

63. Berger and others, *The Homeless Mind* [note 2], page 180

64. Hunter, *The New Religions* [note 2], page 11

65. Hunter, *The New Religion* [note 2], page 12

66. Hunter, *American Evangelicalism* [note 1], page 92

67. Berger and others, *The Homeless Mind,* page 190. On contemporary assumptions about the self and identity, see also, R. Bellah, R. Madsen, W. Sullivan, A. Swindler, and S. Tipton, *Habits of the Heart,* University of California Press, 1985

68. Martin L . Gross, 'The Psychological Society'. Reference made to the Swedish edition, *Det psykologiska samället,* tema nov, 1980, page 15

69. Anthony Clare and Sally Thompson, *Lets Talk About Me. A Critical Examination of the New Psychotherapies,* BBC, 1981. Reference made to the Swedish edition, *Nu talar vi om mig, en granskning av de nya psykoterapierna,* Forum, Borås, 1983, pages 227; Paul C. Vitz, *Psychology as Religion, The Cult of Self-worship,* Eerdmans, 1982

70. Roszak [note 25], page 18

71. Nevill Drury, *The Elements of Human Potentia,* Element Books, 1989, pages 115, 123

72. Harman/Rheingold [note 20], page 218

73. Rupert Sheldrake, 'Rediscovering the Sacred', in Eddie and Debbie Shapiro, editors, *The Way Ahead,* Element Books, 1992, page 194

74. Thompson, *Reimagination,* [note 49], page 111

75. Joseph Campbell, *The Power of Myth,* Doubleday, 1988. References are made to the Swedish edition, *Myternas makt,* SvD Förlag, 1990, pages 28, 87

76. Kenneth Wapnick, 'A Talk given On A Course in Miracles, An Introduction', Foundation for 'A Course in Miracles', 1992, page 23. In several discussions with adherents of ACIM it has been almost impossible to agree on differences since they are thoroughly programmed towards monism.

77. Mark Satin, *New Age Politics, Healing Self and Society,* Delta Books, 1979, page 99

78. Maxine Birch, 'The Goddess/God Within: an initial exploration into alternative health seeking practices and spirituality', paper presented to the BSA Sociology of Religion Study Group Conference, 'Postmodernity and Religion', Bristol, 1993, page 5

79. James W. Sire, *The Universe Next Door, a basic Worldview Catalog,* updated and expanded version, InterVarsity Press, 1988, page 168

80. Shakti Gawain, *Creative Visualization,* Whatever Publishing, 1978. References made to the Swedish edition, *Kreativ Visualisering,* Energica, Orsa, 1987, page 96. See also MacLaine, *Going Within* [note 42], pages 88, 329

81. Observing this and the further development of Gawain towards an emphasis on spiritual contact (Drury [note 71], page 112), one can conclude that the Higher Self as a paranormal channel for information is congruent with the spirit guides we find in Spiritism (Arlebrand [note 19], page 85).

82. Solomon [note 54], page 44

83. Benjamin Creme, *The Reappearence of the Christ and the Masters of Wisdom*, Tara Press, 1980, page 132

84. Osborn, *Angels of Light* [note 35], page 129

85. Gawain [note 80], page 57; Hay [note 43], page 19; MacLaine [note 42], page 199. Creative affimations and visualization are materialized and you can even choose your own parents and moment of death.

86. Compare Clarke, *New Religious Movements* [note 2], page 19

87. Hay [note 43], page 81

88. Compare Osborn, *Angels of Light* [note 35], page 130

89. Hans-Jürgen Ruppert, *Ockultismus, Geisterwelt oder neuer Weltgeist?* Edition Coprint/R B Brockhaus, Wiesbaden und Wuppertal, 1990, page 143

90. Birch [note 78], page 9

91. Ruppert [note 89], page 144

92. J. Stillson Judah, 'From Political Activism to Religious Participation', in *UPDATE, a Quarterly Journal on New Religious Movements*, vol.6, March 1982, Aarhus, Denmark, page 11

93. Heelas, *The New Age in a Cultural Context* [note 9], 1993, page 105

94. the same, page 106

95. the same, page 110

96. Heelas, *The Limits of Consumption* [note 59], page 1. Besides the previously noted articles by Paul Heelas see also:
'Californian Self-Religions and Socialising the Subjective', in E. Barker, editor, *New Religious Movements: A perspective for Understanding Society*, The Edwin Mellen Press, 1982, pages 69–85
'Cults for Capitalism? Self Religions, Magic and the Empowerment of Business', in Peter Gee and John Fulton, editors, *Religion and Power, Decline and Growth*, British Sociological Association, 1991, pages 27–41
'The New Age, Values, and Modernity', paper delivered to the UNESCO conference on 'People in Search of Fundamentals', 1991
'God's Company: New Age ethics and the Bank of Credit and Commerce International', *Religion Today*, volume 8, number 1, autumn/winter. 1992
On Religion and the Contemporary climate, see also:
Richard H. Roberts, 'Religion and the "Enterprise Culture": the British Experience in the Thatcher era (1979–90)', paper delivered at the SISR Conference, August 1991, Maynouth, Ireland

E. Barker, 'New Lines in the supra-market, How much can we buy?', in *Religious Pluralism & Unbelief, Studies critical and comparative*, Ian Hammet, editor, Routledge, 1990.

97. Berger, *The Sacred Canopy* [note 1], page 138

98. Philip A. Mellor and Chris Shilling, 'Reflexive Modernity and the Religious Body', paper presented to the BSA, Sociology of Religion Study Group Conference, Postmodernity and Religion, Bristol, 1993, page 4

99. Keyes, *Handbook to Higher Consciousness* [note 44], page 129

100. Solomon [note 54], page 202

101. Gordon Melton, 'The Coming of the New Age: A Social Vision invades the Occult', Paper presented at the meeting of the American Academy of Religion, Oakland, California, March 30–31, 1990, pages 1, 8

102. Hubbard [note 26], page 4.

103. Ulli Olvedi, 'Neue Zeit mit alten Fehlen', *Esotera*, Freiburg, March 1988, page 6

104. Melton, *The Coming of the New Age* [note 101], page 8

105. Mellor/Shilling [note 98], page 4

106. David Lyon, 'A bit of a Circus: Notes on postmodernity and New Age', *Religion*, volume 23, number 2, April 1993, page 122

107. the same, page 123

108. the same

109. Bednarowski [note 16], page 168

110. First, there are, for example, several different interpretations of the new physics. None of them unanimously validates a particular religious philosophy (Clifton/Regehr [note 31], pages 55). Many of the metaphysical implications of the new science, for example, the inter-connectedness of all things, do not conflict with the Christian belief in a creator that constantly sustains an orderly universe (Lucas [note 30], page 24).

111. Alan J. Roxburgh, *Reaching a New Generation, Strategies for Tomorrow's Church*, InterVarsity Press, 1993, page 51

112. the same, page 75

113. Colin E. Gunton, 'The Church on earth: The roots of Community', in Colin Gunton and Daniel Hardy, editors, *On Being The Church—Essays on the Christian Community*, T. & T. Clark, 1989, page 67

114. The quotation as well as the distinctions from Romans 8 are from the very valuable article: 'The Trinity and the New Age Movement', in *Third Way*, July/August, 1991, page 30, by Jeremy Begbie. This article and Roxburgh's book, *Reaching a New Generation*, are some of the most creative responses to NA spirituality that I have found so far, besides some of the more apologetic books that have been published.

115. Lucas [note 30], page 25

116. Alvin Plantinga and Nicholas Wolterstorff, in Kelly James Clark, *Return to Reason*, Eerdmans Publishing Company, 1990, page 3

117. Nancy Murphy, *Theology in the Age of Scientific Reasoning*, Cornell University Press, 1990, page 201

118. Several attempts are already being made, for example in: Reformed epistemology (A. Plantinga, N. Wolsterstorff, etc), Postliberal theology (G. Lindbeck, H. Frei, R. Thieman, etc), Lakatosian theology (Nancy Murphy), different Polanyian approaches by Andy F. Sanders, T.F. Torrance, Colin Gunton, Jerry H. Gill and Lesslie Newbigin. A.C. Thiselton's work in hermeneutics is also valuable.

119. Colin E. Gunton, 'Knowledge and culture: towards an epistemology of the concrete', in Hugh Montefiori, editor, *The Gospel and Contemporary Culture*, Mowbray, 1992, page 92

120. the same, page 98

121. J. Campbell [note 75], page 105

122. Roxburgh [note 111], page 116

123. The stories of an original feminine spirituality with a Mother Goddess is an example of the speculative. The many esoteric christologies and the claim that the church originally embraced reincarnation are examples of theories which include a lot of data without any historical support.

124. Alister McGrath, *The Enigma of the Cross*, Hodder, 1987, page 123

125. Colin E. Gunton, *Christ and Creation*, Paternoster, Eerdmans, 1992, page 89

126. John Stott, *The Cross of Christ*, InterVarsity Press, 1986, page 212

127. Stanley Hauerwas and William H. Willimon, *Resident Aliens, Life in the Christian Colony*, Abingdon Press, 1990, page 47

128. the same, page 43

129. Roxburgh [note 111], page 95

130. Begbie [note 114], page 31

131. the same

132. Colin E. Gunton, *The Promise of Trinitarian Theology*, T. & T. Clark, 1991, page 116

133. Begbie [note 114], page 31

134. John D. Zizioulas, *Being as Communion: studies in personhood and the church*, St Vladimir's Seminary Press, 1985, page 18

135. the same, page 2

136. Roxburgh [note 111], page 99

137. Gunton, *The Church on Earth* [note 113], page 78

138. in Gregory L. Jones, *Transformed Judgement—Toward a Trinitarian account of the Moral Life*, University of Notre Dame Press, 1990, page 161

139. Maciej Zaremba, 'Vår paniska skräck för beroende' *Moderna Tider*, nr 31, maj 1993, page 15

140. Elliot Miller, *A Crash Course on The New Age Movement*, Baker Book House, 1989, page 137

141. the same, page 138

142. Roxburgh [note 111], page 96

143. David F. Wells, 'The Future', in *Christian Faith & Practice in the Modern World*, Mark A. Noll and David F. Wells, editors, Eerdmans, 1988, page 300

144. Roxburgh [note 111], page 100

11

An ironic cage: the rationalization of modern economic life

CRAIG M. GAY

At the conclusion of his celebrated essay *The Protestant Ethic and the Spirit of Capitalism*, Max Weber submitted that the modern economic order, linked as it is to technology and the conditions of machine production, had become a kind of 'iron cage' from which there was very little hope of escape. Capitalism, Weber felt, had become a most fateful and irresistible force in modern life, a force that might possibly continue to determine the shape of modern existence until, as he put it, 'the last ton of fossilized coal is burnt'.[1] Weber's comments about modernity's 'iron cage' are grounded in an analytical framework that goes some distance toward helping us to understand some of the peculiar features of modern society. The conceptual key to this framework, and indeed the conceptual key to Weber's understanding of the process of modernization, lay in his understanding of 'rationality' and, in particular, in his understanding of the process of 'rationalization', a process in which the appropriateness of social action ceases to be determined by tradition (including religious tradition) and/or custom and comes to be determined instead by abstract, calculable, and largely impersonal that is, 'rational' criteria. I propose to examine this process of 'rationalization' in the following essay, but with an eye toward assessing our chances of escaping modernity's 'iron cage'. For it just may be that the present moment calls somewhat ironically for a rediscovery of one of the very notions that Weber held responsible for the rationalization of economic life: the Christian notion of 'calling'. As this notion implies an intentional and personal address on the part of One who calls for a personal and covenantal response, the Christian conception of 'calling' requires the radical expansion of some of the very horizons of existence which have been drastically limited by, and indeed imprisoned within, the 'iron cage' of modern rationalized existence.

Types of rationality

'Rational' conduct, according to Weber, entails the purposive orientation of one's actions with respect to the actions of others and with respect to the means employed in achieving freely chosen ends.[2] One acts 'rationally,' in other words, if one employs the appropriate means to achieve ends deemed in advance to be desirable. Hence rational conduct is conduct that strives to master and/or shape reality in some subjectively meaningful way and it strives to eliminate uncertainty and contingency. Along this line, Weber distinguished 'rational' conduct from that prescribed unthinkingly by tradition as well as from conduct resulting from affective or emotional states.

Weber also understood the term 'rationality' to be of rhetorical significance in that it can be attached to actions retrospectively to justify them. This is why rationality must be understood not simply as an instrument of will but as a direct reflection of will. Rationality, in other words, is perspectival. The use of the term 'rational' always masks a prior determination as to what it is appropriate to seek by acting rationally.

The perspectival character of 'rationality' owes to the fact that there are actually a number of different types of rationality. Weber identified four of them (though these are not the exact words he used): practical, theoretical, formal, and substantive.[3] Each type is geared toward a different kind of end and, as a result, the different types are often in tension with each other as well as with 'traditional' and/or 'affective' conduct generally. Along this line, Weber held that many of the most characteristic and ironic features of modernity reflect conflicts between different types of 'rationality.'

'Practical' rationality is perhaps most familiar to us as it simply involves trying to employ the appropriate means toward the realization of subjectively determined ends. This kind of practical and self-interested caste of mind most commonly characterizes the daily lives of merchants, artisans, traders, and others who are commonly suspicious of the impracticality of other ways of assessing the rationality of action. In this regard, Weber observed that the disposition toward practical rationality tends to surface in situations where religious understanding does not inhibit the pragmatic caste of mind required for 'business as usual,' as it were.

'Theoretical' rationality involves the attempt to understand and to 'make sense' of the world by means of theoretical abstraction. Theoretical rationality may be applied to specific problems or to the construction of entire worldviews. It may depend upon or develop religious doctrines or it may generate purely secular understandings. Theoretical rationality ultimately finds its impetus, Weber felt, in humanity's irrepressible quest for meaning.

'Formal' rationality is oriented toward adherence to formally established rules, principles, and procedures. It is largely (though not entirely) unique to the modern situation. Similar in many respects to practical rationality, formal rationality relies upon simple means-ends calculation, but instead of applying this calculation to the solution of problems of self-interest, it tries to solve problems by ordering them under universal and abstract rules.[4] Bureaucracy requires formal rationality and bureacratic administration is the most conspicuous example of the process of formal rationalization.

'Substantive' rationality is oriented toward ultimate ends and purposes. Because of its 'values' orientation, 'substantive' rationality often gives rise to the active reformation of social life, and frequently lies behind social change. Weber observed that only 'substantive' rationality possesses the strength to discipline effectively both the practical caste of mind oriented toward purely subjective and egoistic interests, and the purely formal orientation to rules.

The process of rationalization

Each of the four different types of rationality have given rise to episodes of 'rationalization,' that is, to the evacuation of traditional and/or affective conduct from different spheres of social life. Such episodes have usually occurred in isolation. The fact that a number of modernity's central institutions have been rationalized simultaneously and in a synergistic manner is notable. Modern science, for example, owes its success to the expansion of a certain kind of theoretical and formal rationality in the modern period; the modern state could not exist except for the formal (bureaucratic) rationalization of political administration; the modern economy, furthermore, requires the practical-rational actions of pragmatic and self-interested producers and consumers; and all of these crucial institutions and endeavors have their origins in and to some extent still depend in the West at least upon a substantively-rational worldview provided initially by the Christian religion.

Yet the rationalization of modern life has been marked by a number of ironies. For all of their claims to 'rationality' and to having enhanced human freedom to pursue certain ends, many ostensibly 'rational' institutions appear to function quite irrationally and to permit very little freedom. Indeed, the 'rational' means we have employed as instruments to enhance our freedom have not only failed, at times, to yield this freedom, but these very means have had an insidious tendency to become ends in and of themselves, even to the extent that their continued use has become a kind of fateful necessity.

There is an additional irony which the modern situation confronts us with particularly if we are Christians. It is that the theoretical, formal, and especially practical rationalization of such things as science and technology, politics, and the economy have undermined the originally substantive and largely Christian understanding of the world which appears to have given rise to these developments in the first place.

The rationalization of economic life

The 'rationalization' of economic life has not simply required the elimination of tradition and custom from exchange relationships but has entailed the actual ordering of exchange relationships such that they are geared toward practical and pragmatic ends in a consistent and disciplined fashion. The principles necessary for this consistent and disciplined ordering, furthermore, have become central to the theoretically-rational and, perhaps even more importantly, to the formally-rational legitimation of enterprise. Hence—and this is very important—mcdern economic activity is theoretically conceived and formally required to be practical-rational.

Weber understood the rationalization of the modern economy

to require the following:[5] the existence of a market in which competition is possible; individual ownership of property; a method of rational accounting based upon a money economy; and formally free labor dependent largely upon wage-labor for survival. What this list suggests is that the rationalization of modern economic life depended, at least initially, upon social conditions which encouraged the freedom of practical-rational (i.e. individualistically and subjectively determined) exchange within the boundaries of formal predictability. Given the importance of substantive rationality in catalyzing social change, furthermore, it appears likely that the encouragement of practical rationality in economic life must at one time have been substantively legitimated. Ironically, the process of rationalization seems to have resulted in a situation in which we now have very little choice *but* to pursue practical-rational exchange within the confines of the formally-rational requirement of 'growth' legitimated only by theoretically-rational notions of 'progress'. Why this ironic and puzzling reversal? Important clues appear to lie in the way in which modern enterprise is organized and administered, in the rhetorical aspects of rational accounting, in the peculiar habits of mind fostered by the use of money, and in the increased degree of specialization that rational economic exchange naturally gives rise to.

Because practical rationality seeks to coordinate means and ends as precisely as possible, it tends toward the elimination of uncertainty and contingency. One obvious yet critical source of uncertainty and contingency in economic life has to do with the people involved in economic enterprises and the extent to which enterprises are disrupted by the death of those responsible for them or by the entry of new personnel into them. A number of institutional strategies have been developed to shield organizations from this sort of uncertainty, the most effective of which is probably the modern limited-liability corporation which received legal definition toward the end of the nineteenth century. The development of the corporation has contributed quite substantially to the practical rationalization of modern life for at least two reasons. First, the logic of the modern corporation is such that practical, formal, and theoretical rationality are essentially fused within it. The modern firm is formally required to pursue its own self-interest in a practical-rational fashion in the context of a market which, in theory, needs its participants to act in just such a fashion in order to function properly. The second reason is simply that the logic of the firm is, at least in principle, 'eternal' and hence somewhat immune to substantively-rational considerations which, as we have seen, must hold ultimate ends in view. The only real 'end' against which the modern firm's substantive progress may be assessed is that of continued growth.

As far as the rhetorical aspects of rational accounting are concerned, recall that the terms 'rational' and 'irrational' are often used to justify or condemn alternative courses of action. And yet given that the use of these terms is perspectival, how is it possible for them to carry any real rhetorical weight? The answer to this question, at least insofar as economic activity is concerned, has to do with the conventions we have adopted to account for economic activity. The development of rational accounting, and particularly of double-entry bookkeeping, was critical in the development of early capitalism, and it is important to recognize that rational accounting continues to be crucial to capitalism, not simply because it enables us to measure the relative effects of economic actions accurately, but also because it enables us to 'give account' for these actions.[6] Rational accounting does this by abstracting away from the complexity of real life, which process renders important criteria for economic decision-making relatively easy to interpret and to act upon. In terms of the types of rationality discussed above, we typically say that economic action is 'rational' or 'justified' when it can be shown to be so in terms of formally-rational accounting procedures. Again, this simply means that practical rationality is formally and theoretically required in modern enterprise.

Rational accounting presupposes the kind of reduction of quality to quantity already made possible by the use of money. Along this line, Georg Simmel linked the self-consciousness, intellectuality, and rationality of modern urban life directly to the pervasive use of money.[7] He contended that money's mathematical character enables it to reduce the concrete and qualitative relationships between things with precision and reliability and in terms of parity and disparity. This reduction has had a significant psychological impact in the modern situation, captured in the term 'blasé', an outlook in which considerations of 'value' and 'quality' are increasingly collapsed into the consideration of 'quantity'. The subjective impact of the use of money combined with the formal necessity of monetary abstraction for rational accounting goes some distance toward explaining the peculiar 'habit of rationality' that has become such a prominent characteristic of modern life. This peculiar outlook is captured in the phrase, reputedly coined to describe Singaporean merchants: 'they know the price of everything, but the value of nothing'.

Lastly, the practical-rationalization of modern economic life has been exacerbated by the increasingly complex division of labor that rational economic exchange inevitably gives rise to. The on-going specialization of enterprise, which has become such a central feature of modern economies, effectively hinders the ability of any kind of substantive rationality to discipline the process. It is not surprising that modern ethicists have found it so difficult to keep pace with the issues and problems generated by the modern technological economy, for the pace with which the practical-rationalization of economic life issues forth in new products, roles, and social relationships seems to increase at an almost exponential rate.

In sum, if modern economic existence is often experienced as a kind of 'iron cage' this is because it is dominated by a peculiar kind of practical-rational outlook, an outlook that has become the standard for assessing the 'rationality' or 'irrationality' of economic actions, and an outlook that has been essentially 'built in' to the logic of modern economic enterprise in any number of fascinating ways. While this pragmatic outlook is only formally required in 'accounting for' economic decisions by means of rational accounting procedures, it has had a tendency to spill over into other areas of life in such a way that the practical-rational virtues of 'efficiency', 'maximization', 'least cost', 'productivity', etc., characterize much of what has been called bourgeois culture, including even the subjective consciousness of bourgeois individuals. Furthermore, the application of this practical-rational outlook in science and politics as well as in economic life has been consistently legitimated in the modern period by way of a theoretically-rational quest for mastery often discussed under the banner of 'liberalism', an ideological outlook which took shape toward the end of the seventeenth-century in Europe. Along this line, Weber contended that Protestantism, and especially Calvinist Protestantism, contributed quite significantly to this development.

The ideational origins of the rationalization of economic life

The ascendancy of the practical-rational outlook in recent centuries, particularly in the area of economic life, begs an interesting question. How can this have happened, given the fact that practical rationality, depending as it does upon individualistically and subjectively determined ends, normally possesses only a very limited capacity to catalyze historical social change? Weber felt that the answer to this important question lay in the fact that at a particular juncture in Western history practical rationality became substantively important within a larger theoretical (indeed theological) conception of the world. Specifically, he contended that Calvinist Protestantism first gave rise to the uniquely practical, disciplined, and this-worldly 'spirit' that would eventually issue forth in capitalistic economic enterprise and the rationalization of modern economic life.

Weber suggested that Calvinism's powerful synthesis of practical and substantive rationality was both intentional and unintentional. It was intended to the extent that it was implied in the Protestant elimination of the distinction between sacred and secular 'callings'. The Reformers insisted that all practical activity in the world, or at least all practical activity not otherwise at odds with the moral law, was not only morally justified but was to be considered an essential aspect of God's 'call' to individual Christians. For Lutherans, the radical implications of this new understanding were partially mitigated by Luther's static conception of individual 'callings' in terms of the traditional framework of late-medieval society. Calvinists, however, unleashed the radical social potential of the Protestant redefinition of 'calling' by insisting that the Christian is called to the deliberate and energetic reform of the social order itself so that it may become in accord with the divine commands. Within this reform process, furthermore, practical and instrumental rationality was held to be vital. As a result, Calvinists tended to be more open to the retrospective assessment of the actual results of innovations than their Roman Catholic and/or Lutheran counterparts. If something proved to be useful and successful as, for example, the rationalization of economic activities inevitably did, it was deemed to be God's will and in accordance with natural law.

Weber also insisted that Calvinism's synthesis of practical and substantive rationality was unintended in that it was a kind of accidental byproduct of practical pastoral advice aimed at lessening the anxiety associated with the doctrine of double-predestination. Such advice suggested that diligent work in the world could help to assuage this anxiety, especially to the extent that this work revealed its consonance with God's purposes by being effective. In practice, Weber concluded, this meant that God helped those who helped themselves.[8] As it turned out, this emphasis upon diligence and discipline proved to be a powerful catalyst of social change and innovation, particularly in the area of economic life.

Of course, Weber has been criticized for misunderstanding and misinterpreting the counsel of the Puritan divines on matters having to do with the pursuit of wealth.[9] Others have wanted to place a stronger emphasis upon the significance of Calvinism's destruction of the traditional feudal order, arguing that this is really where Calvinism's signal contribution to modernity lay.[10] And yet, in spite of all of the criticism and qualification of Weber's analysis, it has undoubtedly served to draw attention to the intriguing similarities between Calvinist (and especially Puritan) thought and the practically, formally, and theoretically-rational secular utilitarianism which emerged toward the end of the seventeenth century.

Basically, the Reformers' affirmation of 'this world' and their redefinition of the Christian notion of 'calling' appear to have suffered a kind of ironic reversal and in a fairly short period of time. While these theological innovations had originally been intended only to refute the medieval distinction between 'sacred' and 'secular' callings, and although the Reformers obviously had no intention of shifting the balance of emphasis away from eternal life toward life in 'this world', this is precisely what eventually happened. The Protestant affirmation of everyday life came to mean the affirmation of the fundamental importance of practical rationality in 'this world' over and against the substantive concerns for 'the world to come'. Indeed, the Christian religion itself came to be understood in an entirely different way, that is, as simply a means to the practical improvement of 'this life'.

The conflict between 'practical' and 'substantive' rationality implicit in this revised understanding of Christianity seems not to have been noticed at first. John Locke and others assumed that

Christian doctrine, at least to the extent that it was rid of mysterious and superstitious encrustations, must function in practice to improve human life, and that obedience to the Law of God must give rise to happiness in the 'present age' as well as, presumably, in the 'age to come'. But Lockean Christianity quite rapidly devolved into Deism, and the emphasis rapidly shifted from the substance of faith to attempting to determine the requirements of happiness understood naturalistically.

Assessing the practical-rationalization of economic life

The practical-rationalization of modern economic life and the pragmatic 'habit of rationality' the modern economy fosters can be assessed from any number of angles. Perhaps the first thing to say is that, in spite of any reservations we may now have about the process, our assessment cannot and should not be entirely negative. This is simply because most of us have benefited so greatly from the process. The practical-rationalization of production and distribution in modern economic life has resulted in sustained economic growth which has, in turn, translated into vastly improved material standards of living for most people in modern societies. And yet, the blame for so much of what appears to be wrong with modern society may be attributed to this same material transformation of the world. The modern market economy's substantial material benefits, in other words, have come at significant cost.

Philosophically speaking, the rationalization of modern economic life may be said to have enhanced human freedom, at least to the extent that we define freedom in terms of freedom from arbitrary customs and/or traditional sources of authority. On the other hand, it is doubtful that this 'liberal' conception of freedom as freedom *from* want or *from* traditional constraints really exhausts the topic of human freedom. Freedom must also be defined positively. It must be *for* something as well as *from* various constraints to action. Freedom must be discussed substantively in terms of ultimate human purposes as well as pragmatically in terms of the absence of constraints. Now it is precisely this substantive consideration of human purpose that, as we have seen, is inhibited by the internal logic of the rationalized economic order.

261

From a theological point-of-view, it has been observed that the practical-rationalization of economic life has contributed quite substantially to the process of secularization in modern societies. There appear to be at least two reasons for this. On the one hand, to the extent that secularization involves a kind of transposition of aspirations from the 'religious' to the 'secular' sphere,[11] the market economy may be said to contribute to this process accidentally by generating affluence so effectively. Only the affluent, it seems, can 'afford' to locate the sum total of their aspirations in temporal reality. But secularity is not just accidental to the modern economy. As Nathan Rosenberg and L. E. Birdzell have noted, it has been the relative autonomy of the economic sphere in the capitalist political-economy, that is, the economy's freedom from religious and political interference that has, among other things, accounted for the remarkable productivity Western economies have experienced in recent centuries.[12] The key elements of the West's 'growth system', Rosenberg and Birdzell argue, 'were the wide diffusion of the authority and resources necessary to experiment; *an absence of more than rudimentary political and religious restrictions on experiment* [my emphasis]; and incentives which combined ample rewards for success ... with a risk of severe penalties for failing to experiment.'[13] Hence to the extent that secularization may be defined as the process by which sectors of society become freed from the decisive influence of religion,[14] the modern rationalized market economy may be said to be secularized by design. Indeed, it appears to work for just this reason. The problem with the secularization of economic life is that those who grow used to the 'absence of religious restriction on experiment' in the marketplace tend to resist such restrictions in other areas of life as well. It is for just this reason that Berger has gone as far as to say that 'economic data on industrial productivity or capital expansion can predict the religious crisis of credibility in a particular society more easily than data derived from the "history of ideas" of that society.'[15]

Yet in addition to undermining the substantive consideration of freedom and contributing to the process of secularization, the practical-rationalization of modern economic life, biased as it is toward subjectivism and egoism, must also be seen as a symptom of the characteristically modern conceit that it is up to us to create either individually or collectively our own meanings and purposes. To have extended the logic of practical rationality as far as we have in modern society means in effect that we must imagine that we possess a kind of 'Archimedean freedom' of self-definition outside of nature and perhaps even over and against God.[16] Along this line, Louis Dupré has noted that modern self-understanding has tended to reduce all ontological relations to those of efficient causality because such relations are rationally manipulable.[17] 'This elimination of ontological dependence,' Dupré contends, 'proceeds from a freely chosen orientation, a deliberate reduction of reality to the status of an object constituted by a mind that [has] come to view itself as the sole source of meaning and value.'[18] It does appear to be the case that the modern preoccupation with practical-rational methods and techniques reflects a deliberately chosen and supremely subjective orientation toward the world. If the appropriate techniques can only be determined for the discovery of 'usable' knowledge, for the engineering of society, for the engineering of the self, etc., the modern mind imagines that it can master nature and ultimately itself. Along this line, it is not difficult to trace a connection between this 'ontological leveling' and the use of abstractions like money which enable us to determine and to attribute 'values' to the stuff of the world. Yet the signal irony in the modern quest for mastery by means of practical rationality is that, in the end, it renders the social world and even the natural world all the more uncontrollable and fearsome. The world, it seems, stubbornly resists our subjectively—and egoistically—determined purposes and retaliates by becoming 'fateful'.[19] As C.S. Lewis put it, man's conquest of nature has turned out to be nature's conquest of man.[20]

And so we face quite a dilemma with respect to the practical-rationalization of economic activity in modern society. The process has proven tremendously productive and we have come to depend upon its continuing productivity, and yet this very productivity appears to be intrinsically and perhaps inextricably linked to the eclipse of substantive rationality in the modern period. The practical, subjectivistic, egoistic, and individualistic orientation toward the world which Max Weber contended is not capable of ordering or 'making sense' of the world in any particular way, now presents itself with the formal force of law and theoretical support of any number of compelling modern ideologies as the only 'rational' way forward, as our fate. While perhaps it would be an overstatement to describe this situation as an 'iron cage', at the very least it is an ironic one.

Conclusion: toward a recovery of a substantive rationality

Immediately following his depressing comments about the 'iron cage' of industrial-capitalistic existence, Weber went on to opine:

> No one knows who will live in this cage in the future or whether at the end of this tremendous development entirely new prophets will arise, or there will be a great rebirth of old ideas and ideals, or, if neither, mechanized petrifaction, embellished with a sort of convulsive self-importance. For of the last stage of this cultural development, it might well be truly said: 'Specialists without spirit, sensualists without heart; this nullity imagines that it has attained a level of civilization never before achieved...' But this brings us to the world of judgments of value and of faith, with which this purely historical discussion need not be burdened...[21]

While Weber refused to 'burden' his purely historical discussion with matters of value and faith, the logic of his analysis of rationality and rationalization suggests that the only way to discipline the practical-rationalization of modern society, that is, the only way to render this process less mechanical and dehumanizing will be to rediscover and to reassert some kind of substantively-rational understanding of the social world. What would such a view of the world have to look like under modern conditions? At a minimum it would need to attempt to render the events of life formally, theoretically, and practically in accordance with ends or purposes deemed to be ultimate. A substantively-rational worldview would necessarily be *teleological* in the sense that it would evaluate present conditions in terms of their movement either toward or away from ultimate and potentially realizable goals. Any number of proposals have been forwarded along this line. Alasdair MacIntyre has recommended, for example, a rediscovery of a kind of modified Aristotelianism.[22] John Milbank has recommended, similarly, the recovery of an Aristotelianism fitted within the larger *mythos* of Augustine's 'city of

God'.[23] Canadian social philosopher George Grant contended for a rediscovery of a kind of medieval 'natural theology' in which we are again enabled to 'admire' and appreciate the creation and createdness.[24] Similarly, R.H. Tawney argued for a return to medievalism by means of a recovery of an understanding of society as 'social organism.'[25] Yet while all of these proposals are worth considering in detail, it is distressing that they all appear to require us to return to a kind of medieval understanding of theological and social authority. All of them seem to imply the requirement of some sort of *magesterium* that would be responsible for determining the substance of the relationships within the social/spiritual organism. The Protestant distinctives of *sola Scriptura, sola gratia, sola fides*, the priesthood of all believers, etc., although they are not condemned or even explicitly addressed in these proposals, tend to be implicitly repudiated by them to the extent that the medieval social order is held up as the ideal of substantively rational social order. In this connection, it is not difficult to see why the burden of modernity has become such a particularly heavy one for modern Protestants. For if Protestantism was, at least in part, responsible for catalyzing the practical-rationalization of modern life, so it would seem that the most obvious 'solution' to the problem would be to try to 'undo' the Reformation by attempting to reintroduce the authoritative social order of Christendom, or at least something like it, to the modern situation. The question arises, then, as to whether or not there is anything to be said about this problem from a distinctively Protestant (and Evangelical) point-of-view.

While a comprehensive answer to this question is far beyond the scope of this paper (and its author), let me make two suggestions as a contribution to the development of such an answer.

Recovering a 'sabbath' attitude

The first, which is obviously not distinctively Protestant, simply has to do with what I have called elsewhere a 'sabbath attitude.'[26] This is an attitude that erects a fence around practical-rational economic activity, and indeed around all human activity. It does not deny the value of human work in the world, but it confines it within substantive limits, relativizing it over and against God's work in the world and the coming of his kingdom. The sabbath

265

attitude is built upon an eschatological understanding in which we are prohibited from expecting an immanent human resolution to the problems of the human condition, including those associated with modern society. This attitude is repulsed by modern (and postmodern) assumptions that it is somehow up to us to 'create ourselves' through our own practically or theoretically rational efforts.

Recovering a Protestant understanding of 'calling'

In addition to recovering a Sabbath attitude, breaking free of the 'ironic cage' of modern rationalized existence may also require, as I mentioned at the outset of this essay, a recovery of the distinctively Protestant notion of 'calling'. There are at least two reasons for this. The first has to do with the degree of abstraction required by the various kinds of rationalization we have discussed. In this connection, recall that practical, formal, and theoretical rationality all require us to abstract away from the complexity and particularity of actual human experience. This abstraction is what accounts for rationality's actual and potential mastery of the world, and the extension of this mastery is what rationalization is all about. But recall also that many of the thorniest problems associated with the practical, formal, and theoretical-rationalization of economic life, especially the impersonal and dehumanizing tendencies of this process, all have to do with abstraction, and particularly with abstracting away from *persons*. For this reason, whatever else we may want to say with respect to the recovery of a substantively rational worldview in the modern context, this worldview will need to be one in which persons are substantially exempted from rationalized abstraction. Ironically, at least in light of the modern use of the term outlined above, the distinctively Protestant understanding of 'calling' is very well-suited to protecting truly personal existence from rationalized abstraction. This is because the term 'calling' implies a personal address on the part of the one who calls to another who is therefore called to a personal response. In Christian understanding it is the personal God who calls sinners to repentance and to the obedience of personal faith and trust in him. Indeed the Christian faith is one in which deeply personal relationships—the love of God and the love of the neighbor—are of ultimate significance. The essential Christian call, then, is to the reconciliation of personal relationships through which the possibility of truly personal existence is opened up. In this connection, although Christians (and Evangelicals in particular) have commonly attended to the doctrinal content of the Christian faith, the significance of that *to* which we are called has sometimes been neglected. Put somewhat differently, Evangelicals have tended to become so preoccupied with a kind of propositional conception of truth that they have neglected the relational purpose, *telos*, of all Christian propositions. This neglect has subsequently led to confusion on the matter of how the dignity of persons is derived, and this confusion has contributed, albeit passively and unintentionally, to the devaluation of persons in the modern rationalized context. What this context calls for, then, is a rediscovery and reassertion of a fully Christian understanding of personhood, an understanding entailed in the Christian notion of 'calling'. As Emil Brunner observed over forty years ago:

> [The] dignity of human personality is not grounded in
> an abstract, general element in all men, namely reason
> [as in Greek thought], but individual personality as
> such is the object of this appreciation because it is
> deemed *worthy of being called by God* [my emphasis].
> Only the personal God can fundamentally establish
> truly personal existence and responsibility,
> responsibility being the inescapable necessity to
> answer God's creative call, and to answer it so that this
> answer is also a decision ... The love of God does not
> create an abstract, impersonal humanity; it calls the
> individual to the most personal responsibility.[27]

As Brunner's comments suggest, the Christian understanding of 'calling' is profoundly individuating and personalizing. Indeed, Brunner contended that we really only become persons to the extent that we respond to God's call to us in love and trust, love and trust which form the obedience of faith. That the concept of 'calling' may have contributed to the rationalization of modern life is not simply ironic, it betrays a serious theological misunderstanding on the part of our early-modern ancestors. If Weber was at all correct about this, it may have had something to do with the logic of double-predestination, a logic which, if pursued too relentlessly (as Calvinists have had a tendency to do) actually has the effect of obliterating human personhood by collapsing human 'response-ability' into the doctrine of election. To the extent that this actually occurred, it is not difficult to imagine why anxious souls might have tried to lose themselves in diligent labor, and why they might have been so willing to submit to the abstraction implicit in the rationalization of early-modern social and economic life. Practical-rational diligence and effectiveness, in a sense, became a way of proving, not really a 'call', but a fate. Of course, it needs to be stressed in this connection that the problem does not appear to have been with the doctrine of divine election *per se*, but instead with the assumption that the logic and workings of God's election were humanly intelligible and hence that a rational theology could be constructed on the basis of this doctrine. In any event, the point to make here is simply that the Christian understanding of 'calling' preserves, or ought to preserve, the centrality of the *person* in Christian substantive and ethical reflection. Indeed, the notion of personhood and personal responsibility must be seen to be central to a truly Trinitarian theology. Were we really to engage in this sort of substantive and ethical reflection on personhood, we might find ourselves better able to come to grips with and to discipline the seemingly autonomous logic of the modern economic order.

The second reason that the Christian and more specifically the Protestant understanding of 'calling' is relevant to the problem of the 'iron cage' of rationalized economic life has to do with the character of modern work and its apparent immunity to qualitative and/or substantive considerations. As mentioned above, the logic of practical-rational enterprise is such that it requires specialization and an ever-increasing differentiation of skills, roles, and relationships in the workplace. Enterprise also requires abstracting away from the uncertainties and contingencies such as death that attach to personal existence. Taken together, these two requirements mean that the narrative structure of the modern workplace is fundamentally at odds with that of the human beings involved in it. Put differently, unlike real human persons, institutions and firms do not possess immortal souls threatened by death and divine judgment, and so they do not really need to question the meaning of their existence in the light of these contingencies. Instead, the logic of the firm is such that it is simply geared toward perpetual, quantitatively-measured growth. The impersonality of this logic goes some distance toward explaining why the modern worker has so often been depicted as a kind of 'cog' in the larger 'machine' of industrial civilization; for while the practical-rationalization of enterprise does require workers to be consistent, predictable, precise, uniform, etc., it does not really require them to be persons, that is, to grow, to develop character, to search for truth, etc. Certainly, the inhumanity of the modern workplace has been exaggerated by those who hoped that the immiseration of the worker predicted by Marx and others would give way to revolutionary social change; and, contrary to these revolutionary expectations, the workplace has by-and-large grown increasingly humane over the course of this last century. And yet, however comfortable the modern workplace might have become, the practical-rationalization of work is still subject to Christian critique insofar as the process of specialization prevents us from being persons 'on the job', as it were. While space does not permit a detailed discussion of this matter here, suffice it to say that our experience of personhood is impeded by work that is simply too narrow and too specialized to do justice to the formation of character. Indeed, many 'jobs' are so specialized and so narrow that it simply doesn't make any sense to talk about them in terms of the construction of character or in terms of the realization of one's calling before God. Instead, such jobs really cannot be discussed in anything but merely functional and/or quantitative terms. Nevertheless, it is important to stress that when the scope of a job is narrowed to the extent that it simply becomes a kind of 'fate', no matter how willingly this fate is accepted and no matter how efficient or necessary the job might be, it must be judged from a Christian perspective to be wasteful. Indeed, it is wasteful of the only thing in 'this world' that really matters: the opportunity to exercise and to develop personal responsibility in the world before God. In this connection, it is undoubtedly true that one of the chief reasons the modern rationalized economic order has so often been experienced as an 'iron cage' is because of its tendency, as Weber put it, to produce 'specialists without spirit' and 'sensualists without heart', that is, mere functionaries who become so thoroughly integrated into the machinery of modern rationalized existence that they cease to be persons. Clearly, the recovery and application of the high standard of personhood implied in the Christian notion of 'calling' could only be experienced as a breath of very fresh air in the modern context.

Reviewing the development of modernity's 'iron cage' reveals that it has only really become a cage to the extent that we have chosen to make it so, that is, to the extent that we have submitted more-or-less willingly to its inherent abstractions and dehumanization in hopes of achieving a kind of collective mastery over the world, mastery that has thus far eluded our grasp. We might have chosen differently; and, indeed, we still can. But, of course, choosing differently requires the reopening of a number of difficult questions that even Christians have gotten out of the habit of asking in the modern period, questions like: Who are we? What are we here for? and How should we live in light of who we are and what we are here for? Along this line, Christians would do well to reconsider the implications of such elementary affirmations as that of Sabbath and of 'calling', especially with reference to modern economic life. The centrality of persons and of personal responsibility implied in both of these crucial Christian doctrines—grounded ultimately in the personal existence of the triune God—may well provide us with the substantive and ethical muscle we will need to discipline the practical rationalization of so much of modern life. Indeed, our only hope of restraining the impersonal logic of the modern rationalized economic order may lie in just this kind of substantive reorientation in which we are able to criticize and reform economic systems on the basis of how persons are treated within them; protesting in order to free persons from imprisonment within modernity's 'iron cage'.

Notes

1. Max Weber, *The Protestant Ethic and the Spirit of Capitalism*, Scribner, 1958, original 1904–05, page 181

2. See, for example, Max Weber, *Economy and Society*, vol. 2, editors, Guenther Roth and Claus Wittich, University of California Press, 1978, pages 1375ff. It is perhaps important to stress that Weber's various discussions and definitions of 'rationality' and 'rationalization' are somewhat confused (or at least confusing). As Stephen Kalberg has noted in his excellent survey article entitled 'Max Weber's Types of Rationality: Cornerstones for the Analysis of Rationalization Processes in History' (*American Journal of Sociology*, 85, 1980, page 1146): 'Weber himself is largely responsible for the lack of clarity that surrounds his analyses of "rationality" and the interplay of multifaceted historical rationalization processes. His scattered and fragmented discussions of this theme are more likely to mystify than to illuminate.'

3. See Kalberg's discussion here in 'Max Weber's Types of Rationality' [note 2], pages 1148ff.

4. the same, page 1158

5. Weber [note 1], page 17

6. Bruce G. Carruthers and Wendy Nelson Espeland, 'Accounting for Rationality: Double-Entry Bookkeeping and the Rhetoric of Economic Rationality,' in *American Journal of Sociology* 97:1 (July), pages 57–58

7. Georg Simmel, 'The Metropolis and Mental Life,' in Kurt Wolff, editor *The Sociology of Georg Simmel*, The Free Press, 1950, page 412

8. Weber [note 1], page 115

9. Charles and Katherine George, 'Protestantism and Capitalism in Pre-Revolutionary England', in S.N. Eisenstadt, editor, *The Protestant Ethic and Modernization: A Comparative View*, Basic Books, 1968, page 165

10. See Michael Walzer, 'Puritanism as a Revolutionary Ideology,' in Eisenstadt [note 9], pages 109–04

11. See Larry Shiner, 'The Meanings of Secularization', in James F. Childress and David B. Harned, editors, *Secularization and the Protestant Prospect*, Westminster, 1970, page 38

12. Nathan Rosenberg and L.E. Birdzell, Jr., *How the West Grew Rich: The Economic Transformation of the Industrial World*, Basic Books, 1986

13. the same, page 33

14. Peter L. Berger, *The Sacred Canopy: Elements of a Sociological Theory of Religion*, Anchor, 1969, page 107

15. the same, page 151

16. George Grant, 'In Defense of North America', in *Technology and Empire: Perspectives on North America*, Anans, 1969, page 32

17. Louis Dupré, 'The Closed World of the Modern Mind', in *Religion and Intellectual Life*, 1 (Summer, 1984), page 26; see also Milbank, *Theology and Social Theory: Beyond Secular Reason*, Blackwell, 1990, page 241

18. Dupré [note 17], page 27

19. See Glenn Tinder, *Against Fate, An Essay on Personal Dignity*, Loyola Series on Political Analysis, Richard Shelley Hartigan, editor, University of Notre Dame Press, 1981, page 131

20. C.S. Lewis, *The Abolition of Man*, Collins, 1978 [original 1943]

21. Weber [note 1], page 182.

22. See Alasdair MacIntyre, 'Nietzsche or Aristotle, Trotsky and St. Benedict', chapter 18 of *After Virtue*, pages 256ff

23. See Milbank [note 17], pages 363 ff

24. See Grant, 'In Defense of North America', [note 16].

25. See R. H. Tawney, *Religion and the Rise of Capitalism: A Historical Study*, Harcourt , Brace & Co., 1952, pages 61–2

26. See Craig M. Gay, *With Liberty and Justice for Whom?: The Recent Evangelical Debate Over Capitalism*, Eerdmans, 1991, pages 236 ff

27. Emil Brunner, *Christianity and Civilisation*, Volume 1, 'Foundations', Scribner, 1948, page 94

12

Modernity, information technology and Christian faith

KNUD JØRGENSEN

The dominating technology today is the information technology which creates our images of the world. These images are secular and commercial and are a universal language spreading to the entire world. The media become the arena for the myths and values of our modern culture. How do we as Christians relate to this global phenomenon?

What sort of church do we need in an information society? This question may imply a critique of the Church. The only biblical point of departure for criticizing the church is the dream of a church which *confronts* our Western worldview and calls it to repentance. We are allowed to dream of such a church—a church on the move, always relevant for today's world, which always relates its task to its historical situation. If the church cannot communicate in the language and culture of this present generation, 'It is tragically out of touch, not only with the world of today but also with the God of today.'[1]

The answer is not a 'service-oriented' church governed by supply and demand, nor a diluted popular church which tones down conversion and personal commitment. Even less do we need a church that adapts to our worldview's haste for instant gratification. Such a consumer mentality results in congregations that become a spiritual smörgåsbord from which people choose dishes according to colour, taste and satisfaction, more than according to nutritional value and a balanced diet.

The true answer is to *let the Church be the Church* in today's world, without being a museum (or a prison) for the Lord's mighty deeds in the past; note what Tor Aukrust says about the 'temple desire' in us and the danger of seeking refuge in the

273

ecclesiastical sphere.[2] We need instead a new exodus from our fear of the future.

The church finds itself in a crisis of communication as we move into an information society.

'Information society' has to do with our Western culture. In the form of 'modernity' it has spread to most parts of the world, via media, multi-national companies, education and mission—in the form of a modern culture—which has grown out of and would be inconceivable without the Christian faith, but which at the same time more than any other culture needs to be confronted with the Gospel.

This modern culture is characterized by a belief in cause and effect, a feverish hunt for an immanent Jerusalem, an indefinite cycle of production for consumption, self-interest and desire as the fuel in a capitalist system. It is, as Lesslie Newbigin asserts,[3] basically without purpose and meaning and therefore corresponds well to New Age religiosity. It has made a dogma of dividing up life into public and private—facts belong in the public realm and values in the private realm (therefore faith has been privatized).

To a large extent the information society and information technology are the *pinnacle* of this modern worldview. Here nature is totally in our power. Here is the technology for an enormous expansion of our hunt for cause and effect. Here are the instruments for our striving towards happiness and welfare. In the same way, our electronic media are the crank in our modern worldview. These media, and especially television, reflect and communicate our modern worldview and all its myths. Within a worldview of striving for happiness and self-interest, the media tell us what 'the world' looks like, how it functions and what it means. In this way television functions as the creator and transmitter of our culture:[4] it takes our history and our present time and interprets them to us. The media provide us with the worldview which not only determines *what* to think, but also *how* to think and *who* we are. In this way media, information society and modernity hang together.

The basis for the information society

The information society is a child of the marriage between tele- and computer technique—the French call this marriage *telematique.* The building blocks are cable, satellite and computer. It is not a question of many new media; instead we are offered new ways of using the media and new combinations of existing media and technologies.

Two other important elements are increased capacity for storage and transfer and miniaturization: sound and light impulses are transformed into digital code and stored or transferred by means of fiber-optic cables; the process of miniaturization implies a development away from the big mass media towards a mini media that soon becomes personal media in home and household. This computerization of home and society will bring a new way of life, moving work and services into our homes (the electronic cottage; 'Home is where the computer is').

There are at least four interrelated reasons why we need to pay attention to information technology:

◇ Information technology is 'a heartland-technology' which will influence all aspects of our life in a much more comprehensive way than the technology of the industrial society.

◇ Information technology raises questions about power and information gulfs—gulfs that tend to follow social and cultural groupings and patterns.

◇ The speed of technological change is accelerating. As a result, the technology, including bio- and gene technology, outruns the political decision processes.

◇ The consequences of the development of information technology are far-reaching and global. The entire society may be transformed into a global village.

Social consequences

The information society will be a different society. The Japanese analyst, Yoneji Masuda,[5] claims that in this different society the production of information values and not material values will determine development. The computer bank will replace the factory as symbol of society, a synergistic economy will replace the industrial exchange economy, the trade union will be replaced by a citizens' movement. Already the major part of the labour force works on creating, handling and distributing information, and the number of jobs will decrease drastically. Before

275

the year 2000 the retirement age in many countries will have gone below fifty years of age—at the same time, unemployment will increase. The computerization of the home will result in an introvert society. Society seems to be moving towards a decentralized society where the hierarchies within politics, trade unions and religion will be replaced by informal networks similar to the co-operative movements of the past.

A shift from supply to being selective is taking place. In most Western homes one can today choose among 10–15 television channels. Even more important are the changes in perception of reality brought about through an increasing media consumption and the media's communication of values. The result is a growing passivity (the plug-in drug). In addition, it looks as if an unlimited supply has the effect that those groups with the highest media consumption (which at the same time are those with lowest social status) obtain less information from a multi-channel system because they choose entertainment and sport and avoid the more information-laden programmes. The end result of the greater variety is simply 'more of the same kind'; look at the tendency in the United States where 'the least objectionable programme' dominates the media scene.

Is the information revolution after all an illusion?[6] We were promised fundamental changes in society. Instead we have so far got more of the same thing via cable and satellite. Firstly, the development has been much slower than promised. Secondly, the man in the street has not received all the new services, all the alternatives and the opportunities for education that he was promised. Where is the socially relevant information and the entertainment for the elderly, the handicapped and for linguistic and cultural minorities? Instead of the electronic participatory democracy there is less participation in politics. The information explosion has become what the Americans term 'infotainment', i.e. information (and education) transformed into entertainment and 'chewing gum for the eyeballs'. The only places one sees the revolution, Traber claims, are in the banks, in the secret services, in the stock market and in the offices of the multinational companies.

One reason is people's insatiable need for entertainment.[7] Our paradigm is less George Orwell's big brother watching us from the wall than Huxley's 'Brave New World' where mankind goes dancing into the abyss. We ourselves choose the entertainment—in the media and in religion.

There are strong indications that the communication revolution so far has consolidated the military, economic and political power élites. That applies particularly to the military forces which dominate 80–90 per cent of all satellites, and it applies to the multinationals. The result can be a closed haven where those in power decide. In turn this implies increasing information-gulfs, both between various social groups and between rich and poor countries. Penguins do not become more human because they get refrigerators! Technological progress does not automatically lead to a change in the quality of human life. Instead such progress in quantity—more computers, more channels, more satellites—reduces the quality of life. In this way the information society may cement the winners and transform the losers into computer-controlled losers.

Technology as the idol of modern culture?

Does the information society represent another concept of technology than the industrial society—an understanding which makes technique the very spirit in our worldview and the organizing idea of society? The theologian and sociologist Jacques Ellul[8] has raised this question. Modern society has become 'technified': its principle of organization is technology or technicism (belief in, dependence on technology). Order, coherence and function are defined technologically. It is not so much that we use the computer as that the computer forms our culture. Within this society and its worldview (which Ellul calls *la technique*), information technology is the heartblood for other technologies. Ellul claims that *la technique* is the logical consequence of our modern culture and of a futile exploration of cause and effect to such a degree that the consequence itself, the technology, has become the idol of our culture.

There is at least little doubt that the technology has become the universal language of modern culture. If you cannot read and talk that language, you have lost even before you start. And the language is primarily that of information technology. Wherever you go in the world, you see the footprints of our technology and hear the sound of its electronics. If you do not master this language, you will drown in Coca Cola and Donald Duck.

The problem is that the worldview of technology turns

everything upside down: it transforms the means into goals, and the good becomes the pragmatic—that which makes things happen. In this way our worldview lures us into ascribing greater power to technology than it actually has (one example is the supercomputers used for the Star Wars programme). If we make technology into the solution of our problems, it has ascended God's throne. Technology is not neutral: it creates our image of the world and defines society and worldview. What is dangerous here is the power we give to technology and the way we combine it with our self-interest, for where this happens technology will assume a religious character. The flaw is not in technology as such; the problem began when we developed technology within a culture that no longer had room for a living God and his purpose for life. The culture in which the technology has been developed has gone astray, and technology becomes an idol for this reason.[9]

Where technology gains a religious character, it becomes a threat to religion. William Fore mentions three threats:

1. The technological worldview will divert our world's interest, motivation, satisfaction and energy away from a religious centre. Examples of this are found in the empty churches in Europe and the growing gulf between faith and practice in American churchgoers.

2. The technological worldview takes the power out of our religious vocabulary. Religious symbols, images and rituals become meaningless. Instead of relating to Abraham, Moses and Paul, technological man relates to the images of 'Dallas' and 'Dynasty'. Our religious images and our biblical language forms become relics from a past culture.

3. The technological surroundings encourage a religiosity which has little or no interest in organized religion. Such a religiosity can be found in New Age, in the movies of Steven Spielberg, in the peace movements and Greenpeace, in the horoscopes of our magazines and similar signs of folk religion. In the United States the scene teems with folk religious magazines where one may read the most fantastic pseudo-religious tales about the baby born with a wooden leg, visits of angels from Mars, women that died five times, etc. When the Christian lid is taken off a culture, the wild fantasies of paganism come teeming up again.

On the threshold of this different society, we need to be aware that we are in the midst of an exodus in which we, as church, must go on to relate to people in a different society. One cannot and should not move backwards into the future as the church did with industrial society. We need orientation lest the experts take over, and we need to choose: what are we going to use it for? who decides? what is the aim? Without clear choices we shall end in idolatry of the electronic horse or in what some have called 'the triumph of convenience'.

We need an alternative worldview that gives synthesis, norms and a genuine vision of the future. A Christian worldview:

◇ which interprets human history with Christ as the centre;

◇ which gives us moral attitudes and values that distinguish between truth and lie, between good and evil;

◇ which gives us a vision of the future as it looks in the perspective of the Kingdom and the return of Christ.

We need a living congregation that challenges our worldview and calls it to repentance—not an electronic church that has adjusted itself to the technological worldview to such a degree that it has become part of the problem rather than part of the solution. The electronic church represents by and large a 'culture Christianity' which has become part and parcel of its host culture to the degree that it is more adjusted-to-culture than Christ-oriented.

Media and myths

The show window of the technological worldview is found in the mass media. Here we find the vocabulary of the technology. Here religious values and persons are commercialized and secularized. Here our message is turned into consumer goods—even news is only interesting if it sells. Everything is trivialized by media that have become tools for production and consumption. The media are not neutral; they function as the cultivator of our culture. Media will 'mirror' reality and make me believe that I am part of this 'reality'. While the printed word gave me a linear experience of reality, our modern picture media give me a visual and fragmented way of seeing reality because while they mirror reality they also select and distort. They function as a window on the world, but a window that limits and colours my experience, a window which lures me into believing that what I see in the dirty window, corresponds to the real world. They give me 'mono-vision' and create a pseudo-reality.

So the media, as tools for the worldview of modernity, usurp a role that used to belong to the church—creating our values, forming our faith and giving expression to our culture. This has to do with the general function and role of television:

◇ We become more dependent on media communication and gain access to more channels and media.

◇ The media become the cornerstone in our economic system and will therefore transform communication into a consumer good.

◇ Within a modern culture we use the media for relaxation and escapism. We therefore welcome the media offer of banality and triviality. In the midst of a hectic world we opt for entertainment.

In the midst of this the media slowly change me. They reflect, verbalize and make visual the myths that tell us who we are and what is of value. They interpret both past and present and thereby become our common memory. The entire media process gives me my worldview. That is why communication and media basically have to do with culture—our culture. Our culture has allowed the media to become our collective nervous system and in this way take over the dominating communication role in our lives, a role which makes the media a pseudo-religion, giving expression to the values and beliefs of human beings and providing us with a worldview in stark contrast to the Christian worldview. Thus the media have become the propaganda tool of our technological society, and the aim of this propaganda is conformity and 'orthodoxy', i.e. to achieve a behaviour which serves the technological society.

A key element in this propaganda is 'packaging'. The important thing is not how things are, but how they appear. You do not sell a car just because it is faster and better. No, the packaging, the presentation sells. Therefore the effects are essential use of sound, light, colour, pacing. It is a matter of illusion and 'credibility' and only to a lesser degree of content and truth. The media paint a picture for the viewer of what sort of person he would like to be and then they make him believe that 'our' product is a necessary ingredient of that picture. In this way you sell Coca Cola without talking about Coca Cola, by presenting a lifestyle. The media sell image—a cosmetic reality without substance. And some Christian media productions make use of similar methods: instead of 'selling Jesus', they sell people who can witness about the therapeutic effects of the Gospel in their successful lives.

This sale of lifestyle and image is wrapped up in myths, symbols, pictures and fantasy. In the past the church played a key role in conveying myths, as in the mystery plays of the Middle Ages. Today our myths come to us via the media. William Fore mentions four main myths:[10]

◇ The survival of the fittest: The theories of Darwin dominate in education, work, politics and leisure. The fittest in society and the media world are not the lowest classes, the coloured or the foreign labour force. They rather play the fall guys.

◇ Power and decision-making start in the centre and move outwards: Washington is the centre for politics and Hollywood for entertainment. We are at the periphery and are allowed to peep into the arena of power.

◇ Happiness consists of limitless material acquisition. Consumption is an absolute good. Property, riches and power are more important than people.

◇ Progress is absolutely imperative. Progress itself becomes the goal. The day progress would stop, our entire worldview and its market economy would collapse. We are still children of the Enlightenment.

These myths turn the biblical revelation upside down. An uncritical use of the media for communicating this biblical revelation runs the risk of sandwiching Jesus between entertainment and sport idols. Christian participation in the modern media scene is therefore a dilemma. Note that it is not a new dilemma, it is the dilemma of the Incarnation: God himself became vulnerable in the world of fallenness and sin. And it is a dilemma which forces us to be realistic and to look carefully: I know that information technology does not create a better life; I know that the aggressive stream of pictures and words and music is like an epidemic that can attack the soul.

Without the salt and light of the Gospel the world will perish. Without the Christian worldview the world will be a wasteland and the media will become a reflected image of ghosts. We alone have what is needed to fight the ghosts. It is our mandate to find room for the divine dimension and, by the same token, the human dimension in the orbit of the satellites.

Do not take this suggestion as implying that I am blind to the major problems facing the church in the media:

1. *Irrelevance*: Christian involvement in the media reveals some of the main problems of the Church. Our often irrelevant proclamation and our failure at crosscultural communication are not media problems, and so they cannot be solved simply in the media. If we try to, we end up with an electronic church.

2. *Secularization*: this is not the world's problem, but the problem of the Church. It is our problem because we have ceased to think Christianly and because we have privatized the faith. The result is isolation of the Christian faith rather than courageously placing God in the midst of the world as Creator and Lord. If we simply bring this way of thinking into the media, we shall be even worse off.

3. *Entertainment*: How do we avoid a process by which the media transform the Gospel into entertainment? The programmes of the electronic church tear away all that makes faith a historical, profound and holy human activity. There are no rituals, no dogmas, no traditions and no sense of spiritual transcendence. Here we need criteria for our practical Christian media work:

◇ **Mystery**: Does our media work acknowledge that the Gospel is something outside me in such a way that it refrains from explaining everything and from judging too quickly and too glibly?

◇ **Change of values**: Does our media work reflect that the Gospel turns accepted values upside down, so that weak comes before mighty, poor before rich, simple before wise?

◇ **Suitability**: Do form and purpose fit together in our media work? Does the technology fit the task or does it create new dependence? Does the choice of media correspond to the audience?

◇ **Purpose:** What do we want our media work to do—to confirm or exploit people? Do we respect the cultural differences? Do we create fellowship or isolation? Does our message contain hidden motives of profit and propaganda?

◇ **Content:** Does our media work further peace, justice and wholeness? Are we inclusive concerning gender, the powerful and the marginal, Christian and non-Christians? Are we sectarian or ecumenical?

◇ **Style:** Is our message characterized by clarity, variation and humour? Do we communicate modesty, genuineness and humaneness? Do we communicate our own vulnerability? Is there room for the surprise that personal faith and existential experience suddenly may break through the stereotypes of the media?

4. *Awareness:* As we enter the media scene (and especially the commercial channels) we need to be aware of their character-istics with regard to communicating the Christian faith:

◇ Appetizers of faith rather than the whole Gospel.

◇ Personal engagement and experiences will supersede official doctrine.

◇ Untraditional views and radical opinions will gain preference.

◇ Questions and doubt will have more room than answers and faith.

◇ Experiential faith of individuals will be in focus at the expense of more collective and sacramental aspects of faith.

◇ Happy testimonies from those who have 'made it', will easily supersede faith as struggle and suffering.

◇ Well-known personalities will come to the front more than the established Christian leadership.

◇ The love of God will overshadow the wrath of God.

◇ The Christian faith will be presented as more successful and entertaining than the Christian life is in everyday life and in normal congregations. There will be limited focus on faith as exodus and radical discipleship.

This media setting calls for creativity and for an intelligent, colourful, inspiring, witnessing perspective. Mediocrity will simply not do, even less poor imitations of the products of modern culture. Here lies perhaps the biggest challenge.

The dream of a living congregation

Confronted with the information society, I dream of a living congregation. This dream does not omit the need for a theological and apologetic confrontation between the structure of faith and the structure of our modern worldview. A shift of paradigm is needed, similar to that Paul experienced on the road to Damascus. Such a paradigm shift (read: conversion) will also result in a totally different plausibility structure which, because it insists that the tomb was empty and Jesus was risen, says an absolute *no* to the plausibility structure of the modern worldview. But just as important as this apologetic clash is the need for a living congregation: a congregation centered around worship celebration, caring groups and discipleship training.

We need a congregation which *celebrates* worship, which gathers as a fellowship in honour of Jesus in the midst of a broken and noisy world. A worship service that provides room for experience and for spontaneity in the midst of fixed rituals. Unless we work on this, the next generation will be absent from the worship. Already today the youth of the information society is often absent because the worship is boring, irrelevant and with neither celebration nor meaning. Along with a reborn worship we need a reborn proclamation—a proclamation which brings me into the marvelous world of Scripture and which places the same world into the midst of my everyday life.

We need a congregation that functions like a family and where this family fellowship finds expression in *small groups*—Bible groups, house cells, mission groups. They are a powerful alternative to the isolation of the information society and its privatization and alienation.

We need a congregation that provides for *discipleship training*. This was the keystone in Jesus' training model. He taught his disciples, built up their faith, encouraged, equipped and commissioned them. Without discipleship training we lose the capability to make faith visible in world, society and culture. Too many of us have become invisible Christians who have drowned in the world and are not able to give an account of the hope within us. Without discipleship training the Church would never have come into being, and without it we shall not win new disciples today. But this implies that other activities must be discarded. A reduction of feverish congregational activism is sorely needed, for many of these activities only add stones to people's burden. In an information society some of our meetings are no longer relevant meeting-points either with one another or with others.

A living congregation comes as a result of renewal. The primary purpose of this renewal is to make us God's people and the body of Christ. A living congregation breaks away from the privatized hunt for happiness-for-myself which marks our culture. It stands as a counterbalance to the isolation of the individual of *la technique* and is the only genuine alternative to the pacifying imprisonment of the media. A living congregation is all this because it is God's people (1 Peter 2:10). As people we are called to communicate his mighty deeds, and this implies the rediscovery of a central biblical perspective: *The service and ministry belong to and involve all God's people.* The separation between clergy and laypeople is a categorization which we have borrowed since the third century from a Graeco-Roman (not Christian) culture which distinguished between clerics (the learned) and 'idiotes' (the ignorant). Ever since, this division has been one of the greatest hindrances to the growth and renewal of the Church. It has made the cleric/priest/pastor a cork in the bottleneck and obscured the primary task of Christian leadership: to equip God's people for ministry in the world.

The information society brings an acute challenge to us to take seriously our Reformation heritage about the priesthood of all believers. All of God's people have a share in the ministry; there is no room for a passive laity which leaves the job to a paid hierarchy. Instead we need to invest in discipleship training: a genuine missionary encounter with our modern culture will require the energetic equipping of a declericalized laypeople.[11] Ordinary Christians must have the opportunity to view their secular everyday life in the light of the Good News. Only in this way shall we join together what the culture has separated into private and public. This is because it is here, in ordinary Christians, that the missionary encounter with the world takes place.

If all of God's people are to participate in the ministry, they must function as *the body of Christ*, which means that the spiritual gifts must function. Since the spiritual gifts are the equipment which the various members of the body need in order to function as body, and since every Christian has spiritual gifts, then if any do not discover and use their gifts, they cripple the body.

We need a new reformation in which we draw the consequences of the Reformation's rediscovery of the Gospel and actually implement the priesthood of all believers. If not, the Church will be unable to encounter our culture and its worldview. Only a congregation structured around spiritual gifts and the involvement of all in ministry, will make it in 'the future shock'. Churches that have fenced themselves behind strict, institutional structures, will soon experience that they are caught up in culture-bound forms which exclude them from the noise and suffering of the world and from growth and mission.

Notes

1. David Watson, *I Believe in the Church*, Eerdmans, 1985, page 74

2. Tor Aukrust, *Exodus, Om forkynnelsesn krise*, Oslo, Land og kirke, 1984, pages 17-18. [The italicized phrase in the sentence is from the title of the 1940 book by Elmer G. Homrighausen, *Let the Church Be the Church*.]

3. Lesslie Newbigin, *Med 1984 i bakspejlet*, Nyt Synspunkt, nr. 19; Hellerup, DMS Forlag, 1984, and *Foolishness to the Greeks*, Eerdmans, 1986

4. William Fore, *Television and Religion*, Augsburg , 1987, pages 21ff; see also David McKenna, *Megatruth. The Church in the Age of Information*, Here's Life Publishers

5. Yoneji Masuda, *Informationssamhaellet*, Malmo, Liber Forlag, 1984

6. See Michael Traber, editor, *The Myth of the Information Revolution*, Sage, 1986

7. See Neil Postman, *Amusing Ourselves to Death*, Viking, 1987

8. Jacques Ellul, *The Technological Society*, Cape, 1964

9. David Lyon, *The Silicon Society*, Lion, 1986, pages 26–27

10. Fore [note 4], pages 64–68

11. Newbigin [note 3], pages 142 ff

13

Modernity and evangelicals: American evangelicalism as a global case study

JOHN SEEL

The distorting lens of anti-Americanism

Canadian novelist Margaret Atwood claims that the U.S. borders are the world's largest one-way mirror. Americans, she claims, look out at the rest of the world and see only themselves. Her criticism is largely true. Americans are enormously parochial, even in the midst of the global economy and the telecommunications revolution. Many Americans still have a school-age naiveté about how others perceive them.

As a result, almost nothing strikes most Americans as more bizarre than anti-Americanism, whether politically motivated anti-Americanism as in parts of Asia or economic anti-Americanism as in Europe. Scenes of French farmers protesting against EuroDisney is somehow seen as a deep affront to our national consciousness as the benevolent purveyor of Big Macs, Levi 501s, Coca-Cola, Madonna, and yes, democracy. In writing this paper I was conscious of living between two worlds: I am an American, but one who has had the privilege of living for over seventeen years in South Korea as the son of medical missionaries.

At the outset of this paper on modernity and its impact on evangelicalism, I begin with a warning to all those who would reject Americanism in order to protect themselves from the spiritual dangers of modernity. This is a common fallacy, especially in the Third World but also in the West, where there is the fervent belief that the West is by definition the problem and the Third World the solution. Modernity, Americanism, and especially American evangelicalism (including its pervasive missionary movement) are deeply interconnected, but modernity is a social reality that knows no national identity, no geographic boundaries, no cultural differences. It is a spiritual pandemic that poses the greatest single challenge to any orthodox belief and any traditional culture in history. To reject Americanism is no protection from modernity and may, in fact, blind one to modernity's subtle encroachments that are not wrapped in red, white, and blue or marked 'Made in the USA'.

This paper will examine American evangelicalism as a world historical case study of the impact of modernity on the evangelical faith. The lessons learned here are sober lessons for all followers of Christ who still await the full onslaught of modernity within their own countries and faith communities. For better or worse, evangelicalism in America is one of the most important storm fronts in the church's confrontation with modernity although one must not confuse the American character of this confrontation with the global challenge of modernity. American evangelicalism is only one illustration of modernity's threat to the church universal and its world-wide evangelistic mission.

Profile of American Evangelicals

America was founded by a profoundly religious people, many of whom came to America explicitly seeking religious liberty. Historically, modern evangelicals are the spiritual heirs of America's first faith community. Compared to other First World countries, the religious character of Americans is striking. One only has to compare attendance at weekly religious services in several countries to see the difference: Scandinavia at 5 percent, England at 10 percent, Canada at 25 percent, and the United States at 40 percent.[1] The United States is unique among First World countries in its affirmation of belief and its publicly attestable religious activity. Highly modernized like the First World, the United States is highly religious like the Third World.

According to recent surveys, those who consider themselves 'born again' include some 60 million Americans, many of whom are in mainline Protestant denominations or the Roman Catholic Church. Those who identify themselves more narrowly as 'evangelicals' represent 40 million Americans, or 16 percent of the U.S. population.[2]

American institutional evangelicalism emerged after World War II from the initiative of such giants as Billy Graham, Howard Pew, Harold Ockenga, Charles Fuller, and Carl F.H. Henry. In the years that followed, evangelical entrepreneurialism has spawned an expansive network of 'parallel organizations': publishing houses (up to eighty publishing houses accounting for a $1-billion-a-year book business), independent Christian schools (up to 18,000 of them), Bible colleges, liberal-arts colleges and seminaries (more than five hundred in all), magazines and newspapers (more than four hundred), special-interest organizations, law firms, a music industry, radio stations, TV programs and networks, and the like.[3] The Chicago-based National Association of Evangelicals celebrated its fifty-year anniversary in 1992, and now represents 74 denominations, 43,000 churches, and a constituency of more than 15 million people. *Christianity Today*, begun in 1954 as an evangelical *Christian Century*, today boasts a subscription base of over 250,000 readers. Yet this vast institutional empire has also given rise to an institutional fragmentation that historian George Marsden compares to a constellation of medieval fiefdoms—superficially friendly but competitive empires that fight for their own expanding turf while professing nominal allegiance to the same distant king.[4]

Today American evangelicals face a quandary. They have been culturally dominant for most of America's history. The number of evangelical churches and evangelicals continues to increase, but their influence within American society is declining. This fact causes confusion among many American evangelical leaders. On the one hand they are prone to be self-congratulatory when comparing their denominational growth to those of mainline Protestant churches, and yet on the other hand there is a growing awareness that, in spite of nearly a hundred-fifty year cultural dominance, continuing demographic strength, aggressive political activism, and generous financial contributions, their impact in American society is diminishing.

Religion in the midst of modernity

Several of the well-known analyses of the relationship between modernity and religion help explain this discrepancy. Sociologist

Thomas Luckmann suggests three typical patterns between religion and society: *diffusion, distinction*, and *dissociation*.[5]

The oldest relationship is characterized by the *diffusion* of religious beliefs and behaviors throughout society. Wherever this happens, either in traditional Christian societies, such as medieval Europe or colonial America, or in many Third World countries today, all of life is endowed with a sense of the supernatural, the spiritual, and the sacred.

Luckmann points out that in these societies 'the maintenance and transmission of the sacred universe are based on the social structure in its entirety'.[6] Modernity, however, progressively undermines the experience of a sacred universe where faith is diffused throughout—what Max Weber described as the 'process of disenchantment.'[7]

It leads to a second pattern, *distinction*, involving the specialization of religion. Religion is made distinct from other aspects of social life; it is given a separate social location with a specialized body of knowledge. Religious institutions are viewed as just one among many institutions that compete for social and cultural influence. They no longer have uncontested dominance or respect within the society.

The third relationship, and the one that is the primary feature of advanced modernity, is the almost complete *dissociation* of religion from society. Under these conditions, religious belief itself may not decline but instead become progressively isolated and irrelevant to everyday life.

Two aspects of modernity have contributed to this uniquely modern pattern: pluralization and privatization. Pluralization is the growing diversity of religious options within a society. Privatization, in contrast, is the marginalization of religion to the individual, private, and personal sphere of life. Princeton sociologist Robert Wuthnow describes this ironically: 'While it may be that a high degree of supernaturalism remains in American religion as a formal tenet, the operational relevance of the supernatural may have largely collapsed into the interior of the self.'[8] Under the conditions of modernity, religious belief not only faces greater competition but is simultaneously removed from the central arenas of social life where its influence formerly made a cultural difference.

This loss of cultural legitimacy has led to numerous anti-modern reactions by believers in many segments of modern and modernizing societies. In general, these reactions have been of two types. The first reaction attempts to maintain a *consistent anti-modernism*, as seen in the publicized resurgence of Islamic fundamentalism. Cambridge sociologist Ernest Gellner writes, 'To say that secularization prevails in Islam is not contentious. It is simply false. Islam is as strong now as it was a century ago. In some ways, it is probably much stronger'.[9] Martin Marty has written extensively on the rise of global fundamentalism from within the numerous faith traditions.[10] He observes that 'fundamentalism is clearly a force of resentment against "intellectuals," "elites," "the media," and the like, people who are at home with modernization and care little for the presumed traditions'.[11] Marty's colleague at the University of Chicago, historian Scott Appleby, adds, 'Traditional cultures, with values based in religious teachings, are finding that those values are undermined by the push to modernize societies. ... Fundamentalists see it as a crisis in which normal procedures must be suspended and they must fight back or their tradition will be lost.'[12]

These same tendencies can be seen in contemporary evangelicalism at times, but with an equally important difference. Evangelicalism more often represents the second type of anti-modernism: *an inconsistent anti-modernism*. Evangelicalism is simultaneously anti-modern and modern, a complex mosaic of both traditional beliefs and modern practices.

From the eighteenth century onward, evangelicalism has shown itself more than a traditional reaffirmation of orthodox belief. It has included explicit accommodations to modernity, such as reliance on technique and technology. Thus contemporary American evangelicalism is distinctly different from not only other orthodox belief systems but from its earlier counterparts. This balancing act between acute anti-modernism and a naive accommodation to modernity shapes the beliefs and behavior of American evangelicalism. This is also what makes evangelicalism particularly prone to the dangers of modernity.

The evangelical myopia

For all modern people modernity represents the assumed, unconscious reality of social life, what Alfred Schutz calls the 'taken-for-granted life world', a person's 'fundamental and paramount reality'.[13] He explains,

In the natural attitude, I always find myself in a world
which is for me taken for granted and self-evidently
'real'. I was born into it and I assume that it existed
before me. It is the unexamined ground of everything
in my experience, as it were, the taken-for-granted
frame in which all the problems which I must
overcome are placed.[14]

Thus modernity is for all modern people an unconscious and
therefore an invisible reality, lived on the basis of recipe knowledge. It is analogous to what the New Testament refers to as
kosmos, the human sociological reality that exists in estrangement from God. Modernity defines what is 'real' for modern
people. It represents today what the medieval world represented
in the years prior to the Reformation or what Confucianism is
today in parts of Asia—simply, the way things are.

In addition, American evangelicals are particularly blind to the
dangers of modernity for three reasons. *First, their own identity is
historically tied to modernity.* Knowing one's past is integral to a
sense of identity; 'the sureness of "I was" is a necessary
component of the sureness of "I am".'[15] Historian Anthony
Brandt observes that a real appreciation of the past 'requires a
sense of the persistence of the past: the manifold ways in which it
penetrates our lives'.[16] Marx correctly noted, 'Men make their
history, but they do not make it just as they please; they do not
make it under circumstances chosen by themselves, but under
circumstances directly encountered, given, and transmitted from
the past.'[17] Or as Pierre Bourdieu states succinctly, 'It is yesterday's man who inevitably predominates [over] us.'[18] For American evangelicalism this has meant that certain historical
experiences and mythical themes have been interwoven into
their psyche, into their sense of self. I have argued elsewhere
that this 'interior history' has a greater relationship to American
evangelical practice than do their theological beliefs or worldviews.[19]

Contemporary American evangelicalism has been deeply
shaped by both Americanism and modernity. The origins of
these tendencies go back to the Second Great Awakening and its
acceptance of the spirit and tools of early modernity. The major
difference between the First Great Awakening under such Pur-
itans as George Whitefield and the Second Great Awakening

under such evangelists as Charles Finney was that revival was no longer seen to be based on God's sovereign work but instead on the application of humanly engineered techniques—nightly meetings, vernacular preaching, gospel choruses, exhortations by women, the use of the 'anxious bench', mass publicity and the like. Finney was so confident in these new techniques that he wrote in his *Lectures on Revival*, 'A revival is not a miracle, or dependent on a miracle, in any sense. It is purely philosophical results of the right use of constituted means as much as any other effect produced by the application of means.'[20] Elsewhere Finney wrote, 'Perhaps it is not too much to say, that it is impossible for God himself to bring about reformation but by new measures.'[21] The scientific application of technology and technique became incorporated into the mainstream of evangelical practice.

Equally important during this period, religion became dominated by business practice. Theological truth became increasingly judged by its results in the marketplace. Numbers came to trump truth. Ministers were evaluated by their ability to 'get results', specifically the saving of souls in measurable amounts. The 'whole counsel of God' was reduced to the 'how-to's' of human reason. By 1886, Rollo Ogden noted, 'Indeed, so far has the church caught the spirit of the age, so far has it become a business enterprise, that the chief test of ministerial success is now the ability to "build up" a church. Executive, managerial success is now more in demand than those which used to be considered the highest in a clergyman.'[22] Sociologist George Thomas concludes, that the revivalist world of the nineteenth century was isomorphic with the rise of early forms of modernity.[23]

The second reason evangelicals are frequently blind to modernity is because they have misunderstood its challenge as simply one of ideas. Evangelical social critique has overlooked the basic premise of the sociology of knowledge: 'Ideas do not succeed in history by virtue of their truth, but their relationship to specific social processes.'[24] Or as Bourdieu writes, 'In the social sciences, the progress of knowledge presupposes progress in our knowledge of the conditions of knowledge.'[25] It is these 'social processes' and 'conditions of knowledge' that evangelicals have not adequately taken into consideration.

Evangelicals have consciously followed the history of ideas school by attempting to grasp the thought and thinkers of the past in a way to communicate the Zeitgeist, or intellectual spirit of the age. Herman Randall's *Making of the Modern Mind*[26] is an example of the type of intellectual synthesis many evangelical leaders learned in Christian colleges and seminaries in the 1940s and 1950s. Trends in theology and culture were studied in exactly the same way. Social change was about ideas that trickled down from centers of learning to popular culture; from Harvard Yard to Mainstreet, USA; from Paris' Left Bank to *Le Monde*. Such a view was described in Francis Schaeffer's *The God Who Is There*.

> First of all it [the loss of the belief in absolutes] spread geographically. The ideas began in Germany and spread outward. They affected the Continent first, then crossed the Channel to England, and then the Atlantic to America. Second, it spread through society, from the real intellectual to the more educated, down to the workers, reaching the upper middle class last of all. Thirdly, it spread from one discipline to another, beginning with philosophy and ending with theology.[27]

Many evangelical writers have explained contemporary culture on the basis of its relationship to the ideas, particularly the past spokespersons, of the Enlightenment project. The challenge to faith has been viewed primarily as cognitive; wrong philosophy is countered with right theology. Rarely has such philosophical analysis been coupled with an equally detailed sociological analysis of the context in which these ideas were written. Descartes or Kant are quoted and applied to contemporary society as if they had just been interviewed on CNN or the BBC.

There is no doubt that ideas, even élitist ideas, have cultural consequences. Since the sixties, however, numerous questions have been raised about the inadequacy of the history of ideas school, yet numerous evangelical apologists and cultural analysts continue to rely on this approach irrespective of scholarly questions raised about its weaknesses.[28] Quentin Skinner wrote critically in the late sixties, 'The history thus written becomes a history not of ideas at all, but of abstractions: a history of thoughts which no one actually succeeded in thinking, at a level of coherence which no one ever actually attained.'[29] Fritz Ringer writes, 'Ideas are never totally separable from their grounding in institutions, practices, and social relations.'[30] Gene Wise adds,

'[I]ntellectual history has waned since the mid-1960s; because it has lacked forms to handle change very well, it can't convey variety effectively, it can't get its ideas into motion, it can't connect ideas into the concrete events of history, it can't detect strains or cracks in an idea; it can't, in short, *ground intellectual abstractions in the life-experiences of people.*'[31]

Practically speaking, this preoccupation with abstract ideas has contributed to evangelicals' uncritical acceptance of modernity. Even now some American evangelicals see modernity only as the legacy of the Enlightenment project. With intellectual collapse of the Enlightenment project, postmodernity is supposed to usher in a new era of opportunity to the church.[32] However, modernity is more than just a set of ideas. It is primarily a social reality—the global culture created by capitalism, technology, and information. At the same time evangelicals were resisting theological modernism, evangelicals were embracing the sociological features of modernity. As historian Nathan Hatch observes, 'Fundamentalists and Pentecostals reject modernity as it is expressed in high culture [ideas and art], but remain stalwart defenders of modern attitudes [commodification and technical rationality] as they build popular constituencies with the most innovative techniques.'[33] Consequently, while evangelicals have been intellectually defiant they have also been prone to practical accommodation. They carefully maintain theological orthodoxy while simultaneously uncritically accommodating to the tools of modernity whether in marketing the church or mending the soul.

Thirdly, evangelicals have overlooked the risks of modernity because they have not realized that modernity is intrinsically double-edged. On the positive side, modernity has brought the church many wonderful benefits and powerful tools. Who is not grateful for mobility and medicine? For computers and fax machines?

Modernity's good gifts, however, are prone to make us less conscious of its dangers. Almost imperceptibly the church begins to conform to the dictates of modernity. Reality is reduced to what is new, instant, controllable, measurable, predictable, and marketable. What fails to fit the grid of modernity is no longer perceived to be real, and is soon abandoned. What is lost, in fact, are those aspects of reality most precious to followers of Christ—the intangible aspects of the spirit and the soul. Modernity is a

295

corrosive acid to the reality of God's transcendence and the deepest longings of humanness.

The uncritical acceptance of modernity within evangelicalism is a serious matter, for modernity does not lead first to heresy, but to idolatry. Modernity's potent rewards will come to replace our need for God. Our measures of success will be limited to the five senses and the most religious evangelical will be little different from a practical atheist. Like the Pharisees, we will be in error not because we do not know the Scriptures, but because we no longer rely on the power of God (Mark 12:24).

Evangelical gospels of modernity

The Christian faith, as evangelicals understand it, is an intrinsically integrative faith, a belief system that seeks to touch all aspects of their lives. Evangelicals are mandated to be 'in' but not 'of' the countervailing world system. They are not to be conformed to the patterns of this world, but transformed by the renewing of their minds (Romans 12:2).

But modernity's social pervasiveness and global reach makes it impossible to isolate oneself or one's community from its reach. Some form of engagement is inevitable. While the benefits of modernity are celebrated by most modern people, few are equally aware of its dangers. Few evangelicals are aware of modernity's subtle challenge to spiritual vitality. If the worldwide evangelical fellowship is to address the benefits and challenges of modernity, then a closer look at the American church's engagement with it is particularly instructive. Modernity is a complex, multifaceted reality, but three aspects illustrate its challenge to evangelical faith. What follows is an examination of forms of modernity represented by three cultural icons—Disney World, McDonald's, and MTV. Each has found a home within American evangelicalism.

GOSPEL OF DISNEY

For most people, Walt Disney World or EuroDisney is simply a fun, children's fantasy land. Disney World, located in Orlando, Florida is enormously popular with tourists, both domestic and foreign, visited annually by 30 million people. Mickey Mouse is arguably the best-known character, human or otherwise on earth.[34] In fact, Disney is not about fantasy, but reality. Disney sells a self-conscious philosophy of life, 'a techno-commercial utopia'. Disney's world is 'the land of more', the symbol of unchecked consumption, the 'middle-class haj, the sun-baked shrine for the corporate world of commodities'. Herein lies its danger.

In the past decade numerous evangelical ministries have moved to Orlando, Florida, most notably Campus Crusade for Christ. One well-known American theologian living in Orlando described it as 'heaven on earth'. Consequently, the practical relevance of Disney World has at least a growing proximity to key gatekeepers and institutions within the American evangelical church. But its impact extends even deeper.

Most American evangelicals are oblivious to the dangers of capitalism or unchecked consumerism. To offer criticism on these points is thought by many to be the ultimate heresy—both un-American and un-Christian. But advanced capitalism and its form of unchecked consumerism has grave dangers for the United States as well as for other countries such as the former Soviet Union. Put simply, the danger of capitalism is that capitalism has no internal checks to capitalism. Capitalism, like the sorcerer's apprentice who is no longer able to control the powers of the spell, relentlessly reduces all reality to its commodity form. Marx correctly warned that capitalism would 'drown the most heavenly ecstasies of religious fervor, of chivalrous enthusiasm, of philistine sentimentality, in the icy water of egotistical calculations... All fixed, fast-frozen relations, with their train of ancient and venerable prejudice and opinion, are swept away, all newly formed ones become antiquated before they can ossify. All that is solid melts into air, all that is holy is profaned.'[35]

Frederic Jameson suggests that advanced modernity has seen the spread of consumerism into perhaps the last two available domains—the unconscious (pornography, therapy, fantasy) and nature (wilderness, parks, anthropology).[36] Everything is for sale. There is no context, however intimate, beautiful, remote, or sacred, that escapes the potential intrusion of the Energizer pink rabbit. Such 'market totalitarianism', a term coined by sociologist Robert Bellah, is characterized by the following values:

◇ All values are market values;

◇ Anything goes if it pays;

297

◇ The consumer is the center of the world;

◇ Meeting 'felt needs' is the chief end;

◇ Any space is a potential place for consumption; and finally

◇ All business is show business.

The logic of advanced capitalism is that entertainment values come to dominate all values. It has produced a 'carnival culture'. Neil Postman argues that entertainment is the language of public discourse.[37] Advertising executive Felix Rohatyn adds, 'Everything in this world has turned into show business. Politics is show business. Running Chrysler is show business. Sports is show business, and Henry Kissinger is show business. You package all these things. That's the reality of the marketplace... And if you're not in show business, you're *really* off Broadway.'[38]

In advanced capitalism, the crassness of market totalitarianism is sometimes softened by linking it with its seemingly more idealistic twin the therapeutic ideal of self-fulfillment. The therapeutic ideal reinforces the culture of consumption; they are mutually reinforcing. 'Recognizing the cash value of a therapeutic sensibility,' historian Jackson Lears writes, '[the advertising industry] has manipulated needs and underwritten a notion of self-fulfillment through voracious acquisition.'[39] Business thus becomes the delivery system for actualizing the therapeutic vision. Advertising no longer sells a product but a philosophy of life, the promise of self-actualized existence.

Note the similarities between the advertiser and the therapist. Both are centered on the self. Both focus on addressing 'felt needs'. Both represent an assault on traditional religion. Consider, for example, this advertisement for Avia running shoes, which asks 'Is fitness a new religion?' The ad continues, 'This is not about guilt. It is about joy. Strength. The revival of the spirit. I come here seeking redemption in sweat. And it is here I am forgiven my sinful calories. Others may never understand my dedication. But for me, fitness training is something much more powerful than exercise. It is what keeps my body healthy. It is what keeps my mind clear. And it is where I learn the one true lesson. To believe in myself.'[40] Such is the narcissistic gospel of health and wealth.

These twin challenges do not enter the evangelical bloodstream by a malevolent conspiracy of élites or alien religions, but through its own leaders, institutions, and publications. What began with the organizing of evangelistic crusades and spread with the growth of evangelical publishing has reached its zenith in the megachurch movement. Here it is not uncommon to find the mission of the church uncritically accommodated to the premises of the felt-needs of the consumer. Church is analyzed by these advocates as a service business. Marketing consultant George Barna, for example, says that church is 'the transaction in service of felt needs'.[41] The four 'P's' of marketing follow naturally: product, price, place, and promotion. Barna describes the church's task solely in marketing categories—the product is relationships (with Jesus and others); the price is commitment; the place is with believers; and promotion is by word-of-mouth.[42]

Traditional churches are severely criticized for their lack of market sensitivity and savvy. They are variously described as backward, boring, superficial, ritualistic, and embarrassing.[43] In short, they have an inward product-orientation rather than an outward market-orientation. These new entrepreneurial churches, Leith Anderson writes, 'are market-sensitive and attempt to take current trends and needs into consideration, using such up-to-date methodology as telemarketing, advertising, and high-tech communications. These churches seek to be highly relational. They plan to be big and offer full services from the start. Part of the attraction is the lack of tradition. There is no one to say, "We've never done it that way before." No creeds, no liturgy, no building, no history. Everything is new and fresh.'[44] Kenneth Woodward of *Newsweek* summarizes the church-growth phenomenon as the 1990s' response to 'an age of mix'em, match'em salad-bar spirituality where brand loyalty is a doctrine of the past and the customer is king'.[45] A minister's success is measured by 'nickels and noses'.

Or consider evangelical publishing. Benny Hinn's 1991 best-seller was published by Thomas Nelson Publishers, the largest Bible publisher in America, in spite of the management acknowledging that what they were publishing was widely viewed as heretical (nine persons in the godhead, for example). A senior executive of Thomas Nelson is reported to have said, 'After *Good Morning, Holy Spirit* has sold 750,000 copies, you will forget about your theological concerns.' Christian publishing today has little concern for theological truth or serious thought. Here the evangelical bottom line is the commercial bottom line; as one advertisement stated crassly, 'Here is spirituality that sells.'

Thus it was not considered inconceivable for a Sunday church service to be held in a suburban megamall—they were seen as being in the same business. When Wooddale Church held a Sunday morning worship celebration at the newly opened Mall of America, Kathy Duran stated to a reporter from the Minneapolis *Star Tribune* that she saw it as a natural fit. 'We live in the malls, we might as well go to church here,' she said.[46]

The Mall of America is the largest fully-enclosed retail/ entertainment complex in the United States, with 4.2 million square feet of stores, restaurants, nightclubs, amusement rides, and much more. It has enough floor space to fill 88 football fields. To window shop all its stores requires a three mile hike. It employs twice the number of employees as the city of Minneapolis and is expected to be visited by 40 million people annually, nine times the population of Minnesota. This temple of consumerism is located just a few miles from the nation's first enclosed shopping mall built in 1958.[47]

During the mall's opening weeks, Wooddale Church, an evangelical megachurch affiliated with the Baptist General Conference, arranged to hold a worship celebration in the mall's rotunda located between Bloomingdale's and Sears. Six thousand worshippers thronged the space usually booked for baseball card shows and in-line roller skating. Participants were encouraged to wear comfortable clothes in order to do any shopping they had in mind after the service. Anderson preached on 'The Unknown God of the Mall'.

Unrecognized by Anderson and many other evangelicals is the degree to which he had inadvertently preached another message—the gospel of modernity. Disney World is not the Forum and the mall is not the first-century marketplace: a common center of public discourse and exchange of information. It is instead a specialized space designed to relativize all ideas to consumer choices, to trivialize the spiritual with clatter of the money changers. 'The landscapes of the consumer's world,' writes University of Wisconsin geographer Robert Sack, 'are volatile and disposable, they actually accelerate destabilization by making the contradictions of modernity more visible and real.'[48] 'The purpose of the [mall] environment is not relaxation, but titillation. The mall is there to stimulate desire for commodities. . . .They can be stimulating, entertaining, and magical, but they can also be superficial, weightless, and inauthentic.'[49]

Worship services in the mall? The scope of commodification today makes Marx's understanding of alienation seem Pollyanna-ish. It makes the biblical account of money-changers in the temple pale in comparison. In spite of lip-service to theological orthodoxy, many American evangelicals are uncritically accommodating to the gospel of consumerism.

GOSPEL OF McDONALD'S

Seventy years ago, Max Weber observed that the Western world had created a unique form of rationality. Rather than being guided by a set of values, this form of rationality was concerned only to find an optimum means to a given end. Max Weber thought that the supreme example of rationality was bureaucracy. Much of his analysis anticipated the rise of advanced modernity, except that today the paradigm case of rationality is not bureaucracy but the fast-food restaurant, most notably McDonald's. Numerous scholars have suggested that McDonald's is one of the most influential developments in twentieth century America. It is important because it illustrates a wide ranging social process; what sociologist George Ritzer calls 'McDonaldization.' McDonaldization is the process by which the principles of the fast-food restaurant business are coming to dominate more and more sectors of American society as well as of the rest of the world.[50] From food to newspapers, from diet centers to health care delivery, the rationality of McDonaldization dominates modern existence. Today McDonald's Golden Arches represent one of the most visible global icons of modernity. On the opening of the McDonald's in Moscow, one journalist described it as the 'ultimate icon of Americana', while a worker spoke of it 'as if it were the Cathedral in Chartres—a place to experience "celestial joy"'.[51]

Like the consumer ethic of Disney World and the megamall, McDonald's philosophy of life has also found a ready audience with evangelicals who, as we have noted, shifted their emphasis from 'spiritual faithfulness' to 'spiritual fruit' a century earlier. Today the values of McDonald's are frequently accepted without dispute as the criteria of the 'really real', even within the evangelical church. Said one Southern Baptist leader about American evangelicals, 'There is today a bifurcation among the evangelical leaders between those committed to techniques versus those committed to truth.'[52]

What is the gospel of McDonald's, this process of rationalization? And how has it found its way into the church? The McDonaldization of society is based on four distinct values: *efficiency* the optimum way of achieving a specific goal; *calculability* quantity as quality, the measurable as the really real; *predictability* a world with no surprises, with consistent expectations; and *control* understood as the substitution of machines for humans wherever possible. In short, McDonald's sells technological humanism: any problem can be figured out and any goal can be achieved.

As this has entered the church we have progressively created institutions with such organizational potential that an awareness of the invisible spiritual reality, the need for prayer, or even God himself is no longer needed to achieve maximum results. The advertising executive who directed the 'I Found It' evangelistic campaign stated boldly, 'Back in Jerusalem where the church started, God performed a miracle there on the day of Pentecost. They didn't have the benefits of buttons and media, so God had to do a little supernatural work there. But today, with our technology, we have available to us the opportunity to create the same kind of interest in a secular society.' Nor is it surprising that many members attracted to megachurches come from sales or technical professions. Willow Creek Community Church in Chicago is surrounded by major corporate offices of Motorola, Ameritech, Siemens, Data General, and Cellular One. The pastor summarizes his message with the words, 'Let me net it out for you.' Participants at leadership conferences are advised, 'If you have only $500 to spend on your church budget, spend $300 on multimedia.' A pastor confesses to other pastors, 'I lose 15 to 20 per cent of my effectiveness in preaching if I don't have a good lighting and sound system.'

Today those gifted in the tools of modernity are the emerging patrons of power. A quick glance at positions-wanted advertisements outlines the new criteria for pastoral leadership 'Programming Director, BA (Communications/Theater)'; 'Will develop programming teams (Music, Drama, Dance, Lighting, etc.) and creatively coordinate all elements of the service'; 'Attended church growth and Fuller Seminary sponsored seminars'; 'Just completed tenure with 4000 + member church'; 'Is your vision to create a contemporary church for the unchurched? Maybe this married, male conservative-evangelical, seminary-graduated baby boomer can help'; 'Masters degrees in Educational Ministries and Marriage and Family Therapy'; and 'BA in Fine Arts/ Humanities, Masters in Management. Eight years arts admin. Experience includes fund raising, gallery/performance mgmt., PR, marketing, advertising & teaching'.[53]

It is also seen in the evangelical churches' growing reliance on statistical data. Once the purview of denominational mission boards, now every church is advised to conduct a market survey. 'Unchurched baby boomers' have in the United States received the greatest research attention because, as in consumer products, they hold significant market potential. One is instructed that baby boomers don't convert, have low product loyalty, and instead choose against a shopping list of values including quality, convenience, flexibility, proof of integrity, and individuality. In the avalanche of statistical data that covers the typical evangelical pastor's desk, there is frequently a subtle but real ethical shift that occurs: a blurring of the 'is' and the 'ought'. The statistical reality comes to determine the behavioral imperative. Consider, for example, this discussion in a major evangelical seminary's magazine regarding church membership. Boomers, we are told, have low product loyalty as well as a low degree of commitment to programs. Thus the writer concludes, 'It will make obsolete the traditional definition of a church home. In other words, people will no longer have a single church home but multiple church homes. On any given Sunday they will wake up and choose a particular church which they feel will meet the needs they feel most keenly that morning.'[54] Rather than exhort members to biblical faithfulness and commitment, the church is exhorted to accommodate to the prevailing trends. On the basis of this logic, serial church homes will soon be followed by the equal acceptance of serial marriages. For the premise of meeting 'felt-needs' finally justifies the subjective criteria by which modern Americans make their personal choices whether in church homes or marriage partners.

Again we see the corrosive effects of modernity, not only in the power it provides in achieving a specific goal but also in the subtle way it changes the substance of that goal.

GOSPEL OF MTV

Sometimes someone suggests that 'there is nothing new under the sun' implying that the challenges facing modern people are just about the same as in all previous civilizations. This is simply not true. Modernity has created a radically new world and a distinctly unprecedented challenge to biblical faith. Perhaps this is seen most clearly in the impact of the communications revolution, as seen in the gospel of MTV. Never before has society been so dominated by images and never before has there been such an idolatry of images as today. It is evidenced in two important changes: first, the devaluation of words, and second, the rise of the celebrity. As with the gospel of Disney reality is what can be bought and sold; as with the gospel of McDonald's reality can be controlled and measured; here, reality is reduced to what can be seen.

Bob Pittman, the founder of MTV, is the son of a Methodist minister. But it was television, not his parents or their faith that shaped his world, 'Television prob'ly showed me more of the world than my parents did. I can't get enough of television.'[55] In 1981, at the age of 27, Pittman introduced to America and later to the world a popular-cultural sensibility defined by the 'anti-authoritarian child'. The MTV philosophy that emerged was simple: provide programming that is nonrational, cynical, anti-traditional, hedonistic, anti-authoritarian, and consumer-oriented. Pittman states, 'I do attitude-based programming. It's all attitude. The attitude is: Nothing is sacred.'[56] Veteran TV critic Ron Powers described MTV as 'the LSD of the Reagan Revolution'. *Rolling Stone* magazine describes the drug-like purpose of MTV as to create arousal and to avoid boredom.[57] Powers concludes, 'This is the aesthetic of the perpetual child: self as the star of the universe, appetite as the locus of endeavor, consumption as art, advertising as education, the grotesque as amusement, defiance as moral vision.'[58]

*First, the image revolution has brought about a devaluation of words.*Thus it has become a truism in an MTV-dominated world that reading and words are passé. Pittman says, 'This is a non-narrative generation. You communicate to them via sense-impressions. There are two groups of people in this world: those who grew up with television and those didn't grow up with sense-impressions.'[59] Or consider this statement from the French newspaper, *Le Monde*, 'We must learn to resign ourselves to living in an audiovisual age. Most people, especially youth, read little, have poor memories, forget what they learned in school and barely remember what they see on television. Words draw behind images everyday. Not just any image gets watched: only the moving, speaking image. It's not like pictures in books, but like life itself.'[60] French sociologist Jacques Ellul summarizes the shift in expectation, 'Images once were illustrations of a text. Now the text has become the explanation of the images.'[61]

What does this mean for modern evangelicals? Historically evangelicals have been committed to propositional revelation, to truth, to words, and to the Word. Thus these changes have profound implications for the gospel. Yet many evangelical institutions are uncritically following this image-oriented cultural shift.

At the 1990 Inter-Varsity Urbana Student Missionary Convention (involving seventeen thousand university students) the Bible expositors were specifically instructed not to use didactic expository preaching methods, previously modeled by the British evangelical leader John Stott. They were told that students today were incapable of linear thinking and required more stories and entertainment in order to make the Bible messages more relevant. Expository preaching, once seen as the voice of traditional confessional evangelicalism, is becoming viewed as a postmodern irrelevance.

It is also changing the notion of Bible translation. According to an article in the *Wall Street Journal* new, simpler translations of the Bible and video Bibles are being marketed increasingly to appeal to the young, biblically 'post-literate' generation.[62] The First United Methodist Church of Houston, Texas has plans to build a 'biblical theater' a three hundred-seat rotunda with a floor-sized map of the Holy Land, onto which computer-guided lights will trace the path of the Israelites' wanderings in the wilderness or spotlight the towns where Jesus preached. 'People don't want to read anymore, they want you to show them,' explained the church's pastor, the Rev. William Hinson.[63]

Film evangelism showing movies about the life of Jesus is replacing both the traditional missionary evangelist and the missionary educator. Dayspring International, a Virginia Beach-based ministry, states that it has shown 'Daya Sagar' ('Oceans of Mercy') to an estimated 30 million people throughout India since 1979. It has plans to stage screenings in all of India's six hundred thousand rural villages. Campus Crusade for Christ announced in its 1991 Annual Report that it plans to show the *Jesus* film to over 475 million people in 216 languages through 325 mission agencies in 1992. This is in direct contrast to traditional missionary strategies involving the painstaking work of literacy education and Bible translation (such as carried on by Wycliffe Bible Translators). One Crusade staff involved in the project said, 'It is sometimes hard to tell whether they are accepting the projector, the screen, or Christ as their Savior.'

Even within evangelical circles, it appears that just as celluloid is replacing books, images are replacing words, and emotions are replacing thoughts. Bill Hybels, senior pastor at Willow Creek Community Church, says this about his communications philosophy: 'A person's resistance to persuasion is very high when spoken to, but very low when exposed to drama and music. We communicate the truth through the back door. People don't even know it's happened.'[64] One megachurch program director publicly advocates copying the MTV format.

In the beginning was the Word, but in the end, it appears, will be the image. Such will be a direct rejection of the Judeo-Christian heritage. Literary critic Camille Paglia, who celebrates television as the 'hearth fire of the modern home' and describes Madonna as the patron saint of modernity, argues that the rise of the image parallels the rebirth of paganism. 'The image which is pagan and expressive of nature's sex and violence was outlawed by Moses in favor of the word. That's where our troubles began. . . . Moses knew that once a people begin to make images of any kind, they fall in love with them and worship them.'[65] What secular critics acknowledge leads to paganism, American evangelicals continue to accept uncritically. Even while evangelicals picket and protest television content, they are accepting the dominance of image and adopting the MTV format for their own communication strategies.

Second, the image revolution has greatly enhanced the rise of the celebrity—people who are known for their well-knownness. Daniel Boorstin writes, 'Since the Graphics Revolution, much of our thinking about human greatness has changed. Two centuries ago when a great man appeared, people looked for God's purpose in him; today we look for his press agent.'[66] Evangelicalism has long been centered around charismatic leaders, gifted evangelists, and popular preachers. But today there is a growing inauthenticity in evangelical leadership. There is a hollowness created by the growing emphasis on the media and image. Evangelicalism has created a culture of religious celebrities. Word Publishers crassly marketed Amy Grant's latest album under the heading, 'Unwrap Amy Grant for Christmas'. The promotional contest coinciding with her release offered a ski weekend in Colorado and hot chocolate on the slopes with Amy herself. A common factor linking evangelical best-selling authors, writes William Griffin in *Publishers Weekly*, 'is undoubtedly the "media ministry" of the authors.'[67] And yet many of their radio programs are written by staff ghostwriters on topics the evangelical celebrity has not even chosen. In one case, two-thirds of the broadcast commentaries by one well-known evangelical leader are selected and written by others.

This inauthenticity extends to books and sermons as well. In some cases confidentiality agreements hide the fact that a celebrity's book has been in fact written by another, such as Thomas Nelson's arrangement with Neil Eskelin who wrote Benny Hinn's bestseller *Good Morning, Holy Spirit.* Cases have been cited of well-known evangelical preachers using ghosted sermons. Evangelical journalist Ed Plowman concludes, 'We may see the ultimate sorry spectacle (if it hasn't happened already): a celebrity preacher's ghost-written book of ghost-written sermons bearing a ghost-written foreword by another celebrity and ghost-written endorsement blurbs on the dust jacket by still more celebrities, none of whom has read the book.'[68] Such inauthenticity obliterates the evangelical commitment to truth or integrity. But the acceptance of the gospel of MTV within evangelicalism increasingly gives license to image over substance, appearance over reality.

What is at stake in these accommodations to modernity is the belief in what is real. Under the conditions of modernity, modern life is reduced to the 'triumph of the superficial', the 'delight in the unreal', an 'orgy of the facade'. As early as 1859, Oliver Wendell Holmes warned of the time when photographic technique would be elevated to the level of social principle. 'Images will become more important than the object itself, and would make the object disposable.... Men will hunt all curious, beautiful grand objects, as they hunt cattle in South America, for their skins and leave the carcasses as of little worth.'[69] Now today we see transcendence, revelation, and humanness reduced to commodities, statistics, and images. That there are values other than market values, that there are realities beyond what can be quantified, that there are truths deeper than celluloid is what is increasingly forgotten. Thus the challenge of modernity is not in its direct confrontation with theology or faith but in the subtle shifts in the basic assumptions that govern evangelical practice.

Responding to modernity

The American evangelical movement is deeply infiltrated by the spirit and tools of modernity. Oblivious to its dangers, American evangelicalism continues as one of the leading global apologists for modernity through its publications and mission agencies. There is virtually no systematic training within American evangelical seminaries on the challenge of modernity. Until Professor David Wells' recently released book, *No Place for Truth*,[70] there has been no critical assessment of the impact of modernity on theology.

Confronting this challenge must not be left to the scholars. The seriousness of modernity for the life of the church is so significant that one of the greatest dangers is for the analysis of modernity to remain at the level of elite knowledge—the focus of specialized consultations, the purview of academics alone. Quite deliberately in this paper I have chosen to look at common aspects of modern life, in this case three icons of American modernity, to bring home the inescapable challenge modernity is to the church and discipleship.

Many are uncertain whether the American evangelical church will be able to develop the critical distance necessary to repent of the idolatrous overreliance on the tools of modernity and develop an integrity of discipleship no longer patterned after the world. Some evangelical leaders are drifting towards Roman Catholicism or Eastern Orthodoxy as a perceived safe haven from the reach of modernity. At present the megachurch movement has the greatest momentum within the American evangelical church. They it is who have brought the Trojan horse of modernity directly within the sanctuary, and their success has thus far drowned out cautionary voices.

Thus the future of evangelicalism and its engagement with modernity may well fall to the now modernizing countries, to Third World Christians, who for the sake of the gospel will save the church from the excesses of the First World followers of Christ. If evangelicalism is to remain a viable religious community under these conditions, it must first engage in serious self-examination so as to become again people who are serious about the first things of the gospel.

The engagement with modernity by the American evangelical church is a harbinger of the coming challenges to the church worldwide. From this struggle the wider evangelical community has much it can learn so as to avoid the mistakes of their American brothers and sisters. They need your prayers and may need your exhortation. But those who clearly see the excesses and mistakes of American evangelicals should remember the warning of Galatians 6:1b, 'Watch yourselves, or you also may be tempted.'

Notes

1. George Gallup, *Religion in America 1979–80*, Princeton Religion Research Center, 1980, pages 90–92; see also *Religion in America, 1990*.

2. James Davison Hunter, *American Evangelicalism: Conservative Religion and the Quandary of Modernity*, Rutgers, 1983, page 49

3. Donald G. Bloesch, *The Future of Evangelical Christianity*, Doubleday, 1983, pages 23–54; see also Hunter [note 2]

4. George Marsden, editor, *Evangelicalism and Modern America*, Eerdmans, 1984, page xiv

5. Thomas Luckmann, 'The New and the Old in Religion', in Pierre Bourdieu and James S. Coleman, editors, *Social Theory for a Changing Society*, Westview, 1991

6. the same, page 174

7. See Scott Lash and Sam Whimster, *Max Weber, Rationality and Modernity*, Allen & Unwin, 1987

8. Robert Wuthnow, *The Restructuring of American Religion*, Princeton, 1988, pages 300–301

9. Ernest Gellner, *Postmodernism, Reason, and Religion*, Routledge, 1992, page 5

10. Martin E. Marty, 'Fundamentalism as a Social Phenomena', in George Marsden, editor, *Evangelicalism and Modern America*, Eerdmans, 1984

11. the same, page 66

12. Scott Appleby, 'Fundamentalism Storms Back', in George W. Cornell, *Washington Post*, 24 April 1993, pages D9–10

13. Alfred Schutz, *The Structures of the Life-World*, Northwestern, 1973, page 3

14. the same, page 4

15. David Lowenthal, *The Past is a Foreign Country*, Cambridge, 1985, page 41

16. Anthony Brandt, in Christopher Lasch, *The True and Only Heaven*, Norton, 1991, page 118

17. Karl Marx, 'The Eighteenth Brumaire of Louis Bonaparte', in McLellan, *Karl Marx: Selected Writings*, Oxford, 1977 , page 300

18. Pierre Bourdieu, *Outline of a Theory of Practice*, Cambridge, 1977, page 79

19. John Seel, *The Evangelical Forfeit: Can We Recover?* Baker, 1993

20. See George M. Thomas, *Revivalism and Cultural Change*, Chicago, 1989, page 71

21. the same, page 72

22. T.J. Jackson Lears, *No Place of Grace*, Pantheon, 1981, page 24

23. Thomas [note 20]

24. Peter L. Berger, *Facing Up to Modernity*, Basic, 1977, page 27

25. Pierre Bourdieu, *The Logic of Practice*, Stanford, 1990, page 1

26. John Herman Randall, Jr., *The Making of the Modern Mind*, Columbia, 1926

27. Francis Schaeffer, *The God Who Is There*, Hodder, 1968, page 16

28. See John Higham and Paul K. Conkin, *New Directions in American Intellectual History*, Johns Hopkins, 1979; and Gene Wise, 'The Contemporary Crisis in Intellectual History Studies', *CLIO*, Winter 1975, pages 55–71

29. Quentin Skinner in James Tully, editor, *Meaning and Context*, Princeton, 1988, page 40

30. Fritz Ringer, 'The Intellectual Field, Intellectual History, and the Sociology of Knowledge', *Theory and Society*, 19, 1990, page 277

31. Gene Wise, *American Historical Explanations*, Minnesota, 1980, page xxxv

32. Thomas C. Oden, *After Modernity What?*, Zondervan, 1990

33. Nathan O. Hatch, *The Democratization of American Christianity*, Yale, 1989, page 219

34. Stephen M. Fjellman, *Vinyl Leaves*, Westview, 1992, page 398

35. Karl Marx, *Communist Manifesto*, Gateway, 1969, pages 19 –20

36. Frederic Jameson, 'Postmodernism, or the Cultural Logic of Late Capitalism', *New Left Review*, 146, 1984, pages 53–92

37. Neil Postman, *Amusing Ourselvess to Death*, Viking, 1985

38. James B. Twitchell, *Carnival Culture*, Columbia, 1992, page i

39. Lears [note 22], page 304

40. *Self*, April 1993, pages 12–13

41. George Barna, 'Marketing the Church' seminar, Atlanta, Georgia, 29 January 1991

42. George Barna, 'The Church of the '90s: Meeting the Needs of a Changing Culture,' *RTS Ministry*, Fall, 1990, pages 47ff

43. Bill Hybels, 'Church Leadership Conference', 12–16 May 1992

44. Leith Anderson, *Dying for Change*, Bethany, 1990, pages 145-46

45. Ken Woodward, 'A Time to Seek', *Newsweek*, 17 December 1990, page 50

46. Sharon Schmickle, 'Thousands Flock to Service at Megamall', *Minneapolis Star Tribune*, 31 August 1992, page A1

47. David Biemesderfer, 'Of Malls and Men', *World Traveler*, August 1992, page 17

48. Robert David Sack, *Place, Modernity, and the Consumer's World*, Johns Hopkins, 1992, page 104

49. the same, pages 144, 148

50. George Ritzer, *The McDonaldization of Society*, Pine Forge, 1993, page 1

51. the same, page 5

52. John Seel, 'Evangelical Leadership Interviews', 1992

53. *The Exchange*, June 1993

54. Barna [note 42], page 11

55. Ron Powers, *The Beast, the Eunuch, and the Glass-eyed Child*, Anchor, 1990, page 27

56. the same, page 24

57. Anthony DeCurtis and James Henke, editors, *The Rolling Stones Illustrated History of Rock & Roll*, Random, 1992, page 646

58. Powers [note 55], page 25

59. Powers [note 55], page 24

60. Jacques Ellul, *The Humiliation of the Word*, Eerdmans, 1985, page 116

61. the same, page 117

62. *Wall Street Journal*, 2 March 1992

63. *Religion Watch*, April 1992, page 4

64. Bill Hybels, 'Bill Hybels Knows How to Coax Folks Back to Church', *Daily Herald*, 1990, section 2, pages 4–5

65. Camille Paglia and Neil Postman, 'She Wants Her TV! He Wants His Book!' *Harper's Magazine*, March 1991, page 45; see also Camille Paglia, *Sex, Art, and American Culture*, Vintage, 1992.

66. Daniel J. Boorstin, *The Image*, Atheneum, 1961, page 45

67. William Griffin, 'Christian Publishers Refashion Their Image', *Publisher's Weekly*, 10 August 1992, pages 42–45

68. Ed Plowman, 'Haunted Houses', *World*, 10 April 1993, page 14

69. Stuart Ewen, *All Consuming Images*, Basic, 1988, page 25

70. David F. Wells, *No Place for Truth*, Eerdmans, 1993

Further reading

Berger, Peter L., *The Sacred Canopy*, Anchor, 1969

Berger, Peter L., *A Rumor of Angels*, Anchor, 1970

Berger, Peter L. and Thomas Luckmann, *The Social Construction of Reality*, Anchor, 1966

Berger, Peter L., Brigitte Berger, and Hansfried Kellner, *The Homeless Mind*, Vintage, 1973

Bourdieu, Pierre, *In Other Words*, Stanford, 1990

Bourdieu, Pierre and Loïc J. D. Wacquant, *An Invitation to Reflexive Sociology*, Chicago, 1992

Brubaker, Rogers, *The Limits of Rationality*, Allen & Unwin, 1984

Carlson, Peter, 'It's an Ad, Ad, Ad, Ad World', *The Washington Post Magazine*, 3 November 1991, pages 15–33

Gergen, Kenneth J., *The Saturated Self*, Basic

Giddens, Anthony, *Capitalism and Modern Social Theory*, Cambridge, 1971

Giddens, Anthony, *The Consequences of Modernity*, Stanford, 1990

Giddens, Anthony, *Modernity and Self-Identity*, Stanford, 1991

Hunter, James Davison, *Evangelicalism: The Coming Generation*, Chicago, 1987

Hunter, James Davison, 'Religious Elites in Advanced Industrial Society', *Comparative Studies in Society and History 29*, 1987, pages 360–74

Hunter, James Davison, *Culture Wars: The Struggle to Define America*, Basic, 1991

Kalberg, Stephen, 'Max Weber's Types of Rationality', *American Journal of Sociology*, 83, 1980, pages 1145–1179

Klobuchar, Jim, 'You Can Get It All At The Megamall Even Religion', *Minneapolis Star Tribune*, August 30 1992, page B3

Kristol, Irving, *Two Cheers for Capitalism*, Basic, 1978

Lasch, Christopher, *The True and Only Heaven*, Norton, 1991

Lears, T. J. Jackson, 'From Salvation to Self-Realization: Advertising and the Therapeutic Roots of the Consumer Culture 1880–1930', in R.W. Fox and T.J. Lears, editors, *The Culture of Consumption: Critical Essays in American History, 1880–1930*, Pantheon, 1983

Luckmann, Thomas, *The Invisible Religion*, Macmillan, 1967

Lyon, David, 'Secularization: The Fate of Faith in the Modern World?' *Themelios*, September 1984, pages 16–22

Lyon, David, 'Rethinking Secularization: Retrospect and Prospect', *Review of Religious Research*, 26, 1985, pages 228–243

Marsden, George M., *Fundamentalism and American Culture*, Oxford, 1980

Marsden, George M., *Reforming Fundamentalism: Fuller Seminary and the New Evangelicalism*, Eerdmans, 1987

Marsden, George M., 'The Evangelical Denomination', in Neuhaus and others, editors, *Piety & Politics: Evangelicals and Fundamentalists Confront the World*, 1988, pages 55–68

Marsden, George M., *Understanding Fundamentalism and Evangelicalism*, Eerdmans, 1991

Oden, Thomas C., 'On Not Whoring After the Spirit of the Age', in Os Guinness and John Seel, editors, *No God But God*, Moody, 1992

Ostling, Richard N., 'Here Come The Megachurches', *Time*, 5 August 1991, page 63

Postman, Neil, 'Television and the Decline of Public Discourse', *The Civic Arts Review*, Winter 1990

Potter, David, *People of Plenty*, Chicago, 1954

Rabb, Theodore K. and Robert I. Rotberg, editors, *The New History*, Princeton, 1982

Reid, Daniel G. and others, editors, 'Great Awakenings', *Dictionary of Christianity in America*, InterVarsity, 1990

Schroeder, Ralph, 'Nietzsche and Weber: Two "Prophets" of the Modern World', in Scott Lash and Sam Whimster, editors, *Max Weber, Rationality and Modernity*, Allen & Unwin, 1987

Smith, Timothy L., *Revivalism and Social Reform*, Johns Hopkins, 1980

Schudson, Michael, *Advertising, the Uneasy Persuasion*, Basic, 1984

Weber, Max, *Economy and Society*, California, 1978

Wells, David F., 'On Being Evangelical: Some Differences and Similarities', Unpublished paper, 1992

Willow Creek Magazine, November/December 1990

14

Modernity, mission and non-Western societies

VINAY SAMUEL

The purpose of this paper is to present an overview of the impact of modernity on Islamic and Hindu societies and to explore the implications for Christian missions in that context.

While the West is going through an advanced stage of modernity and postmodernity, Islamic and Hindu societies are still struggling against the pressures of modernization.

MODERNITY, MISSION AND COLONIALISM

Colonialism drew much of its inspiration from the Enlightenment's universalizing narrative. The Enlightenment's vision was of a unified destiny for humanity with a drive toward universal rationalization, industrial progress and a global expansion of markets. This vision provided a basic justification for colonial advance and existence. A canopy of Western civilization as the expression of an advanced rational and scientific culture provided the ideological legitimacy for colonial rule.

The colonial powers decided very early that they would not interfere with the religious life of Hindu and Islamic societies because their interests were political and economic. After initial suspicion of Christian mission activity, colonial authorities recognised that the educational and health care efforts of the missionaries supported rather than undermined their economic and political interests.

Christian mission also saw itself as part of the enterprise that was designed to bring an advanced civilization to primitive and stagnant cultures. While Islamic and Hindu societies were not regarded as primitive by a few mission groups, they were judged to be stagnant, backward and in need of being shaped by an advanced civilization. Christian mission often projected itself as bringing modern civilization to these cultures. It was also perceived in Islamic and Hindu societies as attempting to introduce Western civilization with its social vision and technology. Christian missions were considered to be the principal bearers of modernization. In India the benefits of modern education, science and health care are regarded as laudable gifts of Christian mission. It is also acknowledged that the social reform of uplifting the status of women and children was initiated by Christian missionaries.

Islamic societies rejected Christian mission because they saw it as the continuation of the crusades of the Middle Ages. Even the benefits of education and health care were not seen, primarily, as modern and advanced but as instruments that would undermine and even destroy traditional achievements in those areas. Most people in Islamic cultures did not see Christian mission as bringing in any benefits. As modernity entered Western colonialism, Western Christian mission introduced modernity into Hindu and Islamic societies. Such an understanding dominates perceptions of modernity in Islamic societies. Islamic and Hindu societies were introduced to a package of human sciences. Anthropology and historicity became essential for understanding human life and history. In Foucault's term, a 'pre-classical *episteme*' ('way of knowing') underpinned these cultures. Knowledge was shaped by analogy (resemblance), sympathy (mood) and convention (custom). A conceptual matrix of critical analysis and rationality as underlying every type of knowledge was stamped upon traditional non-Western societies. A conflictual inter-episteme situation developed, as the two ways of knowledge intersected and dissected each other.

ISLAMIC SOCIETIES AND MODERNITY

> Islam is integrist; it makes imperious demands. It wants
> to rule everything, to manage society, to regiment
> minds and make them impermeable to the swamping
> tides of technological mutations. More than this, it tries
> to make them resistant to research and innovation.[1]

This is the judgement of an Islamic scholar on the relationship between modernity and Islam.

It was not until the French Revolution that modern ideas began to find their way into Islamic societies. Because those ideas came in a secular, religiously neutral ideology they were given a cautious hearing. However their influence was never allowed to permeate beyond the educated elite. Western books were not translated into Arabic or Persian. Even today, an educated Muslim who is not fluent in one of the European languages has very limited access to the creations of the West.

It was soon clear that modern technique could not be learned without acquiring, or at least understanding its metaphysical under-pinnings. The lack of the development of a critical and modern intellectual current in most Islamic societies is the result of attempts to retain technical contributions of modernity while proscribing the metaphysics on which they are based—for example the difference between faith and knowledge, humanism and humans as self-sufficient subjects. Furthermore, the Islamic state is a product of its religion, whereas the modern state is a product of modernity with a marginal role for religion. A modern state presupposes a secular mentality. 'Democracy is not a super-structure, but a popular creation. Moreover it is the condition, the basis, of modern civiliza-tion.'[2] So Islam is totally incompatible with the modern state.

Though Islamic cultures are rich, they are medieval in struc-ture and hardly able to understand the modern age, let alone use it. Yet, there is a desperate desire to use the products of modernity and to furnish their societies with them. But often out of step and unable to understand the transformation affecting the world, they fall into a cultural dependency which is more insidious than economic or political dependency.[3]

Islamic societies appear to be languishing in a no man's land between the meta-reality of their cultures and the dialectical contradictions of the world where they have no power and often no place. The one capital that they possess is oil, which allows them to be tolerated in the world, but it is becoming less and less essential to the world economy.

It would be fair to note that modern education is desired in Islamic societies. After the purging of universities by the Khomeini Revolution, these places of learning in Iran are slowly returning to their former standards of study and research. The critical approach that is at the heart of modern education, is, however out of bounds as far as religion is concerned. As the West finds itself in a post-critical stage, Islam (except for the narrow area of science and technology) remains in the pre-critical stage. The disjuncture that is produced greatly affects the educated classes. It is a disjunction between ideas and attitudes. The ideas are contemporary, while the attitudes are traditional. Trained in the modern school where a true idea instantly overcomes the false in the sphere of thought, they expect the

316

triumph of modern attitudes over old attitudes and customs just as swiftly. When this does not happen, the result is a cultural schizophrenia among the educated classes.[4]

HINDU SOCIETIES AND MODERNITY

In Hindu societies the situation is somewhat different, though modernity has also assaulted Hindu society in the same fashion as it assaulted that of Islam.

Modernity and tradition are the two 'ways of knowing' (*epistemes*) which co-exist and distort one another. They operate in cultures and individuals, producing displacements in ontological, psychological and aesthetic areas.

Hindu traditions are steeped in the paradigm of the earliest visions of being. The stress is on experience, on empathy of social relations, the identity of the individual in the collective self, and the fluidity of space and time with all the modes of existence communing in a united co-existence. All this is reflected in beliefs and customs. On the level of beliefs it constitutes a meta-reality of concepts like *Dharma* (duty–law), *Moksha* (deliverance–salvation), *Karma* (fate–destiny), *Yoga* (state of belief) etc. These are reinforced by intuition rather than by rational argument and analysis.

In the area of customs, it is family rituals and rites of passage that take the centre stage. There is often no consciously worked-out connection between beliefs and customs.

Modern education with its critical method does become a part of the educated Hindu's consciousness but it is also confined to the areas of science, economic and political spheres. Family life and private customs remain traditional and this compartmentalized consciousness does not paralyse their normal activities. The world of religion and family are not allowed to be disenchanted, while modernity is allowed to disenchant the rest of life. The schizophrenia so evident in Islamic societies does not exist among Hindus. Tensions between the modern and the traditional do not break up social consciousness in the same way.

However, I am convinced that this does produce a psychological displacement. Modernity calls for a strong individual ego able to compete and survive in the market place. The Hindu emphasis on the happy family often produces a passive ego based on the memory of happy infancy. The release of the male child from the mother hardly ever takes place and the primary reference of a male is to his mother. The aggressiveness that modernity demands for continuing success is often absent in modernizing Hindu cultures. As soon as a level of security is reached, contentment sets in and perseverance is abandoned.[5]

Myth and reason co-exist as two orders of reality. Reason is rarely used to question unjust or corrupt customs. They always find legitimation in myth which, while providing a measure of transcendence to life, also prevents reason from completing its critical task. So truth resides both in myth as well as reason. It becomes extremely malleable in the hands of people who draw from both orders of reality and make truth whatever they need. The subject is never addressed by a truth from outside.

Hindu mythology as divine narrative creates a mythic world which is identified with meta-reality in popular Hinduism. Myths can be trusted to reflect ultimate reality. They access the transcendent to the believer. The Hindu devotee accepts that world and uses reason only to establish its validity.

IMPLICATIONS FOR MISSION

Living with two paradigms, the traditional and the modern, Islamic and Hindu societies are already making choices.

The educated classes and the intellectuals have been seduced by the quick-frozen, ready-to-eat ideologies from the West. Leftist ideologies are seen as the only weapons provided from the West's own armoury to oppose the West, the source of modernization and those ideologies are grasped as liberating cultural products. Living in the context of disjunctions, the intellectual activist holds the ideology with innate dogmatism. He combines a religious spirit with an absence of criticism and ends up having unshakeable certainties forged by *a priori* notions. Such ideologies flourish in lands where modernity is superficial. The borrowed leftist ideologies of the West are secular in structure; they get poured into pervasively religious societies which then become westernised. The result is a false consciousness alienating the ideologues from the very people they seek to serve. It is little wonder that the common people find little hope in intellectuals or activists.

Another response to modernity in Islamic and Hindu societies is regressive fundamentalism. Religion is made dominant in the public sphere and integrism is pushed to destroy modernity. As religion dominates and becomes an iron cage, civil liberties that are fundamental to modernity come under threat. An atmosphere of menace and violence permeates society, eroding any advance of modernity. It is sad to note that Hindu fundamentalism in India is growing due to the support of Hindus living in affluent Western countries and benefiting from modern society. Their support of fundamentalism will keep the poorer sections of India in a feudal structure, perpetuating the horrors of injustice and oppression.

As long as Islamic societies continue to face the disjunctions of coping with modernity and retaining their traditional identities, more people within them will look for other options. The option of the Christian faith is often not available to them. There is inbuilt prejudice against the Christian faith as the instrument of the very modernity that threatens their society. I believe the Christian option must be presented to these societies not primarily from the West, but from the Church in the Two-Thirds World. Further Western missions to Islam, however subtle and sophisticated, are more likely to increase resistance than to lower it. It is here that we need to recover the tradition of fervent, unceasing prayer for these societies that the contradictions now breaking them will open them to the gospel.

Hindu societies will continue to be stony soil for the Gospel. Moreover, the postmodern view of 'truth' fits well with Hinduism's traditional emphasis that all truth is relative. Hindu approaches have never questioned the content of any belief against a standard of truth. They have never attempted to reveal the truth behind any myth, but merely pointed to other truths as relativizing any claims to universality. The emergence of a postmodern view of truth in the West will confirm Hinduism's sense of the superiority of its own philosophical system.

I believe that the inadequacy of Hinduism will be revealed in the public sphere in the areas of the state, judiciary, education and family life. Hindu societies are eager to be modern economically and politically. It is accepted that democracy, modern legal systems, and scientific education are necessary for a successful modern state but there is a strong attempt to develop those areas from a specifically Hindu perspective. It is an attempt that is doomed to failure because Hinduism has not developed the cultural habits based on democracy and rationality in the public sphere that would make such an enterprise successful, even if it were to draw on its own vast philosophical resources. It is in these areas the Christian Church needs to present a clear perspective and direction.

Traditional Hindu cultures have never rejected intrusions from other religions or ways of life but have received them and transformed them to conform to a broadly Hindu ethos. This happened to Islam and also to the early fourth century Christian mission. It is also happening to some extent to the contemporary Indian Christian Church. What is needed is a church that is uncompromisingly Christian and willing to pay the price for it. Developing authentic Christian communities is the most effective way of mission and evangelism in such a context.

Much of contemporary Christian enterprise is still part of the Western universalizing enterprise. Christian theology, research, communication and mission are still mostly created in the Western church and consumed by the church of the Two-Thirds World. Much of this is marked by the rejoicing over the great evangelistic and mission advance of the Two-Thirds World church. But resources are still unbalanced, with local national theologies, histories and identities marginalized in the process of universal mission created in the West paralleling the creation of other modern and postmodern products.

In some evangelical circles a Two-Thirds World evangelical who dares to unmask the situation is immediately seen as a threat, 'the Other' who is not quite evangelical but who enables the Western Evangelical to define and possess the centre. If the gospel is to be truly liberating in the contemporary world, we need to go beyond these games to being 'in Christ', where there is no East and West, North and South, yet all one in him.

The church in Islamic and Hindu contexts is called to demonstrate the reality of a community where traditions are continued and renewed, and where the dehumanizing effects of modernity are resisted. Traditions which are not shaped by constant reflection become fetishes and lifeless rituals, and the church is called to be a covenant community where both renewal and resistance operate.

Notes

1. D. Shayegan, *Cultural Schizophrenia: Islamic Societies comforting the West*, London 1992, page 23

2. Octavio Paz, *One Earth, Four or Five Worlds, Reflections on Contemporary History*, Manchester, 1985, page 168

3. Compare Shayegan [note 1] page 105.

4. the same, pages 121–55; I have drawn heavily on Shayegan's analysis of intellectuals in modernizing non-Western cultures

5. S. Kalkar, *Moksha, le monde Interieur, enfance et societé en Inde*, Paris, 1985, page 95, quoted in Shayegan [note1], page 64

LEVEL THREE:

STRATEGIES IN CONFRONTING MODERNITY

15

Mission modernity: seven checkpoints on mission in the modern world

A paper originally prepared for Lausanne II in Manila, July 1989, and revised for the Uppsala Consultation on Modernity, June 1993

OS GUINNESS

The outline of this paper is as follows:

Introduction: The Promise and the Threat
1. Exploiting Modernity: Two Opportunities
2. Reading the Signs of the Times: Two Pitfalls
3. Assessing the Damage to Persisting Religion: Two Trends
4. Sizing Up the Competition: Two Rivals
5. Engaging Modernity: Two Master Principles
6. Engaging Modernity: Two Special Prerequisites
7. Overcoming Modernity: Two Points of Reliance
Conclusion: The Reality and the Glory

Introduction: the promise and the threat

Modernity, or the world civilization that the forces of modernization is now producing, represents the greatest single opportunity and the greatest single threat the Christian church has faced since Apostolic times. Yet no great theme concerning Christian discipleship and mission has been more overlooked by more Christians with more consequences than this one. For evangelicals at large, modernity is still an unconfronted problem.

Let me open this momentous subject in a simple way with a story, an observation, a thesis, and a quotation.

First, the story. Soviet leader Nikita Kruschev used to tell of a time when a wave of petty thefts hit the former USSR, and so the authorities put guards at all the factories. At one of the timber-works in Leningrad the guard knew the workers well. The first evening, out came Pyotr Petrovich with a wheelbarrow and, on the wheelbarrow, a great bulky sack with a suspicious-looking shape.

'Come on, Petrovich,' said the guard. 'What have you got there?'

'Just sawdust and shavings,' Petrovich replied.

'Come on,' the guard said, 'I wasn't born yesterday. Tip it out.'

And out it came nothing but sawdust and shavings. So he was allowed to put it all back again and go home.

The same thing happened every night all week, and the guard was getting extremely frustrated. Finally, his curiosity overcame his frustration.

'Petrovich,' he said, 'I know you. Tell me what you're smuggling out of here, and I'll let you go.'

'Wheelbarrows, my friend,' said Petrovich. 'Wheelbarrows.'

We may laugh, but we must remember that in the area where the church and modernity meet, the laugh is on us. Modernity is a new kind of worldliness that has sneaked up on us without our realizing it. We have tried to use the forces of modernization to serve us, but unwittingly we ourselves have been shaped by them. We have set up endless patrols to detect the dangers of the world in our societies, but the devil has trundled this new worldliness right past our eyes and into the church. As Peter Berger warns, whoever sups with the devil of modernity had better have a very long spoon.

Second, the observation. Back in the early seventies, a renowned social scientist at Oxford University turned to me, knowing I was a Christian, and said, 'By the end of the seventies, who will be the worldliest Christians in America?' I must have looked a little puzzled, because he continued, 'I guarantee it will be the fundamentalists.'

At the time such an idea was startling. Worldliest? Funda-mentalism had always been world-denying by definition. But now, as we meet to discuss the task of world mission and look at the impact of modernization two decades later, that impact confronts us bluntly: World-denying conservatism has become virtually impossible. And Christendom's ultimate worldling to-day is not the Christian liberal but the Christian conservative.

The contemporary church's prototypical charlatan is not the mediaeval priest but the modern evangelist. The Tetzels of history and the Elmer Gantrys of fiction pale beside the real-life examples of evangelical and evangelistic worldliness in our own time. In its sweatless, disincarnate, electronic form, modern evangelism has created the ultimate parody of the incarnation.

Third, the thesis. A full account of the relationship of modernity and the church is probably beyond any of us, and certainly beyond the scope of this paper. But just compare the church's position in 1993 with her prospects in AD993 on the eve of the first millennium. In 993 she held only a tiny segment of the globe and had made only a limited impact on the deep paganism that underlay the official layer of 'Christian civilization'. A millennium later she is the world's leading faith and lays the strongest claim to be a truly global religion. And while the Christian faith is currently in recession in Europe, which was once its heartland, it still experiences the most massive worldwide expansion in its history.

At first sight, then, the close relationship between the church and modernity appears to have been overwhelmingly advantageous. The Christian faith has been tied intimately to the most successful, the most nearly global, the most consciously copied of all civilizations in history. Once due allowance has been made for 'Western imperialism' and 'Eurocentrism', the balance sheet from the church's partnership with modernity seems unquestionably positive.

But to anyone who looks more closely, and who examines the contrast between the state of the church in the more modernized and the less modernized parts of the world, a far more sober interpretation is suggested. No persecutor or foe in two thousand years has wreaked such havoc on the church as has modernity. And the strongest theory that explains this analysis is one that was used as a tool by Marx and Engels but which is rooted in Puritanism and the Bible—the 'gravedigger thesis.' Stated briefly, *The Christian church contributed to the rise of the modern world; the modern world, in turn, has undermined the Christian church. Thus, to the degree that the church enters, engages and employs the modern world uncritically, the church becomes her own gravedigger.*

This theme of the church warring against herself in her own worldliness becomes most focused in the discussion of mission and modernity. For if modernity represents the most powerful, the most all-embracing, and the most seductive setting in human history, then 'contextualization' in the setting of modernity is both amplified promise and amplified threat. The desire to witness and the danger of worldliness are enhanced simultaneously and exponentially.

Lastly, the quotation. One hundred years ago, the German philosopher and self-styled Anti-Christ, Friedrich Nietzsche, remarked that when there was 'the death of God' in a culture, that culture became increasingly hollowed out, or 'weightless'. Karl Marx, in his *Communist Manifesto*, had noted the same effect earlier 'All that is solid melts into air, all that is holy is profaned.' But he blamed it on the corrosive acid of modern capitalism, which dissolved the ties and bonds of traditional society.

Today we would place both their insights into the wider framework of modernization, for modern unbelief and modern market economics are simply two related aspects of modernity. But Nietzsche's insight into 'weightlessness' is a telling description of the hollowing out of reality which is characteristic of modernity even upon truths as powerful and precious as the gospel. And it also points in the direction of the sole, ultimate answer to modernity, for the biblical opposite of, and antidote to, 'weightlessness' is 'glory'.

Far more than his renown or radiance, God's glory is his own inexpressible reality, a reality so real that it alone has gravity and weight—the only 'really real reality' in the entire universe. Therefore, when things move away from God, they become hollow and weightless. It can accurately be said of them, '*Ichabod*', 'The glory has departed', or '*Mene, mene, tekel, upharsin*', 'You are weighed in the balance and found weightless or wanting'. That is why idols, by contrast with God, are literally 'nothings'. That is why revival is the refilling of a nation with 'the knowledge of the glory of the Lord, as the waters cover the sea'.

In sum, the civilization of modernity is a world system and spirit that today both encompasses us as individuals and encircles the globe. It therefore raises ultimate questions and requires ultimate responses. We cannot tackle the character and predicament of modernization if we simply summarize trends, marshal statistics, devise strategies, and assess prospects. To do that is to limit things to 'technique', and thus to fall victim to the mesmerizing spell of modernity itself, and to fail to see that modernity's real questions and impact go far deeper.

Modernity is a profound challenge to the church precisely because its menace is not merely to how we communicate, but to what we communicate and who we are to the very character of the gospel and the church itself. At a time when the church is on the threshold of 'reaching the world,' modernity calls into question what it means to reach anyone. We may indeed 'win the whole world, but lose our own soul'. As Jacques Ellul says, those who understand modernity know that it raises the ultimate question—Christ's: 'When the Son of Man comes, will he find faith on the earth?'

This paper was therefore deliberately different from most others presented at Lausanne II in Manila for several reasons. First, it is unashamedly theoretical, but only so that mission can be truly practical and effective in the end. Second, it is undoubtedly difficult because of the sociological terms, but partly because some people have not experienced modernity, many who have have not reflected on it, and even for those who have it is notoriously difficult. And third, its chief focus is a critical view of the character of modernity, but simply because modernity represents a danger of worldliness as strong as any desire to witness. In tempting us with its distinctive secularity, modernity becomes a test of what we believe is ultimately real. Its challenge is to our character and integrity, not simply to our communication and cultural adaptability.

This paper, then, is a call to repentance, prayer, spiritual warfare, and hard thinking as much as to planning and new enterprise. It is a call to a deeper, tougher response to a challenge far greater than most Christians have realized. If we are to engage modernity and 'plunder the Egyptians' without 'setting up a golden calf', we shall have to understand more deeply both modernity and an incarnational theology that alone can overcome it.

DEFINITION AND DESCRIPTION

But what exactly is 'modernization' or 'modernity'? At a rudimentary level, we all have answers to that question, because all of us are to some extent accustomed to many of the components of 'modern society'. For example, think of the fact that those of us born before the end of World War II (1945) actually have preceded many of the advances modern people take for granted: television, penicillin, credit cards, frozen foods, satellites, copying machines, contact lenses, word processors, artificial hearts, tape decks, split atoms, ballpoint pens, fax machines, men walking on the moon, and so on. Such discoveries underscore how far and fast we have come. But this view of modernity remains impressionistic. A far harder and more important task is to move beyond impressions to define what modernization is, and to describe how it arose and what its consequences are.

It is simple to see that the term *modernization* is derived from the Latin word *modo*, 'contemporary' or 'just now'. But modernization and modernity remain widely misunderstood today. Some people, for example, turn them into a kind of 'rich man's Marxism', a deterministic movement that will inevitably sweep the world with prosperity, progress, and democratic revolutions. Christians, however, tend to fall foul of a simpler misunderstanding. Many use the word modernity as if it were a fancy word for 'change' or simply a matter of being 'up to date'. They therefore treat it as something simple and straightforward, as if one can understand it through monitoring the latest trends and statistics and put it to use simply like a new fax machine or laser printer.

But modernity is much more than that. It refers to the character and system of the world produced by the forces of modernization and development centered above all on the premise that the 'bottom up' causation of human designs and products has now decisively replaced the 'top down' causation of God and the supernatural.

Modernity is therefore not a fancy word for 'change' and little of it can be understood merely by watching trends and keeping up with the latest technologies. To grasp modernity is a challenge: it requires an understanding of the whole, not simply just the parts. Ironically, when we wrestle with a tough-minded overview of modernity, it turns out to be far from modern.

Modernity's replacement of 'top down' God-centered living with 'bottom up' human-centered living represents a titanic revolution in human history and experience. We can trace its origins in two main ways. One way is to focus on human beings and the impact of their ideas. Thus, the road to modernity traces from the revolutionary changes in ideas to the way they have affected society throughout the centuries. This mode of analysis goes back at least to the seventeenth-century scientific revolution and follows the story through the eighteenth-century

Enlightenment and the nineteenth-century romantic movement to the modernist and postmodernist movements in the twentieth century.

The rarer but even more important way to analyze modernity and face the challenge is to focus on society and social change. The line is traced in reverse as the story is followed from the revolutionary changes in society to the way they have affected ideas. This mode of analysis goes back to major structural and institutional developments—supremely those that resulted from the capitalist revolution in the fifteenth century, the technological and industrial revolution in the eighteenth century, and the communications revolution in the twentieth century.

This general statement can be made a little sharper by underscoring some of the components that make up the challenge of modernity. The following twelve statements summarize this challenge from the standpoint of North American evangelicals (who are currently and perhaps unenviably on the leading edge of modernity as British evangelicals were a century ago).

1. *Modernity is the central fact of human life today:* Modernity is the first truly global culture in the world and the most powerful culture in history so far. Thus the empire of modernity is the great alternative to the kingdom of God. Extensively, it encircles the planet; intensively, it encompasses more and more of each individual's life. The massiveness and seeming permanence of its imperial systems and ideology threaten us with captivity as surely as the empire of Egypt did Moses and the empires of Assyria and Babylon did exiled Israel.

2. *Modernity is double-edged for human beings:* Modernity simultaneously represents the greatest human advances in history in such benefits as health, speed, power, and convenience and the greatest assaults on humanness in history in such areas as the crisis of identity and the crisis of the family.

3. *Modernity is double-edged for followers of Christ:* Modernity represents the crux of the contemporary challenge to the gospel because it is the greatest single opportunity and the greatest single challenge the church has faced since the apostles. In the first case, it is equivalent of Roman roads in the first century and printing presses in the sixteenth. In the second, it is our equivalent of the challenges of persecution and gnosticism rolled into one.

4. *Modernity is foundational for the character and identity of both Americans and American evangelicals*: The United States as the world's 'first new nation' and American evangelicalism as Protestantism's 'first new tradition' both have features of modernity that are constitutive of their very character and identity (for example, pluralism in the case of America and a reliance on technique in the case of evangelicalism). This close affinity is an advantage because America and American evangelicalism have prospered at the growing edge of modernity. But it is also a disadvantage in a double sense: those most blessed by modernity are most blind to it, and those first hit by modernity are often the worst hurt by modernity. This is one reason why non-Westerners in relation to Americans, and Roman Catholics and Orthodox in relation to evangelicals, consider themselves superior to, and immune from, either the crises facing America or American evangelicals.

5. *Modernity's central challenge to America is focused in America's crisis of cultural authority*: Modernity creates problems far deeper than drugs, crime, illiteracy, AIDS, broken families, or the plight of the inner cities. It creates a crisis of cultural authority in which America's beliefs, ideals, and traditions are losing their compelling power in society. What people believe no longer makes much difference to how they behave. Unless reversed, this hollowing out of beliefs will finally be America's undoing.

6. *Modernity's central challenge to evangelicals is focused in the crisis of the authority of faith*: Modernity undermines the churches' capacity both to demonstrate the integrity and effectiveness of faith and to provide an answer to America's crisis. Their captivity to modernity is the reason why faith's influence on the culture has decreased while culture's influence on faith has increased.

7. *Modernity is a monumental paradox to the everyday practice of faith*: Modernity simultaneously makes evangelism easier——more people at more times in their lives are more open to the gospel—yet makes discipleship harder, because practicing the lordship of Christ runs counter to the fragmentation and specialization of modern life.

8. Modernity pressures the church toward polarized responses: Ever since the early days of modernity in the eighteenth century, a pattern of response to modernity has grown strong. Liberals have generally tended to surrender to modernity

329

without criticizing it; conservatives have tended to defy modernity without understanding it. This tendency has been reversed in the last generation as more progressive evangelicals now court the 'affluent consumers' of the gospel as ardently as liberals once courted the 'cultured despisers' of the gospel. The two main examples today are the megachurch leaders marrying the managerial, as we shall see, and the Christian publishers romancing the therapeutic.

9. *Modernity's challenge cannot be escaped by the common responses to which Christians typically resort*: Those who recognize the deficiencies of the extreme liberal and conservative responses often go onto two further deficient responses. One is a resort to premodernism—looking to the Third World to refresh the West, not realizing that Third World Christians have yet to face the inevitable challenge of modernization. This is true too of our brothers and sisters in Eastern Europe and Russia, who face a greater challenge from modernity than they previously faced from Marxism. The other is the resort to postmodernism—failing to see that though modernism as a set of ideas built on the Enlightenment has collapsed, modernity, as the fruit of capitalism and industrialized technology, is stronger than ever.

10. *Modernity represents a special challenge to the church*: The three strongest national challenges to the gospel in the modern world are Japan, Western Europe, and the United States. Japan has never been won to Christ; Western Europe has been won twice and lost twice; and America, though having the strongest and wealthiest churches, is now experiencing the severest crisis, so represents the clearest test case of Christian responses to modernity.

11. *Modernity represents a special challenge to reformation*: The reason for this special challenge is its central dismissal of the place of words. On the one hand, the overwhelming thrust of modernity has been to replace words with images and reading with viewing. On the other hand, the words that remain have been weakened because they have become technical, specialized, and abstract to most people. At the same time, postmodernism further devalues words by using them to create a pastiche of effect regardless of their original meaning (for example, the multiple cultural uses of 'born-again' in advertising or news programs).

12. *Modernity represents a special challenge to revival*: Quite simply, it is a fact of history that the church of Christ has not experienced any major nationwide revival under the conditions of advanced modernity. On the one hand, modernity undercuts true dependence on God's sovereign awakening by fostering the notion that we can effect revival by human means. On the other hand, modernity makes many people satisfied with privatized, individualistic, and subjective experiences that are pale counterfeits of true revival. While many Christians no longer have a practical expectation of revival, those who count on God's sovereignty over modernity have every reason to look to God for revival once again.

In sum, modernization is not something simple, local, transient or inconsequential. At its most developed level, it confronts us with such relentless power and pervasiveness that it has been aptly described as an 'iron cage' around human life (Max Weber) and 'a gigantic steel hammer' that smashes traditional institutions and traditional communities of faith (Peter Berger). This darker side of modernity raises two fundamental questions. The first is the human question: How can human beings live in a tolerably human way in a world created by modernization? The second is the religious question: How can faith in the modern world retain its traditional authority and integrity and remain the deepest source of a sense of human meaning and belonging? The answers to both questions are vital, of course, to the church in itself as well as to the church in mission. We turn now to a series of fundamental checkpoints to help us engage critically with the opportunity and challenge of modernity to our mission for Christ.

Exploiting modernity: two opportunities

The main accent in this paper is on the challenge of modernity, its threat to the Christian faith and to the humanness of life as traditionally understood. But that of course is only half of the picture, if the most neglected half, and I would like to begin more positively. The fact is that even the sternest critics of modernity would be reluctant to return to the premodern world. And even beyond the undoubtedly positive aspects of modernity, such as its freedoms and conveniences, there are still further aspects of modernization that represent extraordinary opportunities for mission.

331

CULTURAL OPENNESS

The first, and most obvious opportunity grows from the fact that certain features of modernity prompt *cultural openness*. As modernization spreads further and further, particularly in the form of decentralized modern media, the totally closed society is made more and more difficult. The success of the 'second Russian revolution' is the most dramatic example, but even the failure of the Chinese revolution in Tiananmen Square illustrates the same point. Modernization opens up not only traditional closed societies, but even centralized totalitarian states.

No societies are finally immune to modernization. And to any society that would hope to benefit from modernization, centralization is a recognized handicap. Thus, for example, when the decision came down to a choice between Marxist equality and modern efficiency, death by obsolescence or freedom for new ideas, modernity was impossible to resist. So the modernizing trend moves inevitably, if unevenly and against considerable resistance, toward the opening of societies and nations to a myriad of outside influences to which they would once have been impervious. Raisa Gorbachev uses American Express cards and 'Big Macs' have entered the world of the 'Big Brother'.

This point needs to be guarded against distortion, partly because all sin and all sinful cultures are in part a form of 'closure' designed to exclude God, and partly because we should never forget those countries that are still closed and those three hundred thousand brothers and sisters who each year seal their witness to Christ with their own blood. Yet the point itself requires little elaboration. This dramatic cultural openness is partly why the most explosive missionary growth has been outside the influence of missionaries, such as the indigenous working-class movements among people feeling their 'homelessness' in the face of the gale-force winds of modernization (for example, Latin American Pentecostalism in its self-supporting, self-propagating form).

In addition, this extraordinary openness is behind the fact that in the last century and a half, Christians have used every last means, medium, and methodology to reach the unreached in an enterprise in creative ingenuity unrivalled in history. And no Christian tradition has been richer in such ingenuity, enterprise, and pragmatic organization than evangelicalism. What Greek and Roman roads were to the explosion of the gospel in the first century, and the printing presses were to the Reformation in the sixteenth century, everything from steamships in the nineteenth century to radio, television, and satellites are to missionary enterprise in the openness of the modern world. What this openness means overall, then, is that the church faces the greatest opportunity for missionary expansion since the days of the Apostles.

CULTURAL REBOUNDS

The second opportunity is less obvious and only becomes apparent on the far side of the dislocations of modernity. This opportunity stems from the fact that modernization breeds its own distinctive *cultural rebounds*.

The general possibility of these rebounds is grounded in the dynamics of human sin. No one should have a better appreciation of irony, comedy, and unintended consequences than the Christian. Theologically speaking, sin means holding 'the truth in unrighteousness', which means in turn that neither sin nor its philosophies and institutions is ever stable. But our concern here is with the practical consequence. For modernity reinforces the instability so that every rebound contains some speeded-up disillusionment with some false faith or idol, and therefore presents a moment of spiritual openness—that moment which forms the 'today' in which the Gospel addresses every human being.

The list of such cultural rebounds and their ironies is unending. 'God is dead,' people say. 'The modern world has come of age and outgrown the tutelage of faith.' But its prodigal descent has been swift. Modern cities make people closer yet more alienated at once; powerful modern weapons bring their makers to the point of impotence and destruction simultaneously; modern media promise facts but deliver fantasies; modern education introduces mass schooling but fosters subliteracy; modern technologies of communication encourage people to speak more and say less and to hear more and listen less; modern life styles offer do-it-yourself freedom but slavishly follow fads and end often in addictions; modern conveniences, being disposable and ephemeral, bring people closer to happiness but further from joy; modern styles of communication make people hungry for intimacy and authenticity but more fearful than ever of being prey to phoniness, manipulation, and power games. And so on.

Prior to modernity the corruptions of Christendom tended to rebound into anti-Christian hostility. 'I am not a Christian,' Voltaire is supposed to have prayed to Christ, 'but that is so that I can love thee the better.' Today, the shoe is on the other foot. 'Modern people have come of age,' did someone say? Hardly. Modern people are less often humanists, but only so they can be more human. The very *reductio ad absurdum* of modernity is the open door for orthodoxy. Into the ultimate homelessness of our modernized existence breaks in the way to the ultimate home. The shelf life of modern idols is brief. The very openness of modernity is a destroyer even of its own unbeliefs.

Reading the signs of the times: two pitfalls

Raymond Aron's remark that very few people are contemporaries of their own generation has been made even more apt by the modern explosion of knowledge and the capacity-cum-anxiety that comes with it. As more and more is known and communication becomes faster and better, the lag between information and comprehension grows greater and more frustrating at once. The result does more than divide people between the 'knows and the know-nots.' It lures even those who do know toward two pitfalls that are deepened by the knowledge explosion.

THE UNKNOWING

One pitfall of the information age is summed up in the common mentality, 'Happiness is a small circle'. Life is more tolerable, they suggest, if we know as little as we need and care as little as we can. Yet this attitude is the result of knowing too much rather than too little, and in particular the result of an avalanche of 'news' that leaves people blindingly aware of the last twenty-four hours but ignorant of the last twenty-four years, let alone of history.

The resulting state of mind is a form of information without wisdom and of knowing severed from doing. Christians who react to the knowledge explosion by saying, in effect, 'I'm happy with my small world,' grow irresponsible. Their attitude becomes a serious factor in undermining the missionary initiative of the modernized sectors of the church. From that point on, instead of the whole church reaching the whole world, mission becomes a specialized concern of a dedicated minority.

THE ALL-KNOWING

The other pitfall is not found in society at large, but in those for whom thinking is a profession. Summed up in an attitude that David Boorstin mocks as 'Homo-up-to-datum,' this pitfall grows from the belief that harnessing the knowledge explosion offers the key to instant, total information. Its goal is to know everything in order to predict everything in order to control everything. If the first pitfall ends in irresponsibility, the second can end in an idolatry of information that becomes more of a handicap than a help to mission. It pushes mission and mission studies in the direction of the modern specialization and 'professionalization' of knowledge, and eventually toward the creation of a missionary version of the new 'knowledge class'.

The growing numbers and importance of a 'new thinking class' is one of the most distinctive features of the information society, and some of its unhappy consequences for Christians can be noted: (1) Christian thinkers often become closer to the 'cultured despisers' of the faith than to their fellow Christians, (2) expert knowledge is pursued as an end in itself, (3) specialized knowledge (which can be understood only by other specialists) creates a gap between experts and ordinary people, (4) originality and development are so prized that a fallacy is fostered that the newer-is-the-truer and the latest-is-the-greatest, (5) specialization fosters an expertise and professionalism that creates dependency and becomes disabling for anyone but the professional, (6) it is forgotten that ignorance is a constant in human affairs, and the capacity to act is often greatest when the clarity of understanding is smallest (and vice versa), and (7) members of the new 'knowledge class' become slowly adapted to the language and logic of the expanding world of seminars, forums, consultations, and Congresses (like this one) and thus further and further from other (Christianly more important) such styles of discourse as preaching and prayer.

Advocates of modern mission studies who scoff at such a caution should ponder the fate of most university disciplines today and especially the fate of Christian apologetics, liberal theology, evangelical higher education, and seminary training over the past century. Similarly, we can be sure that sophisticated missiology and 'evangelology' without the love of Christ, compassion for the lost, concern for our neighbor, and utter reliance on the Holy Spirit could quickly develop its own élitism, arrogance, and impracticability. If you asked me to search my own heart and choose between the 'simplicity' of mission as I have seen it lived out by my own missionary parents and the 'sophistication' of much of its equivalent today, I would choose my parents' way without hesitating.

Perhaps the most telling evidence for this point is the style of discourse at Lausanne II itself compared with that of Lausanne I. Under the influence of the 'terrible trio' (advertising, television, and pop-culture), modernization has caused profound changes in public discourse: above all in the shift from word to image, action to spectacle, exposition to entertainment, truth to feeling, conviction to sentiment, and authoritative utterance to discussion and sharing. Most of these wider cultural shifts have been well exemplified here, and the general diminishing of any sense of 'Thus saith the Lord' has been marked.

If we are to be unriddlers of our time and, like David's followers to be 'skilled in reading the signs of the times', we need to immerse our studies and strategic thinking in humility, responsibility, and a deep sense of the sovereignty of God and the sinfulness and smallness of our human projects. Just because we are modern does not mean that we have modernity by the scruff of the neck or that any of us knows definitively what our modern context is. We are all always more shortsighted than we realize. Modern culture can never be an exotic subject studied by outside observers, such as a group of anthropologists on a South Sea island. It is the mold in which we are all cast and that we can only recognize, resist, and change by God's outside perspective in the midst of our ignorance, an ignorance in some ways deepened by the overload of modern information.

Assessing the damage to persisting religion: two trends

In earlier days, when secularization was exaggerated as progressive and irreversible, religion was widely thought to have no future. It was pronounced fated to disappear. So today's revised assessment of secularization means a revised prognosis for religion: Religion, it is now said more humbly and more accurately, has not so much disappeared in modern society as changed its character and location. What then are the trends that have effected this change, and continue to shape the religion that still persists in the modern world?

336

PRIVATIZATION

The first trend, which in many ways is the reverse side of secularization, is *privatization*. By privatization I mean *the process by which modernization produces a cleavage between the public and private spheres of life and focuses the private sphere as the special area for the expression of individual freedom and fulfillment.* There has always been a distinction between the more personal and the more public areas of life, but until recently the relationship between them was marked by a continuum rather than a cleavage. Today in many modern cities it might as well be the Pacific Ocean. One one side of the cleavage is the public sphere, the macroworld of giant institutions (such government departments as Britain's Whitehall, such large corporations as Japan's Mitsubishi and Korea's Hyundai, and such military complexes as America's Pentagon). On the other side of the cleavage is the private sphere, the microworld of the family and private associations, the world of personal tastes, sports, hobbies, clubs, and leisure pursuits.

Privatization has its undoubted benefits supremely because it does ensure authentic freedom in the private sphere. Compared with the situation in the past, it permits more people to do more, buy more, and travel more than ever before, free of the constraints of community, tradition, and other people. But for religions such as the Christian faith, the disadvantages outweigh the advantages. Above all, privatization is limited and limiting. Modern society spells freedom for religion, but only so long as it is confined to the private sphere. Far from being an area of true choice and creativity, the modern private sphere is all too often a sort of harmless play area, a sort of spiritual 'Indian reservation' or 'Bantustan', a homeland for separate spiritual development set up obligingly by the architects of secular society's apartheid.

A classic illustration of privatization came in an interview with the founder of McDonald's hamburgers by the New York Times. Asked what he (a Christian) believed in, he replied: 'I speak of faith in McDonald's as if it were a religion. I believe in God, family, and McDonald's and in the office that order is reversed.' The record of the interview gave no indication whether the reply was facetious or not. But whatever the case, the response was a perfect expression of privatized faith that millions of modern Christians practice daily without realizing it.

337

PLURALIZATION

The second modernizing trend that shapes all persisting religion is *pluralization*. By pluralization is meant *the process by which the number of options in the private sphere rapidly multiplies at all levels, especially at the level of worldviews, faiths, and ideologies.*

Unlike secularism, pluralism is by no means new. The church was born in a period of similar pluralism, and modern pluralism even has its roots partly in the Protestant conviction of freedom of conscience. But modernization represents a stupendous enhancement of pluralism that in turn has set off a tidal wave of choice and change. Urban crowding, the knowledge explosion, modern travel, mass media, enormous dispersions of Third World people across the modern West. . . these are only the most obvious of the factors behind the heightened modern sense of 'all those others' and 'all those options'. We have now reached the stage where it can almost be said that 'everyone is now everywhere' and choice is not just a state of affairs, but a state of mind. Choice has become a value in itself, even a priority. Choice and change have become the very essence of modern life.

The side effects of pluralization on religion have been varied. One is that pluralization creates in modern believers a high degree of self-consciousness. Confronted constantly by 'all those others', modern people are constant question marks to each other, and modern faith is rarely as assured as it sounds.

Another effect is that religious believers in the modern world have become conversion-prone. Whereas faith was once rock-like and the turn-around of conversion was radical, complete, and lasting, modern believers are prone to being reconverted and reconverted and reconverted (or 'born again and again. . . and again'). Multiple conversions are now common, being 'born again' is easily trivialized, and even testimonies are reduced to the status of a spiritual visiting card in constant need of updating in a spiritually mobile society.

Yet another effect is that pluralism reduces the necessity of choosing at all. The very extension of choice increases the likelihood of the evasion of choice. But the overall direction is clear. Pluralization means an increase in choice and change that is almost automatically a decrease in commitment, continuity, and conviction. Pluralization now creates as many tensions within each church, denomination, or religion as there once were between them. With picking, choosing, and selectiveness

338

the order of the day, the result of pluralization is a general increase in shallowness, transience, and heresy. Few challenges to Christian discipleship and mission are so subtle yet so corrosive.

Sizing up the competition: two rivals

A common consequence of exaggerating secularization is to jump to the conclusion that modernity is hostile to all religion. Nothing could be further than the truth. Modernity is directly opposed to two defining features of some traditional religions that the Christian faith shares with only a few others—the absoluteness of its notion of *transcendence* and its notion of *totality*. But partly for that reason, modernity is very welcoming to religions without such angular features and such ornery insistence. Indeed, modernity provides an almost perfect setting for reinforcing two potent rivals to the Christian faith. What is common to both rivals, and in strong contrast with the Christian faith, is the implicit relativism in their truth claims and the evolutionary optimism in their view of history, though one tends to be in favor of modernity and the other, at least quietly, against it.

GENERALIZED SECULARISM

The first rival to the Christian faith is a *generalized secularism*, which combines relativism and evolutionary optimism in various types of naturalism that are favorable to modernity. The leading examples today are liberal humanism and Marxism, both being Western in origin, though ironically the second has outgrown its origins and appeals, especially to those repudiating the 'West'.

What needs underscoring is that *secularism* is not the same thing as *secularization*. *Secularism* is a philosophy, with all the strengths and weaknesses of one, not least that it is commonly unemotional and that to subscribe to it demands a considerable effort of mind or will. *Secularization*, by contrast (as we defined it earlier), is not a philosophy; it is a process. Its roots are not in an intellectual concept but in institutional change. It is a process that has actually taken place in the structures of society and cannot be avoided or simply wished away.

Secularization (the process) therefore provides the perfect setting for secularism (the philosophy). Modernity is the new context which enhances the old concept, making the latter seem natural, even necessary. Secularization, therefore, has a double thrust: *It constricts religion, thereby decreasing its power, but it also reinforces secularism, thereby increasing its power.*

Modernity's reinforcement of secularism is the context for a sobering fact. Since 1900, the percentage of the world's atheistic and non-religious peoples (agnostics, secularists, communists, and so on) has grown from 0.2 percent to 21.3 percent—in other words from less than one-fifth of one percent to over one fifth of the world's population. This is the most dramatic change on the entire religious map of the twentieth century. Secularists, or people with no religious commitment, now form the second largest bloc in the world, second only to Christians, and catching up fast (at the rate of 8.5 million 'converts' a year).

GENERALIZED SYNCRETISM

But this is only half the story. Modernization also provides natural reinforcement to a second potent rival to the Christian faith: *generalized syncretism.* Like secularism, modern syncretism in its varied forms often pivots on a relativism and evolutionary optimism that is conducive to modernity. But it takes them in a religious or semi-religious (rather than naturalistic) direction, and one that is often countermodernizing (rather than promodern) in tendency, and collectivist (rather than purely individualistic) in concern.

The leading examples in the West are the science-based mysticisms, such as the New Age movement, as well as socialism and environmentalism in their more mythic form. But elsewhere in the developing world, where resistance to modernization and resistance to Westernization often overlap, the appeal of, and potential for, such syncretisms is even greater. Such are the blandishments of modernity that few religious leaders will have the obstinacy of an Ayatollah Khomeini to reject it outright. Far more are likely to seek to control modernity and cushion its full impact on their society by some variety of local, national, or religious syncretism. Its religion then becomes a key part of any society's selective adaptation to modernity.

Among examples of this trend are the Umbanda movement in Brazil (with its Christian rites and pagan content) and the recent movement in Japan to revitalize State Shinto as a conscious civil religion that will replace 'post-war democratic Japan' and fill the vacuum of values created by modernity. Similar syncretistic movements were Japan's way of adapting to earlier waves of outside influence, such as the introduction of Confucianism from China, Buddhism from India and, in the nineteenth century, the Christian faith from the West.

And, of course, this reinforcement of syncretism by modernity is one reason for the persistence of certain kinds of religion even in highly 'secular' societies. Because of their substratum of magic, superstition, and fatalism at a popular level, modern nations like France and Britain are not so much 'post-Christian' as pre-Christian and pagan. Similarly in Japan, animistic worship of sun, mountains, trees, and rocks was always just below the surface of official State Shinto, so the revitalization of State Shinto will mean a reinforcement of popular animism.

Engaging modernity: two master principles

All engagement in the modern world requires or reveals an answer to the question: How do we view modernity theologically? Modernity is only one more form of human culture, and the view of culture we find in the Scriptures is a bifocal vision. Always and everywhere at once, human culture and therefore modernity is two things: God's gift to us, and the devil's challenge to us to worship him and not Christ.

Two great master principles have characterized the church at its most penetrating, and both are essential today.

PROTAGONIST PRINCIPLE

The first is the *protagonist principle*, which flows from the theme 'Christ *over* all' and has as its key word *total*. The story of the exodus provides an Old Testament example. The whole issue with the Egyptian pharaoh was lordship. He who can liberate is he who is lord. As the bargaining went on, Pharaoh relented enough to let the Israelite men go, at least for worship. Moses said no. 'Let my people go' meant not just the men and not just for worship. Men, women, and children must go, and go for good. Then a remarkable little phrase was added: 'Not a hoof is to be left behind.'

A New Testament example can be found in Luke. Peter, as a fisherman, was glad to allow Jesus to preach from his boat. But

Jesus said to Peter, 'Put out into the deep water, and let down the nets for a catch.' And we can almost hear Peter reply, 'Look, Lord, I'll listen to you as my teacher all day long, but when it comes to fishing, that's my job.'

We know the result. Peter found that Jesus was Lord of nature, too, and he could only respond, 'Go away from me, Lord; I am a sinful man!' Christ was Lord of nature as well as truth. He is the Alpha and the Omega. He is the source, guide, and goal of all there is. That is why every eye will one day see him, every tongue will be stopped, and every knee will bow. After all, as Abraham Kuyper said, expressing the protagonist principle perfectly, 'There is not an inch of any sphere of life of which Jesus Christ the Lord does not say, "Mine." '

This protagonist principle is indispensable today because modernity renders earlier forms of Christian separatism impossible and many newer forms of activism ineffective. So our engagement, whether in work, politics, art, voluntary action, recreation, or mission, will only be faithful and effective to the degree that Christ remains lord of every part of our lives.

ANTAGONIST PRINCIPLE

The second master principle is the *antagonist principle*. It flows from the theme 'Christ *over against* all that which does not bow to him', and the key word here is *tension*. The Lord himself puts the point unmistakably in Exodus 20: 'I am the Lord your God. . . You shall have no other gods before [to set against] me' (verses 2 and 3). Over forty times in Leviticus 18 and the following chapters is the recurring assertion, 'I am the Lord.' Each time it accompanies a strict instruction not to do as the Egyptians or the Canaanites did, neither worshipping their idols nor copying their ideas and institutions.

The reason? The Lord is the jealous one, the one who brooks no rivals. Since he is our 'decisive Other', he demands of us a decisive contrast with everything that is over against him and his ways, his ideals, and his institutions. Most wonderful of all, the deepest reason is personal. It is 'that you may belong to me'.

In short, God and the world stand crosswise. We are in the world but not of it. To be faithful to him we have to be foreign to the world. We are not to be conformed but transformed by the renewing of our minds. Even the much vaunted critical analysis of Marxists should pale beside the obedience-rooted critical commitment of Christians. But Marxist hardliners and Muslim fundamentalists are often wiser than we are in their deep suspicion of modernity. It is the 'Great Satan' to their cause. It does contain 'spiritual pollution', as they say, and Christians should be wary too.

Modernity, in other words, is not 'the holy ground' some urban theologians proclaim. Modernity is the devil's challenge to us. But that is not because we are the innocents and the modern world is so tempting. Rather it is because we are the temptable ones. The modern world is simply our hearts writ large. Our hearts are simply the modern world writ small. So our view of modernity needs to be theologically realistic. God pronounces the no of his judgment over all our human works before he pronounces the yes of his grace. But while his yes transcends his no, it is not because his no is merely temporary or apparent. God's no is his total, radical, continual, and final judgment of all our works that are born of sin and are moving toward death.

Of course, the protagonist principle and the antagonist principle must never be separated. They go hand in hand. Without the former, the latter would create a 'we/they' division that is Manichean and not biblical. The Protagonist principle means there must be no hatred of the world or false asceticism with us. Yes, the world is passing away, and we are passing through the world. But the responsible realism of that bifocal vision should shape our perspective. Holding these two truths together, we are to be, in Peter Berger's memorable phrase, 'against the world for the world'.

Engaging modernity: two special prerequisites

It is characteristic of modernity that its challenges to faith are fundamental. It calls faith into question in a 'do or die' form. Again and again its pressure is so unrelenting that only the deepest truth, only the real thing, is sufficient. Everything less is exposed as shallow, weak, insubstantial, and ineffectual.

Among many of the taken-for-granted strengths from the church's two-thousand-year history, two are special prerequisites for engaging modernity today.

PLAUSIBILITY

In an ideal world, untouched by the effects of the Fall, the credibility of any belief would be determined simply by whether it were true or false. It would be believed if, and only if, it were objectively true; and if it were false, it would be quite literally incredible.

Needless to say, such a state of affairs is not our situation after the Fall. It doesn't take a cynic to see how the truth requirement has weakened to the vanishing point. Thus in the fallen world flagrant nonsense or complete error can be believed, and incontrovertible truth can be disbelieved without the question of their being objectively true or false being raised at all. In short, plausibility, or a thing's seeming to be true, is often mistaken for credibility, or its being true.

The Freudian concept of 'rationalizing' is the best-known application of the essentially biblical theme. But a more fruitful application is Peter Berger's concept of 'plausibility structure'. The degree to which a belief (or disbelief) seems convincing is directly related to its 'plausibility structure' that is, the group or community that provides the social and psychological support for the belief. Seen this way, only a genius or a madman can believe by himself or herself. For most human beings, it is easy to believe if the socially constructed support group is strong, but difficult to believe if it is weak.

The importance of plausibility can easily be defended biblically either through such recurring emphases as the practice of truth or through such statements as the Apostle Paul's description of the church as 'the pillar and bulwark of the truth'. Needless to say, Paul did not mean that the Christian faith was true because the church was strong. But since the church is the plausibility structure of the Christian faith, its strength or weakness critically determines the plausibility of the faith at any particular moment.

Modernity has multiple implications for Christian plausibility in the modern world. Well-publicized incidents, such as the sexual scandals of the American televangelists or the bitter controversies of the U.S. Southern Baptist Convention, are the least part of the problem. The effects of such subtle influences as 'privatization' and 'weightlessness' are subtler but far more damaging—the former making the faith 'privately engaging but publicly irrelevant', the latter creating a sort of *Christian Lite*'. At the end of the day, the gospel of Jesus Christ stands or falls by whether or not it is true and therefore credible. But modernity makes the practice of truth absolutely critical. Only through the gravely endangered practice of truth will the gospel become plausible to modern people.

PERSUASION

Evangelicals have characteristically been a people of persuasion; modernity puts a high premium on the place of persuasion; yet many modern evangelicals are strikingly persuasionless. This blatant contradiction lies at the heart of evangelical ineffectiveness in communications today.

One way to gauge this dilemma is through evangelical responses to pluralism, a crucial feature of modernity to the integrity of the gospel as well as to Christian mission. Evangelicals can trace a long and mostly fruitful relationship to pluralism in Christian history. Was it not in the highly pluralistic setting of the first century AD that the early Christians experienced explosive growth without compromise to their exclusive allegiance? Was it not the Protestant principle of freedom of conscience that became the greatest generator of choice and dissent in history, and thus a reinforcement of pluralism? Did not nineteenth-century evangelicals make their greatest headway when they showed themselves ready and able to exploit the 'free market' opportunities for enterprising faiths that were opened up by the First Amendment's separation of church and state?

The full story of the relationship of faith and pluralism is not all positive, of course. But no one who knows it can be other than shocked at the sea change in evangelical attitudes to pluralism today. Pluralism has been confused with relativism and become the evangelical 'P word'. Thus at the very moment when modern pluralism reinforces the grand overall shift from coercion (as in state churches where the state's sword and purse are behind the church) to persuasion, many Christians have abandoned persuasion for non-persuasive styles of communication, such as preaching, pronouncements, protest, and picketing.

A second way to gauge the dilemma of persuasionlessness is through evangelical attitudes to apologetics. Apologetics has usually held an honored, if controversial, place in Christian history. So much so that B.B. Warfield said that the Christian faith 'stands out among all religions as distinctively "the

Apologetick religion"'. Today, however, ignorance of apologetics, and unease with it, are widespread.

On the one hand, the liberal tendency has been to say, 'Don't defend, dialogue!' A declining rational certainty in argument has coincided with a declining historical certainty in evidence and a declining cultural certainty in style. As one Oxford professor said to me in my application interview, 'Don't mention apologetics here. It's a dirty word in Oxford!'

Many would therefore agree with Dietrich Bonhoeffer: 'The attack by Christian apologetics upon the adulthood of the world I consider to be in the first place pointless, in the second ignoble, and in the third unChristian.' Others would agree with Jacques Ellul's equation: 'To suppose that it is still possible to have a crusade or an apologetic is to be out of your mind.'

On the other hand, the equally mistaken though opposite conservative tendency has been to say, 'Don't persuade, proclaim!' Apologetics, they fear, diminishes biblical authority by relying on human wisdom. It dries up spontaneity and spirituality by relying on reason. 'I am not sure,' wrote Martyn Lloyd-Jones in 1958, 'that apologetics has not been the curse of evangelical Christianity for the last twenty to thirty years.' The result is that apologetics needs its own apology. As secularist philosopher Antony Flew says, with some regret, 'Belief cannot argue with unbelief: It can only preach to it.'

Ironically, evangelicals are growing persuasionless at a time of extraordinary apologetic opportunity. After centuries of relentless skepticism and hostility to the gospel, many of the great, post-Christian intellectual rivals to the faith are in deep disarray. But there are all too few evangelicals with the convictions, courage, compassion, and imagination to exploit the vacuum. Yet when all is said and done, the Christian faith is a persuading faith. As Peter Berger says, 'The Christian community consists of those people who keep on telling the story to each other, some of whom climb up on various boxes to tell the story to others.' Today, more than ever, modernity has created a world in which persuasion has to be central to proclamation.

Overcoming modernity: two points of reliance

Additional checkpoints that might be included here are legion. But let me conclude with one last checkpoint that concerns our practical faith and two grounds of our confidence as we seek to wrestle with and overcome modernity.

PRAYER AND FASTING

First, looking at things in terms of our part, we must acknowledge that modernity poses a challenge that can be overcome '*only by prayer and fasting*'. This, for me, is not something that comes naturally. It would be far easier to speak of requirements such as 'thinking Christianly'. For at the very least modernity requires a degree of thoughtful wrestling that is on the level of the prophet Daniel: 'Though this word was true, it cost him much toil to understand it.' But precisely because it is even more difficult, commitment to the spiritual disciplines in general and to prayer and fasting in particular is more than a pious truism. It is an emphatic repudiation of modern technique and an open acknowledgement that when we wrestle with modernity, we do not wrestle with flesh and blood. And to link fasting with prayer is even to press beyond the admirable emphasis on prayer demonstrated in modern missions since the Moravian movement. I think of heroic exemplars from Count von Zinzendorf down through Hudson Taylor to the Dorothea Mission and national movements for intercession in our own time such as Intercessors for Britain.

We have the example and the teaching of our Lord himself as he engaged with the enemy at his deadliest, and taught us how to do the same. We can see that prayer and fasting are singularly appropriate for unmasking modernity because the heart of their spiritual purpose is a direct challenge to the heart of the grand lie of modernity.

Modernity, of course, tries to turn even fasting into a technique. Thus for modern people, fasting has lost its spiritual purpose and become a form of weight control or political protest (such as 'hunger strikes'). Even for many Christians it is either neglected or left at the level of the ascetic, the legalistic, or the purely nominal. All of which are a form of reductionism precisely because they have lost their spiritual point.

But when the spiritual is restored and prayer and fasting are rejoined, they form an indispensable weapon without which we could not unmask or disarm modernity. The reason is theological and can be seen in the contrast between Adam and Jesus. Adam, in eating the forbidden fruit, disobeyed God's Word and 'broke his fast'; whereas the second Adam, overcoming the temptation, sustained both his obedience and his fast and thus demonstrated his repudiation of living on bread alone and his dependency on every word that proceeds out of the mouth of God.

Prayer with fasting is therefore both a statement and a stand— a statement about the ultimate meaning of life and a stand against the ultimate lie and its source. What does life mean? In creating 'a world without windows' (Peter Berger), modernity is history's greatest reinforcement of sin's cosmic lie about life-as-bread-alone (purely biological, naturalistic, secular). But, like Adam, modern people who live their lives eating, working, playing, sleeping 'autonomously' for the sake of these things alone, apart from God, find out that such autonomous life is impossible and such an autonomous culture turns out to be death-producing.

How are prayer and fasting an effective stand against this lie? Fasting quickly brings us to the point of hunger, which is the state when our dependency on something outside ourselves is inescapable. In knowing how much we need food, we know we do not have life in ourselves. But then we encounter the test that only prayer and fasting overcomes: on what, then, do we depend? Bread alone, says the evil one, so Adam believed him and ate. God and his Word alone, said Jesus, so he refused the devil's lie and shifted the principle of life back to its source.

This pivotal victory in the war against evil and its lie shows that prayer and fasting are practical rather than theoretical, yet profound spiritual warfare rather than a facile 'how-to' technique. Decisive victory comes only through severe testing. Christ met and overcame Satan in praying and fasting, and he later told his disciples that the 'Prince of this world' can be overcome only by prayer and fasting. Do we think modernity, with all its strengths and seductions, will be different? Unless we recover the practice of prayer and fasting, our best intentioned use of modern media and methods will end only in assisting the triumph of technique and hastening a new Babylonian captivity, albeit with air-conditioned cells and spiritual Muzak to divert us.

WORD AND SPIRIT

Second, looking at things in terms of God's part, we must acknowledge that modernity poses a challenge that can be overcome *only by God's Word and Spirit.* This reminder, too, is more than a truism, because once again it addresses the heart of the challenge of modernity. In producing Nietzsche's 'last men', Weber's 'iron cage', and Berger's 'world without windows', modernity does more than spawn a crowd of problems. It is a deliberate locking-out of genuine transcendence that constructs a suffocating, air-tight world filled with problems that admit of no internal solution.

Nietzsche saw clearly what this loss of transcendence would mean. 'Alas,' he wrote, 'the time of the most despicable man is coming, he that is no longer able to despise himself. Behold, I show you the *last man*.'

But modernity's repression of transcendence explains not only the triumph of triviality in the 'last men' of Western consumer societies, but the flawed enterprise of spurious forms of transcendence, such as Promethean Marxism. Anyone prepared to believe with Karl Marx that the revolutionary will of history can be incarnate in any human political party is bound to be disillusioned. Addressing this lack of transcendence in Marxism, David Martin points out, 'It is a paradox that a system which claimed that the beginning of all criticism was the criticism of religion should have ended up with a form of religion which was the end of criticism.'

But how is the Christian faith different? As we survey the deepening captivity of the church, is there any lasting escape from modernity? What are the grounds for our confidence? After all, is not our very understanding of God and our listening to his Word dependent on the closed circle of our modern context?

No! A thousand times no, the church cries, because the gospel itself contains the secret of why the Christian faith can survive repeated periods of cultural containment and contamination. On the one hand, it has in God's Word and Spirit an authority that stands higher than history, a judgment that is irreducible to any generation and culture. Which is why, when God speaks, not even the worst or best of our hermeneutics can hold him down. On the other hand, the gospel has in its notion of sin and repentance a doctrine of the church's failure, which can be the wellspring of its ongoing self-criticism and renewal.

Like an eternal jack-in-the-box, Christian truth will always spring back. No power on earth can finally keep it down, not even modernity's power of Babylonian confusion and captivity. 'At least five times,' noted G.K. Chesterton earlier, 'the faith has

349

to all appearances gone to the dogs. In each of these five cases, it was the dog that died.'

To write these things is not to whistle in the dark, but to grapple with modernity with hope and direction. We do not 'put our trust in princes', nor in management-streamlined missions, television evangelism, and computer-planned church growth. Even as we use the best modern media, our reliance from beginning to end must be on God's Word and Spirit and on their grave-opening, jail-breaking power in preaching, revival, reformation, and mission. Only so will modernity be restrained and overcome.

Conclusion: the reality and the glory

We should all be encouraged that many of the most penetrating observers of modernity are Christians—for example, Peter Berger, Jacques Ellul and George Grant. But when all is said and done, we would be foolish to pretend that modernization and modernity are easy either to understand or to engage. Little wonder that first reactions to the 'big picture' are often pessimistic. We feel overwhelmed. Which of us is equal to the challenge? 'Winning the World by 2000,' like John R. Mott's earlier 'The Evangelization of the World in This Generation', is easier to handle as a rhetorical rallying cry than as a job actually to be accomplished before the clock strikes twelve on a certain day in a certain year.

What are my objectives in presenting this burden? Some of the simplest are as follows: As followers of Christ concerned to know him and make him known, we need, first, to put the topic of modernity high on our agendas for our concern, study, and prayer; second, to analyze the local and specific impact of modernization on our own country, region, city, church, ministry, and audience; third, to reform those areas of the church's doctrine and life that modernity has rendered weak or non-existent (for example, the place of truth and the importance of the incarnation in a day of electronic evangelism); fourth, to forswear facile excuses and false evasions (modernization may have hit the West first and worst, but modernity is now a world problem and not simply 'a Western problem'. Besides, the real test of 'Third World spiritual vitality' is not the first modernized generation but the third); and fifth, to deepen the 'reality' of our own faith in both knowledge and experience in order to be able to combat modernity.

The extraordinary burden of mission in the face of modernity makes me think of two men under titanic pressure. One was the great German thinker, Max Weber. He never shut his eyes to the modern world. He wrestled with it, but the more he wrestled, the more pessimistic he became. One day, a friend saw him pacing up and down, nearing the verge of a second breakdown.

'Max,' he said, 'why do you go on thinking like this when your conclusions leave you so depressed?'

Weber's reply has become a classic of intellectual commitment and courage, 'I want to know how much I can stand.'

Admirable in many respects, that is not the way for followers of Christ. If we are not called to be Promethean entrepreneurs of the gospel, we are certainly not called to be stoics or tragic heroes.

A very different response under pressure was that of Moses. Faced with enemies behind, around, and ahead, and finding discontent not only among his own people but within his own family, he suddenly met the ultimate threat to his people and to his task as their leader: God himself. The Lord declared that, because of their sin, he would destroy the Israelites.

His very life and trust in God called into question, Moses countered the challenge daringly by putting God on the line (arguing the covenant), the people on the line (calling for a consecration to the Lord even against families and friends), and finally himself on the line (asking to be blotted out himself, rather than the people).

Then, when the Lord had listened to his prayers, agreeing first to forgive the people and then to come with them in person rather than by an angel, Moses made his supreme request, surely the most audacious prayer in all the Scriptures: 'Show me your glory.' He wanted to know all of God that a fallen sinner could be allowed to know, for nothing less would be enough to see him through the crisis of his calling.

In that prayer, we have our ultimate answer to modernity and to its keenest observers, such as Nietzsche and Weber. When 'God is dead' for a nation, a church, a movement, or an individual, a weightlessness results for which there is only one remedy—ultimate reality, the glory of God refilling them as the waters fill the sea. Wasn't that Jeremiah's message to his generation? To a people who had exchanged their glory for a god who

351

was altogether nothing, he warned, 'Ascribe glory to the Lord your God before the darkness falls.'

If in mission today we stress the spiritual aspects of the gospel without the social, we lose all relevance in modern society. But if we stress the social without the spiritual, we lose our reality altogether. The ultimate factor in the church's engagement with modernity is the church's engagement with God.

Are we still tempted today to believe that we or anyone else can pull off the task of evangelizing the world? We must forget it. On the other hand, are we overwhelmed by the thought of the task, overburdened by the state of modernity and the world? Let us forget modernity and ourselves and turn from the what and where of our calling to the Whom. Then we can follow Moses to the source of the only reality that counts, the one power sufficient for facing up to the Colossus of modernity.

Lord, show me your glory.